THE INCORPOREAL

THE INCORPOREAL

ONTOLOGY, ETHICS,

and the

LIMITS OF MATERIALISM

ELIZABETH GROSZ

Columbia University Press
New York

Columbia University Press
Publishers Since 1893
New York   Chichester, West Sussex
cup.columbia.edu

Copyright © 2017 Columbia University Press
Paperback edition, 2018

Library of Congress Cataloging-in-Publication Data
Names: Grosz, E. A. (Elizabeth A.) author.
Title: The incorporeal : ontology, ethics, and the limits of materialism /
Elizabeth Grosz.
Description: New York : Columbia University Press, 2017. | Includes
bibliographical references and index.
Identifiers: LCCN 2016041211| ISBN 9780231181624 (cloth : alk. paper) |
ISBN 9780231181631 (pbk. : alk. paper) |ISBN 9780231543675 (e-book)
Subjects: LCSH: Materialism. | Idealism. | Ontology. | Ethics.
Classification: LCC B825 .G76 2017 | DDC 111—dc23
LC record available at https://lccn.loc.gov/201604121

Columbia University Press books are printed on permanent
and durable acid-free paper.
Printed in the United States of America

COVER PHOTO: John White © Gettyimages
COVER DESIGN: Milenda Nan Ok Lee
BOOK DESIGN: Lisa Hamm

FOR MY PARENTS,
WHO LIVE IN ETERNITY.

CONTENTS

ACKNOWLEDGMENTS

My special thanks to a number of readers who have commented on chapters in their draft form—Keith Ansell-Pearson, Ed Cohen, Annu Dahiya, Claus Halberg, Rebecca Hill, Philipa Rothfield, Kathy Rudy, Kristin Sampson, Hasana Sharp, and especially Nicole Fermon, as well as Wendy Lochner and Susan Pensak from Columbia University Press. This project has only been enhanced and improved through their comments and suggestions. I would also like to thank the Programs in Women's Studies and Literature at Duke University for providing a sustaining environment for the writing of this very abstract book, whose connections to both women's studies and literature remain tenuous at best.

ABBREVIATIONS

Gilles Deleuze	*LS*	*The Logic of Sense*
Gilles Deleuze	*DR*	*Difference and Repetition*
Gilles Deleuze	*PI*	*Pure Immanence: A Life*
Gilles Deleuze and Félix Guattari	*ATP*	*A Thousand Plateaus*
Gilles Deleuze and Félix Guattari	*WIP*	*What Is Philosophy?*
Friedrich Nietzsche	*GS*	*The Gay Science*
Friedrich Nietzsche	*EH*	*Ecce Homo*
Friedrich Nietzsche	*TI*	*Twilight of the Idols*
Friedrich Nietzsche	*WP*	*The Will to Power*
Friedrich Nietzsche	*Z*	*Thus Spoke Zarathustra*
Benedict de Spinoza	*E*	*Ethics*
Gilbert Simondon	*IGPB*	*L'individu et sa genèse physico-biologique*
Gilbert Simondon	*ILFI*	"L'individuation à la lumière des notions de forme et d'information"
Gilbert Simondon	*IPC*	*L'individuation psychique et collective*
Gilbert Simondon	METO	"On the Mode of Existence of Technical Objects"
Gilbert Simondon	PPO	"The Position of the Problem of Ontogenesis"

THE INCORPOREAL

INTRODUCTION

This is a book on ethics, although it never addresses morality, the question of what is to be done. It is also a book on ontology, the substance, structure, and forms of the world, this one world in which we live and that we share with all forms of life, although it rarely addresses being as such. I aim to develop an ontoethics, a way of thinking about not just how the world is but how it could be, how it is open to change, and, above all, the becomings it may undergo. In this sense, an ethics always passes into and cannot be readily separated from a politics, which addresses social, collective, cultural, and economic life and their possibilities for change. An ontoethics involves an ethics that addresses not just human life in its interhuman relations, but relations between the human and an entire world, both organic and inorganic. Insofar as we create ontologies that reflect not only, or primarily, beings but also becomings, that is, insofar as ontologies can be considered ontogeneses, an ontoethics cannot *but* address the question of how to act in the present and, primarily, how to bring about a future different from the present. This question is simultaneously ontological, ethical, and political; it may require new forms of technology and new kinds of art to prepare for and accompany the transformations of a present that is never fully present, composed of beings existing in their self-identity, always divided and complicated by the becomings that characterize and continually transform them.

The open-ended nature of the future, its capacity to deviate from the present and its forms of domination and normalization, necessarily link an ethics, how one is to live, with a politics, how collectives, and their constituents, are to live and act together and within what protective and limiting parameters. An ethics does not form a politics in itself, though it is a necessary ingredient in the organization and operation of political collectives or movements, those established with a specific project or aim in social life. It is even more unusual that an ethics or politics consider itself in connection with an ontology, an account of what constitutes the real, what exists in this world that we collectively share with all forms of life. Only rarely has ethics been considered a first philosophy, a philosophy logically prior to an ontology (this project has been limited, for over a century, to the writings of Emmanuel Levinas);[1] more commonly, ethics has been reduced to a morality, which I understand as a set of principles, a list of preferred practices, with generalizable or even universalizable criteria of virtue or goodness, by which we should all act and through which we are capable of providing judgments about moral or immoral activities. It is only rarely that ontology is addressed not only in terms of what *is* but also in terms of how what is may enable what *might be*. Ontology has been increasingly directed toward explaining scientific and mathematical models, for which ethical considerations seem conceptually extrinsic. Yet an ontology entails a consideration of the future, not only of what we can guarantee or be certain but above all what virtualities in the present may enable in the future. This is the possibility of the future being otherwise than the present, the openness of a future which is nevertheless tied to, based on but not entirely limited by, the past and present. Such considerations of the future are the concerns of precisely ethics and politics and are the implications—open to heated and frequent dispute, no doubt—of whatever one commits to as an ontology.

For over a century ontology has become increasingly diminished as a concern of philosophical, political, and cultural reflection; it has been submitted to the domination of epistemology, theories of what

knowledge is and does. It is through largely epistemological considerations that ontological hypotheses or claims have been directed and
evaluated. If we know what there is, it makes sense that we come to what
is through what we know. But when epistemology questions itself and its
own conditions of knowledge, its own lacunae and places of nonknow-
ing, there is a residue or remainder of ontological issues and concerns
that is untouched by epistemology and that may not always be submitted
to existing schemas of knowledge, existing forms of grammar and syntax
or forms of representation. This was clearly true of the emergence of
subatomic physics and especially quantum field theory, which seems
to defy the protocols that privilege epistemology over and in place of
ontology. We do not have a clear, rational, logical conception of quantum fields and their components, nor, indeed, of many biological and
especially microbiological processes. We cannot ascertain what position
the knowing observer, the quantum scientist, is to occupy in scientific
knowledges. Atomic and subatomic components and their fields exist
beyond our everyday, and perhaps even scientific, understanding, and
biological processes are far from well-understood and explicable in
terms that mark much of twentieth-century thought and beyond. We
know that there are things we do not know. These things we do not know
confirm the independent reach of ontology outside and beyond what
our current epistemologies allow us to understand—indeed they are the
continuing condition of an ever changing and more refined epistemology. What things are, how they connect with each other, what relations
exist between them may be beyond our capacities for knowing at any
moment in history: this in no way lessens what there is. Indeed these
limits add an ethical and political dimension to the processes of knowing: they signal what is funded, supported, normalized as a research paradigm. They also signal how new forms of knowledge may be developed,
new paradigms can emerge that may address what exists quite differently, even, perhaps, in incommensurable terms. It is because ontologies
have ethical and political—as well as aesthetic and cultural—resonances
that they provide limits and obstacles, an outside, to epistemological
frameworks. Ontologies have ethical and political implications in the
sense that they make a difference to how we live and act, what we value,

and how we produce and create. While I do not consider what follows to be a critique of epistemology, I aim to bypass epistemological questions in favor of a focus on an ontology sensitive to and engaged with the realities of space and time, of events and becomings, not just things and their knowable, determinable relations.

In the following chapters I will explore a counterhistory or genealogy of the conceptual connections between ontology, ethics, and politics, which brings together what is with questions of how to live a good life and a generous and productive collective existence—lives that resist oppression, coercion, and prevailing social constraints—that enhance and produce values, that expand social and collective existence and the lives of nonhuman things. Although such an intimate entwinement of ethics, politics, and ontology is uncommon, especially in contemporary philosophy, it is not without precedents: indeed, it has an illustrious lineage, dating from the very rise of philosophy with the pre-Socratics and undertaking numerous transformations and reformulations between then and the present. I do not undertake a systematic analysis of this lineage, but aim to present more a piecemeal overview of some of its key moments and figures, particularly of the concepts that populate this conjunction of ontology and ethics, the formulation of an ontoethics. There are, of course, many other philosophers that I could have included in this genealogy, the pre-Socratics, the Epicureans, and the Cynics, the work of Leibniz and, most obviously, of Henri Bergson, who, perhaps more than any other philosopher in the last 150 years, aimed to link our thinking about ontology, ethics, and collective existence together. I seriously considered writing a chapter on Bergson's contributions for this book, but I believe that I have dealt with his writings in enough detail in previous work for readers interested in this connection to infer it from these earlier texts.[2]

The kind of genealogy I have undertaken here could be greatly expanded; however, for my purposes, I need to show a long and not always consistent, indeed sometimes erratic, strand of thought in the history in Western philosophy that has tenaciously resisted all forms of reductionism. I have sought the strongest and clearest expressions of a position for which I do not have a proper name but that, however inadequately, I will describe as "the incorporeal," the subsistence of the ideal *in* the material or corporeal; although that is a concept derived directly from the Stoics and not used in the writings of the other philosophers I discuss here. It is an inadequate term for addressing the immanence of the ideal in the material and the material in ideality. These philosophers have understood the problems and limits of the impulse to reductionism, the loss of explanatory force, in any thoroughgoing materialism. This is not, however, an enterprise of antimaterialism; on the contrary, this book is an attempt to produce a more complex, more wide-ranging understanding not only of materiality but the framing conditions of materiality that cannot themselves be material. I propose here to explore the intimate entwinement of the orders of materiality and ideality, the impossibility of a thoroughgoing and nonreductive materialism, a materialism that cannot and should not be opposed to ideality but requires and produces it.[3]

Following the Stoics, I have described as incorporeal the immaterial conditions for the existence and functioning of matter, including those configurations of matter that constitute the varieties of life. This book is an exploration of the incorporeal conditions of corporeality, the excesses beyond and within corporeality that frame, orient, and direct material things and processes, and especially living things and the biological processes they require, so that they occupy space and time, have possible meanings and directions that exceed their corporeality. I am interested here in an *extramaterialism*, in the inherence of ideality, conceptuality, meaning, or orientation that persists in relation to and within materiality as its immaterial or incorporeal conditions. This book explores a philosophical "lineage" that addresses the incorporeal and its relations to materiality, the ways in which materiality (in all its forms) exceeds materialism and requires a different kind of philosophy, available but usually latent within the history of Western thought. The particular philosophies I explore in what follows, however, cannot be understood as idealist either, although each assigns a central place to ideality without subordinating it to materiality. However, none can be considered dualists, those committed to the logical and ontological separation of mind from body or the material from the ideal. For each, the question of how we think materiality and ideality together remains central. These philosophers do not necessary concur; indeed there are a number of differences, even incommensurabilities, that mark their relations. I am not undertaking the analysis of a coherent history but rather precisely seeking the various shifts and forces that have gained purchase on and transformed a concept, the incorporeal, that has no proper name.

I begin with the Stoics. As committed and thoroughgoing materialists, the Greek and Roman Stoics provide a counter to the Platonic separation of materiality from ideality and the Aristotelian impetus to *hylomorphism* that distinguishes form from and privileges it in relation to matter. The Stoics demonstrate that a consistent commitment to materialism is unable to explain the order and cohesion of material things and events—for them, matter itself, whether on a microscopic, social, or a cosmological scale, requires extramaterial conditions by which it is framed and through which it can be thought and spoken about. In chapter 1 I explore this apparently paradoxical materialism which is not one that emerges during the birth of Western philosophy. The Stoics make it clear that another kind of ontology (than Platonism, Aristotelianism, and their many offshoots) is possible, one with cosmological aspirations, that aims to understand not only the orders of our experience but also the orders of the world well beyond our experience and to link this understanding to an ethics of existence and an art of living well, beyond received accounts of morality. The Stoics provide philosophies that follow with an aspirational understanding of what philosophy might do—when practiced at its best, philosophy can address the world, the place of all things, and particularly ourselves, within this world, and invent ways of living that experiment with and develop new forms of living in accord with our understanding.

In chapter 2 I explore Benedict de Spinoza's *Ethics*, aiming to analyze his account of substance, with a particular focus on his understanding of the attributes of mind and body, a relation commonly considered one of parallelism but which understands that every material entity and relation brings with it ideas, concepts more or less adequate to understand material (causal) relations. These ideas are not simply ideas we humans who contemplate the world create; rather they exist in God, or nature, which is to say, in themselves in the same way as things. Spinoza provides a self-conscious alternative to the Cartesian opposition between *res cogitans* or mind, a thinking thing, and *res extensa*, an extended or material thing, a body. Descartes's dualism can be seen as a "modern" philosopher's reconceptualization of Platonic dualism. Spinoza's singular substance provides an alternative to the dualism of Descartes, the belief that mind and body are two irreconcilable and mutually exclusive substances. For Spinoza, there is only one substance, indissolubly both mind and body, under two of its infinite attributes. These are not two different things, nor are they one single thing that is the reduction of diverse forces. For Spinoza, an ethics and a politics follow directly from and are immanent in metaphysics; the better one understands the universe in its complexity, in the connections that link each thing to every other, the more adequate is one's ethical relation in and to it. An ethics does not spring directly from our understanding of the world. Rather, it comes from our affective bonds to and connections with other things in the world, relations that enable us to enhance or diminish forms of life. Providing a reading of Spinoza's *Ethics* from the perspective of its ontological commitments may help open up ways in which his ethics and politics, and our own, may be developed in fuller depth.

I examine some texts of Friedrich Nietzsche in chapter 3. Like the Stoics and Spinoza, he styles his work as a critique of and an alternative to dominant philosophical traditions: primarily, for my purposes here, the writings of Hegel and other philosophers, such as Descartes, who have tended to privilege ideality over materiality. In Nietzsche's writings there is not only a privileging of the energetic forces of the body, there is also a primary focus on the question of orientation, on the direction of the future, on the trajectory of forces and their future effects. Drawing as he does on the Greeks and especially the pre-Socratics, Nietzsche aims to restore to philosophy its ethical and political force as a knowledge of and continuity with the one real world and the creation of an ethics—he calls it a morality as well as a transvaluation—appropriate not to everyone, decidedly non- or even anti-universalist (indeed an elitist activity) open only to those strong enough to create their own ethics, an ethics of affirmation, as their principle of self-regulation, an ethics capable of affirming itself eternally. Nietzsche's concept of *amor fati*, the love of fate, intensifies to its maximum the Stoic concept of being worthy of one's fate, a fate dictated or propelled not only by external causal forces—an impersonal fate—but of one's own cultivated nature. Nietzsche elaborates yet deviates both Stoic and Spinozan ontologies through his own perverse readings, for he reads them, as he does all philosophy, not in terms of the logical consistency or plausibility of their arguments but in terms of their values and limits for life, especially for an affirmative life. One cannot affirm life without also affirming the material world and its forces and without seeking to explore and press to the maximum the conditions under which life and its materialities are intensified. This is the task of Nietzschean philosophy: to bring into being new values that affirm all the forms of life to come, their complexities and their struggles, their forms of self-overcoming, their creativity.

If the Stoics, Spinoza, and Nietzsche form not only part of the history of philosophy but also a strain of counterphilosophy, a philosophy that functions in contradistinction to the dominant forms of reason represented in dualism (not to mention rationalism) that marks Platonism, Cartesianism, and Hegelianism, if their influence on the history of Western thought is less understood than these dominant traditions, nevertheless, their writings have sustained many powerful readings and renewals that could draw out what is missing from or problematic with the traditions to which they offered such compelling but relatively neglected alternatives. They are among the very figures brought together, however indirectly, in the writings of Gilles Deleuze (both alone and in collaboration with Félix Guattari). Through Deleuze's careful and thoroughly innovative readings of the Stoics, Spinoza, and Nietzsche, a number of contemporary theorists have been drawn again to these underappreciated yet immensely intriguing, difficult, and original philosophers.

Deleuze's work serves as both a literal and metaphoric center for this book. It was his readings that drew me first to the writers and positions explored here, and enabled me to use them to address a question that Deleuze did not, at least not directly—the relations between ideality and materiality. It is Deleuze's, and Deleuze and Guattari's, work that I address in chapter 4 (although his and their influence is clear in all the chapters) where once again I look at the question of ideality or the incorporeal through an examination of one of Deleuze and Guattari's most elusive concepts, indeed a concept that marks their own distinctive philosophy of the concept—the plane of immanence. The plane of immanence is what a philosophical concept must attain and address in order to become part of the history of thought; a concept must find for itself a nonlocatable place, an intensive position, among all the other concepts it addresses and disputes, which is also the condition under which it can itself be addressed and disputed, added to and complicated, and misunderstood or redirected by other concepts. The plane of immanence cannot be material, though it is not purely ideal either: rather, it can be conceived as the entirety of materiality, with the entirety of ideality that make this materiality conceivable, that is, capable of forming concepts. It cannot be understood as material in opposition to ideality. Rather, it is immanent in the world itself. It is not a Platonic order but an order of relations and interactions that occur between historically created concepts without the mediation of their "inventors" and freed from the forms of argument that are developed to support them. Concepts are able to address and transform each other, not magically, but through the encounters they undergo, the history in which they develop from one set of components to another. Although Deleuze is almost universally considered a materialist, his fascination with concepts, ideas, and the incorporeal complicates such an understanding.[4] Like many of the philosophers his work directly addresses, Deleuze can neither be classified as a materialist nor as an idealist. His work is oriented in both directions without any assumption of a break between them. An argument could be made, although I will not present it directly here, that Deleuze has addressed this question of the relations between the material and the ideal over and over in his writings without articulating it as such.

Deleuze remains at the heart of this project not only because of his profound and idiosyncratic readings of key figures—the Stoics, Spinoza, and Nietzsche—but also because in his writings he directs us to other philosophers who occupy an invaluable place in the genealogy of the incorporeal, near contemporaries of Deleuze, whose work he has used or referred to in a number of his writings. In chapter 5 I discuss some central concepts in the writings of Gilbert Simondon, whose influence on Deleuze and Guattari is the object of considerable current research. Simondon's writings, as with all the other philosophers addressed here, will not be examined in their breadth and detail, for although he published only two books, they are immensely broad in their interests, which range from the inventions of technics to the principles involved in the generation of art; rather, I look only at his concept of the processes of individuation that direct all kinds of relations, material (as is appropriate for purely material objects and processes), living (all forms of life are generated by processes of individuation), psychic, social, collective, and technical. I focus on the relations between the preindividual, individuations, and the transindividual. Simondon, as with the others I discuss in this book, not only develops a unique ontology that problematizes dualism; he is also interested in the technical, ethical, and aesthetic implications of this ontology, a conception of the world as a totality that is the result of a multiplicity of processes of individuation whose operations and activities are the same at all levels. Simondon's work is at once cosmological, biological, aesthetic, ethical, and sociopolitical. He is also a part of the lineage of thinking about the incorporeal, the immanence of ideality in materiality and of materiality in ideality that I aim to explore here. Like the plane of immanence in Deleuze's work or the will to power in Nietzsche's writings, Simondon invents a concept—the preindividual—that is simultaneously material and ideal, the condition for material bodies and self-standing concepts and the inherence of each in the other.

Chapter 6 focuses on a fragment of the prolific and wide-ranging writings of Raymond Ruyer, a philosopher of biology (especially embryology), physics, information theory, axiology, and cosmology, another of the figures whose writings are addressed, briefly but significantly, in Deleuze's writings. Ruyer is perhaps the least known of the philosophers I discuss here, but his work seems indispensable for thinking about the direction and force of materiality, whether in its inanimate or animate forms, in the processes that link, say, quantum fields, through various levels of organization and scale, to the operations of living beings and a living world. Ruyer's concept of consciousness as immediate self-proximity or self-survey provides us with a way of rendering far more complex the relations between the ideal and the material. If even the most elementary particles have consciousness in his broad antianthropomorphic sense, then consciousness is not a mysterious leap from a nonconscious material antecedent, but the growing forms of autoaffection that mark the coexistence and integration of materiality and ideality. Like Simondon, with whom he was familiar, Ruyer is also interested in the ways in which ontology involves an ethics and a politics, how the forms of interaction of materiality and ideality generate the possibility for the emergence of the arts and sciences, particular human ways of addressing the real, enhancing it, and directing some of its objects and processes to goals and ideals.

This lineage provides at least the briefest outlines of a philosophical alternative to a prevailing tendency to dualism in Western philosophy or to its contemporary successor, reductive materialism, a position that still dominates much of what is called theory today. While Cartesian forms of dualism have been relentlessly criticized and alternatives actively explored (in, for example, the tradition of phenomenology), nevertheless Descartes very clearly articulated some of the qualities or characteristics of thought—its nonspatial, nonlocalizable nature, for example—that even the most sophisticated and contemporary expressions of materialism (materialisms in their genetic, cognitive, or neurological forms) are unable to explain: what is thought, what is a concept, what is thinking? Thinking may be explicable in terms of the brain, neuronal networks, or cognitive connections, but none of these has the incorporeal quality of thought. Thought cannot be *nothing but* neuronal firings, brain processes, or cognitive relations: these are conditions, accompaniments, perhaps, but are not the same as thought (just as genes may condition and accompany all living forms without any specific aspect of life being reducible to a genomic base). In seeking a nonreductive materialism attentive to the conceptual or ideal dimensions of materiality as a whole, and of material things in their particularity, we cannot simply explain away thought, concepts, meanings, ideality, or the incorporeal, as, for example, emergent qualities from some increasing order of material complexity. Instead, to make a more robust and explanatorily rich philosophy, ideality needs to be taken seriously and understood in its own terms, not as the other or binary opposite of body but through its own capacities, qualities, and activities and through its ability to direct, orient, and internally inhabit materiality.

I propose here neither a new form of dualism nor a new reductive version of monism in advocating for a materialism that understands its reliance on ideality or an idealism that is committed to the material organization and conditions for ideality. I seek neither two substances whose connection must be adequately, but can only be mysteriously, explained (all dualisms fall prey to the problem expressed by Plato and Descartes—discerning the mysterious conduit by which mind and body interact) nor a single substance that is capable of both material and immaterial effects, but a way to conceptualize something between these alternatives. In exploring the reality of the incorporeal, I do not want to privilege ideality over materiality, but to think them together, as fundamentally connected and incapable of each being what it is without the other to direct and support it. Ideality frames, directs, and makes meaning from materiality; materiality carries ideality and is never free of the incorporeal forms that constitute and orient it as material. It is this connection that I aim to explore, using the genealogy I have indicated—a way to conceptualize materiality without reducing its ideal dimension, a way to think thought, through and in its material arrangements.

With ideality comes the possibility of collective social life, a kind of magical or religious thinking that seeks the orders of connection that regulate the universe itself and the elaboration of increasingly more complex prostheses or technologies that extend and transform materiality exponentially. Without ideality, a plan, a map, a model, an ideal, a direction, or a theme, materiality could not materialize itself. Only through the capacity of thought to extend itself beyond and through its corporeal limits is it directly implicated in the corporeal forces that constitute bodies as form, force, direction, orientation, or, more simply said, as the future which beckons it. This ideality, religious in its earliest conceptualizations, is also the condition for language, concepts, ideas that constitute discourse; the possibilities of philosophy (which debates the proper use of reason and the creation of concepts adequate to it); the emergence of sensations and perceptions whose organization and transformations constitute art; the functioning of testable conjectures; and the development of formulas and mathematical models that elaborate such conjectures constituting the natural sciences. Ideality provides the cohesion of form, the orientation or direction toward which material things tend, the capacity for the self-expansion of material things and relations into new orders.

With the rise of so-called new materialism, it is perhaps necessary to simultaneously call into being a new idealism, no longer Platonic, Cartesian, or Hegelian in its structure, that refuses to separate materiality from or subordinate it to ideality, resisting any reduction of the qualities and attributes of each to the operations of the other. In what follows I explore the entwinement of ideality and materiality, how each is the implicit condition for the other. As mutually implicated, ideality opens materiality up not just as the collectivity or totality of things but as a cohesive, meaningful world, a universe with a horizon of future possibilities. The philosophers I address here provide concepts and frameworks through which we may understand matter as always more than itself, as containing possibilities for being otherwise. I will explore the direction of materiality, its orientation to the future, and the ethical force of this orientation. This has numerous philosophical implications, among them that there is no definitive break between animals and humans or between animals, plants, and inanimate objects. Mind is not an attribute of a consciousness much like our own but characterizes all primary forms, all forms of the (Nietzschean) will to power, (Simondonian) individuation, or (Ruyerian) primary consciousness. While this order of ideality, sometimes described as pan-psychism, is often viewed in religious terms, through the connective and creative relations to a creator God conceived as the external force of coherence and direction of the world, it may be regarded instead as the material constitution of an ordered world in which the connections between things, between objects and events, come to or always already have meaning or many meanings, values, orientations, potentialities through their own modes of order and organization, without the need to invoke an independent God who exists separately from this world. Perhaps this can begin a *new* new materialism in which ideality has a respected place and where these forces of orientation can now be recognized as a condition for and immanent in materiality. Such an understanding of the world as material-ideal, as incorporeal openness, may provide a way to conceptualize ethics and politics as well as arts and technologies as more than human (but less than otherworldly), as ways of living in a vast world without mastering or properly understanding it, as creative inventions for the elaboration and increasing complexification of life in the world of coexistence with all other forms of life and with a nonliving nature.

1

THE STOICS, MATERIALISM, AND THE INCORPOREAL

An event is neither substance, nor accident, nor quality, nor process; events are not corporeal. And yet, an event is certainly not immaterial; it takes effect, becomes effect, always on the level of materiality. . . . Let us say that the philosophy of event should advance in the direction, at first sight paradoxical, of an incorporeal materialism.

—MICHEL FOUCAULT, "THE DISCOURSE ON LANGUAGE"

The distinction between materialism and idealism, between matter and idea, has pervaded Western philosophy since at least the time of Plato. Matter is commonly considered inert, passive, regulated by mechanical principles and thus regarded as open to calculation and prediction, while, as its opposite or other, mind, the Idea, is regarded as active, form giving, capable of perfection (or already perfect in itself) and capable of directing or informing matter or bodies to approximate in some way the perfection the idea represents. In Platonic thought, matter and idea are two altogether different substances, with the idea providing the outline, the eternal model for particular configurations of matter. This opposition between matter and ideality reaches its culmination in the writings of Descartes in the seventeenth century, where he proposes that material or mechanical causation is the principle that regulates all bodies, including human bodies, while mind or ideas, reason, is the principle that regulates thought. Dualism, the belief in two separate and irreducible substances, tends to dominate philosophical speculation—in spite of some notable exceptions—until well into the nineteenth century and beyond. Matter and mind, things and thoughts, are two incompatible orders that, however miraculously, are capable of connection, given their observable and experienced interrelations.[1]

Dualism comes under assault by the revolution in thought that occurs with the writings of Marx, Darwin, and Nietzsche in the nineteenth century, a revolution which implicitly or explicitly affirms the primacy of materialism over idealism. While each of these canonical and transformational theorists invokes a materialism that, even if it doesn't explain away ideas, or the ideal, subordinates the ideal to an effect, or a direction, of material transformations, whether these are understood as historical and political transformations, biological transformations, or transformations in what we understand as philosophy or thinking. For Marx, ideas are the consequences of the material relations to an economic mode of production; for Darwin, conceptuality, the brain, and the possibility of reason are produced gradually as a result of the interaction of biological descent and the forces of external contingency or chance that he describes as natural selection; for Nietzsche, ideas are material or corporeal forces struggling with other forces for conceptual dominance as much as bodies confronting each other for primacy. Materialism is commonly aligned with empiricist forms of knowledge, knowledge based on generalizations from bodily or perceptual observations, however technologically mediated; while idealism tends to become associated with rationalist forms, to philosophies structured by the internal order of reason. From the beginning of the twentieth century to the present, there seems little doubt that the tradition of materialism (whether identified with empiricist epistemologies or not) has apparently overcome the forces of the idealist tradition (whether identified with rationalist epistemologies or not).

Today just about everyone is a materialist. Not only within the discipline of philosophy, but throughout the humanities and sciences. Marxist models of historical materialism mingled and competed with materialist models of signification and materialist challenges to signification and the dialectic itself. There are a numerous recent books and anthologies announcing a "new feminist materialism," or a new "object-oriented materialism,"[2] as well as new materialist philosophical schools or positions.[3] Beyond the humanities, a sharp reductionism has occurred in the biological sciences, in which the mind is nearly universally assumed (usually without argument) to be the brain or its neural nets, and genes and their constituents are assumed to represent the body and its capacities. While there has been considerable criticism in the last few decades of both mechanical or atomistic materialism (primarily through work in subatomic and quantum physics and critical ecologies) and dialectical materialism (through the ongoing questioning of the idealism of a dialectical telos), it is *almost* impossible to find an explicit and credible contemporary advocate of idealism. Idealism at best lurks unknowingly within avowedly materialist texts.

Yet there is something hasty and unconsidered in the impulse to ignore, demote, or reduce ideas and the ideal to a material substrate, for something important and impossible to ignore is lost in the process. What is it that materialism must assume without being able to acknowledge as material? What intellectual maneuvers must materialism develop to hide what it must assume—concepts, processes, frames that are somehow different from and other than simply material? What must materialism assume, what terms must it develop, in order for it to explain what appears to be immaterial or extramaterial? How, for example, do materialist models consider concepts, thoughts, ideas? Are they simply activated neuronal connections? Isn't there something about concepts, whatever neuronal activity their generation and understanding requires, that is not reducible to even extremely complex material, that is, neurological, alignments? How do materialists understand the conditions of appearance of matter, such as space and time, materially? How do materialists understand meaning or sense in terms beyond their materiality as sonorous or written trace? How can sense, in both its senses, as meaning and as orientation, be possible without some direction in matter itself?

While this book will not attempt to develop a credible idealism (the limit to which idealisms tend is always solipsism), it will direct itself to an exploration of how the opposition between material and ideal complicates itself throughout its history, how, as Derrida notes, that which attempts to rid itself of complicating, or irrelevant, terms finds those terms inevitably returning to haunt the site of their excision.[4] What I am interesting in developing, and will attempt to explore in the following pages, is how materialisms tend to idealism, how at least some forms of materialism, from the time of ancient philosophy through the seventeenth century and the rise of modern philosophy and on to contemporary philosophy, nevertheless, in their most productive and non-reductive moments, do not rid themselves of the ideal but transform their materialism to accommodate a fringe or force of the ideal inevitably surrounding and infiltrating, or even composing, matter. For this investigation I will not attempt a systematic analysis of the history of materialism—an impossible project for me—but will rather seek forms of materialism that refuse to abandon idealism, a way of thinking the inherence of ideality in materiality, a paradoxical position only to the extent that it refuses the binarization, the inherent gap, the mutually exclusive and exhaustive relation between matter and ideal. Using forms of materialism, I will trace a small strain of idealism that nonetheless permeates materialism to enable it to more adequately and less reductively address what is irreducible to the material—what I will call variously, the incorporeal, sense, the immaterial, or the idea(l).

With this aim of developing a partial history of immaterial materialism or corporeal idealism in mind, I want to begin with an examination of a few of the key concepts within Stoic philosophy that have laid the groundwork for a number of philosophers to follow, among them Spinoza, Nietzsche, and Deleuze. In returning to ancient texts—actually only traces and fragments of ancient texts—we will see that there may be an alternative philosophical genealogy of the incorporeal or the ideal within the material. Through the work of Stoics, I will attempt to show that ontology is never disconnected from questions of physics and ethics—that is, our views of what the world is and how it functions make a difference to how we understand ourselves and our place in relation to other living beings and the cosmos itself. Through the Stoics, we will explore the concept of the incorporeal and its relations to materiality before, in the following chapters, addressing other later theorists who further complicate or render impossible the binary division of materialism from idealism.

THE STOICS

Stoicism is one of numerous philosophical schools that emerged in Ancient Greece in the fourth century BCE. Unlike earlier schools, including those comprising the pre-Socratics and flowing from the teachings of Plato and Aristotle, and unlike contemporary positions such as those of the Epicureans and the Cynics, nearly all Stoic philosophers were non-Greeks who came to Athens from various regions around the Mediterranean. Émile Bréhier claims, "All third century Stoics known to us were aliens, born in countries on the periphery of Hellenism. . . . They were subject to many influences other than the Greek, particularly the influence of neighboring Semitic peoples."[5] This position of outsider or foreigner has perhaps directly contributed to the focus of the Stoics on worlds beyond the local, in their cosmological aspirations to a rational, ordered universe, indifferent to living beings, that, nevertheless, human beings, through reason, can come to comprehend, namely to a philosophy that seeks order amidst the fragility, fear, and disorder of migration.

Zeno of Citium (probably c. 334–c. 262 BCE) came from Rhodes;[6] Cleanthes of Assos (c. 330–c. 230 BCE) was one of the few Athenians to head the school (and was reputed to be an impoverished prizefighter before entering), and he maintained the school in close accordance with the teachings of Zeno; Chrisyppus (c. 279–c. 206 BCE), a native of Soli, Cilicia, became a pupil of Cleanthes and was regarded, after Zeno, as the second founder of Stoicism.[7] Stoicism as a philosophical school or tradition not only managed to proliferate and prosper during the rise of philosophy in Athens, with a number of philosophers being sent as emissaries to Rome and elsewhere. It also became a significant force in the later elaboration of Roman Stoicism, which strengthened itself over three centuries. Epictetus (c. 55–c. 135 CE), born a slave in Hierapolis (now Turkey), lived in Rome until his expulsion to Nicopolis and elaborated Stoicism as a way of life in harmony with nature, following the teachings of the Athenian Stoics. Marcus Aurelius (121–180 CE) was adopted by the emperor Antoninus (it is quite significant that all the emperors of early Rome adopted as their successors the brightest of their generation rather than seeking familial or dynastic succession) and became the head of the Roman Empire himself, while stealing time from his duties to undertake philosophy, inspired as he was by the writings of Epictetus and other teachers.

Outlining Stoic philosophy is fraught with difficulties. Not only are the vast bulk of the texts written by the early or Greek Stoics lost (it is not clear that some of the early Stoics even preserved their work in writing, being focused as much as possible on speaking, that is, teaching on the painted porch, or Stoa, where all who wanted to hear were welcome), it is also not clear that what remains, often outlined in the writings of various critics of Stoicism, is an accurate representation of their views on various topics.[8] Nothing remains of the work of Zeno or Chrisyppus, who was reputed to have written 705 books on a wide variety of topics, according to Diogenes Laërtius, through whose writings we have access, second hand, to the ideas of many of the Hellenic and Roman Stoics. The writings of the earlier philosophers are preserved piecemeal in the later writings of Cicero, Philo of Alexandria, and others; and the texts of the later Stoics—Seneca, Epictetus, Marcus Aurelius—are sometimes only available in fragments, though a great many more complete texts have survived. The most accessible surviving texts are highly critical of the Stoic position—such as the writings of Plutarch, Sextus Empiricus, Galen, and Origen.[9] Unlike philosophy since the seventeenth century, much of our understanding of ancient philosophy is wildly speculative and conjectural: most of the key Stoic texts have not survived or have survived in fragments only in the work of those who disagree with them. There can be no sense that one's interpretation of these earlier, and later, texts is secure or accurate, a disconcerting idea at the least. Yet there remains something so attractive and appealing in the remainders left for us by the Stoics, for they outline a new kind of philosophy that is very different from their peers and predecessors, whose works in a sense have come to define even contemporary models of rationality. The Stoics provide an alternative "origin" for a chain of thinking that complicates and problematizes the heritages of Platonism and Aristotelianism.

The Stoics provide another mode of thinking, a more complex beginning, to the history of Western thought that opens up questions which even today have not been adequately addressed. This perhaps explains the appeal Stoicism exerts for the wayward tradition that provides an alternative to the dominant (dualist) philosophies of Descartes, Kant, and Hegel: the writings of Spinoza, Nietzsche, even Darwin, Bergson, and in more contemporary writers such as Foucault, Deleuze, Derrida, and Irigaray. The Stoics, while philosophers par excellence, nevertheless transform what philosophy is and how it is to be undertaken. Philosophy, a love of wisdom, is less a rational reflection on the world than a series of practices of living well in the world. Stoicism becomes a way of engaging ethically in a world that maintains and is part of a cosmic order of which we (humans, let alone living beings) are but a tiny part. Neither masters of matter nor of thought, human beings at their most rational do not order the world but submit to its forces and make them their own.

Deleuze claims that the Stoics invented a new image of the philosopher as well as a new way of doing philosophy, a new orientation to the place of philosophy in life. No longer must the philosopher undertake the Platonic task of bringing our ideas of things and ourselves into the clear light, and height, of Reason, reaching ever higher to the (transcendental) Ideal. "Height," Deleuze suggests, "is the properly Platonic Orient."[10] The Stoics distinguish themselves from the pre-Socratics (even those to whom they owe conceptual debts, especially Empedocles and Heraclitus), who are absorbed by an image of philosophy as an exploration of dark recesses of the earth, caves, or the underground: "The Pre-Socratics placed thought inside the caverns and life, in the deep. They sought the secret of water and fire . . . " (*LS* 128). If the pre-Socratics seek the dark depths, and Platonism seeks clear heights, Deleuze locates the Stoics as philosophers of the surface, between height and depth: "These third Greeks are no longer entirely Greek. They no longer expect salvation from the depths of the earth or from autochthony, any more than they expect it from heaven or from the Idea" (129).[11] While neither ignoring the (physical and ontological) depths nor the illuminating heights, the

Stoics observe them univocally, in the same terms, as the surface and from the surface: "there is no longer depth or height" (130), just a continuous movement of the surface throughout. The concept of philosophy as that which is located on the earth, at its surface, in the cosmos, part of the universe, worth no more nor any less than any other part, this image of the philosopher as one who lives and develops a knowledge of how to live well, traces a movement that will be continually displaced by dualism but also reasserts itself from time to time in the history of philosophy that follows from it. This orientation to the surface, through which depths can be unearthed and a cosmos understood, seeks a life in agreement with nature, a life that knows what it can and that aims to learn what it does not know. Reason is both of the earth, corporeal, and beyond the earth, cosmic or divine, but these are in fact one and the same order, viewed from different perspectives, the order of materiality in its totality, an order that coheres the ideas it generates.

Bréhier claims that the Stoics "evolved a vitalistic cosmology" (33) that moved from a model of health (the body as a balance of the four elements—earth, air, fire, and water—that require the right proportions of hot and cold, wet and dry) into a model of the cosmos. For the early Stoics—Zeno, Cleanthes, and Chrisyppus—the universe is itself a living body, just as all its elements or contents, whether living or nonliving—are animated by breath or pneuma, a fiery soul that inhabits each thing and that, in its totality, comprises Zeus or the Cosmos. Pneuma is the active and rational principle of the universe, it animates the world and enables the world to be regarded as a living thing. Fiery breath activates a universe and also ends it: the Stoics believed that if the cosmos is a transformation of an originary fiery breath that cools and changes itself into the four (somehow less divine, more terrestrial) elements, earth, air, water, and fire, whose mixtures and qualities produce things, both animate and inanimate, the four elements in their various configurations and mixtures also eventually cool themselves into oblivion.[12] Just as pneuma creates the universe, it is that which is restored in the great conflagration or apocalypse that ends the universe and prepares for its (eternal) return. The universe is breath in various states of contraction and expansion, breath cooled down into things which are held together by an inner force, or *tonus*, a tension that give a thing its cohesion and consistency, thus connecting it to all other things from which it becomes distinguished and with which it shares a natural affinity. We have here a fire-logos, a breath-seed, a fire that carries within it seeds, material forces that are greatly compressed which shape and direct the emergence of things. "Zeno and Chrisyppus maintained that the earth and the sky were the substance of God: 'Just as the different parts of the body unite to form the seed, but when a new body grows out of the seed they divide once more, so everything arises out of the One and is reunited with the One,' says Cleanthes. 'All the world is divine; but it may also be said that "God is the soul of the world"' (Cleanthes, I, 532), designating by the word God the rational and active principle in the world."[13] God is the fiery force that makes the universe in its complexity and that remains to redirect its end and breath into the constitution of another.

A PECULIAR MATERIALISM

The Stoics are materialists. Indeed, the Stoics are perhaps the first thoroughgoing materialists, moving beyond the atomism of Democritus and Epicurus, for whom the world is comprised of the combination of the smallest indivisible entity, each corpuscle being surrounded by a void, to an account of material forces that move beyond the concept of matter as made of smallest, irreducible particles or atoms. For the Stoics, the universe, including the *pneumatic force* of fiery breath, is material or corporeal. It is comprised of bodies, things, which can be divided into two kinds—active and passive—that which affects and that which is affected. Active bodies are pneuma, an animating or creative principle; passive bodies are composed of the four elements, which themselves are derivatives of the creative pneuma, remaining unqualified without its animating breath. Pneuma as active principle informs passive matter, but not through an external imposition or imprinting but through causation. Active and passive are not different types of bodies, for both are equally corporeal and both positions exist within one and the same body. As Diogenes Laërtius says of the founding Stoics:

> They believe that there are two principles of the universe, the active and the passive. The passive, then, is unqualified substance, i.e., matter, while the active is a rational principle [logos] in it, i.e. god. For he, being eternal and [penetrating] all of matter, is the craftsman of all things. Zeno of Citium propounds this doctrine in his *On Substance*, Cleanthes in his *On Atoms*, Chrisyppus toward the end of book 1 of his *Physics*, Archedemus in his *On Elements* and Posidinius in book 2 of his *Account of Physics*. They say that there is a difference between principles and elements. For the former are ungenerated and indestructible, whereas the elements are destroyed in the [universal] conflagration. And the principles are bodies and without form, whereas the elements are endowed with form.[14]

Active principles are the corporeal causes that abide within bodies, which are themselves capable of becoming causes for other bodies; the rational ordering principle is not imposed on or extracted from passive substance, as Plato claims, but is itself the same substance, pneuma, now acting rather than being acted on. Active and passive are not two different orders, but one and the same body in relation to other bodies.

What we understand as qualities of bodies are bodies themselves. Chrisyppus, suggests that "'light, whiteness, warmth, are bodies' (II 386). 'Voice is a body, since everything capable of action and influence is a body.' Even virtues and vices, wisdom, etc. were in their opinion bodies."[15] Not only are qualities and attributes bodies, but Zeus himself, God, the full force of fiery pneuma, is entirely material, the purest and most refined, the most fully active, of material forces, a materiality surviving as the apocalyptic fire that ends one universe and begins another.[16] The divine is not beyond matter or bodies but can be identified with the entirety of matter or bodies together with their capacity to sustain themselves and to be created and destroyed and reanimated over and over. The divine is not of a different order than materiality but is coextensive with it.

Bodies are not separated from the Ideas they are supposed to resemble, contrary to Plato; rather, for the Stoics, ideas are themselves bodies, qualities are bodies, and even the soul is a body: insofar as it acts and can be acted on, it is necessarily connected in its specificity to a specific body (for the Stoics, the soul, as a particular, is linked to its particular body as one body or quality linked to another).[17] The world is composed not of Being [*to on*] but of *something* [*to ti*], which exists in two forms.[18] Some-things either exist, in which case they are material bodies (*somata*) that act (as does pneuma) or are acted on (as in the case of inanimate objects). All being is corporeal. Every object, force, quality, and state is corporeal. Divine being induces material being; pneuma and matter mix together to produce specific bodies. According to Chrisyppus, whatever can be is something "that only exists which may be grasped and touched (II, 359)."[19] Or there are nonexistent beings, beings that do not exist but somehow subsist, which condition and surround the existence of things but neither act nor are acted on. It is to these nonexistent things that we turn shortly.

Existing somethings are of two types: they are either things that exist, bodies, along with their tensions (*tonus*), qualities, actions, and states, or things that do not exist but nevertheless can be inferred, which inhere in, make sense of, undergird, and inform bodies. Existing things, separately and in their totality, are always material, imbued with pneuma, and are either active or passive. Anything that exists or is capable of acting or being acted on is a body, whether this is a living body, a nonliving object, or psychological and moral characteristics like the soul, wisdom, virtue, and justice. These are not ideals that operate apart from objects but are the qualities and relations in and between bodies: they are what acts and is acted upon. Even reason, virtue, character, or psychology remains a body (or many), for each acts and can be acted upon.[20]

The world is a material unity, a living being that includes every thing, every body, including those bodies that are ideas. Alexander claims:

> [The Stoics] say that since the world is a unity which includes existing things in itself and is governed by a living, rational, intelligent nature, the government of existing things which it possesses is an everlasting one proceeding in a sequence and ordering. The things which happen

first become causes to those which happen after them. In this way, things are bound together, and neither does anything happen in the world such that something else does not unconditionally follow from it and become causally attached to it. . . . They say that fate, nature and rationale in accordance with which the all is governed is god. It is present in all things which exist and happen, and in this way uses the proper nature of all existing things for the government of all.[21]

Active things, god, the forces of the universe, act, and passive things, objects, and living organisms are acted on and created by these active forces.

Bodies or things, divine or mundane, in acting or being acted upon, constitute the realm of causes. Divine causes are the only cause of all things, originating pneuma, the primordial force of all things in the cosmos; but at the mundane level the Stoics are interested in the complex chain of causal relations that applies to particular bodies.[22] A body that acts causes something, though, as we will see, what it causes is conceived by the Stoics in an utterly idiosyncratic way: causes do not cause effects, as we have assumed since at least the seventeenth century; rather they create predicates. As Stobaeus, one of the major sources for accessing early Stoic thought, writes,

1) Zeno says that a cause is "that because of which," while that of which it is the cause is an attribute; and that the cause is a body, while that of which it is a cause is a predicate. 2) He says that it is impossible that the cause be present yet that of which it is the cause does not belong. 3) This thesis has the following force. A cause is that because of which something occurs, as, for example, it is because of prudence that being prudent occurs, because of the soul that being alive occurs. . . . 4) Chrisyppus says that a cause is "that because of which": and that cause is an existent and a body.[23]

Causes are the reasons for a process, state, or event, even though what they produce are, apparently paradoxically, not bodies. Bodies are bodies to the extent that they have a (relative) causal agency. Causes produce other causes; bodies only interact with other bodies. Fate is understood by the Stoics as the concatenation of causes alone: fate does not include effects (the concept of "effect" is nowhere included in the Stoic definition of *cause*) but only the coming together and collective force of causes in their totality, causes indifferent to effects, bound up only with each other. "Fate is always defined in terms of a series of causes: there is an eternal causal nexus, where cause gives rise to cause. Given the overall coherence between all things in the universe, fate is best understood not as a linear sequence but as a network of interacting causes."[24]

Causes, in other words, connect only to other causes as bodies connect only to other bodies. Bodies are bodies only to the extent that they are capable of acting on each other through collective relations. Bodies, all the bodies in the universe, are causally connected in a fate, a relentless convergence of causes, that carries them with it, culminating in the long run in the conflagration and the repetition of future universes. Fate, though, is not understood as the strictly determined. Determinism is a particular relation between causes and effects in which a cause has a guaranteed and predictable, distinguishable, effect. It is the status of effects that prevents the Stoics from considering fate as necessity, inevitability, or predictability and also distinguishes them from any modern notion of causation, concentrated as it is on effects. Bodies act and are acted upon, are active or passive. Bodies cannot be considered generalizable or part of a class of universals ("bottle," "man," "rock"). Universals are errors in reasoning. It may be that the Stoics are the first nominalists. They resist the universal as an abstraction, an approximation of the Platonic ideal. All that is real are bodies, bodies in their individual particularity, bodies that may share qualities or characteristics but whose shared nature is again individual and particular. "Blue" is what is common in blue things, rather than an ideal blue or a universal blue that blue things approximate or toward which they tend.

Fate, the operation of causes on causes, will become a concept that remains powerful in the ongoing impact of Stoicism on the history of philosophy. It will become the basis of a new kind of ethics. But fate, for the Stoics, never undermines or eliminates an individual's responsibility for acting as he or she does. An individual's actions come from what he or she has "in them" as part of their character, what they cause in themselves. Responsibility does not come from our behaving in accordance with predetermined external causes: rather, what we can control, what is within our nature, our history of behaviors, our experience, what we have learned and assimilated into ourselves, is what changes and directs our nature. We will return to the question of fate later in this chapter.

What is peculiar about the Stoic tradition, what enables it to exceed its own materialism, is the place it accords to nonexisting things, things that are not objects or subjects but what they sometimes call "incorporeals" or not-somethings. While incorporeals (*asomata*) do not exist, they are not nonexistent; they are not-nothing. They still belong to the category of "something."[25] However, unlike something, they do not exist but *subsist* as the incorporeal conditions for the appearance and operation of somethings, objects, subjects, and their qualities and relations. This idea of a nonexisting not-something is the object of ridicule in the writings of Alexander, Sextus Empiricus, and Galen.[26] However, it is central not only to the materialism developed by the Stoics, but, as I will argue in the following chapters, for any kind of materialism that aims to function nonreductively. Every materialism requires a frame, a nonmaterial localization, a becoming-space and time, that cannot exist in the same way and with the same form as the objects or things that they frame. Every materialism, whether this is acknowledged openly or not, requires an incorporeal frame. The appeal of the Stoics, even today, lies in the audacity with which they develop the concept of the incorporeal as the subsisting condition of material existence. Their materialism is rigorous and thoroughgoing, but they are among the very few philosophers in the history of Western thought to openly acknowledge that materialism, their own philosophical commitment, cannot be self-inclusive or self-limiting. The Stoics admit into their ontology not only things with their active and passive, causally structured, relations but also the non-things that frame things, put them in the same field and create a plane or context for their actions and being acted upon. Bodies are both created by the divine breath but cohere, connect to each other, and form a world or universe because they are sustained by a universal sympathy, fate, necessity, a vast web of causes that connect them as a whole.

The Stoics are fascinated with causal actions of various kinds that create mixtures of things. How do bodies mix together? They distinguish three types of mixture: the first is "juxtaposition," where two bodies are mixed together but each remains discernible from the other—like sugar and salt before they are dissolved. The second is "fusion," in which two bodies are entirely mixed together in a way that makes their independent existence no longer possible—this commonly occurs, for example, in cooking. A cake is no longer decomposable into its ingredients, which have been permanently changed in the process of mixing and heating. The third kind of mixture is called "total blending," where two bodies are mixed together in such a way that every element of one is thoroughly mixed with every element of the other, such as pouring a drop of wine into the sea. In this case, although there is a total blending, each body can be extracted from the blend.[27] A third entity is created, which is neither the first body nor the body added to it. It may be, as a number of classical scholars suggest, that the universe itself is to be understood as a "total blending" of the two principles of bodies, divine and mundane. The divine may be conceived as that which is blended with every body, large or small, composing the universe. The divine, Zeus, may be understood as immanent and internal to the universe and all that composes it. It is not so much that the universe is composed of an active divine principle and a separate passive material principle: rather, active and passive, divine and material, are completely blended. Pneuma is not distinct from matter but rather matter is always already infused with pneuma.

We need now to further address the question of bodies as causes and what it is that they cause. We need to ask: why is an effect? What does a cause cause? And why aren't effects considered bodies that are capable of having their own effects? Why is it that the corporeality of the Stoic worldview, the intriguing materialism they elaborate as part of their physics, is limited to causes? To address these questions, we need to turn to the conceptual invention that is alone the Stoics'—the concept of the incorporeal.

INCORPOREALS

If all causes are bodies and only bodies—even if they are qualities or states of bodies—then effects, by contrast, cannot be regarded as material. They are considered by the Stoics to be incorporeal, not-something but not-nothing either. The effects of causes are always incorporeal, real but not material, subsistent rather than existent, inhering in their causes while these causes connect with other bodies, that is, other causes. The Stoics consider effects as incorporeal insofar as effects can be considered as *predicates*. Sextus Empiricus claims, in an example that Deleuze discusses in some detail, that a cause, cutting, has an effect, being cut, but it is not a body that is being cut, it is a body that, by the cutting, is transformed from unwounded to wounded. Its being-cut is an incorporeal effect, an event, an alignment of bodies that produce predicate-effects: "The Stoics say that every cause is a body which becomes the cause to a body of something incorporeal. For instance the scalpel, a body, becomes the cause to the flesh, a body, of the incorporeal predicate 'being cut.' And again, the fire, a body, becomes the cause to the wood, a body, of the incorporeal predicate 'being burnt.'"[28] The body uncut is material; a cut body is equally material. But there is something immaterial about the cutting, the being cut, the is-cutting, which is not so much a process as the acquisition of a new predicate. Bodies functioning as causes do not produce physical properties or qualities (for example, being cut is not a quality of a body) but logical and meaningful relations (relations that Deleuze describes as "sense" throughout his exploration of its strange movements from the Stoics to Lewis Carroll, Alexius Meinong, and Bertrand Russell in *LS*). Being-cut is an alignment of bodies and an incorporeal sense that inheres in this momentary alignment: in short, it is an event, a composition of bodies and sense.

Clement, in his *Miscellanies* (8.9.26.3–4), elaborates: "Hence becoming, and being cut—that of which the cause is a cause—since they are activities, are incorporeal. It can be said, to make the same point, that causes are causes of predicates, or, as some say, of sayables [*lekta*]— for Cleanthes and Archedemus call predicates 'sayables.' Or else, and preferably, that some are causes of predicates, for example, of 'is cut,' whose case [i.e. substantival form] is 'being cut.'"[29] The subject of a proposition is a body (as well as the representation of a body in the case of a spoken or written proposition, which is also a body), but the predicates capable of qualifying the subject are incorporeal, predicates not subjected to causation even though they are its effects, predicates that exist in a different way than their subjects, as nonbodies. *Lekta,* or "sayables," are different from propositions or statements, which are material. They contain not just what we would understand as "meaning," or "the signified," with their immense variability and openness and reliance on both psychology and subjectivity. For the Stoics, lekta are not dependent on minds: they exist, or rather, subsist, independent of consciousness or a community. They subsist, somewhere, not any material place, but with all the incorporeals, never fully present but always past and future.

The Stoics mention four incorporeals. It is not clear whether this is a definitive list, to which no others can be added, or a list of those incorporeals that are of use in particular arguments, to which other terms may be added. They are the *void, space, time,* and *lekton.* These are among the most intriguing—and brilliant—ontological concepts within Western philosophy. They cannot be considered anomalies or contradictions of the Stoic commitment to materialism, but are ways of understanding the immaterial conditions that uphold, enable, and complicate materialism. It may be the case that space, time, and the void are the immaterial conditions for any material something,[30] but lekta are the capacity of bodies or material somethings to become more and other than what they are, the condition of their complexity, their rationality and ordered place in the universe. Lekta are what can be said about a thing, what a statement can do to qualify or modify a subject, what enables it to be conceptualized as undergoing change or becoming other. Lekta are "impassive entities," yet they are not irrelevant to any expression of the actions and passions of bodies. They are not secondary qualities dependent on bodies; nor do I believe, as some suggest, that incorporeals are terms complementary with bodies, existing in a reciprocal relation with them.[31] If incorporeals either derive from bodies or exist in a relation of mutual dependence, then they must be capable of acting or being acted upon, and if they can act, they devolve back to bodies themselves. If they engage with bodies, they must be understood as bodies themselves.

The incorporeals cannot be understood as qualities, generalities (or universals), or even as quasi objects: they neither act nor are acted upon. This disqualifies them from adding to, making up, or directly engaging with bodies. They are more conditions for the possible and actual existence of bodies (and their expression), an imperceptible yet unimposed and constitutive field of cohesion (at least with place, time, and the void) that enables bodies, objects, to come into being, and to come to mean something (in the case of lekta), without these transformations being in any way corporeal themselves. They are the modes of presentation of objects, the conditions under which things exist, extend themselves, live in time, and come to produce effects or sense. They are not a priori categories that we impose on the world but orders by which the world makes and expresses itself. Things are surrounded and suffused by incorporeals, which enable them to have extension or occupy a location (place), have a time or history (time), exert effects beyond themselves (lekta), and have a limit beyond which there can be no things (void). For the sake of convenience, I will discuss each of these terms separately, reserving the most mysterious and obscure—lekta—for the last. This may help explain how the lekton is linked, not to spoken or written language, but to a sense that is both eternal and extended.

VOID AND PLACE

Void is probably the most simple of the incorporeals, even though it remains quite complex in Stoic ontology. Jacques Brunschwig claims that "the void is incorporeal, and even the incorporeal *par excellence*: capable of being occupied by a body, but ceasing to be void when it is actually occupied (hence destroyed as such, not just acted upon and altered by the entering body), it is definitionally 'deprived of body.'"[32] It is difficult to define the void (*kenon*—literally, "the empty")—indeed it is the absence of all things, qualities, states, and events—without also specifying that which connects it to the cosmos, place. Void and place are almost exact counterparts. Place is capable of being occupied by a body; the void is not. Void is thus that which lacks a body, that which is noncorporeal, but is capable of receiving a body, a process that transforms it from void to place. As Sextus Empiricus describes it, void, place, and room are fundamentally linked: "1) The Stoics say that void is what can be occupied by an existent but is not occupied, or an interval empty of body, or an interval unoccupied by body. 2) Place is what is occupied by an existent and made equal to what occupies it (by 'existent' they now mean body, as is clear from the interchange of names). 3) And they say that room is an interval partly occupied by a body and partly unoccupied. Some have said that room is the place of the larger body."[33]

Void and place are closely connected though different incorporeals. Void (*kenon*) is different from place (*topos*) and from room (*chora*): void has no body or thing in it, place is that which is occupied by a thing or body, and room is what is partly occupied by a thing, leaving an empty space, though not a void, capable of being occupied. Void is that which occupies the infinity of extension without being able to be localized anywhere. Place is what is occupied by bodies. Room is what remains of place after the bodies occupying a specific place take it up, leaving, as it were, a border of emptiness. The void is the model of space, space before and as it becomes occupied by things in specific regions or places not as template or ideal but as limit or edge. Room demonstrates that place does not have to be fully occupied by bodies for place to exist. Place marks not only what extension bodies occupy but also what they *could* occupy. The void is the limit (perhaps itself capable of shifting), beyond which no body can occupy place. What each shares is the three-dimensional extensity of bodies, even though void and place cannot be understood as bodies themselves and even though a jar, container, or room could be understood as a body as much as void. Void and place are incorporeal to the extent that they take what qualities they have (dimension, extension, direction) from the bodies they either support or enframe. Rooms can perhaps be understood as "limited" or positioned voids, "intracosmic pockets" that exist within bodies,[34] though these empty places must not be confused with the extracosmic void. Void and place subsist only because of the particular nature of bodies; they are thus themselves particulars, though without body.

The Stoics deny that the void functions within and between things, for example, at the site of the operations of the atom, the space between atoms, and a mode of linkage between objects, as Leucippus and Democritus, suggest, or a field through which things move but do not abide, as the Epicureans, particularly Epicurus and Lucretius, claim. Rather, the Stoic conception is a unique one—the void is singular or one (not surrounding each atom or each thing), the infinite field that exists, without outer boundary, at the edge or the end of the cosmos of things, extending out in all directions.[35] The cosmos, composed of bodies (and some incorporeals), is surrounded by an infinitely extendable void, a pure emptiness or place absent of any thing, a place that may be capable of supporting things but does not do so. Both place and the void, like bodies themselves, exist as three dimensional, extending in breadth, width, and height. The void does so to infinity. The void is not nothing, the absence of all types of something: the incorporeals subsist even in the absence of bodies. The void subsists as a possible condition for place, where things abide: it constitutes the conditions and terms of place with none of the things that occupy or take up place. It is pure extension to infinity. Void is thus considered independent of body, but also independent of mind or reason's capacity to conceptualize it. It is an extracosmic, independently subsisting infinity, an absolute particular incapable of generalization or universalization, extension in itself, orientation in itself, unbounded openness, the openness that enables bodies and their qualities to abide in place that is qualified by its bodies and that disposes bodies to be in certain relations with each other.

Void is thus the model of extension that coheres as place through the actions and passions of objects that abide in that part of it that devolves into place. Place is the region of the void that becomes inhabited or occupied by bodies and their mixtures and, through bodily forces, becomes the field of the unity of bodies, a world of things, a living union of all bodies and the totality of their active and passive relations. This union occupies all of place and defines the limits of place. Surrounding place thus understood is void, in all directions, with no limit, except the edge it shares with place. The void is the condition under and through which divine fire can create and repeat the creation of the universe. Void is what subsists during the expansion and contraction of bodies, qualities, and states, enabling place to be restored as bodies come to occupy it. Void is outside the cosmos; place is coextensive with the cosmos; room is within the cosmos as a particular kind of body, a body capable of containing another body.

TIME

While there is always a temptation to understand time and temporality as a fourth dimension to space, sharing many of its qualities (time does share with place a number of significant features, including continuity, infinity, and infinite divisibility), it is important to understand it, as do the Stoics, as a self-subsisting particular, an incorporeal order that is unique, ontologically separate from the other incorporeals, and exerts its own very particular conditions and effects on material bodies. Time is associated by the Stoics with movement: for Zeno, it "is the dimension of all motion without qualification."[36] It is the dimension or order within which bodies, including the entire universe, move, though it cannot be identified with that movement; rather it conditions this movement. While, for the Stoics, time consists in three directions or orientations, past, present, and future, it is only the present that can be said to exist. The past and future subsist as infinite forms that begin in one direction from the present to the past or in another direction from the present to the future. The present itself is capable of infinite division, making it minutely short or long. "The present moment" may last a millisecond or vast eons of galactic time, but is always bordered by the past stretching back forever and the future infinitely directed ahead. It can be understood as an extended or extensible present bounded by two orders of the infinite.

The present is variously conceived in different Stoic texts as an instant or moment or as that which takes the time it takes,[37] a position that is in some ways remarkably close to Bergson's understanding of the moving direction of the present, which brings with it more and more of the past.[38] The present is edged on one side by the infinite past and on the other by the infinite future:

> [Posidonius's definition] (1) Some things are infinite in every respect like the whole of time. Others in a particular respect, like the past and the future. For each of them is limited only by reference to the present. (2) His definition of time is as follows: dimension of motion or measure of speed and slowness. (3) And he holds that that time which is thought of in terms of "when" is partly past, partly future, and partly present. The last consists of a part of the past and a part of the future, encompassing the actual division. But the division is point-like. 4) Now and the like are thought of broadly and not exactly. 5) But now is also spoken of with reference to the least perceptible time encompassing the division of the future and the past.[39]

The past, present, and future are not mutually exclusive but occur, in a sense, together, the present being continuously divisible into the past and the future, the past pulling the present into itself, with the future imminently pushing on the present. Any "when" will require a measure of all three (nonspatial) coordinates. The present can be understood either as an ongoing process (a day, a season, a year) or an ever divisible instant. The present can be understood readily as contracted or expanded according to the context of our understanding.

The Stoic conception of time as movement focuses on the capacity for change: movement makes it difficult to understand an entirely stable unchanging phenomenon, and the universe must be conceived as in perpetual, if ordered, change. Indeed, the Stoics remain fascinated with the question of time, its nature and effects precisely because of their twin concerns with understanding the universe as a causally ordered whole that is rationally organized, whose principles are comprehensible and may provide rational principles for the regulation of one's life in the best possible manner, and also with providence, not a strict determinism but a commitment to a broadly considered fate or destiny. They avoid a reductive determinism in part through the assertion that causes are bodily, but effects are incorporeal. They also avoid a reductive, mecha-nistically conceived determinism through their conception of an ethical relation that binds us and our behavior and wishes to how the universe is, linking ethics to physics (and logic, a topic we will resist elaborating here) and insisting on the freedom that reason gives to life, and espe-cially human life, as bodies engaging with other bodies from which they learn and which produces change in them. Ethics is a life lived accord-ing to internally understood principles. Rational bodies, in their causal efficacy, also bring with them what is not reducible to fixed causes, an openness that the force of time brings to bodies capable of reason, of understanding themselves and their world.[40]

Time is understood as incorporeal because the measure of the motion of a moving body is not itself material, just as the space a moving body covers is not material. Rather, both time and space (as we now under-stand the Stoic concept of place) are the incorporeal conditions of the causal force of movement. Time is considered the movement of the uni-verse as a totality (as well as all the bodies within it—the sun's move-ments, for example, yield day and night as well as the seasons): yet it persists even in the destruction of the universe as the ongoing possibility (or, as the Stoics imply, the inevitability) of new universes, of the eternal return of the cosmos. Time subsists to the extent that it survives even between universes, just as must the void. It is space that must trans-form itself as parts of the void become filled with bodies: space or place becomes linked to the movement not only of particular bodies but of the unity of all bodies. Time and void, both infinite, divisible, continuous, and eternal, are the abiding, immaterial conditions for the existence, dis-appearance, and return of bodies.

LEKTA

If place, time, and void are objectively subsistent, that is, are in no way dependent on mind, cognition, or recognition, lekta remain difficult to classify this way, though I believe that these are also independent par-ticulars, perhaps formulated or uttered in human speech but subsisting, nevertheless, in the world outside human consciousness and independent of reflection or awareness. Lekta address not only what is part of language, meaning, or sense but also parts of the world, whose sense they render articulable in language. Although lekta have often been considered as psychological, they can more consistently be regarded as a sense that adheres to bodies and their mixtures that minds are capable of comprehending and words are capable of articulating, a mediation between different kinds of body, those making up language, those composing human language speakers and listeners, and the body and qualities about which they speak. Moreover, lekta adhere to events, independent of language: they are the ongoing possibility of sense whether such a sense is thought or said or not.[41]

Lekta, sayables, enable humans to articulate and understand predicates, what can be said of things, changes in states of affairs, and especially effects. As Diogenes Laërtius comments, "saying is different from voicing. For utterances are voiced but it is states of affairs which are said—they, after all, are actually sayables."[42] Sayables articulate states of affairs, that is, what happens to a body, understood in language as the grammatical subject. They are understood as the predicates which qualify a subject, the (incorporeal) event that occurs to a subject (or appellative—"man," "Cato," "horse"). The predicate depicts the action or event that occurs to a subject, a subject which abides (as a body) while the changes occur to it. "Cato walks." That is to say, the state of affairs of walking, the event of walking, is something that occurs to the subject rather than an effect of the subject's action or a modification the subject undergoes. Cato abides while walking or not. Walking is the state that comes upon him when he walks, a predicate. It is capable of being represented in language with the statement "Cato walks," but Cato himself remains unchanged in the walking. Cato and walking are each bodies, but Cato's walking is an incorporeal effect, an event that subsists even in the separation of Cato from walking. I am not talking here of something that exists purely in language, a purely propositional relation (this returns us to the Ideal). The Stoics are interested in what of the universe, and of the causal relations between bodies (and their incorporeal effects), is capable of being expressed.

Language becomes oriented in two directions incapable of reconciliation, material and incorporeal. Language, as utterance, is material, and every statement it makes possible is material. Written traces, articulated breath, neurological connections, sign languages, computer screens are all material means by which language expresses. Utterance and sonic breath in itself are not language, but, in Stoic conceptions, the animal conditions of language. Human language, however brings thought to bear on what is or acts.[43] What language *expresses* (rather than refers to, denotes, or designates, which is itself material) is incorporeal, a process, an event, a change of state, a modification, something that adheres to or floats on the surface without penetrating the identity and continuity of the body, a "thin film at the limit of things and words" (*LS* 31). This almost imperceptible layer is the condition of language and its capacity to represent what happens or could happen: "Language is rendered possible by that which distinguishes it. What separates sounds from bodies makes sounds into the elements of language. What separates speaking from eating renders speech possible; what separates propositions from things renders propositions possible. The surface and that which takes place at the surface is what 'renders possible'—in other words, the events as that which is expressed. The expressed makes possible the expression" (*LS* 186).

Something happens. As sense, the sayable may preexist the proposition which articulates this something. The question that intrigued the Stoics is how language is capable of expressing events even as it remains bodily and articulates itself only as body. How is it that language can express this happening of or to bodies? What is it about this happening or event that exceeds the materials to and through which it occurs. That is, how are events, effects, significant? What sense can be given to them if not in language? Isn't the emergence of language, an incorporeal excess over uttering or writing, itself an event? Isn't language the means by which we establish a conceptual connection with, and ways of living in, the universe through the utilization of the logos that orders propositions and that reflects the world?

Language is no doubt capable of stating truths with greater nuance and veracity, the more complex and refined the development of logic.

The Stoics invented propositional logic which enabled them to distinguish states of affairs, changes, processes, what occurs to a body, and what effects a body makes possible.[44] They understood language as the most subtle of nonsubstances, the incorporeal effect of the occasional alignment of bodies, the extra-sense of the world that must be added to materiality to enable it to be spoken:

> It is this new world of incorporeal effects or surface effects which makes language possible, . . . [It] is this world which draws the sounds from their simple state of corporeal actions and passions. It is this new world which distinguishes language, prevents it from being confused with sound-effects of bodies and abstracts it from their oral-anal determinations. Pure events ground language because they wait for it as much as they wait for us, and have a pure, singular, impersonal, and pre-individual existence only inside the language which expresses them. It is what is expressed in its independence that grounds language—that is, the metaphysical property that sounds acquire in order to have a sense, and secondarily, to signify, manifest, and denote, rather than to belong to bodies as physical qualities.
>
> (*LS* 166)

Deleuze indicates that it is materiality itself that contains this extramaterial dynamic, sense, which, in residing on the surface of events, can connect these events to the inside of statements, their propositional content. Language is the invention of a means by which this incorporeal sense can become articulable and capable of transmission, a capitalization on the order of lekta.

Sayables or lekta are what compose the predicates of propositions. The Stoics suggest that propositions are the means by which something can be true or false: "A proposition is that which is true or false, or a complete state of affairs, which, so far as itself is concerned, can be asserted."[45] To be true or false is to be sayable. The lekton is thus a basic element of logic and of language that links them to each other. While a proposition can refer to or denote a state of affairs, making it true or false, both the proposition and its object, its referent, are bodies or mixtures of bodies. The lekton is that excess left over when the referent and the proposition are removed, when the predicate remains. Stobaeus claims that, for the Stoics, "propositions are the objects of acts of assent." Diogenes suggests that an impression arises from perceiving an event, then a statement or proposition, through the power of talking, is capable of expressing in language "what it experiences by the agency of the impression."[46] Language is informed by the agency of assent to an impression. Language refers to the object of this impression, which enables it to create true or false propositions about it.[47] What it creates in propositions or statements is not only an expression of that perception but above all a sense others can also share that is no longer linked to the impression or the particular speech act or perceiving subject.

A number of scholars have suggested that the lekton can be understood in terms of Gottlob Frege's distinction between sense (*Sinn*) and reference (*Bedeutung*): the lekton can be seen as a self-subsistence existing independently of thought yet accessible to it.[48] It is not a psychological meaning (in which case it would be difficult to see how it can be transmitted to others, how others hearing or reading a proposition could also assent to it, disagree with it, or even understand it), although it is made possible by the capacity of language to speak about things. In speaking about things, language also enables something in excess of things to erupt, sense, which may exist independent of reference and possibly through contradictory impressions. Sense inheres in language, in the propositions that make up language, which is why it is possible, so long after all the material references the Stoics made have disappeared (something that they themselves were well aware of—the inevitable decay of all that is material), that we can still attempt to seek what sense there remains, even in scattered fragments, even in secondary or hearsay texts. Even if we are not the intended or foreseen receivers of their writings and teachings, sense is directed to anyone, to any language. Something remains, eternally, from the proposition, not reducible to its truth or falsity, not explicable in relation to its referents or things signified, or its conditions of utterance—sense that prevails, as Deleuze explores in connecting the paradoxes of sense devised by Lewis Carroll to the surface adventures of the Stoic operations of incorporeal sense. Non-sense is possible only because, beyond reference and even with paradox or contradiction, sense subsists, is accessible to speaking beings, though not always fully. Sense subsists because it is not identical with the utterance, it is an extradimension of the proposition, the sayable of an utterance, not the material of its saying. What makes it shareable or accessible to others is the capacity of the utterance, read or spoken, to bring forth sense, to make accessible the sayable by stating the proposition. That it is sayable implies that it may subsist even without propositions, though it is through language and its capacity to state while expressing that we can access sense most easily. Sayables are what can be said of something without being something themselves; they are how we categorize, evaluate, and frame bodies and enable them to become recategorized, reframed, and reevaluated, to be disputed, developed, and used elsewhere.

In the example that Sextus Empiricus uses, the body being cut by a scalpel, "being cut" is incorporeal, a predicate that can be said of a body's modification. "Being cut" subsists as one of the conditions of a body, whether it is cut or not. The body abides; its being cut is one of many possible predicates that inform us of what a body is and what its particular qualities are (being cut, capable of walking, able to run, etc.). Predicates are nontautological qualities, capacities, actions, processes that are capable of qualifying or modifying a subject. The capacity to be cut is a condition of being alive in a world in which metal can pierce flesh. But metal and flesh are bodies, even as the cutting by the metal of the flesh is an event and, as such, incorporeal. Long and Sedley elaborate:

> The scalpel, by acting on another body, flesh, generates an effect, being cut. This effect is not another body but an incorporeal predicate, or "sayable." Why so? The alternative was presumably to say that thanks to the scalpel one body, uncut flesh, ceases to exist and is replaced by a new body, cut flesh. But that would imply that *no* body persists through the process, so that there is no body in which we can say that the change has been brought about. Since the object changed, must, normally speaking, persist through the change, it proved more palatable for them to say that the effect is not a new body but the incorporeal predicate "is cut" (or "being cut"), which comes to be true of the persisting flesh.

The predicate should perhaps be thought of less as an extra entity that appears on the scene than as an aspect of the cut flesh which we abstract in order to present a proper causal analysis.[49]

Where is "being cut" to be located? Where are events in relation to bodies? Sense must link the inside of bodies—their nature, qualities, their inclinations—to the outside of events, to the incorporeal sense that somehow hovers over the flesh and scalpel, over the battle waged among soldiers, horses, weapons, and territory—all material. Sense resides on the surface of events and in the depths of bodies. This is the work of the proposition: to link the inside of bodies (their conceptual and rational abilities, their ability to act and be acted on) with the outside of events. And this is where sense is to be located: in one sense, nowhere, nowhere in particular, no determinable place; but in another understanding, everywhere, residing on and around ("like a mist over the prairie (even less than a mist, since a mist is, after all, a body)" (LS 5), surface of events, events that everywhere, and taken together, make up the entire universe in its smallest and largest movements. Sense is not subjective, nor is it the quality of objects, but the way in which each is capable of being separated yet fundamentally engaged.[50] We can know of events only to the extent that language enables us to invent propositions which contain some of the sense that is the very excess of the event itself. Language, both material and incorporeal, subjects and predicates, enables the sense that inheres in events to be the objects of conscious and collective contemplation and engagement, linking human minds to the world, but also the world to the possibility and actuality of events that may in turn transform bodies. Language links the depth of bodies to the surface of events, not through reference, not through the truth conditions it provides, but through the sense that erupts or is emitted by both. Not regulated by the other incorporeals—that is, free to ignore (or address) void, place, and time and thus not regulated or ordered as bodies are—language is the clearest mode of matter that expresses sense. All bodies contain sense, or, rather, sense subsists around bodies as their possibility for being the object of action of other bodies and the possibility of their being represented. Bodies, in other words, are the subjects of many predicates while still abiding as the subject of propositions. These predicates describe what, under particular circumstances, could be true or false of the subjects of propositions. One must also argue that the other representational arts (theater, the visual arts, dance, cinema, and so on) share this bringing together of bodies and sense as much as the proposition. And, like propositions, they serve the purposes of bringing human assent to the ways of the universe, to living harmoniously in and according to a nature that they, at their wisest, may accomplish.

STOIC ETHICS

No discussion of the Stoics would be complete without adding to or extracting from our overview of Stoic conceptions of physics and logic/language a brief analysis of Stoic ethics, the part of their philosophical system that seems to have had the greatest influence on our current understanding of them. A number of texts from the Roman Stoa exist on questions of wisdom, which explain how the most sage understand, act, and provide reflections on how one might acquire wisdom and live sagaciously. While I do not have the space to undertake this topic with adequate detail, I do want to elaborate some of its key ingredients, which we have occasion to explore further in the following chapters. Only the sage, the wisest, the most steeped in a knowledge of the world, and a knowledge of ourselves (and the difference between them), is capable of living a good life; though every human subject, even slaves (as was Epictetus), is capable of attaining a wisdom of him- or herself and of the world through undertaking philosophy and the rigorous techniques of self-regulation that enable a well-ordered mind to engage with and address a well-regulated body and ennobling practices. In many ways, ethics is at the center of philosophy for the Stoics, for it addresses how we live by the knowledge of ourselves and the world that we have attained while informing and directing us to its practical use. Ethics is not so much a system of moral evaluation of others but a form of self-regulation and self-production.[51] Stoic ethics is less interested in the more conventional questions of morality—What is to be done? How do I act? What should I do?—than the question of how to live well, how to live up to one's fate, how to address, with one's nature, character, and knowledge, the complexities that others, and the universe itself, imply. Ethics is one's way of living life rationally, with as much understanding of nature's forces and its providential orientation as possible. Such knowledge is not simply learned, the mechanical application of principles derived from elsewhere, but rather comes from a critical self-understanding or apprehension of one's tiny place within an enormously vast, inconceivable but existent universe regulated by divine, that is, ordered, principles: "You exist but as a part of the Whole. You will disappear into the Whole which created you, or rather you will be taken up into the creative Reason when the change comes";[52] or, with more elaboration:

> Remember that such was, and is, and will be the nature of the universe, and that it is not possible that the things which come into being can come into being otherwise than they do now; and that not only men have participated in this change and transmutation, and all other living things which are on the earth, but also the things which are divine. And indeed the very four elements are changed and transmuted into other things, and the same manner of transmutation takes place from above to below. If a man attempts to turn his mind toward these thoughts, and to persuade himself to accept with willingness that which is necessary, he will pass through life with complete moderation and harmony.[53]

There are many facets to a fuller understanding of Stoic ethics than we can develop here.[54] What seems most unusual and significant for our purposes is the intimate connection between ethics and ontology, ways of living, and the orders with or in which the living should harmonize or participate. Nature, a name for the universe as a totality, and not just our own (human) nature, comes first and is the primary force and field from which a human (self-)regulation becomes possible. Human self-regulation is not directed by human nature but by the human recognition of an inhuman order, an order of living beings, both terrestrial and divine, and of material coexistence that is far from human control (and will always remain so, even in our current moment in the "anthropocene," the age of the destruction invented by man). Marcus Aurelius reiterates in *The Meditations* that each of us is doomed to almost instantaneous oblivion, even the richest, the most powerful, and the wisest. In the big picture all humanity amounts to a tiny, almost insignificant, role: "You are a little soul carrying a corpse, as Epictetus says."[55] In outlining Zeno's and Chrisyppus's concepts of ethics, Diogenes Laërtius reports that "living in accordance with virtue is equivalent to living in accordance with experience of the natural course of events, as Chrisyppus says in *On Goals*, Book 1 . . . for our own natures are parts of the nature of the whole. . . . Therefore, the end turns out to be living in agreement with nature, taken as living in accordance both with one's own nature and with the nature of the whole."[56]

Living in agreement with nature is one of the core beliefs of Stoic ethics. This is a regulated and ordered nature functioning independent of the human. The task of the human—one of them, at least—is to understand the principles and elements that make up the universe, the mixtures that make up bodies and the complex entwinement of bodies with other bodies, to understand, to the extent that it is possible, not just the universe, but the divine order within it. This, in turn involves coming to understand one's own nature, one's ability to extend these capacities, the forces and dynamics that make up the two bodies—corporeal and soul—that compose everyone. If we could acquire knowledge of the principles of the divine order of the universe as providential, we could understand the ways in which past and future, things and incorporeals together form a single unified, even living, being. It is a history or chronology of cascading and interacting causes that has a distinct beginning and that will come to a definitive and fiery end. If the death of the individual is part of its inner nature and the death of the universe preordained, then what we must aim at is as full a knowledge as we can attain of the causes and their interrelations outside of us in order to know those causes and bodies that constitute our own nature. To know ourselves, we must know the world that exists before and without us, something made considerably easier with the careful study of the wisest writers of the past (and the lekta they elaborate). The virtues are natural inclinations that become ordered through reason into one's very practices and, "according to Cleanthes, are like half lines of iambic verse; hence, if they remain incomplete they are base, but if they are completed, they are virtuous."[57] As part of the universe, we have within us the order that also regulates the universe beyond us. The virtues are the potentials for action bestowed upon us by nature, modes of acting in accordance with our own nature that, with practice, are capable of harmonious interactions with others and the world surrounding us.

"The goal of all these virtues is to live consistently with nature. Each one enables a human being to achieve this goal in his own way: for [a human] has from nature inclinations to discover what is appropriate and to stabilize his impulses and to stand firm and to distribute [fairly]. And each of the virtues does what is consonant [with these inclinations] and does its own job, thus enabling a human being to live consistently with nature."[58] It is nature that makes life possible. All living things, in concert with the orders of the natural world, participate in the universe and add to its order through living in accordance with its principles. Animals, as much as humans, thus have an ethical as well as an ontological status. They are given by nature an inner nature, needs, requirements, that they know how to protect and let flourish. Man, containing both animal and plantlike qualities, is the rational continuation and elaboration of an order by which even the animal abides, an ethics of self-sustenance and self-maintenance that will also form the center of Spinoza's ontology, as we will see in the next chapter:

1] They [the Stoics] say that an animal has self-preservation as the object of its first impulse, since nature from the beginning appropriates it, as Chrisyppus says in his *On Ends* book 1. 2] The first thing appropriate to every animal, he says, is its own constitution and the consciousness of this. For nature was not likely either to alienate the animal itself, or to make it and then neither alienate it nor appropriate it. So it remains to say that in constituting the animal, nature appropriated it to itself. 3] They hold it false to say, as some people do [the Epicureans in particular], that pleasure is the object of the animals' first impulse. For pleasure, they say, if it does occur, is a by-product which arises only when nature all by itself has searched out and adopted the proper requirements for a creature's constitution, just as animals frolic and plants bloom.[59]

Plants, animals, and humans are connected together and participate in the same nature which produces and provides a way for each to live (and live optimally), using the resources that its own inner nature and the natural world together provide it. The natural world provides modes of appropriation that enable life to sustain itself, techniques and inclinations that life has toward what nourishes and protects it and that orients life always to the others with which it shares its world. Self-preservation, the preservation of one's being through the instincts and inclinations nature provides, indicates that we are—each species and perhaps each individual in its own way—able to provide for our needs according to our specific capacities, even if it is at the expense of other forms of life. We can appropriate from nature what we need to live and thrive: nature dictates this as a good. There is no virtue or good outside this sphere of living, which is why Stoic ethics is less to be understood, contemplated, considered than practiced or lived. The child has not yet the capacity to undertake only reasonable action; but even the animal has an orientation to reason, a becoming-reason that is capable of considerable development in the more intelligent species.

There are things within our power and things that are not within our power: we can control only what is up to us, what we believe, desire, dislike, do. We are not capable of controlling what is not within our power—what we are as bodies, how others perceive us, what nature has given to us or bestowed upon us, fate, necessity. Ethics is the organization and understanding of what, in our power, we can do to expand our nature and that of other humans, living beings, and things themselves. It thus addresses humans in their relations to each other and to every component of the cosmos. Epictetus begins his *Handbook* by acknowledging this distinction:

Of things some are in our power, and others are not. In our power are opinion, movement toward a thing, desire, aversion (turning from a thing); in a word, whatever are our own acts: not in our power are the body, property, reputation, offices (magisterial power), and in a word, whatever are not our own acts. And the things that are in our power are by nature free, not subject to restraint nor hindrance: but the things not in our power are weak, slavish, subject to restraint, in the power of others. . . . If you think that only which is your own to be your own, you will be hindered, you will lament, you will be disturbed, you will blame the gods and men; but if you think that only which is your own to be your own, and if you think that what is another's, as it really is, belongs to another, no man will ever compel you, no man will hinder you . . . [60]

Ethics is the domain of operation of what is in our power to accomplish—beliefs, desires, wishes, inclinations: and knowing its difference from what is not in our power—indifferents, as the Stoics call them—that which we cannot control: death, our bodies, the past, our reputations, wealth, and even health. Distress or anxiety may result from our mistaking what is not in our power with what is, that is, from our attitudes or beliefs about what is not in our control, though not from these indifferents themselves. Assenting to the false impressions that are marked by sense-perception, for example, can do little but make one unhappy and lead to the inadequate or improper use of reason. Among the indifferents—all those things, qualities, and processes beyond one's power—there are preferred indifferents, secondary values, as Zeno described them,[61] things like health, wealth, reputation, that, while morally neutral and not in one's own power, help in maintaining a good life, even as they are also capable of supporting a foolish one (and, moreover, one is perfectly capable of a happy life without them); and there are indifferents that may be contrary to nature, unpreferred indifferents that harm and lead to false beliefs and are the opposite of what is good.

If we knew for certain all that makes up the web of causes that is focused on our day-to-day lives, we could live up to our fate, welcome it warmly, whatever it may be. Epictetus, in the *Discourses,* claims that Chrisyppus, as sage a person as one might know, affirms this *amor fati,* that, as we will see, prefigures Nietzsche's understanding of this term: "Therefore Chrisyppus was right to say: 'As long as the future is uncertain to me I will always hold to those things which are better adapted to obtaining the things in accordance with nature; for god himself has made me disposed to select these. But if I actually knew that I was fated now to be ill, I would even have an impulse to be ill. For my foot too, if it had intelligence, would have an impulse to get muddy.'"[62] If we properly understand the web of causes that operate in the world and the intensity of sense that adheres to the events generated by these causes, that is, to all the possible and actual predicates that cause or are caused by bodies located within incorporeal frameworks, we could understand the operations of providence, of the god or gods immanent in the world that direct and frame our own actions as much as they do the other bodies with which we coexist. Such a perfect knowledge would not yield determinism, in which everything, including the living being is caused by determinable causes, but rather, a knowable order in which we can harmoniously find our own place, not as a master of the world but as one of its objects, destined, as are all others, to oblivion, partaking, as do all others, in the corporeal and the divine simultaneously. The task of ethics is to elaborate those impressions adequately derived from the ways the world is into ways of living that coordinate with, complement, and render comprehensible the divine breath that links everything to a common destiny. Ethics is not a recognition of the causes that bind life to destiny, but rather the destiny that binds life to itself and to the world. To live well, in a manner of agreement with nature, is to live up to one's destiny, to be worthy of the events one undergoes, to chose them even as they are already in place, to make them one's goal and desire, to will, to affirm, in advance, what is yet to come.

Ethics is the elaboration, in other words, of freedom, not a freedom from cause or constraint, but a freedom because of it. Freedom in and with necessity. This is, for Deleuze, "one of the boldest moments of the Stoic thought" in which the Stoics both "affirm destiny and . . . deny necessity" (LS 169). Destiny comes from the unending chain of causes, but it is the incorporeal, that which is effect rather than cause, that affirms freedom, the collapse of necessity or the determined. Effects are not determined (determination operates in the sphere of bodies only) but is subsistent and in some sense preexistent, having always existed and yet to come into being, that is, operating as part of the infinite past and the infinite future. This is not an ethics that distinguishes "is" from "ought," an ethics that decrees the conditions under which correct behavior occurs. Rather, it is a manner of living in and with oneself and amidst others in a world that also exhibits order and reason, a manner of making oneself as worthy as one can of what is to come, the incorporeal future that hovers over the moving present: "Either ethics makes no sense at all, or this is what it means and has nothing else to say: not to be unworthy of what happens to us. To grasp whatever happens as unjust and unwarranted (it is always someone else's fault) is, on the contrary, what renders our sores repugnant—veritable *ressentiment*, resentment of the event. There is no other ill will. . . . It is in this sense that the *Amor fati* is one of the struggles of free men" (*LS* 149).

This is to live in the present as if one's fate depended on it, with complexity, obscurity, unknown causes, imponderable effects, with concern for what one can control and indifference to what one cannot. There is no formula for such a life, only preparations, exercises, in body and soul, in learning and doing. These are the aims that come with life but cannot be addressed before it or independent of the processes of living it. The good life is a wise life in which we address what we can control with thorough preparation, through the cultivation of our virtues and the appropriate actions it engenders, extending further and further, through our own body, into the social and collective bodies we share with others and through to all the bodies that constitute the universe.

The Stoics have produced an ethics of the event, an ethics that produces indifference at what becomes of one and joy at what one accomplishes, an ethics that prepares us to live with the events that befall us, the fate that awaits us.[63] It is an ethics that is teleological, directed to an end or finality, one's place in the cosmos as ordered by divine living pneuma:

As Chrisyppus says in the first book of his *On Ends*: for our natures are part of the nature of the whole. Hence the end comes to be living in accordance with nature, that is, in accordance with our own nature and that of the universe, doing no action usually forbidden by the common law, which is right reason, pervading all things and the same as Zeus, who is this ruler of the ordering of the universe. And this very thing is

the virtue of the happy person and a good flow of life, when everything
is done in accordance with harmony of each person's spirit in relation to
the will of the orderer of the universe.[64]

This is an ethics derived from the nature of the things that exist and
subsist in the universe and from a human understanding of one's place
in it. It is a rich view, one that enables humans not only to make the most
of their corporeal abilities—to grow, sustain themselves, reproduce, act,
make—but also to make the most of that body within us that is the soul
or psyche, which is capable, through language, of apprehending the
ordered nature of the world, its possibilities, and the inevitability of its
changing. Stoic ethics aims to produce in oneself a knowledge of both
oneself and all the bodies that occupy the world. It aims to be worthy of
the events destined to be: to live, in the present, the eternity of the past
which has always contained the event or advent of this present (and all
presents) and the eternity of the future that comes from it.

Deleuze makes clear that an ethics of the event such as the Stoics propose is an ethics mindful of the temporal registers, indeed, all the incorporeal registers that the event implies:

> With every event, there is indeed the present moment of its actualiza-
> tion, the moment in which the event is embodied in a state of affairs, an
> individual, or a person, the moment we designate by saying "*here*, the
> moment has come." The future and the past of the event are evaluated
> only with respect to this definitive present and from the point of view
> of that which embodies it. But, on the other hand, there is the future
> and the past of the event considered in itself, sidestepping each present,
> being free of the limitations of a state of affairs, impersonal and pre-in-
> dividual, neutral, neither general nor particular, *eventum tantum*. . . . It
> has no other present than that of the mobile instant which represents it,
> always divided into past-future.

> (*LS* 151)

Stoic ethics is concerned, fundamentally, with the question of whether
I am worthy of my life, whether I am too weak for it or it is too weak

for me. The present instant, the event of which I am worthy (or not), is that which structures my place, in the past and future, on the basis of this instant. Ethics, in a sense, is the mental training, the rigor, of reason operating in bodily practice to mark and live the eternity of the events that happen to oneself and one's social and natural world. It makes a way to live in spite of as well as because of the order of the event and the force it may have on our destiny.

2

SPINOZA, SUBSTANCE, AND ATTRIBUTES

I would like to make you understand why Spinoza has had such a strong reputation for materialism even though he never ceased to speak of the mind and the soul, a reputation for atheism even though he never ceased to speak of God, it's quite curious. One sees quite well why people have said that this is purely materialist.

—GILLES DELEUZE, "LECTURE TRANSCRIPTS ON SPINOZA'S CONCEPT OF AFFECT"

If the Stoics can be understood as one of the earliest exponents of a philosophy of immanence, by which order, purpose, value, and even the gods are understood not as beyond or above this world but existing within it, where the orientations of life, and its accomplishments complicate and come to their fruition in this world and no other, then Deleuze and Guattari's statement that Spinoza is the "prince of philosophers,"[1] the "Christ of philosophers" (*WIP* 48) makes perfect sense.[2] Spinoza is *the* philosopher of immanence, perhaps the only philosopher in Western history to take immanence as a concept as far as it can go, to make immanence the orientation of substance itself. His work can be described as the most thorough and abstract analysis of the functioning of the concept of "something being *in* something," perhaps interested less in thinking the operations of substance than the concept of "in." Spinoza seeks an immanence in which the world is immanent to or in itself, immanent in God, or, equally, God is immanent in the world, nature, in which there is only one world, one order, one substance, but a world and substance that is infinite, ordered, and capable of being understood by us, however imperfectly. Through his radical emphasis on immanence, Spinoza restores the connections between materiality and ideality that Cartesian (and Platonic) dualism keeps apart; indeed he presents the first systematic analysis of the thorough entwinements of the material and the ideal. Although Spinoza is commonly portrayed as committed to the parallelism of material objects and ideas, this restores a dualism that he is at pains to problematize. What he demonstrates is not that objects always have accompanying or parallel ideas (this is simply another form of Cartesianism); rather, he argues that the entirety of the material order expresses precisely what the entirety of the order of ideas expresses. Neither the same as nor reducible to one another, nor separable, the orders of materiality and ideality express one and the same world, one and the same God, or nature, in two of perhaps numerous ways. It is to an exploration of his understanding of this relation that this chapter is devoted.

There is much that Spinoza shares with Stoic philosophy, in spite of a number of contemporary commentators suggesting that what separates and divides them is more striking.[3] However, there is considerable research that connects them (and others) together into an intellectual lineage.[4] Leibniz understood Spinoza, his contemporary, as a leader of a "sect of new Stoics";[5] others are more optimistic, seeing in Spinoza the culmination of a trajectory that began with the pre-Socratics and was fortified through the Stoics. Spinoza himself says little about them, except in a well-known passage in the preface to the final book of the *Ethics* where he claims that the Stoics rely too heavily on the notion of the will's capacity to restrain affects.[6] In this chapter I look at some of the affinities between Stoic ontology and Spinoza's ontology while exploring in more detail Spinoza's understanding of the relations between materiality and ideality.

By carefully examining Spinoza's ontology in this chapter (and Nietzsche's, in the next), I will be in a better position to articulate a more general relation between ontology and ethics that both the Stoics and Spinoza (along with Nietzsche) share, for if an immanent ontology is elaborated, the very nature of ethics is transformed. It is the ontological grounding of ethics, the belonging together of things and values, the inherence of the ideal in the material, the material and immaterial conditions under which a life, let alone a good life, can be lived that I hope to clarify in increasing detail. The common understanding of the world as a living being, a unified whole, an order in which the human in general, let alone individual humans, plays a very small (if self-important) role, underpins the quite different ethical qualities that the Stoics, Spinoza, and Nietzsche elaborate. If God, or nature, is the impersonal internal ordering principle of the universe, as the Stoics claim, such a God or nature is immanent and accessible to rational thought. It, or at least part of this order, is knowable and can form the basis for not only a logical and causal understanding of the world but for better ways to live in the world in accordance with this understanding. Spinoza utilizes something of the Stoics to bypass the ways in which early Christian theology reoriented Stoicism through a transcendent and external God, understood on the model of a superhuman will. The Stoics provide him with an immanent rather than transcendent order and with vast causal networks that bring all things into connection with each other.[7]

There are no doubt many ways in which the work of Spinoza and that of the Stoics can be compared and differentiated, as there are with comparisons between any two positions. Of course there are differences in how they understand central concepts. Most notable, perhaps, are their different understandings of what an ethical life entails: for the Stoics, ethics is a movement beyond both passions and affections, that is, a life that is internally regulated to accord as closely as possible with the nature of the universe rather than one that responds to, is enlivened or deadened by, encounters with otherness, whether the otherness of family bonds, the otherness of our encounters with other beings like ourselves, our fellow man, or beings that are unlike us but to which we may be connected: others that are fundamentally indifferents, neither good nor bad. For Spinoza, ethics is a movement oriented by encounters with others, other humans and human institutions, other living beings, and the nonliving material order that constitutes the whole of nature, an ethics not based on autonomy and self-containment, the quelling of external impingements, but through engagements that enhance or deplete one's powers. The encounters a body undergoes elaborate, develop, transform the powers of the nature of bodies and thought to act and be acted upon; living beings are not autonomous entities but capacities for embodied engagement, action, and conceptualization that are strengthened or weakened by their relations with other forces and powers.

The Stoics understood the universe as a regime of causes, an ordered and providential force that provides for man the natural conditions for living a sage life, that, if man follows the promptings of reason, give him (always male!) peace and self-contentment. For Spinoza, however, although the universe is governed by an order of causes that it is possible to comprehend (even if not completely), the universe is fundamentally indifferent to the fate of man or of any particular thing and is not directed providentially to any specific outcome: man is caused as much as he causes, an effect of a vast and infinite network of causes that has no telos, aim, or end.[8] Spinoza understands that we live in an indifferent universe that is nevertheless ordered, or is itself order, and that provides us with reason that we can use in the ongoing processes of understanding it and in acting in accordance with it to increase our powers. Both the Stoics and Spinoza share a belief that freedom is based on causal necessity rather than on its absence, on an understanding and utilization of the very causal chains that order the universe as a whole.[9] Freedom is not opposed to necessity but is conditioned by it. By understanding how we are affected by the relations in which we engage, we come to understand our powers to act, our capacity to transform passions, which affect us passively, into activity, the capacity to affect.

This different understanding of the ordering of the universe, by gods who have a benevolent aim and by a God whose order is creative rather than directive, and for whom *good* and *bad* are relative terms, no doubt signals many other differences in the worldviews of the Stoics and Spinoza as well as a number of shared concerns and conceptual commitments.[10] Yet, in spite of some obvious differences, there is an affinity in both the nonnormative ethical tasks they envision and, most significantly here, the shared ontological frameworks of the Stoics and Spinoza. Each elaborates an immanent God, or nature, an order of (material) causes and (conceptual) reasons that is the same throughout the universe, an order that binds God as much as it does us to causal chains and networks of order, an order of cohesion and interrelation that is amenable to or interpretable by reason because reason itself is part of this order.

In what follows I intend to elaborate the peculiar belonging together of matter and conceptuality in Spinoza's *Ethics* that provides a continuing strain of resistance to both dualism and reductionism. This refusal of reductionism, in either one direction or the other, marks the very peculiar, unique, and uncompromising radicalism of Spinoza's understanding of *substance*, his reading of the Stoic concept of *something*, that is, his understanding of the relations between corporeal and incorporeal orders or attributes. And, like the Stoics, there is an irreducible and creative incoherence or excess in Spinoza's monism that, while it advocates one order, one universe, one reason, nevertheless articulates an excess that cannot be directly accommodated or reduced to the One.[11] His monism is a dualism, and, equally strangely, his dualism is a monism, for he affirms that the orders of thought and matter are two different attributes of a single, cosmological, immanent substance made up of many parts, many orders and capacities.

SUBSTANCE

There is perhaps no stranger and more perplexing book in the history of philosophy than Spinoza's *Ethics*. While it is well known that it was written under dangerous conditions and that Spinoza faced very real personal threats for his philosophical undertakings and sought to leave many of his key texts unpublished in his lifetime for his own protection, this does not entirely explain the text's peculiarities. There seems little doubt that Spinoza wrote the *Ethics* in geometrical style, the *more geometrico*, following the format of Euclidean geometry, using definitions, axioms, proofs, and other apparently logical and geometrical, that is, nontheological and nonpolitical, conceptual apparatuses in order to evade not only censure but imprisonment or worse. It is also true that the appearance of a dry, detailed, and obscure metaphysical tract

on God's infinite existence and powers, which elaborates claims in logical form through definitions and arguments, served to protect his work
against philosophical and religious charges, most especially the charges
of atheism that served to disqualify his work from being understood as
part of philosophy.[12] Spinoza's *Ethics* can in fact be understood, in Errol
Harris's phrase, "not [as] the linear formal deduction of traditional logic,
but as a crypto-dialectical development,"[13] a paradox that elucidates or
indicates a difficult-to-grasp concept as it is wrested from theological
and dogmatic interpretations, that cannot be simply said without a
sometimes bizarre overlay to protect it from too easy an understanding.
As Spinoza explains key terms, articulates axioms, and develops their
implications, he is already working well beyond them in a conceptual
order where connectedness, the impossibility of separating either things
or ideas, is such that a logical or geometrical analysis of them can only
indicate something beyond logic or geometry, though not necessarily
against them.

The concept of substance is the central tenet of Spinoza's metaphysics.
All things exist and are conceived through substance, or God, or nature,
which exists and is conceived only through itself. Substance represents
the singular binding force that connects things, no matter how small
or disconnected in space and time they might be, for every thing participates in and is a part of a complex totality. Substance has infinite
attributes, ways in which it expresses itself through the world, but we, as
humans, as terrestrial beings limited by the relations between things that
affect us, can only perceive and conceive two—extension, the order and
connection of things; and thought, the order and connection of ideas.
These are, however, not two different types of substance or things (as
Descartes claims) but the two attributes that express a single substance.
The order and connection of things *is* the order and connection of ideas.
These are not two substances but two irreducible "perspectives," two
forms of emanation or expression of a single substance. Each attribute—
there may be countless others beyond thought and extension—equally
expresses the essence of substance in its univocity; each attribute "speaks
substance" in the same way. One substance, with at least two attributes,
numberless finite things, which entail and require each other: "By God

I understand a being absolutely infinite, that is, a substance consisting of an infinity of attributes, of which each one expresses an eternal and infinite essence."[14]

God, substance, or nature, is that which is cause of itself, cannot be conceived as not existing (*E* ID1); is conceived in itself and without any other thing (*E* ID3); is free because it exists only from the necessity of its nature (*E* ID7); is infinite, both temporally and in its attributes (*E* ID6, P11); and can have no cause or reason outside itself (*E* ID2). This is substance that is singular (*E* IP5 and 6), infinite, eternal, self-causing, all-encompassing, with no outside. Perhaps Spinoza's most significant term is the word *in*, one of the signifiers of immanence. His first axiom regarding God, or substance, is "Whatever is, is either in itself, or in another" (*E* IA1), "Whatever is, is in God, and nothing can be or be conceived without God" (*E* IP15). So if there is a finite thing (and for Spinoza, there are very many), then, by definition, it exists in another; all things exists "in" God, "in" nature, "in" the world of which they are a part or component. They do not aspire to and cannot accomplish a place beyond nature or substance, a transcendental movement beyond, because God is precisely this totality within which all things abide. Every thing exists *in* substance that encompasses and, through minute and infinitely linked chains of causes, determines it, which in turn exerts causal force on the whole ("if, in Nature, a certain number of individuals exists, there must be a cause why those individuals, and why neither more nor fewer, exist"(*E* IP8,S2)).

Substance is not only the totality of all finite things but also the uncaused causal force that makes each thing, and each kind of thing, able to exist. Although God or substance is the cause of each thing in its particularity without being caused, a "free cause" (*E* IP17, C2), and each thing is created or caused through infinite causal chains that are themselves made possible by earlier causal chains, Spinoza refuses God, or substance, the capacity for division into parts, into acts, into the order of calculation. As infinite, eternal, uncaused, God is indivisible (*E* IP13, P14C1). To calculate the infinite that is God is to misunderstand its indivisible nature, for God, or substance, is already the vast number of finite things, as well as the network of forces that cause and connect them. Spinoza mocks those, "my opponents" (*E* IP15S1V), who try to understand substance, or matter/idea, by dividing it into parts so that it may be measured by finite means.[15] Spinoza refutes these arguments regarding the divisibility of matter and thus the impossibility of attributing a divine character to it: "I do not know why [matter] would be unworthy of the divine nature. . . . All things, I say, are in God" (*E* IP15, SVI). Division and numerical calculation, while always possible, mischaracterize substance and misunderstand infinity as solely quantitative or numerical, instead of understanding its qualitative or intensive nature.[16] Nothing of this world is not in God. Substance is not the despised materiality of bodies that must be separated from God; it *is* God, God under the attribute of extension or materiality. Descartes is thus mistaken, according to Spinoza, in defining matter as extension, for matter must necessarily have a conceptual equivalent, an idea, not in opposition to extension but as one of the attributes of substance. This is Spinoza's claim in a rather terse letter to the German mathematician Ehrenfried Walther von Tschirnhausen in which he argues it is reductive to assume that matter is adequately defined by extension: "Distinguished Sir,—With regard to your question as to whether the variety of the universe can be deduced *a priori* from the conception of extension only, I believe I have shown clearly enough already that it cannot; and that, therefore, matter has been ill-defined by Descartes as extension; it must necessarily be explained through an attribute, which expresses eternal and infinite essence."[17]

Substance is indivisible even if it is composed of great numbers of finite specific things; for each thing, in its own ways, is part of substance and adds to its capacity to act, though in a way that is not amenable to division, and subsequent addition cannot reconstitute it. Things are *in* substance to the extent that they are always already an indivisible part of substance. Substance is the whole that contains and magnifies its "parts" by enabling them to resonate with each other. Substance is both material and incorporeal, both objects and ideas (and more), the whole within which both things and ideas exists.

ATTRIBUTES

If substance is singular, incapable, by definition, of multiple parts, if, that is, it is an indivisible one, it nonetheless expresses itself in infinite ways. The attributes, to which we have access only as extension and thought, are the infinite ways in which substance is expressed: "what the intellect perceives of a substance, as constituting its essence" (*E* ID4), what the intellect as passive effect finds is cause of itself (this is what differentiates a conception, which arises endogeneously, from a perception, which impinges from the outside and of which the perception is an effect).[18] Attributes are what is perceived (and cannot be denied) as constitutive aspects of the essence of substance. These essences are not subjective interpretations or qualities of substance; they have no dependence on particular minds or bodies.[19] They are attributes of substance, two attributes not so much of substance as "in" it, and, as such, the intellect is capable of perceiving and accessing them, whether accurately or unclearly. Whether there are infinite attributes or only the forms of extension and thought with which we are familiar, attributes are the essence of substance and substance expresses itself equally in all its attributes, which can be attributes of a substance only insofar as they address and are made possible by the essence of substance. They are not qualities or characteristics, which are always particular features of finite things or examples of subjective or idealist images imposed by the perceiver or the mind on the perceived, but universal modes by which substance is objectively capable of being perceived under one aspect or another (or under all of them). The attributes distribute substance, enable substance to proliferate and change itself through the encounters between finite things that its attributes frame and make possible. Without extension, substance would remain in itself alone (perhaps like the Einsteinian universe before the big bang), unable to spread itself in varying ways across the universe, defying the void, rendering the void impossible. Substance expresses its materiality through extension, which enables us to perceive that extended qualities of material things are part of their very materiality; it expresses its conceptuality, rendering the thoughtless impossible.

Substance expresses its ideality through its capacity to be thought and to inspire and emend thought, to direct thought to think extension adequately and thereby to cohere it more adequately, not as thing or property, but as an indivisible part, an attribute, of substance.

Attributes *express* substance; they are substance involved in itself. To say that they express substance, as Pierre Macherey argues, is not to say that they "represent it in the form of a predicate, a property, or a name."[20] For Spinoza, in opposition to the Stoics for whom predicates express an incorporeal effect, the attributes do not express something different from themselves, nor is substance involved in the attributes as something different from itself. The attributes partake in all of substance and express all of it, in their own ways or of their own kind: "the attributes are included within substance, and, just as much, it is included in them; they are not at all external and arbitrary manifestations, dependent on the free will of an intellect that would reflect it according to its own categories. . . . *Involvere*: attributes and substances are inseparable in that they cannot be conceived without one another, outside of one another; and this reciprocal dependence expresses nothing but the fact of their real unity."[21] The attributes are *in* substance just as substance expresses itself in them. In other words, the attributes are essences of substance, seen from a certain angle; extension explicates substance from one angle, thought explicates it from another, but it is the same substance that is expressed one way or another, or, rather, necessarily in both (and in the infinite ways we do not access). The attributes *are* substance, but extension and thought may not exhaust how substance may be attributed. Substance is not Being comprised of beings. It is the totality, affirmed through each of the attributes, that makes all things exist in connection with and require each other. As one that is also many, that has many, perhaps infinite attributes "in" it, substance is thus, by necessity, nonnumerical.[22]

For Deleuze, expressionism, the idea that substance (God), consisting of infinite attributes, can be expressed in each of them, is perhaps the central idea driving the *Ethics*; for not only do attributes, such as extension and thought, express the essence of substance, essences are actual, real, for each attribute expresses "a *certain* infinite and eternal *essence*, an essence corresponding to that particular kind of attribute. ... [Or]: each attribute expresses the infinity and necessity of substantial *existence*, that is, expresses eternity."[23] This is the basis of Spinoza's immanent understanding of the order of nature that he designates as God. God expresses attributes, which remain a part of God that expresses all of God as well as the necessity of his actualization in real things, the potential of real things, subjects and objects, to become different as they engage in encounters with other things, all equally "in" God.

Attributes express (that is, manifest, show, dilate, or unfold) the essence of substance, its existence and eternity. Deleuze understands expression in terms of the contrary relations that map immanence— relations of involvement and explication/expression—relations of inherence and elaboration, movements that enfold and unfold substance and its attributes. Deleuze refers to systolic and diastolic rhythms, contraction and dilation, as two contrary but equally necessary movements by which all attributes, and all things, express one and the same substance, and exist on the same level, though in greater or lesser degrees of elaboration. If all things exist on the same level, in the same order, with the same reality, that is, through the same operation of causes, then inherence and expression are the two directions available for any relation between substance and attributes and, as we will see, any relation between attributes and modes, as well as any relation between modes and finite things. This movement of enfolding or inherence and its corresponding process of unfolding or expression connect all the terms, from the top down as much as from the bottom up, to substance and are thus a part of substance, a noncalculable component of substance.[24] Substance unfolds itself in its attributes; attributes inhere in and elaborate substance, movements "in" and "out" at the same time and of the same substance, involving and explicating without elaborating new orders, new heights or depths. The expressive and implicative relations between substance and attributes, between attributes and modes, and between modes and specific things entail that all of substance is equally expressed in every order or level, in every thing, that no thing is more humble, wretched, or valuable than any other in the order of substance. Substance is as real and active as its attributes, and they too are as real and active as its modes, and so on, all the way up to the most abstract terms and all the way down to the most specific and concrete.

For Spinoza, we who are part of divine nature are nevertheless limited in our access to and knowledge of both substance and attributes, although perception and action rely upon both and give us some of the most basic forms of knowledge that reason can develop through its rigorous self-emendation. Thought and extension are not binaries, opposites, mutually exclusive and exhaustive terms. For Descartes, the qualities and activities of mind and body are dichotomous: the problem his work bequeaths the history of philosophy is how to understand the ways in which mind and extension, defined as mutually exclusive, can somehow be connected or their relation explained.[25] Spinoza offers a way out of dualism, but only on condition that the relation is entirely reconceived, by being *more dualist*, by taking dualism to its limits, by conceiving the attributes as different rather than opposed, as positivities rather than as one term (mind) and its negation or denigration (body). Dualism does not rotate around two terms, but around one whose negation defines its other. All dualisms, as Irigaray has often claimed, have been conceived on the model of the one and its lack or negation, the other it requires to be one.[26] Spinoza's attributes are *at least* two, and two that are irreducible to each other and not mutually exhaustive, insofar as there may be many, even infinitely, more than two attributes, but where each participates in and expresses in its own way all of the one substance. These are two that cannot be added together, do not consolidate each other, and cannot be understood as representative, let alone exhaustive, of substance. They are its expressions, the manner in which substance explicates or dilates itself.

THOUGHT AND EXTENSION

Neither mind nor body are separate from each other or from substance itself. As attributes of and in substance, they are two orders that do not require mediation to act together, for they always accompany each other.

Thought is the thought of extension, ideas are ideas of the body, ideas in God as much as extension is in God: "the order and connection of ideas is the same as the order and connection of causes" (*E* II, P7, P9D). The operations of extension and thought are inseparable, neither elaborating the other or complementing it, but each expressing, explicating, or elaborating the whole of substance. Each attribute expresses equally the infinity of substance itself and each expresses in the same way, through univocity, the whole that substance is.[27]

If the order and connection of ideas is the same as the order and connection of causes, and yet if ideas do not function simply as parasitic representations of causes or bodies, nor bodies function as exemplifications of ideas, that is, if each is autonomous in its way of acting, then ideas are not simply ideas of the body. The human mind does not know the human body in any direct way (if it did, our knowledge of our own bodies and those like us would be much more advanced: we would understand our physiology, the most difficult of all tasks, as Nietzsche understood). The mind knows the body and has ideas through the body, not in itself but only insofar as the body is affected, that is, only insofar as the body acts and is acted upon by other bodies. The mind is not the mental effect or accompaniment of the body and thus tied to ideas which come only from "its" body; rather the mind operates in and is affected by all sorts of ideas just as the body is affected by all sorts of bodies, each with a relative autonomy. Ideas arise first from perceptions, limited and naive in infancy and childhood, but then, through learning, that is, access to other ideas, they may move beyond or in complication of what appears in perception. Spinoza twice uses the example of the sun, which appears to us, following only the coordinates provided by perception, as two hundred feet away when, with the help of science, we understand it to be millions of miles away (see *E* IIP35S and *E* IVP1S). Ideas thrive on other ideas. They are enhanced or diminished, revivified or problematized by other ideas, more and more remote from those provided directly by the body. The body is not the locus of ideas, nor do ideas reside in a body: ideas connect with and are affected by other ideas, and bodies connect with and are affected by other bodies. It is clear that, for Spinoza, "having" a mind, or ideas, gives us no special knowledge of our own bodies or other bodies. This is learned through the relations between ideas.

The body is not a thing any more than the mind is a thing; the nature of each is continually modified by the creative encounters that bodies undergo with other bodies and that ideas undergo with other ideas: "The human mind does not know the human body itself, nor does it know that it exists, except through ideas of affections by which the human body is affected" (*E* IIP19). The mind knows the body through its ideas of the affections of the body. The mind cannot know the body directly; it is in no way the scene of knowledge production. All that it knows it comes to know, whether erroneously or correctly, through the ways in which the body is affected by other bodies that enable ideas to understand the body's capacities only as they operate and are subjected to encounters that transform it. The body is not a thing, even an extended thing, as Descartes defines it, because it is a process of encounters that change bodies and enable them to undergo new affects and new encounters. Likewise, the mind is not a thing, even a thinking thing, because ideas undergo encounters with other ideas, and particularly other ideas generated by the affections by which the body is affected. Each involves cohesive processes that center around a body, made of many capacities to act and be acted on. Even God knows the human body not in itself, but insofar as the body is affected by many other bodies, the mind by many other ideas.[28]

While ideas exist in themselves in mind or thought and are thus capable of being connected, caused, or transformed by other ideas, and while bodies exist in themselves in extension (which is "in" bodies as much as bodies are "in" extension), they are nevertheless connected in a number of different ways. Ideas are able to come "into" mind because they are ideas of a specific body, my body. Not ideas about a body, but ideas that address and are dependent on the ways in which bodies are affected. "The first thing which constitutes the actual being of a human Mind is nothing but the idea of a singular thing which actually exists" (*E* IIP11), by which Spinoza means "an idea is the first thing which constitutes the being of a human mind. But not the idea of a thing which does not exist. . . . The first thing which constitutes the actual being of the human mind is the idea of a singular thing which actually exists" (*E* IIP11D). This first idea, the first content of an actual human mind, is an actual existent, based on an encounter, a bodily and perceptual encounter, with something actual.

This relation is the basis of increasing scales and complexities of knowledge in Spinoza's understanding. Knowledge consists of three types or orders: that which, following this idea of the first thing constituting a mind, is a knowledge based upon perception; the second is that which, following the emendation of the intellect, becomes a knowledge based on reason, on a capacity to generalize from perception; and the third one based on the order and intricacy of a place in the infinite mind of God, is "intuition," a knowledge of the place a thing or an idea has in the whole that is God or substance. Perception is an intimation of the thing, our first engagement, which always carries a degree of truth, but which, in imagination, may be prone to overstepping its authority and in need of correction. Whether the imagination, open to the association of ideas and to the privilege of the body's affects and experiences, is enabling, in spite of its limits, or not, it is in need of emendation, capable of greater rigor and an expansion beyond the limits of experience through the operation of reason, which provides a different ordering and connection between ideas, which follows the connection of ideas not for me, or for my use, but in God or nature. Imagination is "the only cause of falsity" (*E* IIP41), even if it is also the personal condition under which reason can be attained.

The first type of knowledge is described as opinion or imagination. It is based on perception of singular or specific things. From these specific things we attempt to generalize to form universal notions that in some cases may be correct but in other cases may be "mutilated, confused, and without order for the intellect" (*E* IIP40, S2, I). Imagination may be perceptually adequate but nevertheless disordered, partial, or confused for reason. Opinion, which may be gained from "having heard or read certain words" (*E* S2, II), seems to offer a secondhand perception, the representation or signs of another's perceptions. Together these produce common notions and adequate ideas. Common notions are ideas of things "which are common to all, and which are equally in the part as in the whole" (*E* II, P38); that is, ideas we share about the general features of physical objects. To the extent that the body and its sensory capacities are not subjected to a malicious God or to inherent error and unjustified assumptions, as Descartes conjectures, imagination or opinion provide conditions for a more adequate knowledge, however partial, experiential, and perspectival. When we have adequate ideas and the capacity for generalization, that is, when we have added to our own perception an order and a number of other cases, supportive or otherwise of our general notions, we may attain a second type of knowledge, a knowledge not just of particular things but of the "properties of things" (E S III), something that is common between things, properties, generalizations which enable us to expand our perceptual awareness to encompass the essence of things, their capacity to act and be acted upon.

The third kind of knowledge, which Spinoza describes as intuitive, "proceeds from an adequate idea of the formal essence of certain attributes of God to the adequate knowledge of the formal essence of things" (*E* S2, IV). The second and third kinds of knowledge are "necessarily true" to the extent that they are "adequate" either to the essence of things (in the second kind of knowledge) or to the formal essence of attributes, that is, to God (in the third kind of knowledge). What seems contingent, accidental, providential at the level of imagination, at the level of the second and third types of knowledge, turns out to be necessary when seen in its connections to past and future (*E* IIP44, S). When we can attain something like this third type of knowledge—a rarity in Spinoza's universe as much as in the Stoics'—we attain a knowledge of the order of connection and necessity that binds even the smallest and most apparently trivial things, extended or conceptual, to the entire order of substance; we gain an understanding *sub specie aeternitatis*, under the aspect of eternity. We are capable of distinguishing what appears contingent, minor, or irrelevant from the rational and causal order that creates and connects it to the whole.

MODES

Under the attribute of thought, substance can be conceived as an infinite intellect whose action is identical with its capacities to reason, to logically connect and order ideas. As infinite thinker, God is identical to what he thinks, his infinite essence is his infinite intellect, and ideas, even human fallible ideas, perceptual ideas, are, to that extent, eternal. Under the attribute of extension, substance must be conceived as an infinite causal power, the power to bring into existence and to locate in space and time, that is, to induce in a thing the powers of a determinate existence and the powers of movement that determine relations of motion and rest. Bodies are the ongoing and constantly changing relations of movement and rest, speed and slowness, succession and coexistence. Just as the idea is eternal and partakes, with all other ideas, in nature's or God's eternity, so all that is extended, all that constitute events, while they create history as unique and unrepeatable, also participate in the eternal: "It is the configuration of the whole [of extension] that is the infinite mode, not the particular changes, which produce, and occur, among the finite modes. Motion-and-rest must be conceived as a single indivisible 'state' of the entire physical world, an all-inclusive energy system which at once involves a structure, a dynamic pattern, of matter and interchange."[29]

If the attributes express God's essence and infinite modes, that is, if they are God's powers, the modes are the most direct way in which they manifest themselves. While substance or God is the primary form from which the attributes act, infinite modes are a consequence of or preconditioned by the attributes, and finite modes are a consequence of infinite ones. They are lower on the cosmic scale that Spinoza addresses from the top down in the *Ethics*; modes are logically and causally derived from the attributes and have among themselves relations of causation, derivation, and entailment that provide an order to connect these modes. Among the very first definitions Spinoza provides is that of modes: "By modes I understand the affections of substance; *or* that which is in another through which it is also conceived"(*E* ID5): modes are the ways in which things affect other things, the concrete and often far-reaching relations of action and passion in which things find their causes. Modes have their being in another; they are constituted, in the attributes, through their relations with other things, even very far-reaching things. Modes are forms of modification that things undergo in their creation and existence. They are, along with substance, what is actual, an actual existence for which the attributes, extension and thought, are necessary conditions. Modes are what require God or substance to think them, for they are not self-produced but created through the interaction of previous modes: "modes can neither be nor be conceived without substance. So they can be in the divine nature alone; and can be conceived through it alone. But except for substances and modes there is nothing" (E I P15D).

Modes cannot be identified with things, material objects, or ideas, though they are the means by which we can know and access them. Modes are the manner in which things interact, their types of relation. If God alone is self-caused and encompasses everything within himself, then the things, which are "in" God, are also "in" interaction with each other, forming encounters, or events, becomings that are modified by each other. If God, or nature (more exactly *natura naturans*, a "naturing nature," nature as production) is the cause of all attributes and modes, and if the infinite modes (*natura naturata*, a "natured nature," nature as effect, that is, as modes) are effects which have their causes outside themselves, then modes must distinguish between infinite and finite forms, and this distinction, significantly, will introduce the problem of temporality and a determinate duration, that is, finitude, to Spinoza's eternal and infinite substance and with it the problem of death (see also E IP21D), just as much as it will provide Spinoza with a way of conceiving nature, or substance, or God as both what acts and is acted upon, a nature that includes actions and passions, causes and what remains peculiar, even in Spinoza, effects.[30]

The attributes ensure that every mode must have a cause outside itself, and, further, there must be an adequate idea that expresses the essence of a body, at least "in" God (E IP23). Deleuze explains that if the ontological relation between substance and modes is paralleled by or rather, has its equivalent in the level of thought with an epistemological conception of (eternal) essences and (infinite) properties, while, at the level of extension, it is paralleled by the relation of cause and effect, all are fundamentally the same relation, represented from different angles or frameworks.[31] Modes are *the manner of relation* that exists between things, the relations by which things affect and are affected. One way to understand modes is that they are properties of things; another way is to understand modes as what inhere in substance such that they could be understood as predicates. In many ways modes are not clearly identified with things, but with what things do and have done to them, the manner of their existing with each other, which involves their causal interactions,[32] but above all, in the relations of affect that link things, the capacity of things being transformed both in extension and in thought. This is quite close to the Stoic conception of lekta, the inherence of an excess, a sense, in things beyond their current state, the condition under which things change, the becoming of things, whether material or ideal, the conditions under which they can be thought and spoken.

There are both finite and infinite modes. The "things" Spinoza discusses are not clearly differentiated in his writings, for they may include objects, material processes, ideas, as well as properties like envy and pity, roundness and yellowness, things that are limited (concrete objects) as well as things that are unlimited (such as time or substance itself). Spinoza does explicitly distinguish between two kinds of modes, infinite and finite. Infinite modes are necessary for they necessarily follow from any of God's attributes: "Every mode which exists necessarily and is infinite has necessarily had to follow either from the absolute nature of some attribute of God, or from some attribute, modified by a modification which exists necessarily and is infinite" (*E* IP23). An infinite mode exists in and though another, God alone, through one of his attributes or a necessary modification of an attribute. An infinite immediate mode is one that follows directly from God's attributes (in the case of thought, infinite intellect; in the case of extension, motion and rest). It is infinite not because it includes an infinite number of instances (i.e., it is not a universal) but because it is caused by God and is incapable of other explanation.

By contrast, mediated infinite modes are the operations made possible by thought, and motion and rest, insofar as they can be understood as nonnumerical parts of infinite modes, general participants in the movements of thought and bodies: every thought, every relation of motion and rest, is not only finite and particular but, at the same time, a "part" of the totality of things, infinite and eternal. Mediated infinite modes are those modes of existence and operation of things, thoughts, and movements that do not simply follow from the essence of the attributes but are modifications, "parts" of the attribute. Curley, Spinoza's English translator, identifies these as "the laws of nature."

Finite things, while we can understand them as part of and caused by these infinite modes, by the nonnormative laws of nature, are only finite in their existence, duration, and capacity; for, from the angle of eternity, they too are an inevitable part of the whole. But, from the point of view of their existence (existence can never be inferred from essence—see *E* IP24), finite things are determined by things that preexist them and coexist with them, relations that appear to us contingent, or accidental, but that, in the order of causes, are organized and ordered in relation to the entire network of causes. If infinite modes are determined directly or indirectly through God's essence, then God's essence is no less expressed in the causal chains that link the existence of finite things to an infinite causal chain, a chain that is fundamentally extensive (and historical) but also at the same time, eternal, intensive, unchanging, determined by a vast web of causes: "Every singular thing, or any thing which is finite and has a determinate existence, can neither exist nor be determined to produce an effect unless it is determined to exist and produce an effect by another cause, which is also finite and has a determinate existence; and again, this cause also can neither exist nor be determined to produce an effect unless it is determined to exist and effect by another . . . and so on to infinity" (*E* IP28). Finite things are determined not directly by God but by "remote causes" that are themselves "in" God.

Finite things, objects, living beings, planets, and all that occupies them are determined by vast, infinite, chains of causes in extension and generate ideas for an actual intellect, whether the infinite intellect of God or the more limited intellect of living beings. Of course, for Spinoza, even nonliving finite things have, are accompanied by, or generate ideas: even the rock or stone has a kind of consciousness, ideas at their most elementary, insofar as ideas are ideas of a body and their complexity mirrors the complexity of the parts of the body. Finite things, under the attribute of extension, have particular forms of motion and rest within their various parts which contribute to or are coextensive with the powers of that thing. Under the attribute of thought, finite things have particular modalities of thought, particular degrees of reason or imagination, that are also the powers of thought that are part of the thing. There can be no finite (or infinite) thing that is not *both* extensive and conceptual.

No essence, or degree of power, requires existence (*E* IP24);[33] existence is the expression of essences under particular modes, the coming into existence and the persevering in its being (and also the passing out of existence) that each finite thing requires for its actual existence. Its existence brings nothing to the essence that it expresses, but existence enables the capacity to affect and to be affected to enter into and shape a thing's actual existence, to produce a "nature," a "history" and "community" of things. A mode is a "certain and determinate way" of expressing God's attributes (*E* IID1). Each existent thing, made up itself of many parts, many things, makes up a part of the totality of things through its interconnectedness with every other thing, a collection of infinite finite things, especially as we consider things over the course of an eternity. Each determinate thing is thus thought and understood, exists and has its causes, has an essence and an existence that can confirm each itself, others like it, and others it requires, all located "in" substance as its intensive and extensive expressions. Finite things, in congruence with the laws of nature, with, that is, infinite mediated modes, find their existence in the causes linking each thing to increasingly large numbers of other things. Even finite things, things that appear contingent to us, are connected to and flow from one and the same principle, that which regulates substance, that is, by necessity, which we tend to mistake for contingency (*E* IP17S).

AFFECTS AND POWERS

Substance and its attributes have no need to exercise their power, to act on things, for they are the unconditioned conditions of things; substance and its attributes express themselves, act themselves and their power, and they have no "need" for other acts (than, say, thought and extension or any other attributes). There need not be any extended things or thoughts in other beings, whether human or not, than the attributes as they are "in" God. Attributes, and substance itself, are indifferent to what is extended and what is thought, but they remain the conditions for the existence and perseverance of thought and extension. Like substance, they *are* their power, they act their power without requiring further action. Modes require action or enactment, which bring things, thought or extended, into existence and mark their encounters, their passive and active relations with other things.

Power (as *potentia*) is understood, in a disarming simple manner, as capacity or ability. God's power "is his essence itself" (*E* IP34). Spinoza explains that it is not that God acts and is nothing but action; God's power, as God's essence, has no further need for action than its existence, no hidden will, no unrecognized intention, no required telos. God's essence, expressed in every thing, does not act beyond this "every thing." His essence entails that God is cause of himself and cause of all things, not proximately, but directly and internally, at every stage, without beginning or end. God, creative force, substance, nature (all at times interchangeable terms), is not outside the world but its order of immanence. God does not withhold his activity or begin it: rather, God, or substance, operates in every thing, as every thing functions within it: "Whatever we conceive to be in God's power necessarily exists" (*E* I, P35); "Nothing exists from whose nature some effect does not follow" (*E* I, P36). Here Spinoza argues that things, in God, express the essence of God, God's power, in some respect but not in all—each thing in its own way expresses God's power (and thus has a certain power as well): "Whatever exists expresses the nature, *or* essence of God in a certain and determinate way (by P25C), that is (by P34), whatever exists expresses in a certain and determinate way the power of God, which is the cause of all things" (*E* IP36D).

If God is cause of himself and his expressions, his essence is identical with his power. For man, and for all things, "the potentiality of existence is a power," and the greater a thing's essence "so also will it increase its strength for existence" (*E* IP11*n*), thus the greater its power. The essence of God or substance gives rise to an infinity of modes in an infinity of ways. Substance is not the power to generate effects but *is* those effects: the more causes it produces, the greater its power, the more perfect it is. Each thing expresses the power of God, who is thus both active, insofar as he produces modes, and passive, insofar as the effects generated are not separate from God. Expression is the power of the movement of unfolding acts that are both in God (as active force) and effected by God (as passive effect).

Modes can be understood as *degrees* of power that an infinite number of things (each thing itself is an infinity insofar as it expresses God's attributes), understood as a whole, express. Modes are the manner in which things are affected, the capacities that are imparted to or part of the nature of things, the ways in which they can act and are acted upon: "The idea of any mode in which the human body is affected by external bodies must involve the nature of the human body and at the same time the nature of the external body" (*E* II, P16). Taking, for the first time in our discussion of Spinoza, human bodies as specific examples of extended bodies (though with the advantage of language and collective knowledges), when human bodies, like all other types of corporeal being, are affected by external bodies, the mode is the manner of their engagement and the possibilities, or capacities, the powers, that such encounters bring to bodies. Bodies are affected by other bodies. Insofar as they encounter other bodies, their bodies are changed, undergo new mixtures, yielding both new physical arrangements, a change in the "parts," also changing and affecting ideas.

Deleuze is particularly focused in his writings on Spinoza on the question of affects and affections. It not only takes up a good deal of space in his books solely devoted to Spinoza; it is also the major object of some of his seminars, now available online,[34] and in many of his references to Spinoza throughout his writings. The question of affect is also clearly being revived in present writings in part as a way of addressing more directly the mind-body relation.[35] Deleuze is careful to distinguish affect or affection from ideas, a mode of thought that is capable of addressing real things, that is, that has an object and perhaps an objective reality.

Ideas, in short, represent something, whether existing things or not. They have an object. Affects, in Deleuze's reading of Spinoza, are modes of ideas that have no object. Of course, one may feel sadness or joy, and it may be that something or someone prompts this feeling. But sadness and joy, strictly speaking, have no object. "Every mode of thought insofar as it is non-representational will be termed affect."[36] Affect is thus nonintentional, related to the idea but not its equivalent; nor can it be understood simply as a state of the body, though it is related to the body's actions and passions. One side is (nonrepresentational) idea, the other is body. So whereas affect occurs both "in" or to a body and an idea, unlike the idea, affect has no object, although it is itself, like the idea, an object. An idea has not only referential possibilities, objects of representation, but is itself a thing, an objective reality. And, as a thing, it has degrees of perfection both insofar as it represents its objects adequately and insofar as it is a thing with its own degrees of reality, its own forces, its relations to other ideas.

Ideas follow one another in rapid succession, largely but not solely dependent on the flow of the perception of objects. Likewise, affects arise from the flow of objects, from the increase and decrease of our powers of connection and influence that constitute the "identity" of any thing, an identity of endless variation or difference. This is both the endless variations that constitute, in our own case, the human body, in all its possibilities of connection or engagement with other bodies, and consciousness, the mind, a flow of continually varying ideas. Life itself may be understood as the continuous variation or self-differentiation of ideas and bodily encounters that enhance (or diminish) our degrees of perfection by elaborating further encounters which add to and continue the movements of perfection that are part of the nature of the idea and the body. There is no perfect body or mind other than that of God. There are degrees of perfection, which are not directed to a pregiven ideal or model, which cannot aspire to emulate God, but are linked to the ongoing discovery of one's possibilities of acting (and being acted on) and thinking (and being thought about). There are only endless and continuing variations that both retroactively and prospectively constitute ever more degrees of perfection, that is, degrees of connection, with everything else. Affect may be understood as the lived movement of transition from one degree of perfection to another (not always an enhancing move, as in sad encounters), the lived transition that occurs in body and idea from their encounters with others and in the affects these encounters engender that continually transform the body.

Spinoza talks a number of times about the movement of blood through the body as a movement of continual variation where nutrients, other bodies, are added, and different bodies are removed as blood circulates through the body's organs. It is pure difference while nevertheless maintaining an "identity," an ongoing cohesion even in the face of continuous change:

> All natural bodies can and ought to be considered in the same way as we
> have here considered the blood, for all bodies are surrounded by others,
> and are mutually determined to exist and operate in a fixed and defi-
> nite proportion, while the relations between motion and rest in the sum
> total of them, that is, in the whole universe, remain unchanged. Hence
> it follows that each body, in so far as it exists as modified in a particular
> manner, must be considered as a part of the whole universe, as agreeing
> with the whole, and associated with the remaining parts.[37]

Spinoza further explains to Henry Oldenberg that this power of affecting and being affected applies as much to ideas as it does to bodies:

> You see, therefore, how and why I think that the human body is part of
> nature. As regards the human mind, I believe it is also a part of nature;
> for I maintain that there exists in nature an infinite power of thinking,
> which, insofar as it is infinite, contains subjectively the whole of nature,
> and its thoughts proceed in the same manner as nature—that is, in the
> sphere of ideas. Further, I take the human mind to be identical with
> this said power, not in so far as it is infinite, and perceives the whole of
> nature, but in so far as it is finite, and perceives only the human body.[38]

This is a fundamentally fluid conception of bodies, in which what a body is made of is less significant than what it can do, and with it corresponds the flow of ideas, which are enhanced and made more perfect, not to the extent that they adequately reflect on or refer to reality, but only to the extent that they encounter, engage with, and transform themselves through other ideas. Affect is the movement of this variation of bodies and their constantly changing parts as well as of ideas, their modes of flow and their ever-changing relations. When I feel the sun on my body, or when I see its bright aura in the sky, it affects me, changes me, transforms chemicals in my body (sometimes in a conducive way, producing vitamin D, and sometimes in a harmful way, producing sunburn or even skin cancer). It is a mode of affection that mixes with the many smaller, sometimes infinitesimally small, objects and flows that make up my body. It is also a source of knowledge, at first limited to how it feels on my skin and in my eyes, which can be developed and elaborated the more informed I am about other ideas regarding the sun.

My body is a composite relation of many coordinated forms of movement and rest. Its identity as a body is not provided by the cohesion produced by memory, as John Locke suggests, but by the preservation of these relations of movement and rest even amid the continually changing relations of objects entering and leaving the body. Bodies, like ideas, are made of mixtures. There is no clear and distinct idea on which to found knowledge (as Descartes believed). Ideas only become clear and distinct in their relations to other ideas. There is no bodily integrity in the sense of an unchanging continuity over time, only mixtures, ideas encountering each other and bodies affecting each other, each transforming and being transformed by its engagements. This conception of bodies and ideas as open forms of engagement, capable of being expanded or diminished, means that, in a strict sense, Spinoza can be understood neither as a materialist nor as an idealist. Perhaps, *per impossible,* he must be considered to have elements of both. Or rather, to have developed a philosophy that refuses to reduce any element of the world, or nature, to any other. A materialist needs to explain how ideas operate materially, and an idealist needs to explain how matter is, contrary to appearances, idea or driven by an idea. Spinoza undertakes neither of these projects: ideas are irreducible to bodies even if they always accompany bodies and begin as ideas of a body. And bodies retain not only an irreducible extensive character, they remain corporeal in all the mixtures they undergo and the relations they encounter. There is no direct parallel between an idea and a bodily action, even neuronal. Descartes is right to suggest that there are two orders of existence, but, as far as Spinoza is concerned, he makes the ridiculous assumption that the two orders can be linked directly, that there is a causal passageway from one to the other. Spinoza's conception of ideas and bodies is neither dualist (if there are two attributes and the world is divided by them, then there are "at least two," there are infinite attributes in God) nor monist (in the sense that these two are never one in themselves but only "in" God or nature). Or he is both a dualist *and* a monist simultaneously: a single substance that speaks in (at least) two attributes.

Not only do ideas have a force, an energy, an order of connection of their own, bodies, even the most simple—Spinoza frequently invokes a stone—can be construed to have an intent, an incipient idea, even if it is an inadequate one. They cannot be detached from a component of the idea: "Further conceive, I beg, that a stone, while continuing in motion, should be capable of thinking and knowing, that it is endeavoring, as far as it can, to continue to move. Such a stone, being conscious merely of its own endeavor and not at all indifferent, would believe itself to be completely free, and would think that it continued in motion solely because of its own wish. This is that human freedom, which all boast that they possess, and which consists solely in the fact, that men are conscious of their own desire, but are ignorant of the causes whereby that desire has been determined."[39] Human bodies and rocks are all bodies of the same kind, in the same world and governed by the same order of causes and the same forms of self-ignorance. Ideas, whether the ideas of a human, the ideas of all humans, the ideas of a rock or that of God, are also governed by the order of reason and in the same way. Each expresses, in its own way, the same order.

What ideas and bodies share is a capacity to be affected, which in turn may enable ideas and bodies to transform themselves, to affect others. Spinoza understands ethics as an analysis of the relations of composition into which ideas and bodies may enter and the transformations that bodies and minds undergo in these relations. Good and bad encounters are relations that respectively enhance or diminish a thing's powers to persist in acting in its own way. Good encounters enhance our powers, and bad diminish them. There is no good or evil in itself, for all that exists is "in" God: there are only good or bad relations, relations that positively or negatively act on us or are acted by us. Evil itself is not an active force, in Spinoza's conception, so much as the deprivation of good.

Food, sex, and good company are positives for Spinoza (rather than indifferents as they are for the Stoics) insofar as they benefit us and enhance our powers, insofar are they are useful for our well-being; they may become bad to the extent that they harm our capacities, slow down or speed up our relations: "As far as good and evil are concerned, they ... indicate nothing positive in things, considered in themselves, nor are they anything other than modes of thinking, or notions we form because we compare things to one another. For one and the same thing can, at the same time, be good, and bad, and also indifferent. For example, music is good for me who is melancholy, bad for one in mourning, and neither good nor bad for one who is deaf." (*E* IV preface, 209/18–22). This is less a form of relativism—what is good (for you) may be bad (for me)—than it is a therapeutic conception of terms that are usually considered moral or religious. Good benefits me; evil deprives me of what benefits I might gain as well as diminishes my power to act: "By good I shall understand what we certainly know to be useful to us" (*E* IVD1), and "By evil, however, I shall understand what we certainly know prevents us from being masters of some good" (*E* IVD2).

This conception of good and evil is therapeutic, not in the sense that Spinoza advocates a general model of good health, but in the sense that good is what is useful to our being and our ability to become more, and evil is what inhibits us to the point of our becoming less. There is no virtue, no measure of good and evil above and beyond our actions (this is true no less for animal and plant existence than it is for humans): it lies immanent in the relations a being undergoes that enable certain actions and their consequences: "the more each [man] strives, and is able, to preserve his being, the more he is endowed with virtue. And consequently, insofar as someone neglects to preserve his being, he lacks power, q.e.d." (*E* IV, P20D). Food, sex, and good company, for example, enhance our capacities, though they may also, depending on who, what, and how, lead us to neglect them.[40] What is good is what enhances me; what is evil is what prevents such an enhancement, what deprives me of the ability to preserve and enhance my being.

This may be considered an entirely selfish philosophy, in which what is "good for me" is the only criterion for judging an action. But this is so only to the extent that the selfish subject is considered a self-contained entity rather than something whose being is possible and thrives only within a network of relations that ultimately reaches every aspect of the universe. In acting "for myself," I am not thereby acting against a world or against others, though in fact the human and animal worlds abound in selfish actions. Each thing desires to persist in and enhance its being. This desire characterizes the dynamism of the world (but also entails the conflict between different forms of dynamism and its different aims and practices). Each thing, body, or idea strives to enhance itself and does not seek to destroy itself (except through an external cause). The actual essence of each thing is precisely this striving, this desire (see E IIIP7 and P8, and D1), that is, *conatus*.

Spinoza claims that there are only three primary affections from which all the others can be logically derived: desire, or the striving in one's being, joy, and sadness (E IIIP11S). Much of book 3 of the *Ethics* shows how affections such as envy, love, disdain, fear, pity, compassion, veneration, hatred, and so on (commonly considered virtues and vices) are convoluted expressions of the primary three, ways of expanding on or concatenating them. Surprisingly, given that the basis of morality since the rise of Christianity has been the suppression of most affections, for Spinoza, our inability to restrain these affections or emotions may not be the cause of our bondage; it is through our inability to adequately understand affections, our willingness to understand them only as I experience them (the first kind of knowledge) instead of seeing their place within the whole (the second kind of knowledge), that they engender or constrain my actions.

Acting on our affects brings us a certain freedom and being unable to act on them may result in our bondage.[41] Pleasure, for example, is a joy that, when acted upon, may enhance our powers to affect and be affected: but it is also a joy that may inhibit other affects from their actions. The same is true for pain. It is a sadness that in itself diminishes our powers, but it may reveal other powers and capacities: "Pleasure is a joy which insofar as it is related to the body, consists in this, that one (or several) of its parts are affected more than others. The power of this affect can be so great that it surpasses the other actions of the body, remains stubbornly fixed in the body, and so prevents the body of being capable of being affected in a great many other ways. Hence, it can be evil" (*E* IVP43D). Neither joy nor sadness is in itself good or evil. It depends on what these affects enable us to do or prevent us from doing. It is a question of what a particular body and idea is enabled to do or prevented from doing by particular relations that constitute good or evil. Even "evil" is that which can be readily replaced, without any battles, through an understanding of what affects enable, a confusion that, at least in principle, can be overcome.

Affects are events that occur to or between bodies/ideas or that transform bodies/ideas in the intensity of their powers of persistence, in their conatus. This is not a *will* to persist but a(n impersonal) power of persisting. Affects enable conjunctions to occur which strengthen and broaden my powers of persisting, and others, the passions in particular, those affects that we must bear passively, tend to weaken my powers of persisting. Powers are not powers over other things, but capacities to act in particular ways, either at the level of corporeal behavior or at the level of mental elaboration. They are powers to act *with* and *within* things, not powers that can act against mind or body. These are the powers the body and mind have to make connections, to expand themselves, to acquire both understanding and bodily achievement that enable more active affects, that overcome passions. Sometimes we mistake this striving for will, as if somehow consciousness controlled these actions. Spinoza prefers to understand will in terms of appetites, strivings that are both corporeal and conceptual, orientations to those things which will expand our capacities rather than acts that exhibit conscious control over the body, as the term *will* implies.[42]

NECESSITY AND FREEDOM

The question of will is central to Spinoza's conception of our errors regarding God and ourselves. Will is what we falsely attribute to God as our explanation for earthly events we do not understand; will is also what we attribute to ourselves when we do not adequately understand the causes that precede and surround us. Will is a concept that demonstrates our ignorance of causes. Spinoza shows that although our minds are ignorant of our bodies and the chain of causes that supports the body (as much as it is ignorant of the order of ideas that precedes and surrounds ideas), we do not require a concept of will, not even "free will," in order to understand freedom. Indeed, paradoxically, Spinoza demonstrates, in some echo of the Stoics, that freedom is only possible within the constraints of necessity. Our own limits, both bodily and conceptual, render us unable, without more adequate ideas, to understand the vast webs of causes that make nothing random, accidental, or unconstrained.

The concept of "free will," or "will," is, for Spinoza, an imaginary conception, a first kind of knowledge, possibly misleading, even as it may explain the experience of volition, unless it is complicated by further knowledge. For Spinoza will is a certain kind of perception that, in the light of more knowledge, would be understood as simply one link in a causal chain, a name that marks nothing different from the movement of this chain: "The will cannot be called a free cause, but only a necessary one" (E IP32).

Not even God can be attributed freedom of the will, for this is to misunderstand the nature of a God who is not separate from his attributes and modes, who inheres in, is, his attributes and modes, that is, who is not outside nature but its inner principle. God has no need to will to do or think anything, for that entails there is something extra in addition to existence: "From this it follows . . . that God does not produce any effect by freedom of the will." Freedom of the will, if it could be possible, would be a capricious intervention into the causal networks that condition each thing, including each thought, a break in the causal order. It is not the case that things that exist could have been otherwise, even in the case of God, who is subjected to the same order as all things in the world: "Things that have been produced by God in no other way, and in no other order than they have been produced" (*E* IP33). To believe that something is contingent, or that God could have willed it otherwise, for example, "is a defect of our knowledge" (*E* IP33S1).

It is this "defective" or incomplete belief that enables us to believe in miracles and divine intervention, such as the scriptures suggest, or to believe that God is pleased with or displeased by our behavior, as much as it allows us to think that our (human) will acts and produces separately from chain of causes that regulate all other things, as if humans were somehow exempt from being conceived as effects and can only consider themselves as causes or active agents. Man projects onto God his own ignorance about the chain of causation, assuming that because man feels as if he acts from will and from need and towards certain ends, God must also. This imbues our human understanding of the world with a telos, a heavenly reward, that the chain of causes in no way suggests. Man assumes he is made in "the image" of God, which is to say that man's naive conception of God is a man projected into an infinite order beyond this world. The entire appendix of book 1 is devoted to demonstrating that it is only man's ignorance of himself, the world of which he is a part, and God in whom he exists that enables him to understand God as a suprasensible megahuman: "they [such theological and humanist interpretations of God] seem to have shown only that Nature and the gods are as mad as men" (*E* I, P36, A).

For Spinoza, it is only if we can move away from superstitious or magical thinking, in which divine or human beings can break the causal order to insert "free causes," that is, only if we come to a reasonable understanding of affects, the manner in which we are affected by other things and affect them, that we can understand the causal network within which we are embedded and in which we participate as actants as much as effects. The more careful and accurate our understanding of the natural order, that is, God or substance, the more adequate our understanding of the affects that represent our powers of actions and passion. To convert passions, in which the human is subjected to forces and things, bodies and ideas, external to itself, into affects, in which humans attain something like an expansion of their power, Spinoza claims that the mind is capable of ordering and organizing passions and in this way converting them to active affects and enhancing joyous encounters.

As long as the affects we seek to understand are not "contrary to our nature," that is, produce bad encounters, encounters that disagree with our nature,[43] our understanding can only help to convert what we passively experience as outside of ourselves into an active component of our self-understanding, which is necessarily linked to an understanding of the order of nature. "As long as we are not torn by affects contrary to our nature, we have the power of ordering and connecting the affections of the body to the order of the intellect" (E VP10). These "affects contrary to our nature," bad encounters, prevent us from understanding as much as they impair our powers of acting; they divide us between contrary impulses, those that accord with our nature and those that do not, which hinder us in our possibilities for comprehension. These are noxious encounters rather than the operation of an inexplicable evil, the clash of natures between things, which are neither good nor bad in themselves. To the extent that we can learn which things do not agree with our nature, we can also learn to maximize our encounters with different things that enhance our capacity to act.

If love or joy is the most general name for positive and active affects (and, correlatively, hatred or sadness is the name for bad or toxic encounters), then Spinoza claims that the love of one's fellow man is an obvious good, an obvious benefit to man. This love of man for other men, the expansion in man's powers that occur in the community of other men, is an obvious good,[44] even with its potential lapses such as Spinoza himself directly experienced in the political and religious upheavals of his time. But a greater benefit, not surprisingly, is a love of God, as nature, which provides us with the clearest comprehension of ourselves and our place in the world and thus the strongest ability to act for good, that is, for our own well-being, which involves the well-being of others, of the community, or of the state. A love of God is a love of oneself and the whole of existence (E VP16). A love of God, or nature, provides, not a returned love (such a thing is impossible—see E V P19), but an understanding of the place of causes in their interactions and of those relations which tend to maximize our active affects and thus our powers. A good life consists in maximizing our powers of body and mind while avoiding those bad encounters that diminish our powers.

Spinoza summarizes the powers the mind can exert over affects: it can gain knowledge of the affects; it can separate an affect from the idea of an external cause; it can overcome confusions of affect; it can see not just one but multiple causes for its affects (the greater the number of causes, the stronger the affect, the more these affects have in common, the more easily we can understand their causal force on us); and it can order and organize affects (see *E* VP20S I–V). The more active the mind is in the constitution of adequate ideas, the greater its power becomes not in overcoming affects, as the Stoics suggest, but in enabling them to enhance our powers.

This is why the third kind of knowledge, one not clearly defined or explained in the *Ethics,* involves a knowledge of things not just as they are or in themselves, but as they are in God, in nature amidst the infinite connections that condition it. Intuition provides clear and distinct ideas of things as an expression of the immanence of the order of the world:

> We easily conceive what clear and distinct knowledge—and especially that third kind of knowledge (see *E* IIP47S) whose foundation and beginning is the knowledge of God or nature—can accomplish against the affects. Insofar as affects are passions, if clear and distinct knowledge does not absolutely remove them, at least it brings it about that they constitute the smallest part of the mind. And then it begets a love toward a thing immutable and eternal, which we really fully possess, and which therefore cannot be tainted by any of the vices, which are in ordinary love, but can always be greater and greater, and occupy the greatest part of the mind and affect it extensively.
>
> (*E* VP20S [II/294])

The knowledge and love of God, the understanding that we participate in God as much as God is in us, enhances our power, connects us to other human beings, individually and collectively, and to the world of nature. It enables us not to quell the passions but to convert them into active affects, to understand how they come into composition with our nature, and what they can elaborate and develop in us (*E* VP25–26).

This third kind of knowledge is made possible by a second kind that is based on the generalization of experience and perception and the attainment of the laws of nature that regulate our experience. The third kind of knowledge begins, as Spinoza does, from God or nature, a movement "from an adequate idea of certain attributes of God to an adequate knowledge of the essence of things" (*E* VP25D). This is a movement from an adequate understanding of the whole organization of nature to an adequate understanding of the essence of things to the nature of things in particular, a movement that provides us an ever greater knowledge of nature, or God. While the human mind cannot grasp the entirety of God, it can attain an adequate knowledge of the orders of causes and reasons, bodies and ideas, that sharpen and add to knowledge with each empirical encounter—an empiricist rationalism or a rationalist empiricism.

A knowledge of the causal order regulating durational events down to every detail, that is, an order that knows life and death, the duration of things, is God's alone. A human mind, through its ordered use, through reason, can come to understand the order of things, their connections, but not their place in God or their duration or life span. Extension, as the order of spatialized corporealities, exists in time or history, which extends forever in both past and future, but ideas exist in eternity directly. They are what survive the death of a particular body, not as disembodied thoughts but as eternal. This third kind of knowledge is not only empirical, based on observation and generalization, it is a knowledge that is now under the aspect of eternity: "Whatever the mind understands under a species of eternity, it understands not from the fact that it conceives the body's present actual existence, but from the fact that it conceives the body's essence under a species of eternity" (*E* VP29).

It is only the body's "present actual existence," the body here and now, that "conceives duration, which can be determined by time, and to that extent only it has the power of conceiving things in relation to time" (*E* V29D), that is, duration or the flow of time is perceived only through the flow of perception in the body here and now. Memories, recollections, associations, imagination are all provisional ideas of the body, not part of the materiality of the body (even as its organs and circulatory system are continually changing and modifying themselves); they are parts of the soul. Duration is marked by the existence of modes and pertains only to them. A mode exists only through the ongoing relation between a thing's extensive parts. These parts, which are capable of continually changing, do not constitute a thing's essence, which can be understood in terms of its intensive and thus eternal parts, that is, its degrees of power. Hence, under the aspect of eternity, ideas exist in eternity, which is to say, in God. Not all ideas exist in eternity; most ideas we humans have are confused, disorganized, and appear haphazard. Only those ideas adequate to the essence of things are eternal, to the extent that the essence of things, rather than their existence, is in God and exists eternally.

In death we lose all the extensive parts that compose our bodies and we lose all the faculties of the soul insofar as they express these extensive parts. We lose all passive affects as well as our powers of acting. What is retained are the ideas that are necessarily adequate to God and, to that extent, that abide *sub specie aeternitatis*. Eternity coincides with duration, not as a separate temporal stream, a divine or heavenly eternity. Rather it is the infinite duration within which each thing's temporality is located. But each thing comes into existence and goes out of existence in its own way. Something of it, its ideas insofar as they express the essence of God, abides beyond death and in all of time, every moment of it: "This third kind of knowledge depends on the mind, as on a formal cause, insofar as the mind itself is eternal" (*E* VP30D). Spinoza explains that the mind requires the body to give it ongoing impressions, new encounters, passive affects. When the body dies, the mind ceases to undergo affections (*E* VP34). Its "contents" or "parts," ideas, join the infinity of all ideas that are adequate to essences, that are part of a divine essence eternally, that is, within the continuous flow of all durations.

There is no life after death in the sense that we commonly understand. There is no ghostly double of the body that persists, there are no further actions and passions, except for the eternity of ideas that a body's experience may have enabled its mind to begin to comprehend. The greater the body's experiences, the more capable it is of extending its power, the more it is capable of acting. Spinoza argues that the greater the mind perceives and understands the modes and affects of the body, the more it may be able to engage in active affects and the less it may be led to passive encounters and bad relations (*E* VP39D). The more the mind is directed, not by imagination, the first and most naive ally of the body, but by reason, the more it is able to convert passions into actions, inadequate ideas into ideas adequate to essences: "it follows that the part of the mind that remains [after death] however great it is, is more perfect than the rest. For the eternal part of the mind is the intellect through which alone we are said to act. But what we have shown to perish is the imagination, through which alone we are said to be acted on. So the intellect, however extensive it is, is more perfect than the imagination" (*E* VP40C). Our ideas, as adequate ideas of God's essence, are as eternal as God's essence: "our mind, insofar as it understands, is an eternal mode of thinking, which is determined by another eternal mode of thinking, and this again by another, and so on, to infinity; so that together, they all constitute God's eternal and infinite essence" (*E* VP40S).

Freedom consists in the joy at comprehension of the order of causes, the order of ideas and their place within the whole that is nature or God. Freedom is the enjoyment of the eternal order of thought that, in comprehending and growing with the body's encounters, especially those which enhance its power, also enhances the encounters of ideas. Freedom is the comprehension of a place in the universe, not necessarily a preordained place, but a place that is within the order that is God. Freedom is not "free choice," the choice between already existing objects or actions, nor is it the absence of causes, indetermination; it consists in understanding necessity, the necessity that causes my own existence and the whole of existence that I require, directly or indirectly, to persist in my being. From a knowledge of God or the universe itself to a knowledge of each particular thing, from the top down, to the extent that our bodies have ordered and understood passions and maximized active affects, maximized our powers, by interaction with other bodies and other ideas, we attain a place, not only in history as a momentary event but in eternity as an adequate idea of essences, as it were, from the bottom up. Freedom is the freedom to act, encounter, enhance, learn, grow, make, do, with as many of those objects, material and conceptual, that agree with our natures as we are able. Wisdom is the attainment of ways of acting and thinking that are conscious of themselves and of God or nature.

Spinoza ends the *Ethics* in a Stoic frame: the wise person, the sage, is calmed in a sea of change and waves of passion, for such a person understands more and more of himself, is capable of acting with greater clarity to convert sad passions into joyous affects and is thus engaged in the eternity of God:

> From what has been shown, it is clear how much the wise man is capable of, and how much more powerful he is than one who is ignorant and is driven only by lust. For not only is the ignorant man troubled in many ways by external causes, and unable to ever possess true peace of mind, but he also lives as if he knew neither himself, nor God, nor things: and as soon as he ceases to be acted upon, he ceases to be. On the other hand, the wise man, insofar as he is considered as such, is hardly troubled in spirit, but being, by a certain eternal necessity, conscious of himself, and of God, and of things, he never ceases to be, but always possesses true peace of mind.
>
> (*E* VP42S)

Wisdom is not an abstract knowledge of things in general, but a knowledge of what enhances and expands as well as what diminishes or contracts our beings and that of the world.

3

NIETZSCHE AND *AMOR FATI*

I am utterly amazed, utterly enchanted! I have a precursor,
and what a precursor! I hardly knew Spinoza: that I should
have turned to him just now, was inspired by "instinct." Not
only is his overtendency like mine—namely to make all
knowledge the most powerful affect—but in five main points
of his doctrine I recognize myself; this most unusual and
loneliest thinker is closest to me precisely in these matters: he
denies the freedom of the will, teleology, the moral world-
order, the unegoistic, and evil. Even though the divergencies
are admittedly tremendous, they are due more to the differ-
ence in time, culture, and science. In summa: my lonesome-
ness, which, as on very high mountains, often made it hard
for me to breathe and make my blood rush out, is now at
least a twosomeness.

—NIETZSCHE, POSTCARD TO FRANZ OVERBECK IN SILS-MARIA, JULY 30,
1881, TRANS. YIRMIYAHU YOVEL, IN *SPINOZA AND OTHER HERETICS*

I am in the mood of a fatalistic "surrender to God"—I call it
amor fati, so much so, that I would rush into a lion's jaw."

—NIETZSCHE, LETTER TO OVERBECK, IN *SELECTED LETTERS OF
FRIEDRICH NIETZSCHE*, ED. AND TRANS. OSCAR LEVY

There is no doubt that the joy Nietzsche expresses to his friend
Franz Overbeck is genuine, a delight at finding a kindred spirit
who understood affects and power, who could be something of
a companion, a "twosomeness," for Nietzsche in his singular struggles.
Perhaps even more than Spinoza, Nietzsche immersed himself in the

full implications of power, seeing power, rather than substance, as what runs through and adheres together all things. Nietzsche no longer sees an ordered world that is rationally structured through the inner order of things, corporeal and conceptual. For Nietzsche, it is force fields instead of the orders of substance that give us the greatest opportunities for self-expansion, for a good life, that is, a life lived in its intensity without regret, a life that the human cannot bear but, that perhaps the best of humans, the last humans, may foresee, the overcoming of man through the creation of the overman, the one who can bear the eternal recurrence of the universe and all its exhilarating, quirky, and shameful moments. For Nietzsche, the order that the world exhibits, while we may be able to extract principles which mark its regularities, is primarily chaotic, conflictual, excessive, open-ended, not dominated by things, which may be understood as the corporeal effects of forces and force fields. The world is no longer ordered rationally, with our forms of reason concurring with and produced by this world, as Spinoza believed. With the death of God, the world has no order other than that imposed on it by the various forces that make things and seize hold of their utility. If there is no divine order, if there is no knowledge we can have of the entire chain of causes that condition all things, and the sea of ideas carried alongside it, if, as finite beings, we are but specks of insignificance in the conflicting orders that compose the world, our task is less to know this world, to apprehend it *sub specie aeternitatis*, than it is to assent to and create a life that lives in the world with full intensity, that seeks both healthy or good encounters as well as struggles and challenges that bring with them bad health and bad encounters. Instead of loving God, substance or nature as a divine order in the world and in us, Nietzsche proposes that we, his future readers, enhance ourselves through affects, through both suffering and joy, through solitude and in alliances, through living the intensity of the forces that compose us, and, above all, he teaches us to love necessity, the necessity of our living in a world that does not reflect us, and whose order and causal chains we cannot understand but whose existence we affirm as much as it affirms our own powers. We become "divine," to the extent that humans can, through affect rather than thought, through feeling and acting more than thinking (for thought itself, and particularly consciousness, is a kind of action, a force, turned inward, a force that delays its action through the mediation of reflection).[1] For Nietzsche, force is unconscious and bodily, indeed ideas themselves have forces, energies, invested in their contestation. Many affects come to be turned inward rather than acted on, and inaccessible to consciousness, that is, reactive, a function of normalization, or "the herd," the more "civilized" man becomes.

Nietzsche's extraordinarily rich and strange writings—for which there is no counterpart in Western philosophy—provide a clear addition to the genealogy of philosophers I am exploring here, those who are difficult to classify as clear-cut materialists or idealists, whose work confounds and exceeds a binarized representation of these terms and who actively invent key terms, unique in each case, that insist on the belonging together of the orders of materiality and ideality. In Nietzsche's case, it is not only the opposition between mind and body but the binary structure itself he challenges, often using contrary expressions or analyses to address the same question that binary thought considers in contradictory terms, commonly invoking the no-man's-land between polarities. This is perhaps why he so welcomes a "twosomeness" to address his own loneliness. Nietzsche, alone and misunderstood in his time, needed a history of those who preceded him in order to understand the future that his work, especially through the figure of Zarathustra, prophesies—the overcoming of man and the birth of a new type of human. Nietzsche acknowledges many in the lineage that makes him possible, the Greeks, Spinoza, Goethe, Darwin (though he has no peers, in his conception), but he always adds a perspective that no longer makes any of these works comfortable in its own history, that shakes each text with the extraction and explication of its unrecognized forces, its own excesses and limits. This is a lineage that requires seeking out; it is both a genealogy and therapeutics of the history of philosophy (and of the sciences and languages, philology, Nietzsche's own specialization), that overcomes the history of philosophy, even those whose work on such a history he deeply admires. In announcing a new kind of human, the evolutionary overcoming of man by man-to-come, Nietzsche sees this lineage as preparatory for those beings, overmen, who will replace us. Although he does not invent the idea of the being to come, he is the one to see its inevitability most directly.

In this chapter I will elaborate the relations, as Nietzsche understands them, between body and idea and explore in further detail the concepts of freedom, self-making, self-overcoming, *amor fati*, and the overman that articulate Nietzsche's understanding of the conjunction of ontology and ethics. A fascination with this conjunction also connects him to the genealogy of philosophers he both affirms and criticizes, the Greeks, including the pre-Socratics, the Stoics, as well as Spinoza. Each articulates a connection between ethics and necessity, a fine line between determinism and freedom, in which freedom cannot be understood as the absence of causes but is conceptualized only through and because of the operation of causal chains. Freedom is the understanding of and capacity to utilize for oneself the chain of causes, the lines of linkage, that connect any thing to all others. Freedom is that which we attain only to the extent that its enemies—custom, politeness, civility, social clichés and opinions, the "herd morality," normalization—can be overcome and the convergence of causes used for oneself. Each of these traditions articulates not a freedom *from* determination but a freedom to act *because* of the orders of determination, a freedom enhanced by a philosophy or knowledge appropriate to it. In Nietzsche this freedom to act is not so much enabled, affected, by the general knowledge of the regularities that mark our perception and thus accessible through the knowledge that the sciences may provide for us, as they are for the Greeks and Spinoza, but a kind of knowledge that is primarily expressed in and enabled by art.

The arts even more than the sciences enable life to overcome itself, to evolve beyond itself, to make and live up to new ideals, a new morality, a new kind of life, not beyond this one but already manifest in some members of each species. Moreover, art provides a counterbalance to the sciences, insofar as each of the arts makes clear the constructed nature of all production, the literary and linguistic characteristics of even the most mathematically bound sciences. Art, and science, not only physics and chemistry but also biology, provide us with forces by which we can expand our own forces, if we can use what they provide us.

Each alone, and taken together, are merely preliminaries, for Nietzsche, to the creation of a new morality that will emerge from the transvaluation of values that his own writings accomplish, a true creation in the art of life. Reviewing and renewing the value of the arts, sciences, and other human practices can move us forward, as individuals and as a species, in developing a new morality, a new understanding of how to live in accordance with a nature that is neither benevolent nor only lawlike. Nietzsche continues, in the manner of the nineteenth century, that is, in the wake of Hegel, Marx, and Darwin, to affirm, with Spinoza, a life as pure immanence. He provides us with an updated and transformed immanence, a single ever recurring, continually changing universe with nothing else beyond it and thus also nothing new in it, while, paradoxically, each being must create itself and live up to its fate as artfully as it can.

NIETZSCHE, SPINOZA, AND THE STOICS

Like the pre-Socratics, the Stoics, and Spinoza, Nietzsche is fascinated by an ethics that is naturally involved in and expressive of an ontology, a model of the real, which does not provide a moral code but does provide the kind of knowledge that may enable our self-transformation in a larger movement that also acts and transforms the real. Ethics is a question linked to what the world is rather than a question directed to how it should be: it is, for him, linked to the *is* as much as to the *ought*. Like the Stoics, and Spinoza, Nietzsche is committed to the concept of a single world, a vast universe that is the only one we or any other being inhabit: there is no other world beyond this one, there are no possibilities of transcendence, no existence in another realm, no religious or divine order, only immanence, the inherence of forms of order in the flow of objects, processes, and ideas. Nietzsche is committed to a radical rewriting of the moral norms of his contemporaries through the creation of a new kind of philosophy and, with it, the constitution of a new morality, or, as I would call it, a new ethics.

Like the Stoics and Spinoza, Nietzsche is committed to both an order of material causes but also an extramaterial force, an orientation or inner telos, the will to power (not to be confused with willing power, having a powerful will or any psychological characteristics), that orients or organizes material forces, those with a quantity and a quality, from within, a vector according to which a direction or mode of action, that is to say, the will (or many competing wills) comprising a thing can elaborate itself. The will to power is a force more powerful than conatus in the sense that it desires not only its perseverance and maximization, as does conatus, but to overcome its obstacles, overcome itself, conquer, whether this is at the level of the simplest object or the most complex human and collective actions. As Yirmiyahu Yovel argues, if Spinoza sees conatus as the power of self-preservation and self-enhancement, a power always at work in life, Nietzsche regards the will to power not as an instrument of life but as what life does, what life makes of other wills to power.[2]

Like the Stoics and Spinoza, Nietzsche believes that an ethical life, a life that achieves its own overcoming and links its future or destiny to that of the whole of the universe, is a great rarity. This is not a life lived in accordance with religious or moral precepts that are given, either from on high or from one's fellow beings, in which morality preexists and to which a life conforms. An ethical life is different from, and often opposed to, a religious life. It is only a singular individual who may personify such an ethics, a rare being who not only exists but profoundly affects others and teaches others to find their own way—Chrisyppus, Christ (?), perhaps Spinoza himself, and, above all, Zarathustra—all beings who in some way exist out of their own time, who prefigure the future while remaining ghosts, no longer able to live or to be put to death, but inspiring our understanding of a certain way to life, a life of overcoming: "*A kind of atavism.*—I prefer to understand the rare human beings of an age as suddenly emerging late ghosts of past cultures and their powers—an atavisms of a people and its *mores*: that way one really can *understand* a little about them. Now they seem strange, rare, extraordinary; and whoever feels these powers in himself must nurse, defend, honor, and cultivate them against another world that resists them, until he becomes a great human being, or a mad and eccentric one—or perishes early."[3]

Such a rare individual fights against the norms of an age, perishing only in the knowledge that something is destined to return again, to be read again, to teach others who are themselves a little out of their time, living as ghosts or angels of the future. This rare individual, one who has adequately digested the specific forces of the past that produces him or her, who refuses to rely on consciousness or on an accretion of social opinions, acts his or her affects and suffers his or her passions fully, is a kind of beacon to the future of the species, an outlier who invents new ways to live, new moralities by which to live. The history of such rare individuals prepares us for the kind of transvaluation of values by which new humans, still rare, can prepare for this future. And this history must, by definition, be antidemocratic, anticollective, a singular being operating against prevailing forces by resistance through creation, the construction of new values.

Nietzsche is fascinated with and entranced by Greek philosophy, whatever criticisms he has about particular philosophers. The place that thought was accorded in Ancient Greece and Imperial Rome made it truly the birth of Western philosophy, where philosophy struggled with competing ideas and formed part of the lifeblood of society, not just a specialized profession of philosophers working in their isolation. As is well known, Nietzsche studied philology and became immersed in Greek texts, their translations and later reception. His earliest publications dating from 1868 deal with early Greek texts, especially the pre-Socratics, which he would invoke in arguing against elements of Plato and Aristotle; his third philological essay analyzed the sources for Diogenes' "The Lives of Philosophers," through which we have the most direct access to many ancient texts otherwise lost.[4] Even into his more mature writings through the 1870s, Nietzsche draws extensively on Stoic practices, and particularly their therapeutic techniques of self-analysis, as a kind of counterweight to the Christian hold on human suffering that converts suffering into punishment. Nietzsche wants to develop an alternative to religion, a treatment for misery that relies on a central Stoic insight: that one must change one's values from within, one must revalue all existing values for oneself, given that the universe is as it is.[5]

In relation to the Stoics, Nietzsche understands the power of Stoic fortitude or indifference, not always and in every context, but particularly in violent times. Such fortitude, however, misleads one in conditions of peace and plenty (in these circumstances, Nietzsche prefers Epicureanism, the enjoyment of one's well-being!), but the Stoics too have a place in his path as prophet of the future. The Stoics have developed a "hedgehog skin," a toughness to external elements, which the Epicurean may find irritating to his sensitive nature.[6] This may prove useful in conditions of struggle. The Stoic understands resistance: "The Stoic . . . trains himself to swallow stones and worms, slivers of glass and scorpions without nausea: he wants his stomach to become ultimately indifferent to what the accidents of existence might pour into it. . . . For those with whom fate attempts improvisations—those who live in violent ages and depend on sudden and mercurial people—Stoicism may be advisable. But anyone who foresees more or less that fate permits him to spin a *long thread* does well to make Epicurean arrangements" (*GS* #306). The Stoics prepare themselves for the worst; they understand what the world may throw at them, the small position each of us have in a vastly larger world. This is their strength, from which Nietzsche has undoubtedly learned a good deal; perseverance in one's project, seeking understanding, even in the face of a sometimes vicious and difficult-to-comprehend world, become key methodologies and principles regulating his own writings.

Their renunciation of all that is outside them, of all they cannot control, including the passions, is also, unlike the Epicureans, a form of life denial, a minimization of one's powers, their restriction to the body of thought. The Stoics elaborate perhaps the first systematic philosophy in which philosophy, as a calling and as a practice, stands in defiance of established order, as political opposition (this is why Socrates remains the exemplary figure for both the Stoics and Nietzsche). Nevertheless, beyond their ethics of self-satisfaction, an ethics that, for Nietzsche, diminishes their capacities, lies an ontology of a dynamic, changing, and providential world, a world with a destiny, a fate, which dictates also the fate of each of us that Nietzsche will rediscover as a kind of "solution" to his project. [7] From the Stoics, Nietzsche utilizes the idea of living up to one's destiny, affirming one's fate, in defiance of Spinoza's idea of knowledge as the possibility of eternity, of knowledge and ideas that live on. Forces live on, and knowledge, for Nietzsche is merely one among many competing forces, each with its own wills to power, none destined for eternity, except in infinite repetitions. Nietzsche seems to invoke the possibilities of Stoicism to upset Spinozism and, equally, the possibilities of Spinozism to unsettle Stoic thought. Yet he is nevertheless fully entwined with their respective works, he, as his own Diogenes, must include these "eminent philosophers" as part of his own (lost) history, and they form part of the assault that Nietzsche undertakes on the morality and politics of his own time, and ours. They help Nietzsche to remain "untimely," to resist his present, to be born "posthumously" ("The time for me hasn't come yet: some are born posthumously),"[8] that is, through the power of the unexhausted past and the call to a future transvaluation of all existing values, a future not deducible from the present.[9]

If it is obvious that there is a kind of lineage between the Ancient Greeks, including the Stoics, Spinoza and Nietzsche (among others), it is also important to recognize that there are very clear differences between Nietzsche and his predecessors, and especially Spinoza, in spite of the affinity so joyously proclaimed in Nietzsche's excited card to Overbeck. Perhaps the most significant is his difference from Spinoza's advocacy of an *amor dei intellectualis*, the conceptual love of God, a love under the aspect of eternity that is the goal of his *Ethics*. Nietzsche replaces this love of God with amor fati, the love of fate, the love that overcomes the present to embrace the eternal return.[10] With the death of God, it is only the order of causes and the possibilities of overcoming such an order—fate and its embrace—that remain possible. Once God is fully dissolved into nature, its order becomes contestable. Nietzsche seeks out a more full-bodied relation to nature in which intellectual contemplation is not enough for an adequate understanding. We need to invoke our animal impulses, so readily directed internally by cultural forces and habits, to enhance our capacity to feel (both joy and hardship); we need to revivify our capacity to act. Spinoza's mistake, for Nietzsche, is his severing of feeling (or imagination) from understanding (or the third kind of knowledge):

Nonridere, no lugere, neque detestari, sed intelligere! [Not to laugh, not to lament, not to detest, but to understand],[11] says Spinoza as simply and sublimely as is his wont. Yet in the last analysis, what else is this *intelligere* than the form in which we come to feel the other three at once? One result of the different and mutually opposed desires to laugh, lament, and curse? . . . We suppose that *intelligere* must be something conciliatory, just, good—something that stands essentially opposed to the instincts, while it is actually nothing, but a *certain behavior of the instincts toward one another.*

(*GS* #333)

For Nietzsche, Spinoza has intellectualized our instincts, perhaps mistaking mind for body, certainly substituting mind for body. He misunderstands that the forces of the body produce the mind, making whatever thinking it has—and thinking is difficult—possible only through various bodily imperatives. Nietzsche also charges Spinoza with the creation of an immanent God but not the demise of such a God. The "shadows of God" still darken Spinoza's thought, "And we—we still have to vanquish his shadow, too" (see *GS* #108, see also #109). We need to see knowledge not as a means for an eternal (partial) life, the eternity of ideas of the third kind, but "life as a means to knowledge" (*GS* #324), life and knowledge always bound together.

Spinoza, for Nietzsche, has disembodied ideas and made them pale. In a section of *The Gay Science* titled "Why We Are Not Idealists" (#372), he argues that ideas need to be fed not just on other ideas but on bodies: they need to insinuate themselves into a body in order to be thought, to be felt, to live, for ideas are fundamentally parasites or vampires which live on blood, which require full-bloodedness to have any power:

Ideas are worse seductresses than our senses, for all their cold and anemic appearance, and not even in spite of this appearance: they have always lived on the "blood" of the philosopher, they always consumed his senses and even, if you will believe us, his "heart." These old philosophers were heartless: philosophizing was always a kind of vampirism. Looking at these figures, even Spinoza, don't you have a sense of something profoundly enigmatic and uncanny? Don't you notice the spectacle that unrolls before you, how they *become ever paler*—how desensualization is interpreted more and more ideally. Don't you sense a long concealed vampire in the background who begins with the senses and in the end is left with, and leaves, mere bones, mere clatter? I mean categories, formulas, *words* (for, forgive me, what was left of Spinoza, *amor intellectualis dei*, is mere clatter and no more than that: What is *amor*, what is *deus*, if there isn't a drop of blood in them?)."

Ideas need bodies: for only bodies in their struggles for life invent thought, energize it and enable thought to act, enabling ideas to effect each other. Further, the concept of substance, the center of Spinoza's ontology, is the slowing down, the normalization, the rending equal of what is merely similar, the production of an identity for what is always varying:

> In order that the concept of substance could originate—which is indispensable for logic though in the strictest sense nothing real corresponds to it—it was likewise necessary that for a long time one did not see nor perceive the changes in things. The beings that did not see so precisely had an advantage over those that saw everything "in flux." . . . The course of logical ideas and inferences in our brain today corresponds to a process and struggle among impulses that are, taken very singly, very illogical and unjust. We generally experience only the result of this struggle because this primeval mechanism now runs its course so quickly and is so well concealed.
>
> (*GS* #111)

Ideas and their connections, logical or propositional, are results, effects, not causes, for they are residues of the body's forces, the complicated and by no means clear and distinct, effects of a body's relations. Thinking is not contemplation but struggle, not learning and acquiring but wrenching and transforming, war by other means.

Nietzsche is perhaps the most forceful, energetic, and wry reader of philosophical history and the one most directed to exploding the often unacknowledged assumptions of human or heavenly primacy in the order of the world. Neither an empiricist (or, if he is considered an empiricist, it is in a very different sense than any other philosopher) nor a rationalist who believes in the primacy of mind or reason, neither a materialist (our conception of matter is no less an invention than any other thought) nor an idealist (idealism ignores the senses—see *GS* # 371), Nietzsche, in effect, ends both the naive empiricism of pure observational objectivity and the naive rationalism that claims to know the conditions of knowledge, to know the mind and its order only through itself. Like the others addressed here, he refuses to separate one from the other.

He seeks a physics of being, vowing at one stage of his teaching career to leave philosophy in order to study physics more thoroughly. Indeed in his understanding, a study of the way that the world is, is a condition for a moral life, a life of self-overcoming and self-expansion. For it provides a way for not only understanding ourselves, a fundamentally reactive project, but for understanding what we are capable of becoming:

> We, [who want to live outside the great majority] however, want to become who we are,—the new, unique, incomparable ones, who give themselves their own laws, who create themselves! And to that end we must become the best learners and discoverers of everything that is lawful and necessary in the world: we must become physicists in order to be able to be creators in this sense,—while hitherto all valuations and ideals have been based on ignorance of physics or were constructed so as to contradict it. Therefore: long live physics! And even more so that which compels us to turn to physics,—our honesty!
>
> (*GS* #335)

To become who we are, to become "the new, unique, incomparable ones," we must become "the best learners," we must understand, not abstractly, not through reason alone, but through our bodies and behavior what the world is so that we can expand ourselves, create ourselves, through its resources. A physics is needed to create ourselves beyond ourselves, for such creation cannot occur internally, through merely wishing or desiring it, but only by acting and understanding the world as it is. A critical physics is needed, a physics that understands that all of science is man's way of inserting himself into and claiming to understand the forces and ways of the world, even when he may not.

SCIENCE AND ART

We need a physics that tells us of the world of matter; but we also require an understanding of the nonscientific origins of science, the religious conditions that science, or physics as the "purest of the sciences," must disavow, its superstitious, magical, religious origins. In a section entitled, "Preludes of Science," Nietzsche amuses himself by considering the necessary but irrational or intuitive preconditions of all the sciences: "Do you really believe that the sciences would ever have originated and grown if the way had not been prepared by magicians, alchemists, astrologers, and witches whose promises and pretensions first had to create a thirst, a hunger, a taste for *hidden* and the *forbidden* powers? Indeed, infinitely more had to be *promised* than could ever be fulfilled in order that anything at all might be fulfilled in the realm of knowledge. . . . The whole of *religion* might yet appear as a prelude and exercise to some distant age" (*GS* #300).

Science alone cannot model an ontology and cannot understand the coming together and excess that characterizes itself and its own very unscientific origins and present, let alone the world it aims to know truthfully. The more science, especially, the physical sciences, explain matter and its organization in the universe, the more it tends toward art; the more science gains in "truth," the more it loses in "objectivity." Art understands, as science does not, that human constructions, including science and art, function to enhance our ways of living and that this is their "truth effect," their will to truth.[12] Science, whatever its truths, its protocols, training, and "regulative fictions" (*GS* #344), functions at its best only with such an enhancement, for it is a set of practices that is capable of supporting life. But science also brings with it the danger of supplanting a morality of life affirmation, with its own morality of objectivity, by affirming not this one life but another, not the order (or chaos) of this world, but the perfection of another:

> No doubt, those who are truthful in that audacious and ultimate sense that is presupposed by the faith in science, *thus affirms another world* than the world of life, nature and history and insofar as they affirm this "other world"—look, must they not by the same token negate its counterpart, this world, *our* world?—But you will have gathered what I am driving at, namely, that it is still a *metaphysical faith* upon which our faith in science rests—that even we seekers after knowledge, we godless metaphysicians still take our fire, too, from the flame lit by a faith thousands of years old, that Christian faith, which was also the faith of Plato, that God is the truth, that truth is divine.
>
> (*GS* #344)

Science is a faith in truth that feigns objectivity while veiling the values and unargued-for beliefs that undergird it. Science is a way of addressing the world, making the world accessible to us in a particular way. Causality is a human invention for addressing the ever complex interrelations between objects which cannot be readily divided from each other and which cannot be known in their entwinement:

> Cause and effect: such a duality probably never exists: in truth we are confronted by a continuum out of which we isolate a couple of pieces, just as we perceive motion only as isolated points and then infer it without ever actually seeing it. The suddenness with which many effects stand out misleads us: actually, it is sudden only for us. In this moment of suddenness, there is an infinite number of processes that elude us. An intellect that could see cause and effect as a continuum and a flux and not as we do, in terms of arbitrary division and dismemberment, would repudiate the concept of cause and effect and deny all conditionality.[13]
>
> (*GS* #112)

If causation is a habit of thought, a convenience more than a truth, if it is convenient for us to understand one cause and its separate effect, this is because the science that relies on concepts of causation has not yet advanced to its postcausal complexity.

To the Stoics and Spinoza's understanding of the place of the (causal) sciences, a knowledge of the order and regularity of the universe, Nietzsche poses the necessity of art, not as distraction or pleasure, as it is for both the Stoics and Spinoza,[14] but as an augmentation and transformation of science and, above all, as a force of life and a means to a better life. Thus, in counterbalance to the delusions of all the sciences and the metaphysical systems that uphold them, which consider themselves unconstructed by human artfulness or undirected by human need, Nietzsche proposes the arts, and especially the most festive, to make clear that sensation and affect are the human conditions of science and its (historical) limits.[15] Art has a power to affirm the magical and the superstitious, error and illusion, without falling prey to it, for it has the power to convert superstition or irrationality into something more significant than reason; art can convert lies, errors, and superstitions into art works, whether theatrical, musical, or visual, whose forces have the capacity to affirm life in all its intensities. Art speaks the body's instincts and forces directly, invigorating or irritating them. It is a greater aid to action, and to ethics, than the sciences, which certainly have their place in our actions and understanding, but which, as Nietzsche sees them, harness the faith that had previously propped up religion. Science, as the most "objective" and "vaunted" of human accomplishments, tends to inherit the faith and awe that religion once inspired: with the death of God (not his nonexistence but his annihilation), the herd must find new objects for its faith.

Art provokes a thirst for reason, for the kinds of knowledge science produces, although it is never content to turn itself into science, that is, to decorporealize itself. For Nietzsche, the trick is to undertake science artistically, to produce a new kind of science, a gay science, new forms of knowledge, to create what we can use to understand ourselves, not a new kind of psychology, but a new ontology, and with it a new set of values: "We others, who thirst after reason, are determined to scrutinize our experiences as severely as a scientific experiment—hour after hour, day after day. We ourselves wish to be our experiments and guinea pigs"

(*GS* #319). Life is part of a universe. To love it, to be fully part of this one and only universe, to affirm one's place in it amounts not only to a love of truth, but also a taste for deception, error, and lies, for confabulation and invention, for all that life encounters.[16]

While there are undeniable affinities between Stoic, Spinozan, and Nietzschean philosophies and a lineage of influence, it is also true that, in his transvaluation of values. Nietzsche's aim to live outside the customs and social norms that mark contemporary religious and cultural life and characterize the sciences and political relations of his day makes his work very unlike that of his predecessors and "ancestors." His aim is to soar into the future and to welcome it entirely, while acknowledging the power and inevitability of the past that produced him as such. His aim is to breed a "higher" human, a human no longer recognizable to us but perhaps anticipated in the bravest, the most imaginative and open of our contemporaries. His transvaluation will also revalue all of philosophy, including those positions and claims that have helped create his own. Nothing is immune to Nietzsche's withering, and scathingly accurate, dismissals of many of the key concepts in each. He seeks a philosophy not based on God, nor man and his fantasies of self-production and self-importance, but a philosophy, both ethics and ontology at the same time, that heralds a new kind of being, that enables such a new kind of being to bring itself into existence.[17]

Spinoza's affirmation of the singularity of substance, and its identification with the whole of nature, and the Stoics' understanding of the universe as a living being, while powerful metaphors, belie the fact that, for Nietzsche, the universe must be understood, both through science and the arts, not as a natural order governed by nature's laws, not an external magnification of our own ordered self-image, that is, by God, but chaos, a tangle of causes, that generates excesses of order rather than a moral order.

> Let us be aware of thinking that the world is a living being. Where should it expand? On what should it feed? How could it grow and multiply.... Let us even beware of believing that the universe is a machine: it is certainly not constructed for one purpose and calling it a "machine"

does it far too much honor. . . . The total character of the world . . . is in all eternity chaos—in the sense not of a lack of necessity but of a lack of order, arrangement, form, beauty, and whatever other names there are for our aesthetic anthropomorphisms. . . . When will we complete our de-deification of nature? When may we begin to "naturalize" humanity in terms of a pure, newly discovered, newly redeemed nature?

(*GS* #109)

Nietzsche dedeifies nature. He makes nature neither law nor order but only necessity: "There are only necessities: there is nobody who commands, nobody who obeys, nobody who trespasses. Once you know that there are no purposes, you also know that there is no accident" (*GS* #109). Nietzsche develops a radical Spinozism that, in the wake of Darwinism, sees life endlessly overcoming itself, without divine direction or orientation. If there is order in the struggle for existence, it is the order of the body and its forms, its varieties, its strengths in practice, *in situ*. In spite of his resistances to the Darwin he inherits, Nietzsche places bodily impulses, instincts, the preservation of the species, and the excessive desires of living things above the operations of reason, not annihilating reason but inevitably orienting it to questions of life, even as thought may rebel against or be ignorant of these questions, ensuring that reason is always tinged with the aura of the "unreason or counterreason of passion" (*GS* #3), that even bad or evil intentions function to preserve the species.

In other words, if we have misunderstood the role of passions and actions, if we have misrepresented the immense creativity of evil, of disruption, of conquering, then a new kind of ethics or morality is required. If God is dead, if we have killed him, then it is no longer an order under the aspect of eternity that directs our actions but precisely the opposite: we are directed to become what we are, to affirm our instincts and passions, to develop them for ourselves, not according to a general good but according to their own intensities and directions. Following Spinoza in the sense that Spinoza understands conatus, self-preservation and self-expansion, as the essence of our being, Nietzsche refuses to accept that acting according to our passions and desires is bad, needs

careful consideration, and should be tempered by reason or calculation. Such a mode of action is dangerous to life: life needs to act—or
suffer—its needs, whatever the consequences, if it is to survive, not as
an individual but as a self-sustaining species. Action needs to overcome
consciousness in order to instill and confirm instincts, direct modes of
action, a new nature that intensifies our inherited instincts and creates
new instincts.

THE NIETZSCHEAN TRANSVALUATION OF VALUES

Nietzsche invents, or refashions from earlier sources and makes his
own, a new ontology, one in which things, whether bodies or ideas, are
not inert beings that simply exist in themselves or are caused from outside. Bodies, ideas, identities of all kinds are the provisional alignment
of a physics of forces, which gives "blood," that is power, energy, to all
things. His challenge to thought is to conceptualize a universe now freed
of identities, names, human and religious categories, to understand
the universe in terms of the one order that underlies and runs through
everything. In contradistinction to Spinoza's substance and its deducible
operations, Nietzsche affirms a concept much closer to the Stoics' fiery
pneuma. He terms it "the will to power," a force that is neither will nor
power in its usual sense. Will must be understood, not as intentionality
or as teleology, not as living or the product of life. It is the impersonal
condition of life that makes life, including the human, possible and that
each life lives in its own way. And power cannot be conceived as a quality or condition of a living or divine being, something it "has," for it
cannot be possessed but only exercised. The will to power is the vast network of impersonal forces that make up the world that acts and strives to
become. The will to power ensures that nothing remains fully what it is,
that each thing, each object, thought, nation, people, is forever becoming, never absolutely stable, never the self-same but always engaging in
activities and passions that necessarily transform it. The will to power
is both the active and passive forces that underlie everything, that run

within all causal relations and relations between ideas. Such relations are henceforth political, forces that act, react, command, or obey in relation to other forces. The contestation of bodies and bodily forces is no more fierce than the contestation of ideas.

The human has been bound by two forces, two forms of power, that function to instill obedience: the forces of social arrangement which become more intense the more "European," the more, we might say now, internationalized or globalized social and economic mores, or the less Greek or Roman, they become.[18] The Greeks are more in tune with their animal instincts, with the forces that activate them, than modern Europeans (and particularly, Nietzsche insists, the modern German). The Greeks elaborated a Dionysian condition, a physiology and praxis, a will to life, in the arts, which involve a joyous expression of instincts and pleasures, a festive orgy of life: "it is only in the Dionysian mysteries, in the psychology of the Dionysian condition, that the *fundamental fact* of the Hellenic instinct expresses itself—its 'will to life.' *What* did the Hellene guarantee to himself with these mysteries? *Eternal* life, the eternal recurrence of life; the future promised and consecrated in the past; the triumphant Yes to life beyond death and change."[19] The more that collective social order requires conformity, the more civilized man becomes, the more consciousness replaces thought, the more our animal instincts, those which enable us to thrive, are overcome.

The second force that instills obedience, and whose only function is the production of obedience, is religion, especially Christianity, which aims to exchange all the conditions of this life for the promise of another life after death. An Anti-Christ is required to announce not only the death of God but what will replace him—the self-organizing forces of the will to power, the forces of the impersonal, a morality or ethics beyond morality. Christianity invents, as its most powerful weapon, pity, that most debilitating of affects, the affect most opposed to life, which poses itself as a solution to suffering but functions as a diminution of the power suffering may produce, for nothing new can be produced without suffering. Not all suffering is a debilitation, for it is the greatest spur to self-overcoming: "Christianity is called the religion of *pity*.—Pity stands in antithesis to the tonic emotions that enhance the energy and feeling of life: it has a depressing effect. One loses force when one pities. The loss of force which life has already sustained through suffering is increased and multiplied even further by pity."[20]

The will to power is the "will," the orientation or direction, in which a body or thought is taken when it acts, the force of its actions, the possibilities of its affecting and being affected. The will is the direction of a force; power is the quantum of force, the amount of energy it can expend or attract. The will to power is what expresses the *inner* force of each thing, its powers and capacities and their degrees of force relative to each other. The totality of wills in play provide a map of force fields, an ever-changing movement of force relations that ebb and flow, that create "things" as their human faces but which function through the interaction of differential forces. This will to power is not just power or force oriented in a particular direction: it is a "will," something internal that has its objects of willing (those it commands or obeys, those it utilizes or is utilized by). It is called "will" by Nietzsche in part to designate its irreducibility to the forces composing materiality. The will guides the power it "wills"; it is its inner orientation, an inner goal, even if this will has nothing to do with the concept of "free will," that is, a causeless will. The will to power is power directed from a (spatiotemporal) location, a force field, to a (spatiotemporal) location, another force field, with a different quantum of energy. If force fields, the constituents of things, can be understood materially (certainly not in any mechanistic model of materiality, which Nietzsche demonstrates is incoherent),[21] then the will that organizes and orients them cannot be understood materially. The will can be located within any form of matter, any form of thought, any practice as a push in certain directions and not others. It is incorporeal, the direction that the corporeal or the conceptual takes, the direction of its movement *to* something or somewhere. Like cause and effect, power and its will, its inner direction form "a continuum out of which we isolate a couple of pieces." This inner will cannot be identified with the quantity or degree of forces but only with the capacity for the *self-organization* of forces, their modus vivendi.

In the final pages of *The Will to Power*,[22] Nietzsche invokes a breathtaking world of ever-intensifying, ever-transforming force relations that compose everything large and small, noble and servile, equally, a world no longer made up of things, which are now dissolved into the various forces that compose them:

> This world: a monster of energy, without beginning, without end; a firm, iron magnitude of force that does not grow bigger or smaller, that does not expend itself but only transforms itself; . . . as force throughout, as a play of forces and waves of forces, at the same time one and many, increasing here and at the same time decreasing there; a sea of forces, flowing and rushing together, eternally changing, eternally flooding back, with tremendous years of recurrence, with an ebb and a flood of its forms. . . . [This], my *Dionysian* world of eternally self-creating, the eternally self-destroying, this mystery world of the twofold voluptuous delight, my "beyond good and evil," without goal, unless the joy of the circle is itself a goal; without will, unless a ring feels good will toward itself—do you want a *name* for this world? A *solution* for its riddles? A *light* for you, too, you best-concealed, strongest, most intrepid, most midnightly men? *This world is the will to power—and nothing besides!* And you yourselves are also this will to power—and nothing besides!
>
> (*WP* #1067)

Nietzsche's transvaluation of existing values consists in seeking out the various wills or interests at stake in existing values, the various forces of reaction and inhibition that overtake values, in order to create a new set of values, untimely, untamed by the inhibitions that the social entails and requires. He proposes a new kind of philosophy (one, for example, cut off neither from the sciences nor the arts, but able to resonate and add to each of these its own perspective without identifying itself with either) to understand the world and ourselves, a new therapeutics that will overturn the regime of the individual, and of cause, by which modern individuals consider themselves free. Such a new philosophy, which is both an ontology and an ethics inseparably, functions to affirm life and what is beyond life, to affirm the will to accumulate and intensify force that characterizes life: "The will to accumulate force is special to the phenomena of life, to nourishment, procreation, inheritance—to society, state, custom, authority. Should we not be permitted to assume this will as a motive cause in chemistry, too?—and in the cosmic order?" (*WP* #689). New perspectives, which is to say, new wills, new forms of knowledge, new modes of seizing hold of particular forces, must be created through the internal critique of prevailing forces, whether conceptual, material, natural, or social. Only this can bring about new values, new ideals, beyond consciousness, beyond man—values that affirm life and its capacity to accumulate and multiply energy, that affirm the will to power and all its consequences—the eternal return and the love of fate.

The task of Nietzsche's philosophy is to provide a diagnosis of the malaise which marks Western humanity, the malaise of yearning for a different world which more properly reflects the individual's most common and herdlike feeling of his own autonomy and agency. For him, "We are *more* than the individuals; we are the whole chain as well, with the tasks of all the futures of that chain" (*WP* #687). Nietzsche asks: what if a certain kind of agency pervades not only human life but every organ, every process, every ingredient that composes human life, including the long history of animal life and the nonanimate universe that are all the way through regulated not only by forces but by the provisional alignments of microforces, the forces that operate below the level of a singular being? What new kinds of individual may be spawned by such a recognition, what kinds of man comes with the demise of man?

In opposition to both an ever-burgeoning humanism that has grown from the Greeks to present day, and a recently decaying religiosity that affirms this humanism by providing it with a God in its image, Nietzsche proposes the ever-changing movement of impersonal forces, forces that align themselves with others, forces that are conquered by others, forces that aim to conquer, a movement that resists the stasis of an identity. He argues that "all driving force is will to power, that there is no other physical, dynamic or psychical force except this" (*WP* #688). To live in this one world is to address and encounter these forces. The sciences sometimes allow us to understand these forces, or at least their effects; the arts, and especially music, enable us to feel these forces and to be enhanced by them bodily. The antidote for this disorder is an affirmation of the will to power and its chaotic, conflictual order. The transvaluation of values aims to restore health and vigor to the power of willing, the power of suffering and overcoming, to correct the assumption that the world is for-us, for-anything other than itself: "I have seen above me, glittering under the stars, the tremendous rat's tail of errors that has hitherto counted as the highest inspiration of humanity: 'All happiness is a consequence of virtue, all virtue is a consequence of free will.' *Let us reverse the values*: all fitness the result of fortunate organization, all freedom, the result of fitness (—freedom here understood as facility in self-direction. Every artist will understand me)" (*WP* #705).

MAN BEYOND MAN

Nietzsche foretells of a time when man evolves beyond man as we have known him; indeed, he sees Zarathustra, one of his own masks, as the herald, the prophet, of the overman who will inevitably overcome "European" sensibility, the herd, and the forces of reaction that grow ever stronger, who is the inheritor of human history (and prehistory) and is able to digest it adequately and robustly transform it. Such a human can make of life a new morality, a new order that affirms its own forces and this world of whirring, interacting forces. This human of the future is bred through the most rigorous regimes, undergoing the most intense experiences of suffering and joy, a self-created Dionysian.[23]

This human beyond the human is healthy, in the sense that even sickness enhances the overman, bringing with it a new affirmation of life;[24] it eats well, digests adequately, exercises, lives in a healthy invigorating environment, and has a rigor in living with both good and bad "luck" as equal stimuli for action. Nietzsche poses a veritable system of self-regulation and self-management that involves not only a care of the self but a dynamic connection with all the orders of existence that enable this being to persist, to digest, to become more and more energetic, to continue its ongoing self-overcoming: "The *tempo* of the metabolism is strictly proportionate to the mobility or lameness of the spirit's *feet*; the 'spirit' itself is after all merely as aspect of this metabolism."[25] Not only must the body be able to digest well, rapidly, without sluggishness, but it must find a conducive climate (dry air was essential, Nietzsche believed, for one to best undertake the work of philosophy)—thought itself comes from struggle, from addressing problems, though now considered not as a reflection on life but as an ingredient in life. Nourishing food, a climate and environment that is conducive to good health, exercise, a love of the arts, especially music and dancing, movement, generosity, openness: these are the conditions under which humans as we know them thrive. They are also the preconditions under which humans can breed themselves into a new kind of species.[26]

The overman is not man who has overcome the reactive, but man who has used what is reactive as a spur to act, fearing neither passivity nor passions. This being after the human does not fear affects, even contrary ones, for they are the inducements to ever greater becomings. Everything experienced is useful for the task, even that which appears as an interruption, for the only task is becoming what one is, which must be carried out without the slightest consciousness: to become what one is, to aim at this task without knowing it, without directing oneself to it, and to welcome it with full affirmation. This can only be undertaken to the extent that one overcomes the constraints of consciousness, prevailing moralities, man as he is: the task of becoming who one is, that is, becoming what one is destined—without knowing it—to be can only be undertaken by the strongest individuals, those who have developed the impulse to say "No as rarely as possible" ("Why I Am So Clever," *EH* #8). Given certain preconditions outside the individual, forces with which such a rare individual must engage, the overman is bred primarily through immersion in selfishness, in the revelry of his inner forces:

At this point the real answer to the question, *how one becomes what one is*, can no longer be avoided. And thus I touch on the masterpiece of the art of self-preservation—of *selfishness*. For let us assume the task, the destiny, the fate of the task transcends the average very significantly: in that case, nothing could be more dangerous than catching sight of oneself *with* this task. To become what one is, one must not have the faintest notion *what* one is. From this point of view, even the *blunders* of life have their own meaning and value—the occasional side roads and wrong roads, the delays, "modesties," seriousness wasted on tasks that are remote from *the* task.

("Why I Am So Clever," *EH* #9)

One needs to breed oneself, not through reproduction but through self-cultivation, for the task of being worthy of one's fate. With certain preconditions for good health and vigor in place, even then, only the most rare of individuals attain the capacity to love one's fate, whatever it might be. The tool for this task of the self-production of the human-to-come is the eternal return, Nietzsche's rewriting of the pre-Christian Stoic conception of providence. The eternal return or recurrence is the indistinguishably ontological and moral concept that Nietzsche understands as the working of fate, the operation of the physical principles of the world. I have discussed elsewhere the distinction between the eternal return as ontological, a fundamental principle of physics (the principle of the conservation of energy, Newton's second law) entailed by the universe being considered a finite quantum of energy: the eternal return is an inevitable consequence, for Nietzsche, of the finiteness of matter and the infinity of time. Given enough time, every thing, every relation, every thought that has occurred will occur again, even given their random combinations: eternity entails recurrence. This means that, in terms of the physics of his time—and our own,[27] the universe never began to become, never finished becoming, but is in a perpetual cycle of eruption, heat-death, and re-eruption ad infinitum.[28] The universe not only recurs; in its many forms of repetition it also recurs in precisely the manner of our world, our thoughts, our being. If everything recurs, if every possible combination of elements has already occurred, then it must occur again, and again, an infinite number of times.[29] All that has been will come again: all that has passed will pass again an infinite number of times. Our task as beings living on the verge of a new morality is to love this inevitability, even as we cannot know its consequences.

The moral dimensions of the eternal return are perhaps its most significant implication. They are tied directly to its ontological claims. It becomes the very means by which self-cultivation exceeds itself.

Nietzsche asks, what kind of human can face the eternal return, what kind of self-overcoming does an affirmation of this principle entail? What kind of being can bear the eternal return? What test of the human does it impose? In what way is the eternal return the litmus test of the overman? Nietzsche asks the crucial question:

> What if, some day or night a demon were to steal after you into your loneliest loneliness and say to you: "This life as you know it and have lived it, you will have to live once more and innumerable times more; and there will be nothing new in it, but every pain and every joy and every thought and sigh and everything unutterably small or great in your life will have to return to you, all in the same succession and sequence—even this spider and this moonlight between the trees, and even this moment and I myself. The eternal hourglass of existence is turned upside down again and again, and you with it, speck of dust!" Would you not throw yourself down and gnash your teeth and curse the demon who spoke thus? Or you once experienced a tremendous moment when you would have answered him: "You are a god and never have I heard anything more divine." If this thought gained a posses-sion of you, it would change you as you are or perhaps crush you. The question in each and every thing, "Do you desire this once more and innumerable times more?" would lie upon your actions as the greatest weight. Or how well disposed would you have to become to yourself and to life *to crave nothing more fervently* than this ultimate eternal con-firmation and seal?
>
> (GS #341)

The eternal return is the most heavy weight for a life that is lived reac-tively, in relation to another's action. How could any average human, any civilized human, bear what this "demon" has to say? To live every thing, every mortification, embarrassment, stupidity, lie, self-justification as well as every joy, intensity, pleasure, to live every act and affect again, in precisely the same order as the life one has (as well as every universe without me, without any particular actions and affects, for everything, every possibility, will return again) is entailed by the eternal return. In thinking the eternal return as primary ethical principle, Nietzsche asks the question: who is strong enough to bear such a "great weight," who in the human race, and beyond it, can will this return of everything high and low, rather than fight against it? The question "do you live your life without regret, without wishes for something else at some time in your life?" is the question of will: do you will your life again, with all its details and all its humiliations? Do you fully affirm the life that is yours, the one life you have, this one and only life, such that you will to live it and everything that constitutes and makes it possible an infinite number of times over? To even think this thought, as Nietzsche has, is to be on the brink of overcoming oneself, and man more generally, foreseeing what man may become and entering that process oneself. What in us now is overcoming ourselves, affirming the will to eternity of all our actions and passions, never actions indeed without passions (Nietzsche's corrective to Spinoza!)?

Through the ontophysicist understanding of the eternal return, the universe inevitably recurs an infinite number of times. This happens whether we have any consciousness of it or not (and, at some level, our consciousness, an effect of the universe's forces, is always incapable of understanding anything but the enumerable, even if we can sometimes *feel* its forces). It becomes an ethical principle insofar as we can live this principle as a necessary part of our becoming, whether it can be actively affirmed, as it is for those who see the demon as a god, or whether it must be covered over, lived reluctantly and in bad conscience, for those who curse the demon, who seek a different life than the one they have lived. The eternal return is the ultimate affirmation, not of life, but of endless becoming, endless movement, endless return, of which life is a consequence rather than cause.

It is not man alone who may experience and come to understand the eternal return. Zarathustra's animals remind him of this principle and its capacity to run through and touch every thing, every will:

"Now I die and vanish," you [Zarathustra] would say, "and all at once I am nothing. The soul is as mortal as the body. But the knot of causes in which I am entangled recurs and will create me again. I myself belong to the causes of the eternal recurrence. I come again, with this sun, this earth, with this eagle and this serpent—*not* to a new life or a better life or a similar life: I come back eternally to this same, selfsame life, in what is greatest as in what is smallest, to teach again the eternal recurrence of all things, to speak again the word of the great noon of earth and man, to proclaim the overman again to men."[30]

If this is the principle that regulates the universe—the idea of an infinite time and a finite amount of energy entail recurrence—then it is lived by every living thing, every field of forces. We don't have to understand it to affirm our lives and all that is bloody and improper that constitutes our lives: but we can only rise above the lot of the herd, the moralities of religion, capital, and civilization, to the extent that we affirm them to their limits and affirm our capacities to overcome in the same affirmation. That is, only to the extent that we can cultivate a new kind of being, oneself, can a new order and a new morality take place.

Luce Irigaray's careful reading of the eternal return in Nietzsche's writing, itself an act of love and affirmation, articulates a devastating critique, one that strikes at the heart of Nietzsche's philosophical project. Isn't the affirmation of the eternal return precisely the affirmation of another life (this time an identical life) that Nietzsche so powerfully criticizes in others? Isn't the consolation of a life eternally repeated—Zarathustra's great insight—the residue of a life lived alone, a life without the other, and especially the sexed other? Where sex has a place in Nietzsche's writings as part of our Dionysian heritage, it is pastime, rather than fundamental otherness, and its possibilities of bodily procreation. Nietzsche's circle of eternal return is a circle of self-love and self-affirmation that destroys life, this life, as much as it seems to affirm it. To live without others, to not see the place of otherness in the strength of the self (something that Spinoza affirms as the most basic good) and part of its capacity for self-overcoming represents the (feminist and, indeed more generally, the political) limit of Nietzsche's world: "And your whole will, your eternal recurrence, are these anything more than the dream of one who neither wants to have been born, nor to continue being born, at every instant, of a female other? Does your joy in becoming not result from annihilating her from whom you are tearing yourself away?"[31] For Irigaray, the eternal return is a ring: an enclosed, self-sustained circle, a wedding ring, in which there is only one spouse, an endless play of mirrors in which there is only one figure.[32]

This love of eternity, this yearning to return, not again but infinitely, is, in Irigaray's diagnosis, Nietzsche's limit: a disdain of the body even while he affirms its impersonal forces; a refusal to recognize that bodies, even as each lives in its own way, do not recur, they live only once; a failure to recognize that the other sex, and other types of body more generally, are what enhance life and make philosophy possible as much as a love of the infinite: "He who repeats so that time will come back has already separated himself from time."[33]

Yet, as much as Irigaray sees Nietzsche within the history of phallocentrism, she undertakes a Nietzschean transvaluation of Nietzsche himself; she is his "marine lover," the watery element that is needed, to add to the mountainous heights he seeks. She affirms his project of a new humanity to overcome existing man; she insists, though, that such a project must involve not only man overcoming himself; even more urgently, man must no longer contain woman, and woman, beyond being the ground of man's becoming, must be free to undergo her own self-overcomings, the limits she too must overcome in order to become what she is. Nietzsche, perhaps too, has a glimmer of what he owes, of the maternal debt, the debt of life, lived in every messy detail: "The good fortune of my existence, its uniqueness perhaps, lies in its fatality: I am, to express it in the form of a riddle, already dead as my father, while as my mother I am still living and becoming old" ("Why I Am So Wise," *EH* # 1).[34] His father and the line of paternity is always already dead; it is only his mother who represents the possibility of living on, the capacity to, in becoming old, become more, become other. The future can be welcomed only by the living (and the dead on whom their living existence is posited) and what can create the living.

AMOR FATI

The nature of forces, their relations of commanding and obeying and the various changing hierarchies created and destroyed by these interactions, is the condition of a new morality that is no longer prey to illusions of a better world, but is fully prepared to revel in this one. Eternal recurrence is an ontological effect of the will to power, one of the consequences of the play of the will to power over the (incorporeal) eternity that is time. The question is: how can we, humans of the present, "preparatory human beings" (*GS* #283), come to a different understanding of ourselves, poised between the dead father and the living mother, between the weight of the past (including our own) and the lightness of the future? Before an overman can create himself—or herself!—by overcoming history as a weight, by finding in history, in unorthodox histories, new forces that have not had their impact blunted, man must begin this movement or has always already begun it. "Prophetic human beings" (*GS* #316), unlike we who at best can prepare, beings like Zarathustra and, above all, like Nietzsche himself, who can incant the future, bring it into existence through a formula palatable only for the strongest, like themselves: amor fati, love of fate, love and fate, the affect and object that lies immanent in all others. If the eternal return is the doctrine or philosophy of the future, its ethics lies in a love of what must be, a love of what has been and what will be.

We must not confuse fate with causation, although casual regularities and the interaction of causes, incalculable as they may be, are bound up with fate and are its agents.[35] Fate is not providential, directed by anything benevolent (or malevolent), nor, in Spinozan terms, is it the attainment of something that partakes in the eternal. It is more to be understood as the orientations to which one's character, one's history and particular configuration of forces, is directed, the inner direction of a convergence of wills, the alignment of inner wills and external causes. Like will, fate is a direction or orientation, and, like will, it must be understood as an *incorporeal* or ideal direction or orientation, the force of a cohesive trajectory, cohesive not prospectively (which would entail knowledge of the entire causal order), but only ever retrospectively, in terms of the causes (wills) that activate other wills, a more specified and singular focus. Supported by the configuration of causes (or prevailing forces, dominant causes), fate is the interaction of causation and character, the orientation that one's character takes through its encounters with the world, however random. There is no such thing as fate, if it is understood merely as determinism, the long-range consequence of chains of causes, even though it may be true that such causal chains condition one's fate; fate is that to which we are directed from within and which external causes can facilitate or impede. If the eternal return (not the chain of causation) characterizes everything in the universe, then amor fati is the only appropriate affect one can feel to understanding one's place in the universe, as bound up as it is with one's own forces and the forces of the world, forces one cannot control but whose internal effects constitute who and how we become.

Ecce Homo is subtitled "How to become who one is," and this indicates what the love of fate may be—a love of what external forces open up in me, a love of what becomes of me, in which "I" am as much an agent, or agents, as external forces. How to cultivate oneself and one's capacities to the maximum? That is Nietzsche's question for all of us—given that we have natures of our own, each of us with our weakness, strength, fortitude, abundance, height, digestive system, identifications, sex, race, class, and nationality—how can we give value to our existence, how can we live artistically, how can we overcome what we must and live with what we cannot overcome? His only answer is: with style, with self-fashioning, with art, by making ourselves living works of art, living forms of resistance to the herd's resentful normalization: "To 'give style' to one's character—a great and rare art! It is practiced by those who survey all the strengths and weaknesses of their nature and then fit them into an artistic plan until every one of them appears as art and reason and even weakness delights the eye. Here a large mass of second nature has been added; there a piece of original nature has been removed—both times through long practice and daily work at it. Here the ugly that could not be removed is concealed; there is has been reinterpreted and made sublime" (*GS* #290). Self-stylization, self-creation is the work that creates an acquired "second nature," an artful self, to supplement and at times replace one's "original nature," relying on nature itself, on one's "character," one's "gifts" and capacities. It is Nietzsche's hope that such a constructed "nature" is itself the condition under which man can make himself higher, can more readily overcome his all-too-human nature.

In even the most lavish displays of wealth and artistic creativity, in the building of palaces and gardens, Nietzsche claims, gaiety, a gay science, is the result not of an overcoming and annihilation of nature but of its stylization, its transformation, and our own. Nietzsche asks: how can we overcome ourselves and, in this process, come to love ourselves, to attain some kind of satisfaction?[36] How can we develop "brief habits," improvisations, behavior that is stylized for short periods of time, to replace "enduring habits," our given and acquired behavior and that which culture assumes for us? How can we acquire a "personal providence," one not directed from outside but from within, which creates in us those habits that generate new experiences, new intensities, new actions?[37] "What does your conscience say? 'You shall become the person you are'" (*GS* #270); we who seek beyond ourselves, who seek to know and affirm ourselves and all the forces of the world, "want to become those we are—human beings who are new, unique, incomparable, who give themselves laws, who create themselves" (*GS* #335).

These self-created human beings capable of loving fate, these rare humans (perhaps only Nietzsche himself has ever truly achieved this love!) created by a knowledge of and love for the very orders of necessity that govern the universe, love themselves as they become other and more than they are. This love involves both suffering and joy, both good and bad health, both opportunity and threat: it involves *learning* to love necessity, to love not only what one accomplishes in processes of self-stylization but also all the indignities to which one may be subjected, to love the eternal return of everything, however dull, fleeting, and insignificant, however horrible, world-transforming, and destructive. The lesson of the eternal return is not resignation and acceptance, but joyous affirmation, gaiety. And love itself cannot be adoration, the passive delight in being in proximity with love's object, but only full affirmation, upholding. Love that works, that creates, that is, love that is artistic, that makes: "I want to learn more and more to see as beautiful what is necessary in things: then I shall be one of those who make things beautiful. *Amor fati*: let that be my love henceforth!" (*GS* #276).

To see as beautiful what is necessary in things: this is art, science, and philosophy together, ordering, knowing, feeling the order of necessity, not the determinable causal relations that condition each thing, but the necessity, within each thing, each relation, each state of affairs, that it be what it is in the manner in which it is. Causation is not the impersonal order running between things, living or nonliving: rather, causation is itself conditioned by and possible because of the forces that inhabit and are activated by the engagements of things with each other, that is, by the will to power. Loving fate, loving necessity, is loving this specific thing in its history, nature, and capacities (for no thing is itself except for an instant); it is loving what is most internal: "What is necessary does not hurt me: *amor fati* is my innermost nature" ("The Case of Wagner," *EH* #4). This is not the Stoics' indifference to fate, an acceptance of providence, a rendering passive of one's impulses to act; it is the converse— amor fati is emboldened love of all that one is and all that has produced one, a joyous strengthening knowledge and love.[38]

Amor fati is not only the love of necessity or fate (scientists, moralists, and historians may all share in such a love), but the more difficult, perhaps impossible, love of the eternal return of fate—the same fate— endless reiterated. It is a love of fate that eternally returns: "My formula for greatness in a human being is *amor fati*: that one wants nothing to be different, not forward, not backward, not in all eternity. Not merely bear what is necessary, still less conceal it—all idealism is mendaciousness in the face of what is necessary—but *love* it" ("Why I Am So Clever," *EH* #10). If all idealism is mendacious from the point of view of necessity, if idealism "unbloods" thought, nevertheless, it is the force of return that is ideal, both necessary and ideal, a whirling series of centers of force, but centers that, whatever their chaotic movements, are still directed by an ideal, as we shall see, by a "theme," by repetition to eternity. What repeats is not only the relations between things (or between ideas) but also the direction of repetitions, their force to eternity, which cannot itself be material. All that is material is destined for repetition, but cannot induce eternal repetition: this is the relentless and untamable force of time itself, which orders and organizes all things in terms of "before" and "after" and "now," which is not material itself but its immaterial or incorporeal accompaniment.

The movement of time, the returns its eternity entails, are never material, but the conditions under which materiality returns. Space and time, the immaterial conditions of repetition, are precisely the incorporeal forces that we must assume (and which provide for our potential well-being) for our material organization. To the extent that Nietzsche loves eternity and not just this particular convergence of forces that are linked to his own history (and all the ethical and ontological implications that repetition involves), he also loves the ideal that remains to order the return of matter and life. It is perhaps for this reason that Nietzsche proposes that art may better address what science has up to now explored, a time and space only ever understood numerically. The arts of movement, music, dance, theater, poetry, opera (in his time, though in ours one could proliferate all the technically mediated and performative arts as well) provide, not an analysis of forces and the space and time they require (as the sciences do), but great joy in their affirmation. Art is a moral remedy to science, just as science may be a moral remedy for everyday misconceptions.

But art is able to undertake its joys and intensities only to the extent that a philosophy, perhaps even a psychology, can come to understand the ways in which the illusions that constitute art ennoble and invigorate us. Art is a creative untruth that functions as a counterweight to a world in which appearance hides everything; it is the "good will to appearance" that bring us closer to the eternal return and its affirmation than science, which can pose itself as frameless truth that corrects art only when it overlooks its own productive untruths. As it revels in appearance and untruth, as its existence is a creative and inventive lie, art is not "truth," but rather overflows into and makes possible new kinds of science, especially a gay science: "We possess art lest we *perish of the truth*" (*WP* #822).

Philosophy as transvaluation of all existing values, is the counterweight to art's taste for untruth. Nietzsche does not understand art as correctible or that art should direct itself to truth in place of untruth; art is the highest form of the intensification of feelings, even though it also contains the possibility, indeed likelihood, for a religious infusion

of soul. Art has perhaps only retraced the outlines of an outworn theology.[39] Art requires no further truth than its own techniques, though
art may resist the impulse to truth that concerns most of philosophy.
It contains whatever feelings it may harness, the most fully affirmative
of human practices: "What is essential in art remains its perfection of
existence, its production of perfection and plenitude; art is essentially
affirmation, blessing, deification of existence—What does a *pessimistic art*
signify?" (*WP* #821). If science, art, and religion are remnants of a time
when our life-affirming forces were turned against life and its values,
pre-Enlightenment values, then Nietzsche's own philosophy, sharing
this affirmative force with the arts, is the corrective to these residues,
which tend to reappear with great frequency through philosophy, politics, and social life.

Only a fully affirmative philosophy, one that is artistic in its own ways,
can bring to thought this joyous affirmation. Philosophy can aspire to
the forms of intensity that art invents, while also directing itself to questions of truth and order that science produces, incorporating elements
of both where necessary but providing something neither art nor science can develop—a way to live, an ethics for life. While art and science
participate in and are products of the ways in which humans live, they
do not provide a way for a new kind of humanity, or beings beyond the
human, to come into existence. They do not create new moralities, new
forms of self-creation and self-expansion, even if they do help provide
some of the forces for such contemporary becomings. This still needs to
be thought, written, considered. It is in the company of, and by being
permeated by, the highest accomplishments of the arts and sciences that
a new kind of philosophy, the highest kind of philosophy—one that fully
affirms life and this world in all its detail—can come into being. Nietzsche witnesses its birth. Indeed, he can be understood as its midwife!

Amor fati is the "highest state a philosopher can attain" (*WP* #1041),
the "formula for greatness in a human being" (*EH* #258), the love of
and wish to comply joyously with the order that regulates everything,
the movement of fate that is the concurrence of external causes and
the movement of inner wills. My fate is that for which I am destined,
a movement linking my existence and its inner operations to the chain

of causal connections that runs along but never quite coincides with it. My destiny is not simply all that happens to me, whatever high and low elements that may contain: that is my history, the forces that make me what I am now. It is what is in me that overcomes my history, that awaits (perhaps unknowingly), to become my future, including that which postdates me. This destiny calls me, even though I do not in any way control it. Most humans no longer believe they have a destiny, a purpose, a reason, or calling. But destiny is not within us but what calls to us in the future. To love this destiny or fate is to move beyond the inner wills that are "mine" to answer to something, some force, time itself, eternity, outside me, something that calls these wills. Destiny is self-overcoming by a self that happily submits itself to the orders of time and necessity, gives itself up to the play of eternity, the work of the eternal return, and affirms it with joy.

We have no other model for such a joyous affirmation of the impersonal within the personal than Nietzsche himself, who affirmed every part of his life, every misery and sickness, every failure to be recognized and understood, every joyous and sad moment, to eternity. Nietzsche understood his own untimeliness, his position between two cultures— the ancients and the overman to come—and his fate is to be misunderstood in spite of the powers of affirmation of nothing but immanence in every part of life. Nietzsche provides not only the most powerful remedy for the sickness of thought and body generated by European sensibility (one that is not healed even today), the life of the modern self-entitled herd within society, but also the most joyous affirmation of its alternatives. To stand apart, one must no doubt suffer; to stand alone, or with only a few, is also to resist a normalization, a becoming-herd, that only a few can overcome and with its suffering and joy produce new perspectives, new insights, new awareness. Nietzsche produces a new kind of ethics, not without its antecedents (the Greeks, Spinoza, Goethe), but which is linked to and based on the immanent principles that order this world. Amor fati is the most direct expression of these principles, not a submission to fate but a love of its power.

This new kind of ethics is not the imposition of principles on life from outside, from *ressentiment* and reactive forces, but the extraction of ways to live well from the order of the universe itself. This is an ontoethics, without any recourse to a concept like "should," but always embedded in and dependent on what is and what will be. Life is ethics; life affirmed fully, each in its own way, each with its own nature and fate, is what ethics reflects on and philosophizes. Philosophy, at its best—Nietzschean philosophy—is how one comes to understand the nature of the world, the nature of life, and the nature of this particular life. It expresses and articulates, sometimes in poetry, sometimes in aphorisms, sometimes in exclamations or even arguments, the inner wills' affirmation of the external causal chains that confront them and which they must address. A new kind of philosophy will rely on "inspiration," revelation, or intuition, that is, what is sensual in life, what we feel, some inner orientation; and its cohesion and force comes from outside, from the world itself: "The concept of revelation—in the sense that suddenly, with indescribable certainty and subtlety, something becomes *visible*, audible, something that shakes one to the last depths and throws one down—that merely describes the facts. One hears, one does not seek; one accepts, one does not ask who gives; like lightning, a thought flashes up, with necessity, without hesitation regarding its form—I never had any choice" ("Thus Spoke Zarathustra," *EH* #3). The artist will also describe the process of artistic creation as "beyond my choice," as an inhabitation by outside forces that speak directly to one's inner wills without the mediation of consciousness (we will return to this question of the impersonality of artistic production in the following chapters). Philosophy too, more art than science, more ethics than epistemology, is this being taken over by outside forces, concepts, ideas, arguments and finding something within that affirms them or experiences their crushing force. Philosophy. in this sense, is the thinking and writing of the impact of chaotic forces, events, on bodies, and the individual, social, cultural, political, artistic, and scientific inventions that life has created to address them.

In producing a new kind of philosophy, Nietzsche has not only challenged idealist philosophies (such as those developed by Berkeley, Kant, and Hegel) that reduce body to thought or mind, rendering thinking anemic, but also materialist philosophies that range from the atomism of Leucippus and Democritus to the mechanism of Newtonianism and

Thompsonian conceptions of the universe. Above all, he produces a philosophy that, while it is commonly characterized and mischaracterized as materialist, is neither dualist, monist, idealist nor strictly materialist. I have described him as one of a number of philosophers in the history of philosophy who could be labeled, for want of a better formulation, incorporeal, for not only is he fully committed to a philosophy of material forces, he is also equally committed to a philosophy of inner wills, wills to power, inner orientations, the directionality of fate, of return that makes his philosophy always exceed materialism. Nietzsche argues that his own life personifies this process, in which one's will has nothing to do, nothing to will, where understanding comes suddenly from the outside and from the slow and dawning understanding of its implications in experience. Will is the direction(s) of the world that we can make our own. Philosophy may come to understand something of this will, which science has thus far neglected: "So many dangers that the instinct comes to 'understand itself'—. Meanwhile the organizing 'idea' that is destined to rule keeps growing deep down—it begins to command; *slowly* it leads us *back* from side roads and wrong roads: it prepares *single* qualities and fitnesses that will one day prove to be indispensable as means toward a whole—one by one, it trains all subservient capacities before giving any hint of the dominant task, 'goal,' 'aim' or 'meaning'" ("Why I Am So Clever, *EH* #9).

Nietzsche has created a new kind of philosophy, aware of its debt to history, to life, to the philosopher's singular life, that engages us in our highest becomings and overcomings in a project that takes us from the most internal and minute forces that regulate an individual life to the furthest reaches of the universe while celebrating their most intimate connections. Life is directed to something (many things that affirm its capacities), to both the world in its great complexity and to the expansion of its own powers. It is not aimless and without purpose, although no external purpose can be given to life. Life and the universe in which it emerges do have a goal, aim, or meaning—an ideal—even if it is not the ones in which we have, up to now, believed. This goal or aim, eternal recurrence, *is* the transvaluation of all values, the value that revalues all others.

4

DELEUZE AND THE PLANE OF IMMANENCE

To affirm is not to take responsibility for, to take on the
burden of what is, but to release, to set free what lives.
To affirm is to unburden: not to load life with the weight
of higher values, but to create new values which are those
of life, which make life light and active. There is creation,
properly speaking, only insofar as we make use of excess
in order to invent new forms of life rather than separating
life from what it can do.

—GILLES DELEUZE, *NIETZSCHE AND PHILOSOPHY*,
TRANS. HUGH TOMLINSON

Nietzsche had a tiny audience in Germany: minimal numbers of his books were sold and only his closest friends seemed to communicate with him about his researches. This is hardly surprising, given the severity of his judgments about German philosophy and culture. He had developed a devastating (self-)analysis of German morality, practices, arts, and everyday life and their place in an equally problematic "Europe." He was excited at the prospect of a new audience, perhaps from France, that would appreciate and understand his writings. From 1877, when his "Richard Wagner in Bayreuth" was translated into French, he believed that the French might have a better understanding of his nuggets of aphoristic insight. He wrote to Peter Gast that "the Panama canal to France has been opened,"[1] although it took until the 1890s, shortly after Nietzsche's breakdown, for his work to be not only widely discussed, but to be appropriated by the French, particularly in literary circles, as one of their own. The first article discussing Nietzsche's work appeared in French in 1888 (a rather critical article by Jean Bourdeau, whose existence elated Nietzsche!), but it was only after the 1892 translation of *The Case Against Wagner* that Nietzsche began to claim a larger readership.[2] Or rather, to be claimed as French by French writers, such as Jules de Gaultier, who asserted that "we have to recognize that Nietzsche's thought is of a purely French inspiration and brings us back to ourselves."[3] Not only was the reception of Nietzsche in France strong, it grew with each decade of the twentieth century through the works of Georges Bataille, Roger Caillois, and other members of the College of Sociology, and on to the work of the 1960s and after in the writings of Foucault, Derrida, Deleuze, and Irigaray, among many others.

It is Deleuze's use of Nietzsche, as well as Spinoza and the Stoics (not to mention Simondon and Ruyer, whose work will be examined in the following chapters), that makes him the most appropriate figure to include in my genealogy of the impossible division between the material and the immaterial. Along with Jacques Derrida and Luce Irigaray, and particularly his long-term collaborator Félix Guattari, he is among a few major contemporary philosophers to insist on the impossibility of dualistic and dichotomous distinctions that rely on an either/or model. Deleuze had long suggested that binarized or dichotomous terms are only one kind of disjunctive relation and that we need to understand the cooperation of more complex disjunctive syntheses with conjunctive relations as phases or forms of becoming. Instead of dividing concepts into mutually exclusive and mutually exhaustive binary pairs, such as mind/body, reason/passion, material/ideal (and, of course, underlying them and providing a political, though not intellectual, explanation of their existence is the binarization of the relations between male and female, one of the primary techniques of patriarchal thought, which has been coextensive with Western philosophy), Deleuze, Derrida, Irigaray, and others insist that many concepts refuse to abide on one side or the other of binary divisions, terms that entail both sides or require many terms without one functioning as the regulative ideal for the others (as *man* has served for *woman, child, animal,* and *God*). In this sense they are the contemporary heirs of a movement, nascent in the pre-Socratics,

self-consciously developed in the Stoics, fully systematized and philo-
sophically ordered in Spinoza, and given blood and life in the writings
(and life) of Nietzsche.

Ethics, for Deleuze, and others I discuss, is based on a knowledge of
the implications and consequences of living a life here, in this world,
with its own forces with which ours are bound up. Foucault well understood that Deleuze's ontological and historical writings were in fact ethical texts as well. In his preface to the English translation of *Anti-Oedipus.
Capitalism and Schizophrenia*, vol. 1,[4] he states: "I would say that *Anti-
Oedipus* (may its authors forgive me) is a book of ethics, the first book
of ethics to be written in France for quite a long time" (xiii). While not
the first book of ethics to be written in France for a long time (Foucault
forgets here the work of Levinas), it is perhaps Deleuze's most explicitly
ethically oriented book: all of his work, from his earliest writings on
Hume, *Empiricism and Subjectivity*,[5] to his final text with Guattari, *What
Is Philosophy?*, are involved in the question of ethics, but an ethics that
is reconfigured outside and beyond theories of good or moral laws or
ethical obligations. This is an immanent ethics of joy, an ethics enhanced
and made more powerful the greater our understanding of the world is
and the greater our power of acting in it. It is an ethics that is an elaboration, a maximization, of the ontological forces which support and enable
life.[6] Such an ethics cannot be conflated with norms, universal principles
of thought or action, ideals of behavior, or even medical prescriptions,
as many of Deleuze's critics have assumed any ethics should be; [7] rather,
it is a broader view that makes no assumptions about health, well-being,
happiness, or freedom in human life. It is a set of concepts that lie within
how we live and that can be developed only in our encounters with others and with the world and its forces. There is nothing prescriptive in his
work, only an analysis, like his predecessors, of what is and can become,
nothing of the "should," but only the virtual "could."

What further links the current generation of French thinkers such
as Derrida, Irigaray, and Deleuze (and, to a lesser extent, Foucault) is
a common commitment to develop, all at once, an ontology, a politics,
and an ethics (or many).[8] These are not separate tasks or projects, but
one project that has many facets. This connects them all to the traditions

of thought that have been explored in the previous chapters. All three are interested in developing elements of an immanent ethics and distinguish this project from a morality, that is, they are more concerned with the kind of work developed by the Stoics about how to live a good life than with the question of moral law that is developed by Kant.[9] Deleuze will frequently use the term *morality,* following Nietzsche's use of this term (Nietzsche rarely speaks of an "ethics"; it is the genealogy of morality and its overthrow by a new morality that interests him! But such a Nietzschean morality is what Deleuze understands as an ethics). By it, Deleuze will often designate, not a generalizable code of conduct, but a set of self-defined parameters that individuals of all kinds may develop to regulate their encounters with others and the world in the most positive manner, self-imposed limits such as artists (or philosophers) may use to regulate what and how they produce, which may be regarded as their "style," their manner of dealing with the world. These are, as Nietzsche recognized, interpretations of the world, our manner or mode of living, our "artistic" impulses. Rather than a morality, Deleuze (along with Foucault) seeks a life which regulates itself, develops its own "style," it own modes of self-enhancement and expression of the world:

> Establishing ways of existing or styles of life isn't just an aesthetic matter, it's what Foucault called ethics, as opposed to morality. The difference is that morality presents us with a set of constraining rules of a special sort, ones that judge actions and intentions by considering them in relation to transcendent values (this is good, that's bad . . .); ethics is a set of optional rules that assess what we do, what we say, in relation to the ways of existing involved. We say this, we do that: what way of existing does it involve. . . . It's the styles of life involved in everything that makes us this or that. You get this already in Spinoza's idea of "modes." And is it not present in Foucault's philosophy from the outset: What are we capable of seeing and saying . . . ? But if there is a whole ethics in this, there is also an aesthetics too.[10]

In other words, Deleuze aims to elaborate a system of self-assay, in which one's actions are undertaken and regulated according to principles immanent to them, that, together with the acts they regulate and enable, make up one's style, one's ethics *and* one's aesthetics inseparably. Political struggle, less a question of style, is nevertheless linked to the production of principles of regulation (and various practices) that are shared or collective, that define a purpose, values, targets for change, and potential techniques of change. The political is not the result of the collectivity or sharing of individual (transcendent) aspirations or ideals, but of the collectivity producing new (immanent) ways of living, an *ethos*, fundamentally impersonal: "Style, in a great writer, is always a style of life too, not anything personal, but inventing a possibility of life, a way of existing."[11] Deleuze aims to create an ethics that is an ethology, that is immanent in the variety of lives and forms of living—in their fundamental differences. It asks: what am I capable of doing, what is my degree of power and how can I act to enhance and maintain an active use of it? How can I intensify, become more active, go to the limit, without diminishing my powers through sad/bad encounters? How can I regulate myself according to the principles that I have taken for my actions?

In this chapter and the two following, I will explore Deleuze and some of his other key sources and contemporaries, Gilbert Simondon and Raymond Ruyer in particular, who each address this almost impossible-to-conceive concept of the incorporeal, whether it is understood as the preindividual, finality, or the orientation and direction of becomings. For Deleuze, it is the irrepressible elements of the ideal, and of rationalism, that cannot be reduced to the material that also constitutes the conditions for an ethics of life enhancement, an ethics as the will to power. Deleuze's work (chronologically) follows all the others I discuss here; it provides a way of reading the texts that have come before him and to which he owes (and acknowledges that he owes) an intellectual debt. It may be that Nietzsche, who understood his destiny to be misunderstood, Spinoza, who saw his necessary task as to say without saying it directly, and the Stoics, who produced philosophy as a way of ethical living, can be more directly and powerfully accessed, and reassessed, through Deleuze's reanimation of their writings. Inspired directly and openly by the more submerged tradition of immanence that surfaces at times in the history of philosophy, Deleuze is perhaps its keenest detector and most explicit advocate. He continues Nietzsche's task of exploring the immanence of "a life," of developing an ethics/aesthetics of ontology or an ontology of ethics/aesthetics.

Rarely is Deleuze understood as a philosopher who works not only on the big questions of ontology but, throughout his works, from beginning to end, on questions of ethics, an ethics or *ethos* linked to self-regulation and to immanence rather than transcendence. His project is just as clearly involved in the questions of ethics as are the writings of the Stoics, Spinoza, and Nietzsche. For each of them, providing an understanding of the way this and only this one world is, an understanding that refuses to privilege any central or organizing term, is the key to a different way of living, one that understands and feels things in their specificity, that lives with difference and welcomes the becomings that all things, including life, including its own life, involve. Each creates an ontology that *is* an ethics, that does not produce an ethics in reaction to or after ontology but an ethics that understands itself as always already implicated in and responsible for the maintenance of the various orders of existence (and thus also their transformations or overcoming), whether these are social and political or natural and physical.[12] Deleuze, utilizing the Stoic concept of being worthy of or living up to one's fate, the Spinozist concept of *amor dei* (understood as a love of nature in its complexity), and the Nietzschean concept of amor fati, elaborates a new ontoethics, a new way of understanding the world, and a new ethics by which to live in it.[13]

THE PLANE OF IMMANENCE

Deleuze and Guattari elaborate a new concept, to be found nowhere else: the plane of immanence, which has also been described as the plane of consistency or the plane of expression. A number of Deleuze's commentators have suggested that the plane of immanence is Deleuze's reconfiguration of Spinoza's substance, an immanent order expressed equally in all that exists or could exist, that the plane of immanence is his translation of Spinozan substance.[14] In this case, however, it seems strange that Deleuze would aim to represent the richness and variety of things that each help to constitute Spinoza's concept of substance, which consists in an infinite number of attributes, on a single plane, a plane of immanence that Deleuze and Guattari distinguish from a plane of composition that characterizes art works and a plane of percepts that characterize the works of the sciences. Why would substance constitute only one plane? What would be achieved, conceptually or politically, by flattening Spinoza's infinitely variable substance? If this is indeed how Deleuze "rereads" Spinoza, then he is responsible for a new philosophy of presence (and, with it, a new idealism) in which immanence is conceived as one (plane, order, voice, force). As we will see, *substance, the universe, nature, destiny, fate* are all terms that require not only numerous interlocking things, objects, living beings, and causal networks, but that can no more be adequately represented on one plane than they can on many. Moreover, Deleuze never suggests that the plane of immanence is coextensive with substance or being: rather, it is the direction or order, binding force and point of connection that enables all concepts, ideas, thoughts, the Ideal, the incorporeal to connect, to be related to each other, to form points of convergence and divergence, to create alliances and tensions independent of the history of their formation or evaluation. It is the orientation of the ideal that subsists in materiality, the force, direction, or movement of ideas relative to each other and outside history (even as concepts are only ever created in and with a history). It is the "plane," "field," or, more abstractly and temporally, the eternity where concepts can address each other and can be used by us to make claims, propositions, hypotheses, arguments. The plane of immanence is the virtual adhesion of ideas, the belonging together of concepts, even as they are produced and developed in different times and places, the possibility of thinking engendered by other thinking. This is the plane of consistency, not in the logical sense of consistency but in its culinary sense: the order or systematicity, the texture and capacity to affect and be affected of ideas. This is not any simple form of idealism; rather it is a Spinozist commitment to the irreducibility of thought to the orders of causation that connect things. It is an idealism that is a necessary (but not sufficient) condition for the emergence of events and of their capacity to be represented or spoken. Nor is this a form of dualism, although idealism is often taken as the binary opposite of materialism. Following the Stoics, Spinoza, and Nietzsche (and many others), Deleuze suggests an ideal subsistence in materiality, a plane that orients, connects, and/or disconnects ideas without any evaluation or measure.

While there has been remarkably little work devoted to understanding Deleuze and Guattari's concept of the plane of immanence within current interpretations of their writings, it is central to both an understanding of their ontology (and its historical and conceptual place relative to their source texts) and to Deleuze's quiet elaboration of a new kind of ontoethics, an ethics immanent in life.[15] The plane of immanence or consistency is abstract: it cannot be understood as a dimension, a flat surface, a volume, or, more generally, in spatial terms. Rather it is the order in which all ideas take place, the "place" where one concept can encounter another, enhance or diminish it, and which other concepts must attain in order to engage in the domain of concepts. This is not a Platonic order, in which ideas exist in their perfection, but an actual order in which the particular, true or false, well-formed or not, concepts and texts—each historically produced work of thought—can function beyond the context of its production. It is matched, Deleuze and Guattari suggest, by a plane of composition, in which art works and the affects they induce can be located relative to each other independent of any external valuation, and by a plane of reference in which formulae, experiments, and scientific hypotheses abide, again independent of their origin and contemporary value, exerting or not exerting effects on any particular scientific act, hypothesis, or work.[16] These are not different dimensions or orders but abstract representations of different types of practice, each embedded in both material practices and the production of ideality, each a way of thinking/feeling/acting.

Philosophy, the various arts, and the different sciences develop different practices for the production of sense, different types of sense and its regimentation and ordering and different techniques of evaluation, different expressions and modes of the capture of sense, but each is implicated in the production of a world order in sense, a sense that transparently covers the orders of nature, thought, and affect. Each of the human modes of the organization of chaos by sense must touch the limit of space and time, as well as the orders of materiality and ideality. The type of ordering, evaluation, and organization that each field or discipline creates with may be understood as the plane it occupies, the "plan" or order in which it comes to have sense or in which its sense can come to change. The planes or plans are, in other words, directions or orientations that align different types of entity (concepts, affects, percepts, and prospects) in any possible way, for any possible use. It is in this sense that planes may be understood as virtual, as unactualized (and continually actualizing) potentials for a particular type of autonomous existence, the existence of concepts, of affects and percepts *in themselves*. As orientations or directions, it is hardly surprising that the planes rely on and attempt to limit chaos by extracting space and time, our necessary conditions for ordering anything. This is what they share, the organization of a space-time and the invention of a protocol to address this organization: "The limit common to all of these series of inventions—inventions of functions, inventions of blocks of duration/ movement, inventions of concepts—is space-time. All of these disciplines communicate at the level of something that never emerges for its own sake, but is engaged in every creative discipline: the formation of space-times."[17]

The eternity that constitutes Spinoza's third kind of knowledge also characterizes the plane of immanence. Not that it is eternal or unchanging in Spinoza's sense, but because it is both separate from other possible planes, a "pure" plane, and because it preserves thought "there," that is, in no space in particular or in virtuality. It is eternal insofar as thought persists anywhere and in any form. The concepts that populate the plane of immanence—and populate it "nomadically," that is, without a given location, free to connect with or disconnect from relations to any other element or idea—do not perish as thinkers do. Nor do they persist forever unchanged: the intensities that comprise relations that constitute the plane of immanence are ever changing, capable of alliances with other terms, undergoing endless change, permutations, engagements, revivifications, or quieting down. It is the plane that subsists and provides cohesion for concepts that, as incommensurable as they might be, can nevertheless form connections, change or moderate themselves, grow stronger or weaker, affect and be affected by other concepts, and thus be available for new uses or for the historical reconstruction of its former uses. The plane ensures the persistence of concepts beyond their creation. These terms or concepts, while produced historically, and by particular individuals through their brilliance, torment, and originality, persist beyond the history of their production and are the condition under which any history of thought, history of ideas, is possible and functions in actuality. The practice of philosophy is possible only to the extent that concepts can find a position there. The plane of immanence is thus the incorporeal uncontaining frame that coheres concepts, not together, not into a "community of ideas," but away from other processes that may involve altogether different connections, speeds and slownesses, between living bodies and their objects (such as percepts and affects); it is the principle of the autonomous self-produced cohesion of ideas without the direct interference of any thinker. A concept stands up, exists in its own terms, without external support: only then can it be considered a concept (something that can take a place on the plane).

Like affects and percepts, concepts require bodily or corporeal forces, bodies that think, and the incorporeal order of sense, ideality, "meaning," or direction in which they think. Deleuze rather surprisingly retains the Stoic incorporeals, though the concept of the void seems to be subsumed in his work under concepts of space: space, duration, sense provide the incorporeal framework under and through which both material objects and incorporeal ideas become possible. The plane of immanence derives in some part from the Stoic concept of lekta, the Spinozan concept of a third, intuitive kind of knowledge, a knowledge sub specie aeternitatis, and from Nietzsche's concept of a foreknowledge, a prophecy of what must come, the overcoming of mankind by a higher man, something both within and beyond time. Neither rationalist nor empiricist, neither idealist nor materialist, the plane of immanence is the condition for their emergence, their opposition and any rethinking of their relations.

Deleuze and Guattari discuss the concept of the plane (if it is a concept)[18] in some detail in *A Thousand Plateaus. Capitalism and Schizophrenia*, vol. 2,[19] and elaborate it further in *What Is Philosophy?* They suggest that there are (at least) two conflicting philosophical planes. One is a transcendental plane or plan, a hidden principle that causes or enables things to appear but in no way appears itself. It can only be inferred as either the genetic or structural condition for what appears: concepts, signs, an unconscious and invisible structure in which things, especially subjects and the signs they generate, are made possible and through which they develop. Such a plane is supplementary to and separate from the things it conditions: it is "a plan(e) that cannot be given as such, that can only be inferred from the forms it develops and the subjects it forms, for it is *for* these forms and these subjects" (*ATP* 266). Against this transcendental and teleological organization, Deleuze and Guattari counterpose the plane of immanence. Here all notions of subject, inherent form, signification, secret origins, genesis, and structure disappear, to be replaced by what life and matter share, not what enables their bifurcation. There is no underlying structure, no hidden genesis, no given border or boundary. Instead this plane is populated only by Spinozan/Nietzschean forces: "There are only relations of movement and rest, speed and slowness between unformed elements, or at least between elements that are relatively informed, molecules and particles of all kinds. There are only haecceities, affects, subjectless individuations that constitute collective assemblages. Nothing develops, but things arrive late or early, and form this or that assemblage depending of their compositions of speed" (*ATP* 266). The plane of immanence is not the order in which things are formed from ideals, external models, pregiven forms, but rather the order in which the degrees of movement and force produce a self-structuring that orders real things, concepts as much as material objects, through their own characteristics, without need for recourse to another order.

This is why it is a "plane of Nature" (as much as it is a plane of "culture"), a plane of consistency even amidst contradiction: "However many dimensions it may have, it never has a supplementary dimension to that which transpires upon it. That alone makes it natural and immanent"

(*ATP* 266). Understood in the spirit of Spinoza, as a geometrical plan(e) (though like Spinoza, a geometry that always addresses more than spatial and numerical relations), it is no longer to be seen as an ideal plan(e), according to which the real objects that populate it perform, but instead an abstract plane in which, and through which, all real things (and their virtual tendencies) can be located. It is a "fixed plane," not in the sense of rigid, tied, or planted in some specific location: "Here, fixed does not mean immobile: it is the absolute state of movement as well as rest, from which all relative speeds and slownesses spring, and nothing but them" (*ATP* 267). We can understand not only Spinoza's *Ethics* as a rigorous and systematic analysis of the modes of existence of the plane of immanence and the ways in which various terms, all of those that comprise the universe, populate the plane; perhaps even more strikingly, Zarathustra is himself, unformed, asubjective, impersonal, nothing but speeds and slowness. It is not that he lacks depth or "personality"; rather, it is that everything in him moves at its own pace, becomes on its own. Zarathustra becomes the spectator of his own becomings: "Zarathustra is only speeds and slownesses, and the eternal return, the life of the eternal return, is the first great concrete freeing of nonpulsed time" (*ATP* 269).

The plane of immanence is in precarious balance with the plane of transcendence. Immanence is immensely difficult to sustain, especially when separated from the theological and philosophical avatars of another world and a higher order. Transcendence appears not only as height to be aspired to but also as the ground of possibility, a hidden depth or foundation. Immanence, a movement of the surface, is always perilously positioned, tenuously thought, so that the slightest orientation above or below draws it into the plane of transcendence and returns to it the ideals of a "dead god." Stratification, the distinguishing or separation of planes, serves the interests of transcendence, which requires not one but several orders or levels. The plane of immanence must remain flat, rigorously without depth, if it is to avoid the ever active traps of transcendence: "all we need to do is sink the floating plane of immanence, bury it in the depths of Nature instead of allowing it to play freely on the surface, for it to pass to the other side and assume the role of a ground" (*ATP* 269).

THE CONCEPT

If the concept, or "quasi concept," of the plane of immanence is first developed in *A Thousand Plateaus*, it is more carefully elaborated in Deleuze and Guattari's final collaboration, *What Is Philosophy?* There Deleuze and Guattari claim that concepts, the philosophical elementary particle, are constituents, or populations, of the plane of immanence and find both their history—the historical, social, cultural, and political influences that induce a philosopher to produce a concept at a particular time and place—and their completion—for each concept, as a historical object, has a history in the concepts that precede it and from which it borrows ingredients for its own, capable of being taken over and used long after the death of its "author"—in the plane of immanence. Concepts are the "contents" of the plane of immanence, its population, that which is rendered out from any historical context and made capable of being used elsewhere, in other philosophies and outside of philosophy. It is because there is a plane of immanence or consistency that we can access the work of the Ancient Greeks, with or without an adequate and detailed knowledge of their texts, that we can access Spinoza's writings in Latin and address all the texts that constitute the history of philosophical thought—because such concepts have an extrahistorical existence, a persistence (or subsistence) elsewhere than where they were generated and sustained. Concepts live on, in eternity, on the plane of immanence, where they remain continually available, without regard for any particulars of their production or circulation, even as they require a historical emergence insofar as they are created. This differentiates Deleuze and Guattari's understanding of the eternity of the plane of immanence from the eternity and perfection of the Platonic ideal: for Deleuze and Guattari, the plane of immanence is occupied not by perfect ideas or truthful ideas or eternal verities but precisely by imperfect, historically produced ideas, which mix with and help to form also imperfect, historically produced ideas through their use elsewhere.

Deleuze and Guattari devote the first chapter of *What Is Philosophy?* to explaining their unique concept of the concept. They note that each philosophical concept—a term carefully differentiated from an "idea," "opinion," or "belief"—has a number of features. First, it has a history, sometimes erratic and wayward, in which a concept may produce off-shoots and developments as it is elaborated within different philosophical frameworks and contexts. Second, the concept has a becoming, which, as Spinoza and Nietzsche recognized, is not self-generated but the result of the encounters it undergoes with other concepts, including those on which it relies as well as those it contests.[20] Third, each concept is intensive, and, as we will see, self-surveying. It provides an internal consistency, a cohesion without external perspective, as it is elaborated in different philosophical systems. Fourth, it is incorporeal and, as such, lacks any historical and geographical location ("spatiotemporal coordinates" as Deleuze and Guattari call it *WIP* 21) for it is intensive: "The concept is therefore both absolute and relative: it is relative to its own components, to other concepts, to the plane on which it is defined, and to the problems it is supposed to resolve' but it is absolute through the condensation it carries out, the site it occupies on the plane, and the conditions it assigns to the problem. As a whole it is absolute, but insofar as it is fragmentary it is relative" (*WIP* 21). And fifth, Deleuze and Guattari claim, in opposition to analytic, structuralist, and poststructuralist traditions informing philosophy today, that the concept is neither discursive nor propositional, neither intentional nor referential: it is not of the order of representation at all. Rather, concepts, like bodies, are consistent or cohesive totalities capable of entering into relations with other concepts. They comprise neither propositions nor philosophical systems: in fact, they suggest, propositions and systems often hide the concept or betray it, which may explain Deleuze and Guattari's fondness for the paradoxical and the nonsensical.[21] Concepts are internally regulated consistencies, which are created by the reworking of fragments or components of other, previous concepts that, once (re-)created, stand as a concept without this history and are thus open enticements or provocations to other concepts insofar as they may help them to better address a problem that can be "located" in proximity with a concept. Concepts are how we address events: "Every concept shapes and reshapes the event in its own way. The greatness of a philosophy is measured by the nature of the events to which its concepts summon us or that it enables us to release in concepts" (*WIP* 34).

Concepts are peculiar. They are not uniquely human by any means. But it is perhaps their complexity, their consistency, and their capacity to maintain a certain speed and slowness that grants human thought access to the plane of cohesion or consistency for all concepts, enabling them to address each other, building "movable bridges" (*WIP* 23) between one another, and to resonate, to affect, and be affected in their own way through their nonlocalizable intensive relations on the plane of immanence. Deleuze and Guattari describe the cohesiveness or connectedness that the plane of immanence bestows on concepts in terms of Stoic pneuma—the plane of immanence adds breath, life, animation to the components that are concepts: "Concepts are the archipelago or skeletal frame, a spinal column rather than a skull, whereas the plane is the breath that suffuses separate parts" (*WIP* 36). Concepts are real events, each with their own history, that populate an abstract horizon of pure conceptuality, adding to it, creating of it, an increasingly complex intensive landscape for later concepts and new populations. The plane abides, indivisible, without maps or location, except for those occupied by concepts, a nonmeasurable milieu or conceptual ecology for each concept: "The plane is like a desert that concepts populate without dividing it up. The only regions of the plane are concepts themselves, but the plane is all that holds them together. The plane has no other regions than the tribes populating and moving around on it" (*WIP* 36). The plane is the unconceptualized condition of thought or conceptuality, the means by which even the most disparate and incommensurable concepts can coexist, the means of orientation by which we can access, use, transform or ignore concepts.

Deleuze and Guattari describe the plane of immanence as "an image of thought," one of the prephilosophical conditions under which philosophical concepts can be created. This image of thought, "the image that thought gives itself of what it means to think" (*WIP* 37), is what enables concepts, and we who think them, to distinguish between concepts on the one hand and opinions, beliefs, and thoughts (with which they share a certain ideality but not a particular kind of rigor or consistency) on the other. It enables the concept to address other concepts without the mediation of arguments, propositions, refutations, critique, and the rest of the paraphernalia of institutional philosophy, all of them also concepts. This image, orientation, or dynamic horizon of thought requires of concepts not truth, veracity, plausibility, but the capacity for intensity, the capacity to go as far as they can, to infinity: "The image of thought retains only what thought can claim by right. Thought demands 'only' movement that can be carried to infinity. What thought claims by right, what it selects, is infinite movement or the movement of the infinite. It is this that constitutes the image of thought" (*WIP* 37). The plane of immanence enables the concept's movement, carried to infinity. It enables the concept to orient and reorient itself.

Perhaps most significantly, the plane in its entirety (however we orient ourselves and our concepts to it) is ideal, incorporeal, or virtual.[22] Thought itself, the plane of immanence and all that populates it, is movement, the movement of concepts, their speeds and slownesses, positioned not only relative to other concepts but also to the world in which these concepts exists and which they, in their own way, address. Concepts, which constitute the movement of thought, come from a world which they address, however adequately and however knowingly: they populate the plane of immanence, one that history continually adds to and transforms. For concepts to exist, the plane of immanence must precede them, they must have a prephilosophical "origin," something unthought or without concept, something nonphilosophical, that conditions concepts, makes them possible, and provides them with conceptual coordinates. Something outside philosophy, outside thought, perhaps even outside life, induces or forces thought, which never occurs easily and involves the invention of categories and forms of order to function at all.[23] This nonphilosophical outside—something of the real, outside conceptualization, an event, a problem, a force, something that must be addressed or overcome but cannot be ignored—is the trigger for the elaboration of thought.[24] Something from the outside, a problem, forces thinking to occur. Deleuze recognized, in *The Logic of Sense*, that the problem, the event, and thought are fundamentally linked: "We can speak of events only in the context of the problem whose conditions they determine. We can speak of events only as singularities deployed in

a problematic field, in the vicinity of which the solutions are organized"
(56). Events induce problems for they are erratic, unique, unrepeatable;
and problems, pressing ones, generate not so much solutions as concepts
that may be in the vicinity of the problem, oriented to the problem, that
develop ways of living with the problem. Concepts are inventions to deal
with, not only to solve, problems that we cannot but address.[25]

Thinking does not arise "naturally"—this is the place of "habit." It
arises from what Bergson understands as an intuition and Spinoza
understands as knowledge of the second kind, an awareness of an outside that touches one from the deepest regions of oneself.[26] Intuition
is prephilosophical, the raw material of philosophy (and the arts and
sciences). It is an inner attunement to a force, or many, outside us, the
orientation of thinking in relation to things and the first laying down of
the plane of immanence, a plane that lies between nature or the world—
chaos, which is to say, all that there is at infinite speed—and concepts.

In order for the prephilosophical impulse, the jolt from outside and its
bodily response, to generate concepts, Deleuze and Guattari claim that
the generation of thought often, perhaps usually, requires something
else to help usher the concept into existence. This is something midway
between the plane of immanence and the concepts that occupy it, which
they describe as "conceptual personae," figures within philosophical
texts (and perhaps necessary for their production and understanding),
sites of enunciation which speak in texts, not in place of the philosopher,
but which enable a philosopher to generate a movement of the concept:
"In philosophical enunciations we do not do something by saying it but
produce movement by thinking it, through the intermediary of a conceptual persona. Conceptual personae are also the true agents of enunciation" (WIP 64–65). If Socrates functions as a conceptual persona for
Plato (and the Stoics), the dreamer or madman are two of Descartes's
conceptual personae, and Nietzsche, a master of such figures, elaborates many such personae—Dionysus, Zarathustra, the Anti-Christ, the
priest, the ascetic, the man of ressentiment—it is because these figures or
personages are required to transition and prepare us (and their authors)
for the concept that is being formed.[27] Conceptual personae function
both to condition and enable the plane of immanence to be constructed

by extracting a possible consistency from chaos; they condition concepts to access the plane by enabling various features or qualities to be brought together and located relative to other concepts: "the conceptual persona with its personalized features intervenes between chaos and the diagrammatic features of the plane of immanence and also between the plane and the intensive features that populate it" (*WIP* 75).

Philosophy is only possible because it creates concepts that in some way address these intuitions, most clearly presented through conceptual personae, that arise from problems that we cannot but think. Philosophical concepts are ushered into existence by the images and figures, prephilosophical in themselves, that prepare us for the concept to come. As the rigorous and detailed creation, understanding, and analysis of concepts, philosophy occurs simultaneously with but conditioned by and located on the plane of immanence. Its task, in order to begin as such, is to slow down chaotic forces enough to make them thinkable: "The plane of immanence is like a section of chaos and acts like a sieve. In fact, chaos is characterized less by the absence of determinations than by the infinite speed with which they have taken shape and vanish. . . . The problem of philosophy is to acquire a consistency without losing the infinite into which thought plunges (in this respect chaos has as much a mental as a physical existence)" (*WIP* 42). The plane of immanence is the extraction of a consistency that the Greeks threw over a section of chaos in order to be able to think, to address problems and issues that life before the concept cannot. These problems are intractable, which is why they insist on being thought, or on some mode of address, problems like mortality, collective existence, the struggles of survival, even sexual difference, which do not go away but may be managed or regulated. The plane of immanence, the plane that accompanies and makes possible the invention of philosophical concepts, is the order, plan, or horizon of thought. It makes thinking in concepts possible. But Deleuze and Guattari insist that it is not the only plane and, moreover, that it is itself composed of numerous philosophical planes, forms of the ordering of concepts, gathered from the history of philosophy. It is "interleaved" of many planes for the distribution of concepts, sometimes knotted together and at other times fraying in their connections (*WIP* 50–51).

Alongside of, or perhaps aligned as strata with the plane of immanence, the plane "proper" to philosophy, one mode of addressing chaos
and slowing it down in one manner, are the planes of composition that
characterize all artistic creation, including literature, music, painting,
architecture, cinema, and the performance arts. Here the arts extract
from the world, from chaos, from the excess of order that characterizes the world, qualities, sensations, affects, or forces that, through their
cohesion, become perceptible, immanent both in the work of art and in
the world. Another is the plane of reference that constitute and make
the various sciences and their scientific practices—hypotheses, experimentation, tests, confirmations, results—possible and comprehensible.
If no constructed plane is adequate to the chaos it addresses (without,
that is, collapsing into chaos itself), since chaos abides in whatever
planes are thrown over it to generate a provisional organization, then
there must be a multiplicity of planes, each eternal, ever transforming,
temporally directed, always further populating, available consistency
of the products—artistic, philosophical, scientific—of history, each a
mode of ideality that is part of and yet laid over the real, chaos, that it
partially addresses. Residing between the impulse to transcendence and
the forces of dissolution amidst chaos, the plane of immanence frames
and orients philosophy as active thought, existing in impersonal and
incorporeal concepts, freed from their origins, capable of directing a
movement of thought.

ETHICS AND ETHOLOGY

What are concepts for? What do they accomplish? What do they do?
For Deleuze as much as for Nietzsche, concepts function as affirmations
of life, not only the life of the philosopher, but all life, all materiality, this
and only this world. Concepts are produced or created because of the
impact of an outside, something outside our control that will not allow us
to rest in peace: they are motivated by life's most urgent tasks, surviving
and adequately (though not necessarily truthfully) addressing the most

pressing problems that beset life. We think only because we are forced into invention by external exigencies on which we must rely to live, let alone prosper. Thinking does not come easily and is wrenched not only from the living being's interior but above all from the capacity for sense that the alignment of events—these external exigencies—make possible. Thought, concepts are possible both because living beings are capable of feeling, intuiting, perceiving and also because of the way the world is, the excess of order that also includes sense. The world itself, made up of nothing but infinite numbers of events at different speeds and slownesses, is the condition under which thought, and the later emergence of concepts, can come into being, can create a temporary order, can throw planes over the chaos of these infinite events. Concepts thus have not only a functional or strategic orientation—how to think through a problem—but also the enlivening capacity to provide order to the world from something extracted, or contracted, from it. This gives all thought an ethical dimension: thought functions as an enhancement of life; it enables some modes of life's intensification and self-ordering.

Immanence, the condition of all concepts and, for Deleuze, the only real object of philosophy, gives a life an ethical dimension, even if it is an ethics that we must come to learn for ourselves from living life rather than principles which we use to direct life before it is lived. This is an ethics linked to a self-therapeutics, a maximization of the powers of life, considered at its most impersonal and asubjective. Immanence is "a life": "We will say of pure immanence that it is A LIFE, and nothing else. It is not immanence to life, but the immanent that is in nothing is itself a life. A life is the immanence of immanence, absolute immanence: it is complete power, complete bliss."[28] Immanence is "a life," not life in general, living. There is no life in general, only particular forms of life, particular modes of living, particular milieus in which the encounters of the world enhance and elaborate lives—many many forms of life—from the incipient conditions, the virtuality, contained in the material and natural order. Deleuze describes a state in human life, a life briefly suspended between life and death,[29] as life is being born or is dying, in which what is impersonal and external comes to dominate what remains or is yet to come of subjectivity or consciousness. For a moment, a life erupts, it expresses its singular asubjectivity, its status as event, and it shares in common with everything around it, living or not, the capacity to actualize its potentials, to expand as well as contract itself. This perhaps is the key distinction between the newborn infant Deleuze describes as a singularity without individuality (*PI* 30), a pure virtuality capable of nearly infinite actualizations, fully open, and the dying stranger, an individuality no longer recognized and losing its capacities, becoming purely singular once again.

A life shares with nonlife—both the dying and what has never lived—various types of self-formation, virtual paths to actualization. It is, as Bergson recognized, laden with virtualities, the capacity to become more and other: for Bergson, the past, which coexists virtually with the present, becomes useful to life only to the extent that it can be brought to bear on present and impending events.[30] The smaller one's future, the less one needs to bring the past to life in action and the more one is able to abide in pure recollection. This may also explain the experience of one's history rapidly unrolling in consciousness when facing imminent death: "A life contains only virtuals. It is made up of virtualities, events, singularities. What we call virtual is not something that lacks reality but something that is engaged in a process of actualization following the plane that gives it its particular reality" (*PI* 31). What is alive in this broadest of senses, one that Deleuze shares with the Stoics, Spinoza, Nietzsche, and Bergson, is what becomes, what invents ways of actualizing some of its virtual forces to create new virtuals and new lines of actualization—far more wide-ranging than life understood in its biological sense. Not only do plants and animals have unactualized virtuals, and various paths of actualization, so too do volcanoes, oceans, weather patterns, planets, solar systems. The impersonality of "a life" also inhabits what we consider nonlife, both the inanimate products of life (books, art works, commodities of all kinds)[31] and the inanimate preconditions and milieu for each type of life.[32] It is Nietzsche's will to power, the forces that run through subjects and objects, belying and betraying their apparent unity and integrity and preparing for their eternal recurrence. This life is the life of events, their absolutely particular and never repeated alignments of force, their processes of actualization in states of things and in the sense that adheres to them. This impersonal life is also the Stoics' concept of destiny, the force of the incorporeal within the corporeal: "Events or singularities give to the plane all their virtuality, just as the plane of immanence gives virtual events their full reality. . . . A wound is incarnated or actualized in a state of things or of life; but it is itself a pure virtuality on the plane of immanence that leads us to a life. My wound exists before me: not a transcendence of the wound as a higher actuality, but its immanence as a virtuality always within a milieu (plane or field)" (*PI* 31–32).

Ethics is thus irretrievably bound up with the movement of events, with how events may be "lived" by both a living being and a nonliving milieu, with the corporeal and incorporeal forces they bear. The question of ethics is how can I be worthy of the events that await me, how can I enter into events that sweep me up, preexist me, or that I cannot control? How can I be worthy of my destiny? How can what is impersonal *in* me be worthy of its impersonal fate? "To the extent that events are actualized in us, they wait for us and invite us in. They signal us: 'My wound existed before me and I was born to embody it.' It is a question of attaining this will that the event creates in us, the Operator; of producing surfaces and linings in which the event is reflected, finds itself again as incorporeal and manifests in us the neutral splendor which it possesses in itself in its impersonal and preindividual nature" (*LS* 148). Or, in more Nietzschean language, how can I maximize the impact of the forces of ideas and the forces of bodies such that I can make the most of myself and of them? In a reading of Joë Bousquet, who Deleuze claims "must be called Stoic," he suggests that to fully live the splendor and magnificence of the event is to extract the sense of the event, to liberate a sense, the condition of concepts, that themselves may be able to produce a new self, new events, and a new order of becoming: "to become worthy of what happens to us, and thus to will and release the event, to become the offspring of one's own events, and thereby to be reborn, to have one more birth, and to break with one's carnal birth—to become the offspring of one's events and not of one's actions, for the action is itself produced by the offspring of the event" (*LS* 149–50).[33]

It is because of the sense that is mixed with events that thought is possible, that concepts can be created and conceptual means developed by which we can modify our behavior and environment, survive circumstances beyond our control, and create new orders by which to survive the chaos, the excess of forces, into which we are born. Thinking is thus ethics, one form of ethics (thinking is a form of action that accompanies material action), one mode of directing life in its ability to live up to what happens to it, to be worthy of what occurs, to prepare internally for what externally awaits, and to be impinged upon from the outside to draw out what is most active within.[34] Ethics is the manner in which a life can live in the world, the relations between material forces regulated by casual networks and conceptual relations ordered by the plane of immanence. It thus defines not only a human's conceptualization of moral responsibility (this is only one form of ethics, morality), but the ways in which all forms of life survive and enhance the encounters in which they are bound up, which overcome them. Thought, concepts are one such strategy, not invented by a conscious being, but a condition under which a being can become conscious. Thought, concepts are movements: they generate new ways of acting and being, new kinds of combinations and collectivities. In his earlier writings, especially in *Nietzsche and Philosophy*, Deleuze understood that concepts, thought, function primarily as movement: "Nietzsche snatches thought from the element of truth and falsity. He turns it into an interpretation and an evaluation, interpretation of forces, evaluation of power.—It is a thought-movement . . . in the sense that thought itself must produce movements" (xiii). My birth awaits me, my death the same, and all my encounters, though not predestined and not functional without my actions, are events in which I am not an agent, in which I cannot exercise "free will," but for which I can prepare myself, in which I participate, indeed that make me what I am. Causes and events occur. My life is enabled by them and its conceptual and physical sustenance and enhancement occur through them. They are internal to me, even as I exist only through them. This is why thinking and evaluating are part of life, the part by which I can transform what is given to me so that it can be mine or so that it is other than itself.

Ethics is not so much about living a "good life" (one cannot know a "good life" until it is lived, and living a good life does not require knowing it) as it is about facing what we cannot control and living—or dying—in the process of willing what we cannot control, willing the event without ressentiment, affirming the events with which one is bound. My birth, my death, the bad accidents and moments of good luck that occur to me—ethics is my capacity to affirm, enhance, and intensify them. Ethics represents my capacity to affect and be affected, the enhancement or diminution of my power to act, including my power to think. The greatest affirmation of freedom is the affirmation of the necessities that make me what I am (those both outside and within me). Destiny does not entail necessity, external causes, but (impersonal) will: "It is in this sense that the *Amor fati* is one of the struggles of free men. My misfortune is present in all events, but also the splendor and brightness which dry up misfortune and which bring about that the event, once willed, is actualized on its most contracted point" (*LS* 149). Ethics is the action of the intensification or contraction of what the events that befall us offer, not only in their effects but their excess of sense, living at its most contracted point, life at its most intense. Ethics is thus linked to a life, to every life, and every encounter that shapes, forms, interacts, and transforms the becomings that constitute a life. It is also linked, in a fundamental way, to aesthetics, an aesthetics of existence, a style or art of living, a manner of making one's life into a work of art, an aesthetics without need of an external object.[35]

This is why, instead of identifying ethics with an evaluation of one's life and the lives of others, Deleuze and Guattari have closely linked it to the questions of ethology. Ethics is not simply the domain of human morality, but occupies all forms of life in their encounters with their milieus (and the transformation of their milieus). Using the work of Jakob von Uexküll, Konrad Lorenz, and other founders of ethology—the discipline that explores the behavior and the lifeworlds of living beings, living beings in their environments—Deleuze and Guattari elaborate an ontoethology, an ontoethics. This is an ethics that affirms what a body can do, what a concept/prospect/affect can do, what degrees of power, that is, what degrees of movement and rest, intensify or diminish the capacities of a life. In *ATP* Deleuze and Guattari address the question of ethics/ethology through Spinoza, although they could have done so just as readily using the work of Nietzsche: what latitudes and longitudes compose a body and in what ways are these capable of affecting and being affected?: "We call the *latitude* of a body the affects of which it is capable at a given degree of power or, rather, within the limits of that degree. *Latitude is made up of intensive parts falling under a capacity, and longitude of extensive parts falling under a relation. . . .* This kind of study is called ethology, and this is the sense in which Spinoza wrote a true Ethics" (257). Latitude is the degree to which the intensive parts of a body—its capacity to conceptualize, cognize, or think—is affected, and longitude the degree to which the extensive or material elements of a body or bodies acts, affects, or is affected. In other words, ethics assesses the enhancement or diminution of the body's powers of acting and think-ing. Ethics is an ethology to the extent that each living thing—microbes, viruses, bacteria, plants, animals, humans—is not only constituted by its "own" nature (a nature composed of many other microorganisms, of many forces and vectors, as we will discuss in the following chapters) but also by that of its milieu: each thing lives in a nonreciprocal interchange with a milieu. Ethics names the ethological relations that enable a life to live to its limits, to test the limits of its capacities.

It is not surprising that Deleuze and Guattari invoke Uexküll's work on the mutual constitution of the animal and its *Umwelt*. Uexküll argued that in order to have a better understanding of animals, and particularly those very far from humans in form and evolution—he was particu-larly fascinated with sea urchins, jellyfish, octopods, starfish, flies, ants, honey bees, mosquitoes, and, most famously, ticks and the worlds in which they live,[36] each a kind of self-contained subset or monad, a "bub-bleworld," within a larger environment that cannot even be sensed.[37] Uexküll argued that the problem of life, addressed by all of life in its enor-mous variety, which the organization of an animal or plant attempts to address through its powers, is how to survive, even thrive, in its milieu? He sees the "solution," or mode of address, provided for an organism through the "plan" of its bodily organization, a plan that includes not only organs and parts but above all the integration of capacities and uses. While Uexküll understands his project in Kantian terms, Deleuze and

Guattari read him as Spinozan. As Uexküll says: "Biology is the science of the organization of living beings. Organization is called the conjunction of different elements according to a uniform plan for a common effect. Biology has thus to search in each living form for the plan of its construction and for the elements of this construction."[38] This plan of construction, the plan by which any life elaborates itself in a milieu, is a pattern or order that inheres in and is part of the processes of more or less mapping on the inside of the organism what it requires to live in its world. This plan, neither ideal nor material, is the ordering of the development and growth of forms of life that inheres in each life and gives it is particular characteristics.

An organism is not so much a coherent being, nor even a genetic totality, but the ongoing interchange between sense organs, motor organs, the dynamic connections between them (a plan of bodily organization, following the experiments of Hans Driesch and Hans Spemann, which we will discuss in the final chapter) and the milieu that supports them, an ongoing field (itself oriented by a plane or plan, a direction) that facilitates its continuing existence, while it is to some extent transformed by that existence. This provides a quite precise model of Deleuze's concept of an ethics that is linked to the ways in which animals live in their worlds, the way they generate worlds and, in the process, enhance or diminish themselves. Uexküll's work, steeped though it may be in an explicit Kantianism, provides not only an expanding and narrowed down idealism (expanded insofar as all forms of life now exhibit mind and narrowed insofar as mind is no longer considered rational but is understood as affective), but a way of seeing that bodily form is organized through an ideal plan that always already includes the possibilities of an adaptation and transformation of milieu insofar as the living body is the accretion of the history of prior bodies in their encounters in their milieus. While Uexküll can be regarded as perhaps the first "animal phenomenologist," reconstructing the lived worlds of various species, Deleuze and Guattari understand him instead as a Spinozan, as the theorist of animal affects and the ways in which each species and life folds into its patterns of growth and needs the key (contrapuntal) elements of its environment that it requires to exist as such.

Deleuze and Guattari argue that animal life can be understood—instead of a coupling of mind and body, of individuals created through genealogies or species and genus—as movement, the movement of energy, of impacting forces and counterforces or milieus and the relations of dependence and transformation they pose to life. It is no longer a question of what identity a life form has, what constitutes it genetically or materially, but what it does, how it acts, its modes of affecting and being affected. Using the terminology of strata and deterritorialization, Deleuze and Guattari claim that we can understand life in terms radically different from its reductionist representations as assemblage, as connection: "'Ethology' . . . can be understood as a very privileged molar domain for demonstrating how the most varied components (biochemical, behavioral, perceptive, hereditary, acquired, improvised, social, etc.) can crystallize in assemblages that respect neither the distinction between orders nor the hierarchy of forms" (ATP 336). In short, ethology represents a way to understand the complex movements by which life is born, develops, acquires habits, survives, and thrives (or not) in a milieu that is always in principle open to change: it analyzes the inventions that life elaborates, the obstacles it must overcome, the transformations to its milieu that it creates. Each life lives in a world, opens up and elaborates a world through what it perceives and how it acts: each living thing is an artist (some better or worse at their creations) that invents an *ethos*, a way to live, a style of living in their habitat or milieu.[39]

Life is thus both natural and material, an organization (and deterritorialization) of bodily form, but also conceptual (a condition for any ethics) and artistic creation or invention. It is because each life is affected by and affects its world that it has an ethical existence, one based on its interrelations with a world that includes all sorts of others, in which its capacities are enhanced or diminished. Numerous affective relations mark every living thing: the expression and framing of affect are also the conditions under which art becomes possible, not merely human art with its systems of monetary value but also the creative and artistic productions of animals—nests, elaborate dances and techniques for attraction, competitions for sexual success, the production of various architectural structures, the differentiation and elaboration of sexually pleasing characteristics. Art is an ethics expressed not in action and concepts but through affects and percepts, through the transformation of perception and affection into self-sustaining and self-standing framed and deterritorialized qualities.

Ethics and art, discovering ways to live and intensifying them, are means by which living beings capitalize on the excess of sense that is produced by the problems generated for life by events, by the irregular and unpredictable disruptions to habit and expectation that must somehow be addressed. Ethics and art maximize the powers of living beings. Ethics aims to create an order in which a being can act for its health, well-being, and expansion, and art aims to create an order in which a being can express, and others can find expressed, this power of expansion and this capacity for more. Art expresses the affects that a life focuses or diffracts. If "ethics is an ontology," as Bogue suggests,[40] then ontology also is the condition of an ethology through which an ethics and an aesthetics of existence become possible, understood as life's various evaluations of its own ontological immersion in its world. Ethics and aesthetics are the ways in which we can intensify and live in accordance with what of the sense-laden excesses of materiality—those that constitute events—we can harness.

It is because of this immersion in the world that we can find the forces necessary to compose the intensities that populate the planes of immanence, composition and reference which enhance our capacities to act, to know, and to perceive. The ontology of this one world, an ontology as fully elaborated by Spinoza as any other philosopher past or present, is the condition under which we have the particular natures and habits that we do and the reason that we are able to both cognize and play with the objects and qualities, the things of this world—and their virtualities, their capacity to be otherwise—and to create philosophies, sciences, arts, ways of intensifying and magnifying our capacities for life, as well as ignorance, oppression, war, murder, and all the acts of undoing and uncreating that characterize a life's trajectory. Philosophy, the sciences and the arts, are the ways in which human life extracts an order, a consistency, a plane, a structured or useful excess from the chaotic movement of forces, most of which exist unperceived by any forms of living.[41]

Each does so differently, in its own (plural and contested) ways. But each draws out some order, a consistency, through the construction of a plane, all ultimately different versions of planes of immanence, through which chaos can be divided or ordered enough to enable us to address it through these slivers. Philosophy, art, and science are three modes of thinking in different ways, three forms of address for what cannot be mastered, which, at their most intense and vibrant, can also address something of the others. Because each plane, artificial and abstract as it is, nevertheless addresses one and the same world and its forces, each can bring about transformations or linkages with the others—some artists have been powerfully influenced by, say, physics or biology, philosophers have sometimes come to address scientific or artistic questions, and scientists, perhaps more rarely, may find that literature, art, or philosophy help them to formulate what they see as their scientific tasks. Yet each plane is constructed according to its own requirements, its own particular consistencies:

The three thoughts intersect and intertwine, but without synthesis or identification. With its concepts, philosophy brings forth events. Art erects monuments with its sensations. Science constructs states of affairs with its functions. A rich tissue of correspondences can be established between the planes. But the network has its culminating points where sensation itself becomes sensation of concept or function, where the concept becomes concept of function or sensation, and where the function becomes function of sensation or concept. And none of these elements can appear without the other being still to come, still indeterminate or unknown. Each created element on a plane calls on other heterogeneous elements, which are still to be created on other planes; thought as heterogenesis. It is true that these culminating points contain two extreme dangers: either leading us back to the opinion from which we wanted to escape or precipitating us into the chaos that we wanted to confront (*WIP* 198–99).

These three "rafts," on which human precarity floats, constitute, as Deleuze understands it, a fold, a new organization or reorganization of the constituents life requires so that more than life is served, life to come is also addressed, invoked, and perhaps brought into being. In his reading of Leibniz in *The Fold*, Deleuze argues that the fold is always double, always in two directions or levels at the same time, "the pleats of matter and the folds in the soul."[42] Deleuze's own work may itself may be understood as a fold (sometimes Deleuze himself describes it as an invagination),[43] not only between the material and the ideal, or thought (each itself enfolded and enfolding) but also between, on the one side, Spinoza, Nietzsche, Bergson, who come before, and to whose work he has given a renewed life, and, on the other, his own contemporaries and coexplorers, above all Guattari, but also Simondon and Ruyer, who work alongside of and in congruence with him and with whom he has shared a growing concern for the question of life, at its limits, not only in death but above all at its most creative and self-forming.

AN ETHICS/AESTHETICS OF THE EVENT: OR, HOW I LEARNED TO LOVE MY FATE

The ethics of amor fati, Nietzsche's most cherished principle, is also the basis for at least some key elements of Deleuze's ethics. Long after his work on Nietzsche, in his collaborations with Guattari, Deleuze seeks to temper Nietzsche with the Stoics, to accept that "a life" requires an acceptance of both the inevitability of death, through which all that was personal becomes impersonal, and also the affirmation of something both quite particular but absolutely impersonal, less an individuality, a recognized subjectivity, a personage than a singularity. Below the level of identity, perhaps an ingredient of any molar identity, is the impersonal, the singular, the imperceptible that runs through any identity and can be affirmed only at those moments of birth and death when the subject disappears and only singularity remains. If becomings, human becomings at least, are always mediated by becoming-woman, the animal, all minorities, the mineral, and, above all and ultimately, the imperceptible, if they are always oriented by singularities and intensities that run alongside identities, the unrecognized support for the norm, the selfsame self-conscious (masculine, white, human) subject, if the resistance to the subject/object opposition always occurs through becoming other (than a subject or object), then events and their unpredictable and sometimes uncontainable effects will entail becoming-other, becoming-minoritarian, becoming something in between or neither subject or object, becoming cosmic:

> To go unnoticed is by no means easy. To be a stranger, even to one's doorman or neighbors. If it is so difficult to be "like" everybody else, it is because it is an affair of becoming. Not everybody becomes everybody [and everything: *tout le monde*—trans.], making a becoming of everybody/everything. This requires much ascetism, much sobriety, much creative involution . . . "Eliminate all that is waste, death and superfluity," complaint and grievance, unsatisfied desire, defense or pleading, everything which roots each of us (everybody) in ourselves, in our molarity. Everybody/everything is the molar aggregate, but *becoming everybody/everything* is another affair, one that brings into play the cosmos with its molecular components.
>
> (*ATP* 279–80)

Ethics entails becomings; becomings are the condition under which what is transforms itself or makes itself amenable to transformation. These transformations, including acts of depersonalization, becoming imperceptible, receding in identity, are required in order to think, to write, to paint, to play music, to know scientifically. We need to muster something of this impersonality—to the extent that we can—in order to create, whether in experiments, in art works, or in philosophical texts: we need to undertake at least some becoming imperceptible in order to adequately live and work within our milieu(s), understanding them as much as possible from within. We become impersonal to the extent that we can liberate a thought, create a work, understand an experiment and its implications, to the extent that other impersonal things, impulses, or forces can live within and through us, that is, to the extent that we can walk a precarious line, a line of death that always inhabits life, a line perhaps first understood in the work of Bichat and fully developed in the writings of Foucault, who himself turned to developing an ethics of life as he moved away from his genealogy of power.[44] This is the line, Deleuze indicates, that sometimes precedes but always follows "a life," balanced as it is between the forces of subjectivization, which personalize an individual and make it responsible (Nietzsche's concept of culture itself: brand culture on the skin!) and death, which ends whatever particular line a life might follow, but perhaps liberates other lines, to be taken up by others who come after.

The line that a life may walk in order to liberate concepts, intensities, forces that it cannot control and that will change this life is perilous to the extent that it always hovers close to death: the closer one follows the line (whether as schizo or as perfectly blended in, imperceptible), the more directly one faces death (one's own and that of countless others). This line is the condition of thought and art, but also of madness and self-disintegration: "this line's deadly, too violent and fast, carrying us into breathless regions. It destroys all thinking, like the drugs Henri Michaux had to stop using. . . . We need both to cross the line, to make it endurable, workable, thinkable. To find in it as far as possible, and as long as possible, an art of thinking. How can we protect ourselves, survive, while still confronting this line?"[45] The question of an ethics and aesthetics of existence is not, for Deleuze, the question of quantity—how can I maximize good? how can I maximize beauty?—for these only address a certain kind of consumption; rather, it is a question of the intensive: how can we curve a line that will both enable us the most intense concepts, sensations, percepts, but also some protection and cohesion against the very chaos from which these qualities erupt or the banality of our failures to adequately address this chaos? How can we experience to the maximum, with the maximum reflection and understanding, without tipping into wild deterritorialization or madness, what, with Guattari, Deleuze sometimes calls the full Body-without-Organs through which nothing can flow? How to negotiate this line, while maintaining some consistency in transforming oneself and retaining what remains of the impersonal, the cosmic, the chaotic? How can we maintain "just a little order to protect us from chaos" (*WIP* 201), enough to wrest concepts, affects, and percepts from it while not enough to plunge ourselves into it?

Each plane making philosophy, art, and science possible (there are no doubt many such planes: the plane of governmentality that Foucault elaborated, the plane of management, marketing, and other forms of commodity connectedness that Deleuze and Guattari challenge in *Anti-Oedipus* and *ATP*) involve a rhythm, a timing, a cohesion or consistency, and thinking that somehow impacts life and its worlds because it takes from chaos some of its force in a sometimes manageable (but also sometimes deranging) form. The capacity to invent concepts, to create affects that stand by themselves, without their creator, the tenacity of scientific techniques and principles to withstand experimentation and repetition, signifiess that we have created the means by which to stall our imminent deaths, finite means to access something infinite, and the sometimes, indeed commonly, violently inhuman becomings we undergo to access works of philosophy, art, and science in order to make room for them in our lives: "The philosopher, the scientist, and the artist seem to return from the land of the dead" (*WIP* 202). They return, not as specters, carrying death with them, but as affirmations of this world (conceptual, affectual, perceptual) and of a life that can be lived beyond opinions, clichés, marketing slogans, that has risked entering chaos in order to create something from it, in order to open life up more to its outside.

Perhaps one of the most unexpected and improbable moves Deleuze and Guattari make is their claim that the three planes that constitute philosophy, art, and science are not anchored to or located in the world or over it, but in the brain![46]: "*The brain is the junction—not the unity—of the three planes*" (*WIP* 208). Neuroscience and cognitive psychology are not, however, the discourses to which they turn in rethinking the brain. As we will see in the following chapters, much of their understanding of the brain is derived from the work of Simondon and Ruyer, and the brain that they conceptualize is neither quite neurological/material nor psychological/ideal, though it has elements as it were facing both directions. It is not the brain's capacity to perceive and cognize, to remember or recognize, nor its capacity to assign mental representatives, images, neuronal pathways to things, abstract or concrete, that interest Deleuze and Guattari; the brain is not the highest accomplishment of the human, that which differentiates the human from the animal by a "higher" form of cognition, "deeper" forms of processing of information. The brain is no more clear, rational, or direct than the chaos in which it resides: it too is prey to opinion, belief, chatter, which block thought as readily as institutions like religion.[47] The task of philosophy is to force the brain to think, to shock it into thought, to direct it to think rather than opine. It is not the objective, measurable, mappable brain that interests them but rather the capacity of the brain to remove, to shake up and problematize, the subject. Contrary to the phenomenological insistence that "Man thinks, not the brain" (cited in *WIP* 210), Deleuze and Guattari ask: what would happen to thought if it is no longer a subject who thinks with a brain, but a brain that thinks without a subject, or in place of the subject? "We will speak of the brain as Cézanne spoke of the landscape: man absent from but completely within the brain. Philosophy, art, and science are not the mental objects of an objectified brain but the three aspects under which the brain becomes subject" (*WIP* 210).

If philosophy, art, and science are the means by which a life need no longer be defined by consciousness or received beliefs, feelings, and thoughts, and the most wrenching forms of bravery for these confrontations are always undertaken alone and without guidance, then the brain is that part of us most in touch with the chaotic forces that direct life. The brain is a self-organizing, self-containing microchaos that connects living bodies to the chaotic slices of milieu in which they abide, a point of connection between bodily forces and cosmic ones. This is because, like cosmic forces, it is both material and ideal, both an organ with vast synaptic networks, "fissures, hiatuses, intervals" (*WIP* 210), and the incorporeal condition of thought (as well as sensation, affect, and percept). The brain is not so much a privileged organ, the locus of thought, as the organ which is most prone to and affected by the movement of forces of all kinds, a kind of slowing down, adding consistency and organization to these forces, selecting, highlighting, and intensifying some of them: "Thought is molecular. Molecular speeds make up the slow beings that we are. As Michaux said, '*Man is a slow being, who is only made possible thanks to fantastic speeds.*' The circuits and linkages of the brain don't preexist the stimuli, corpuscles, and particles that trace them."[48]

The brain is the locus, in particular, for the contractile relations by which living bodies (even those without a brain, as they suggest) internalize and make use of the forces and things outside it. Just as the plant synthesizes chlorophyll from the energy of the sun, the nutrients in the soil, water, and the air, so it both contracts and preserves within itself something of these external conditions. They remain as plant, transformed, just as plants are themselves digested, contracted and preserved in the bodies of the microorganisms, insects, and animals that ingest them. This is no different than the contractile conditions for consciousness, memory, cognition, and thought. Each contracts something of what is outside it and is capable of living, perhaps even maximizing, its powers, through the extension in which life prolongs them. The same sun that the plant contracts leaves its trace on my digestive tract, both through my ingestion of the plant and/or the animal that feeds on it and through its direct action on me. But in this contraction there must also be a preservation (even amidst transformation) of the elements synthesized, an excess by which the living being, in whatever form, can feel, think, address, in its own way, what it contracts: "The plant contemplates by contracting the elements from which it originates—light, carbon, and the salts—and it fills itself with colors and odors that in each case qualify its variety, its composition: it is sensation in itself. It is as if flowers smelled themselves by smelling what composes them, first attempts of vision or of sense of smell, before being perceived or even smelled by an agent with a nervous system or a brain" (*WIP* 212). A brain can be created, even without the organ, only to the extent that affects, concepts, percepts are contractions of external forces that line the very details of every cell and organ with the outside which conditions and enables it.

For Deleuze and Guattari, this means that the entwinement of ideality or conceptuality with materiality or corporeality—the nature of the world, substance—is folded in on itself through life and through the process of becoming-alive. There is a process of becoming-brain that runs through all objects, including living ones, that spreads (and highlights) and intensifies as forces are contracted and become integral to life's operations, its becoming-thought and becoming-action. Concepts, percepts, affects are not only human ways of affecting and being affected but also the contractile possibilities of what is nonliving or may be understood as a form of "nonorganic life": "Of course, plants and rocks do not possess a nervous system. But if nerve connections and cerebral integrations pre-suppose a brain-force as faculty of feeling coexistent with the tissues, it is reasonable to suppose also a faculty of feeling that coexists with embryonic tissues and that appears in the Species as a collective brain; or with the vegetal tissues in the 'small species.' . . . Not every organism has a brain, and not all life is organic, but everywhere there are forces that constitute microbrains, or an inorganic life of things" (*WIP* 212–13). Contraction, the condition of habit (which is itself a means of life), is temporal and qualitative: the whole of the past is contracted in every "moment" of the present in different degrees, according to Bergson in *Matter and Memory*,[49] and forces are contracted into organs, actions, and the possibilities of self-affection, which bring the forces of the out-side into organisms, making thought, perception, affection possible. These are the vital modes of connection and contemplation (or self-contemplation) that living beings and "nonorganic life" continuously create with the chaotic order from which they are generated and with which they interact. These habits, multiple forms of contraction, and the behaviors they enable or prevent, constitute whatever cohesion we have as subjects, as bodies, as beings, for we *are* these forces, contracted, and the plan or order in which they interact with other forces: "Underneath the self which acts are little selves which contemplate and which render possible both the action and the active subject. We speak of our 'self' only in virtue of these thousands of little witnesses which contemplate within us: it is always a third party who says 'me.' These contemplative souls must be assigned even to the rat in the labyrinth and to each mus-cle of the rat."[50] We will discuss this peculiar concept of self or soul in the writings of Ruyer in chapter 6.

The brain-subject, the nonsubjective, inorganic brain, is a point of conjunction between the world and its forces, registered on and through a body; and an incorporeal order of sense that enables and conditions thought. This brain may be located in the skull, as it is for primates, in the membranes that regulate tree life and the pincers that regulate the sea urchin: it is the point of conjunction of perceptions and actions, the frontier or barrier connecting a being's interior with its exterior. It may be that many brains or "persons" inhabit all living beings.[51] The brain, or many brains, is the means of connection and disconnection between circuits of perception and action within a living being by which external forces are contracted/preserved and contemplated and internal processes are set into motion and enacted. Subjects are effects of these processes, a residual or bonus consistency that coheres (or doesn't) the sensations, affects, percepts, and concepts that circulate within a body.

What interests Deleuze and Guattari is not so much the operation of these brain-subjects but the question of how the various planes of contemplation and action resonate or interfere with each other, how concepts populating the plane of immanence may induce sensations populating the plane of composition or formulas occupying the plane of reference and vice versa—the manner of their "synesthetic" transformations relative to each other. It is because all the planes address features of the same world, features which pose problems for living beings that must be addressed, that one plane or some of its inhabitants may be enhanced or diminished by the push they exert on another plane or some of its inhabitants. But each plane must nevertheless address its own questions in its own way, according to its principles and protocols. The planes have chaos in common, this world of forces in its monstrous entirety, that underlies them. Each is anchored not in a world (to the extent that these planes protect us from the full force of chaos) but in the living needs they address, in the "objects" of all kinds (conceptual, affective, perceptual) that they house, above all in the futures, future populations, future events, future peoples they welcome. It is, however, no longer clear whether these "world-people" will any longer be human or inhabit a new kind of humanity rather than calling forth the most intense forms of impersonality. Perhaps only an overman, or an after- and beyond-man, whatever this may involve, will be summoned from this shadow.

The kind of ethics that Deleuze and Guattari elaborate, an ethics never strictly separable from an aesthetics, while never explicitly developed as such, runs through their collective writings and through all Deleuze's texts. The love of a destiny that precedes me and that, with the labor of thought, I may come to understand through an understanding of the world, destiny as an event that carries me with it, underlies the Stoic conception of ethics. To love oneself in the best possible way, one must look to nature and come to understand one's own nature as one's destiny, a nature linked to all others by vast chains of causes, a destiny providentially directed. Spinoza's too affirms a love, founded in and belonging to eternity, an *amor dei intellectualis*, in which knowledge finds its proper home in substance, where something of a living being, a rare human, can touch the infinity of substance or nature. Nietzsche, who is philosophy's most forceful advocate of fate, claims that what is highest in life affirms itself in the highest manner possible in the affirmation of eternal recurrence. For only the strongest of humans, those to come after humanity, amor fati is the joyous affirmation that everything that has occurred should occur and will recur—we have the fate we deserve, for there is no other. For Deleuze, as close reader of these traditions, there is no art, no science, no philosophy that is simply rooted in the past and the present. These forms, simultaneously of thought and action, exist in part because the chaos from which they are drawn always beckons new inventions, new thoughts, new practices, and, above all, a "people to come": "There is not work of art [or science, or philosophy] that does not call on a people who do not yet exist."[52] What a Deleuzean ethics affirms is a life that maximizes its engagements with chaos or, as Simondon will call it, "the preindividual," that supports, informs, and extends itself through the creative inventions that all forms of life add back to this chaos, whether it is sustained and given life on the planes of consistency or whether such inventions are destined to return to the chaos from which they were formed. To be worthy of having lived, to be worthy of living the life we have and are, we must extend life and intensify its forces through creative engagements that also extend and intensify the nonliving, making it artistic, giving it a kind of life of its own. To live is thus, for Deleuze, to live the events that constitute "a life" at the point at which it touches most directly the forces that threaten to disintegrate it, but where it is most affected and capable of affecting the most.

"There is a dignity of the event that has always been inseparable from philosophy as *amor fati*: being equal to the event, or becoming the off-spring of one's own events—'my wound existed before me; I was born to embody it.' I was born to embody it as event because I was able to disembody it as a state of affairs or lived situation. There is no other ethic than the *amor fati* of philosophy" (*WIP* 159).

5

SIMONDON AND THE PREINDIVIDUAL

"Ethics exists to the extent that there is information, in other words, signification overcoming a disparation of the elements of being, such that what is interior is also exterior." What Simondon elaborates here is a whole ontology, according to which Being is never One. As pre-individual, being is more than one—metastable, superposed, simultaneous with itself.

—GILLES DELEUZE, "ON GILBERT SIMONDON"

Gilbert Simondon (1924–1989) produced his key texts before the publication most of Deleuze's philosophy writings. He began working on the problem of individuation as early as 1952,[1] a year before the publication of Deleuze's first book, on Hume. In turning to Simondon's conception of individuation, we are reversing the chronology followed so far in this book, in fact, we are unfolding or elaborating what is already enfolded or contracted in many of Deleuze's writings. Along with Ruyer, he is one of the lesser known inspirations for a number of key concepts in Deleuze and Deleuze and Guattari's, writings.[2] He prefigures Deleuze's writings in a number of ways, from his account of an ontogenesis of individuals, his critique of dichotomous thinking, his fascination with machines (and mechanology) to his conception of information as well as his understanding of the increasing orders of scale and complexity that mark the movements constituting material, psychic, and collective existence. He also turns to questions of ethics and aesthetics as ways of addressing the real, which he conceives as connected to and fundamental for philosophy, the thinking of the relations of matter and life. He continues the marginalized tradition of thinking the modes of incorporeal—the ongoing challenge to the distinction between mind and body or form and matter or abstract and concrete—that I have attempted to trace through the writings of the Stoics, Spinoza, and Nietzsche, although he does so very much in his own way. Perhaps the most significant reason for Simondon's position in this book is his desire to produce an ethics that is inseparable from ontology, an ontoethics, that in some ways has the breadth of Spinoza's ethics, and the force of Nietzsche's. His work may also help to articulate more clearly the kind of ethics that lies nascent in Deleuze's writings.

Simondon aims to replace the study of ontology, of what is, with the study of ontogenesis, the various processes of self-formation that create what is. Simondon devoted his earliest writings to the pre-Socratics, for whom nature was the unquestioned source of existence and creativity.[3] He was thoroughly steeped in ancient philosophy, from the writings of Plato, Aristotle, the Epicureans, and the Stoics, in many cases returning to pre-Platonic conceptions of the coexistence of life and nature, to the kind of philosophy that existed before science, poetry, the arts, and philosophy became separated. The separation and privileging of form over matter—*hylomorphism*—which began with Socrates and is accomplished by Aristotle, becomes a significant conceptual obstacle to a thoroughgoing understanding of the continuities and discontinuities, the rising and falling of order and information, that connects the human, and other forms of life, to the orders of the universe.

In this, he is more at home with the pre-Socratics (especially Anaximander),[4] the Stoics, Spinoza, Nietzsche, and especially Bergson; but, to Bergson's distinction between matter and life, Simondon poses degrees of life, punctuated leaps in level, that link the most complex psychic and collective behavior to the most elementary processes of materiality. All of becoming becomes in the same way, not according to universal conceptual or mechanical principles, not according to rational or formal plans which preexist them, but according to the heterogeneous logics of their individuations, and the consistencies, cohesions, and effects across disparity, difference, dispersion that they produce. This is perhaps the single most compelling reason for Deleuze's deep admiration for and use of Simondon's work—Simondon serves as a more or less contemporary interlocutor of Deleuze's and enables him to develop another language by which to speak about the events and becomings.[5] Instead of opposition, Simondon speaks of disparation, the productive tension between two closely related but incompatible orders; instead of identity, or individuality, he speaks of individuations; instead of forces, he speaks of energetic potentials; and instead of the negative, he speaks of creation. By moving from Deleuze to his contemporaries, I explore in more depth the intimate relations between ideality and materiality as well as extend Deleuze's conception of an ethics of the event.

THE PREINDIVIDUAL

Insofar as an individual exists, there must be a process, or many, that produces it. This is Simondon's most basic axiom—to seek out the phases by which, from initial conditions, a being comes into existence, not through an identity, a preformed path, or the imposition of a preexisting form or plan on unformed matter. Such conceptions are hylomorphic: they consider matter to be passive and unformed—indeed, they are considered fundamentally feminine since at least the time of Aristotle, if not before, and form to be a masculine, active, imposing, ordering process. I have suggested elsewhere that the dichotomization of thought through presence and absence into dualistic and mutually exclusive terms—mind and body, reason and passion, self and other—may have its origins in the transformation of sexual difference into sexual opposition (the most elementary gesture of patriarchy).[6] It is the transformation of difference that Simondon addresses. Not only is the hylomorphic schema unable to explain the coming into existence of individuals, its terms, *form* and *matter,* require that their own geneses as individuals be addressed. His challenge to hylomorphism is an analysis of the coming into existence of hylomorphism itself, the ontogenesis of philosophical models that, because of their binarized structure, have lost direct contact with the preindividual forces that are used to produce and sustain the various orders of individuations.

The concept of the preindividual is Simondon's alternative to the problem of Spinoza's substantialism. There is being, huge, magnificent, complicated, perhaps even divine, in its order, regularity, creativity, multiplicity, and logic. But the coming into being of substance still needs to be explained. Simondon's project is to articulate a theory of becoming that accounts for the complex geneses of the becoming of all beings and their different levels of operation through the concrete elaborations of the preindividual, a concept I believe is in fact very close to Spinoza's understanding of substance and the divine. His notion of the preindividual is also closely linked to Nietzsche's understanding of the universe as composed of impersonal wills to power, force fields that constitute and decompose every "thing." Simondon adds post-Einsteinian, quantum conceptions of fields, deformations, singularities to Nietzsche's conception of the will to power. Forces become more subtle, less easily identifiable, shifting terrains, with their points of intensity, dark spots, strange attractors, and vectors and gradients of differentiating forces.

The preindividual is described as "not one," lacking identity, cohesion, not less than one (and not zero) but indeterminately more than one: "it is more than unity and more than identity, capable of expressing itself as a wave and a particle, as matter or energy,"[7] fundamentally open to contradictions, indeed the very ground of their distinction. This is because the preindividual has no individual or collective contents (only potentials for individuation), while it provides the conditions and means by which individual and collective existence comes into being. The preindividual is the center of Simondon's conception of being, but not a being comprised of identities, things, substances. It is the metastable order from which beings, or, rather, becomings, engender themselves. Being is, for him, potential rather than actual. This is the preindividual before there are identities, distinctions, and oppositions, "being" that exists purely as becoming. Such a conception is not possible in the classical age where only stability and instability, regulation or the absence of regulation can be conceived. The ancients could not conceive of an order that is neither stable nor unstable, neither being nor nothing.

Simondon uses a concept from nonequilibrium thermodynamics to describe a mode of being as *metastable*, neither in a state of equilibrium nor in a state of depletion or entropy. It retains unexhausted potentials that require the generation of a new order to explicate or develop these potentials and keep them contained and cohesive. Metastable systems are systems of becoming, dynamic systems which have both energy and information, and enable them to exchange with each other. A physical system, for example, can be understood as metastable when the slightest change in its parameters (in temperature, pressure, electrical charge, magnetic force, etc.) occurs. In such circumstances the system does not behave as it does under conditions of equilibrium but undergoes dramatic transformation. Muriel Combes, one of Simondon's most astute readers, explains: "in super-cooled water (i.e. water remaining liquid at a temperature below its freezing point), the least impurity within a structure isomorphic to that of ice plays the role of a seed for crystallization and suffices to turn the water into ice."[8] In other words, the smallest perturbation of the metastable system generates a powerful change in the system's functioning, and enables it to "evolve." A metastable system is always more than itself, for it contains not only its present capacities but also the ongoing potential for self-transformation or mutation. Its potential energy can be tapped to the extent that it can be actualized, structured, positioned at another level. Metastable systems contain contrary potentials, potentials that are incompatible and require resolution through the creation of a structure, a form or level to express them. Becoming is not the development of being but its conditions and raw materials.[9]

The preindividual is metastable, which is to say, "the notions of order, potential energy in a system, and the notion of an increase in entropy must be used" (PPO 6). If the real can be understood as metastable, then some of its regions, as supersaturated as they can be, become potentially differentiatable systems of individuation. The preindividual constitutes those dynamic sites of metastability whose energetic and informational potentials remain active and unexhausted in change.[10] Much of what is real—dead planets, dead life—has lost its potential for more and becomes subject to entropy, decay. But the preindividual is capable of bearing contrary or even contradictory aims and outcomes as different lines of individuations are created.[11] Reality can express itself in contrary ways. When we binarize the real—that is, understand that it is composed of a presence and its negation or absence (form as the absence of matter, matter as the absence of form, for example)—we misunderstand its ability to induce contrary explanations, fundamentally different and incompatible orders of understanding. The preindividual is an ordering, orienting dimension of the real, its *dynamis*, both, and indistinguishably, form and content, energy and information, wave and particle, conceptual and material.

The preindividual is an excess of energy and information, more than unity and more than individuality. Through the self-organizing forces of the preindividual and the intrusion of a foreign "germ," an element that is introduced from outside to a metastable system, processes of individuation—provisional modes of resolution of tensions within the preindividual—become possible and can operate continuously without exhausting the resources of the preindividual. The preindividual is both the precondition of any individuation, and thus of any individual, but also the extra "charge" that individuation carries with it as it develops and elaborates new orders to address new kinds of problem, a resource for ongoing individuations that may occur within and between individuals. The preindividual may be understood as the indistinguishably mental/material condition for thought and things, mind and matter. It makes every individual, material or mental, living or nonliving, possible. The preindividual is neither material nor ideal but the dynamic forces, the charge of potential, that enable both to come into being and to function in increasing interrelations and orders of complexity.

If the preindividual consists in metastable systems full of energetic/informational potential, supersaturated, if it has no identity, it must be considered an order of pure difference. For Simondon, the preindividual is not the ground of an ontology but of an ontogenesis. The preindividual is more "concrete" and "complete" than the forms of identity that may emerge from it.[12] Without unity or identity, but nevertheless laden with form-matter and their various tendencies, the preindividual provides a clearer way to understand ontology as ontogenesis.

CRYSTALS

The processes of individuation have an order or direction, for they develop levels and dimensions of increasing complexity according to the phases of individuation, such that more complex individuations rely on and require lower order levels of individuation. For ontogenesis to proceed, the preindividual, which is neither localizable nor temporal but the condition under which we may come to understand space, place and time, must, through its energetic potentials begin a process of "dephasing": "becoming is a dimension of being corresponding to a capacity to fall out of phase with itself, that is, to resolve itself by dephasing itself" (PPO 6). The preindividual, or one "region/moment" of it, through the various tensions it generates, that is, its metastability, creates a (provisional) resolution of these tensions through a division into phases, a falling out of step with itself, a movement of becoming something else. Becoming is the connection of phases, the dephasing and temporization that opens up the order of change and a direction for change: "Individuation corresponds to the appearance of phases in being that are phases of being" (PPO 6). In the processes of dephasing, the preindividual generates, through a "germ," two orders of magnitude, two modes of energy/information, between which a new process mediates and whose tensions it resolves in some way. There is always a doubling in becoming, a division of the preindividual into two orders between which an individual may be formed. The plant in its relations to its world, its exterior, enfolds energies from both cosmological and terrestrial orders. These contractile capacities provide it with solar energy, water, and minerals it requires to sustain its own growth—the plant, in Bergson's terms, reaches as far as the sun which it contracts in its organic functions. It is also an internal order of growth and development, a particular pattern of life that requires and participates in its cosmic operations. The plant requires and generates two orders, one internal, related to self-organization, the other external, related to the universe, in order to live, reproduce, and flourish.

Individuation can occur only when the preindividual dephases, that is, acquires temporal and spatial consistency, becomes a specific milieu against and through which individuation may be distinguished. There is no individuation without an individuating milieu, a local or associated milieu created in the process that separates an individual-to-be from its particular environment. Each order of individuation entails a new order of milieu and a new reserve of the preindividual. Individuation, at all levels, requires a process of differentiation of milieu and individual, a differentiation that is itself successively transformed through the emergence and development of an individual. Individuations never cease to be reimmersed in preindividual forces that make them possible and that accompany their development and a milieu which always accompanies them in a manner that sustains them.

Simondon is not so much proposing a history of individuations—history requires already individuated beings—as a conceptual understanding of the processes which bring individuals into being through becomings that are themselves not individuated, that take into account historical changes but focus on what changes and how it changes rather than its contemporary setting. Individuated beings can acquire a history and be understood historically, but the processes of individuation are, in a sense, prehistorical and pregeographical. Instead, he proposes a genealogy of individuations, a reconstructive account of how individuals of all kinds and orders of complexity, physical, biological, technical, psychic, collective, and transindividual, bring themselves into being on the basis of the types of order between which they engage and the milieus from which they draw their particularities.

Simondon uses a series of striking examples to describe the (self-) genesis of individuals of different kinds and complexity. He begins with the most simple, the creation of a brick, used since the ancient Greeks as an example of the form-matter dichotomy. A brick, it is assumed within hylomorphic schemas, is composed of two different elements, formless clay and a forming mold. The clay is considered passive relative to the forming effects of the mold, which imposes, from the outside, a form for the brick, one that is in principle infinitely repeatable. This model is the basis for (or perhaps is based on) an understanding, clear in Aristotle's work, of human and animal conception: the semen functions as form giving and menstrual blood—raw material for the newborn—is matter that requires form. Simondon considers such a model "abstract": it takes no account of the actual qualities that both "form" and "matter" require. Such a model must ignore the careful preparation of both the clay and the mold. Each is indistinguishably already form and matter. In making such a relation between the mold and the clay abstract, we do not understand how each is prepared for their mutual yet nonreciprocal use.[13] That is, the microphysical order of clay must align with the macrophysical forces of the mold for there to be a brick that will stand up as enformed matter, as informational matter and the materials are themselves not raw, for each is already worked on, prepared for its task.[14] Brickmaking or sculpture—another favorite image of hylomorphism—is a very particular bringing together of two orders, that of the mold with its tensile force and that of the clay with its mobile consistency—so that mold can more directly influence the nature of the brick than the brick does the mold. Although their relations are mutual, they are not reciprocal. The mold introduces a manner of organization into the clay's transformation into a brick. Both mold and clay are already well-worked integrations of enformed matter in the process of transformation.

The brick is among the simplest of technical objects, but a hylomorphic understanding necessarily ignores the processes of production of both mold and clay, which each have their own consistency and strength through their interaction. The "two half-chains," as he calls them—the chains that link the production of the mold to the preparation of the clay—are ignored. Clay is reformed according to its own self-forming capacities; the mold is put to use through its repreparation, according to its own particular qualities and characteristics. Simondon suggests that more complex individuations occur, in the same manner as the complex half-chains that constitute the formation of the brick, through an iterative transformation, although at a higher level, with materials provided through earlier individuations. If the brick represents the simplest form of individuation, Simondon claims that the individuation of crystals, a far more complex alignment of forms and materials, functions according to the same principles. Crystals are among the most dynamic and seemingly alive products of inorganic nature, the inorganic at the point of its closest meeting with the organic. Simondon understands the crystal as a "limit-case," occupying the border between the inorganic and the organic (*IGPB* 223), and he retains a fascination with such limit cases insofar as they reveal more clearly the becomings that make possible a leap in order or complexity.

The crystal provides Simondon with a kind of paradigm of individuation, one whose features intensify with the growing complexity of different orders of individuations, physical and biological. In many ways, the brick and other simple technical objects are less complex (though not in all ways—at the subatomic level there is immense complexity) than the requirements and conditions necessary for the creation of crystals, which can now also be created artificially or technically with some ease. The individuation of a crystal elaborates an order that is not at work in the creation of a brick. A brick is produced by the introduction of two externally connected forms of matter—a preprepared mold and already worked on clay. A crystal is a process of self-creation, which begins to elaborate a distinction, or a permeable difference, between an interiority and an exteriority, a distinction or border between two sites unfolded from one, capitalizing on the bifurcation that emerges between energy and information. A crystal can grow from a very small seed, an intrusion or irritant, placed within a saturated aqueous solution. The seed grows in all directions in the solution as each layer of the crystal-in-creation provides a base for the next layer as it forms on top. The aqueous solution contains within itself the potential for processes of crystallization, which are only triggered and aligned layer by layer with amplifying reticulation through the intrusion of the seeding element and can in principle continue until all the potentials of the solution are fully crystallized, that is, individuated. The seed-germ is the eruption of a point of singularity within the solution that transforms the solution, a system of metastability, into a point of disparation. The crystal is a "resolution" of the disparation of the system, the point of individuation that produces a provisional unification of the disparate, an individual. The seed introduces a catalyzing element, an informational or organizational tension: it begins to reorganize the liquid in which it is located through its informational forces so they align, become parallel, adhere molecule by molecule to the emerging form while continuously relying on the unspent forces of the solution. The seed does not give form to the solution: rather the seed and the solution, each "agents" with their own forces, must create a mode of resolution of these energetic differentials. The crystal is their invention; a radiating, iterative order is produced that "grows" slowly as far as it can from its initial point of immersion in the liquid. The "problem" is at the level of the mother-liquid and its differential tensions.[15] The seed introduces a way for the problem to be "formulated," and its genesis devises a possible "solution," the growth of a particular crystal with its characteristic shapes, according to the materials it resolves. This seed does not need to grow all at once. It can be reimmersed in the solution to add growth at a later time. This is because of its reticulating structure and because what growth the crystal undergoes always occurs from its topmost layer. The disrupting energy/information of the seed in the solution causes it to restructure.

The liquid solution is a preindividual system whose energetic and informational forces become organized around a point of singularity, the seed, that has been introduced from outside. The disparate forces and energies that enable crystallization involve a reorganization that can align the metastable order of the liquid and the catalytic qualities of the intrusive seed. These two kinds of forces and informational and energetic orders require a mode of encounter that enables each to transform and separate itself while relying on an accompanying or associated milieu. The crystal is a local solution to the instabilities of the preindividual liquid, one that does not exhaust the liquid's potentialities but that orients them in a particular direction. This is the very heart of invention, not human or conscious invention, but the invention of solutions through local instabilities, regions of excess that resolve their energetic and informational forces through the creation of an individual.

The coming-into-being of the crystal is an individuation that occurs, as it were, at the threshold between material and biological individuations. This is why it serves so emblematically in Simondon's writings. The individuation of higher order individuals—biological individuals, psychic individuals or thoughts, human and technical collectives, the transindividual—all follow closely the formal movements, the movements of transduction and disparation, from a preindividual order (an order of larger scale or different forces in the case of different types of individuation) of the ontogenesis of the crystal. Transduction entails that there are no entities, no terms, no orders of complexity in advance of the relations that are set up between systems and their intruding seeds. It is the "logic" of the forward temporality of creation, a mode of approximation or intuition of a potential result, a knowledgeable guess of an invention, addressing the processes of reconfiguration and restructuring of the stabilities and instabilities of indeterminate systems as they bring forth or give birth to individuations.[16] Transduction can be considered the converse of the dialectic—it analyzes not what must be overcome, negated, and left behind as the detritus of history, as do Hegelian and Marxist dialectical models, but what returns, transforms itself without an unusable residue, and that, if it leaves a remainder, leaves it as dynamic and full of potential, an inexhaustible if changing virtuality. This world is not governed by scarcity and lack, but by an abundance of potential, the endless possibility for becoming, and becoming-more, for continual replenishment and transformation through these inexhaustible potentials.

Disparation is another concept that Simondon uses frequently. He derives it from optics. Each eye sees a slightly disparate visual image, an image that is separated in perspective by a few centimetres, the distance between each eye. When we blink, leaving one eye open, then the other, the image we see with each eye is slightly different. When we look with both eyes open, the two images naturally merge into a single, three-dimensional image that appears the same in both eyes. The slight differences in the image, through resolving themselves in disparation, enable us to see even more acutely with binocular vision, which invents a resolution to the disparity in image. As Simondon says, "a given information is never relative to a unique and homogeneous reality, but to two different orders that are in a state of *disparation*; information, whether it be at the level of the tropistic unity or at the level of the transindividual is never available as a form that could be given; it is the tension between two disparate realities, it is *the signification that will emerge when an operation of individuation will discover the dimension according to which two disparate realities may become a system*" (PPO 9–10). Disparation is difference that may find a higher-order existence not in a future unity but as a future impetus that requires a continual invention of modes of mediation, continuing transductions, inventions, and becomings.

BIOLOGICAL LIFE

The ontogenesis of physical individuals, like that of the brick or the crystal, provides a basis for reconsidering the prevailing models of form and matter, ideality and materiality, and informational and energetic transfers between disparate orders. They provide us with a new way of conceptualizing higher order, more complex ontogeneses, those that constitute living beings and their increasingly complex relations. Simondon's model of a preindividual order, which is as yet without individuality but which, through the intervention or operation of a disparate seed or interruption, can produce emergent individuations that resolve some of the tensions, seems to work as well at the level of organic life as it does with inorganic existence. It is only if physical individuations generate a certain complexity in the individuals they produce that biological and psychic emergence becomes possible. The preindividual is the resource not only for the order of physical being, but for all becomings, all orders of individuation, and all kinds of individuals.[17] Simondon proposes the most profound decentering of identity, hierarchy, and binarization, the terms by which every thing thus far has been understood. He claims that such a model is more concrete than the abstractions that signify an entity is identical to itself, fully self-contained.

If there is an ontogenetic leap in complexity—Simondon calls it a hiatus—between the inorganic and even the simplest organic forms—this is because life reorients physical principles and the chemical flows on which it relies to establish a distinction between a milieu of interiority and a milieu of exteriority. This exists in primitive form even in the production of the crystal, for each crystal molecule becomes the interior on which the next molecule lays itself. But this interiority is only apparent or, rather, is only a phase in the crystal's self-formation.

What distinguishes the crystal from the most elementary forms of life is the distinction between a space or milieu of interiority (that space produced by the most simple membrane or boundary) and a space or milieu outside. Life grows from its interior, unlike the crystal which can only grow from its edges.

Simondon differentiates life from nonlife in at least three primary ways. First, a living being's individuality is never finished or finalized, as a crystal may be. A life coincides with a permanent process of individuation, while the physical individual may be generated through a single quantum leap, structured by a single encounter between two incompatible orders of information and energy.[18] Second, individuations of living beings proceed from an internal resonance and not only through the disparation between internal and external milieus. This is why the crystal, or the physical individual, grows only at its extremities, at the points of surface contact with the outside. A living being, by contrast, grows through the integration of external milieu elements into its internal organization. Life has an internal resonance which requires a permanent engagement with its external milieu: "Within the living itself, there is a more complete regime of *internal resonance*, one that requires permanent communication and that maintains a metastability that is a condition of life. . . . The living is also the being that is the result of an initial individuation and that amplifies this individuation—an activity not undertaken by the technical object" (PPO 7). And third, not only do living individuations become from within themselves, in a manner of permanent individuations, they transform their environments, but above all their own individuating interiority. The inner consistency of a living being is a movement of continuous growth and change from within that coordinates with and transforms features of its external milieu, and thereby addresses problems: a living individual is not only a being that can modify its environment, but also "by modifying itself, by inventing new internal structures and by completely introducing itself to the axiomatic of vital problems. *The living individual is a system of individuation, an individuating system and a system individuating itself:* internal resonance and the translation of the relation to itself into information are in this system of the living" (PPO 7).

In other words, life modifies itself, where the physical individual is modified by its milieu; life exists within itself and not only at the borders of its engagement with its milieu; and life elaborates itself through the ways in which its engagements with its milieu reconstitute or reframe its internal resonances. Life exchanges energy and information in the same manner as material individuals, but from a different level or dimension and directed to different problems and different orders of information and communication. Life builds on and accommodates physical individuations that become part of every biological process—blood circulation, nutrition, growth, muscular contractions and movement, the coordinated operation of organs, if there are organs—but in addition, it generates new orders of spatiality (no longer Euclidean) and new orders of chronology or ontogenesis, the term that replaces it:

> The bodies of organic chemistry do not carry with them a topology different from that of physical relations and habitual energies. However, the topological condition is perhaps primordial in the living being *qua* living. The space of the living being is perhaps not a Euclidean space: the living being can be considered in a Euclidean space, where it is defined as a body among others; even the structure of the living being can be described in Euclidean terms. . . . The essence of the living being is perhaps a certain topological arrangement that cannot be known on the basis of physics and chemistry, which utilize in general a Euclidean space.
>
> (*IGPB* 223)

The necessary condition of vital existence is the individuation of a membrane, itself polarized and oriented by the asymmetrical permeability of cells, whether anatomical or functional, which comes to distinguish two different orders while creating a disparation between them. The cell's permeability in one direction is its means of regulating the flow of information/energy in the other: "The living membrane . . . is characterized as that which separates a region of interiority from a region of exteriority: the membrane is polarized, letting pass one kind of body in a centripetal or centrifugal direction, opposing the passage of another

kind of body" (*IGPB* 223).[19] The constitution of a living membrane produces a new topology, a new order of existence, and a new complexity of
relations: "Life emerges as a fold in the tissue of matter and brings about
a bifurcation in the transductive logic of crystalline individuation."[20] Life
is thus not only a different order of becoming than physical individuations but a new topological and temporal folding, a chronogenesis, as
Sauvagnargues calls it, a new alignment, orientation, and dimensionality, the creation of not only an individual and its environment but also
an interiority and an associated external milieu, which both partake in
physical and vital individuations together, infusing a new order of infor-
mation/energy into the chemical constituents of life and a new orientation to its milieu.

The membrane is usually considered to contain life, but Simondon
suggests that perhaps it constitutes life: "You could say that the living
substance that is on the interior of the membrane regenerates the membrane, but it is the membrane that makes the living being alive at each
moment, because the membrane is selective: it maintains the milieu of
interiority as a milieu of interiority in the relation to the milieu of exteriority" (*IGPB* 223–24). This is as true of the most simple unicellular
organism as it is of complex living beings. The more complex a multicel-
lular organism, the more interior milieus exist in its body, each exterior
to other simultaneously internal processes and organs. The organism is
thus not a simple or single interiority relative to a fixed or given exterior,
but a series of orders or degrees of interiority in which what is exterior
to one system (as a gland is to the flow of blood, for example) is capable
of passing into another—different orders of mediation of interiority and
exteriority, of an exterior temporarily integrated and then expelled from
an interior, of an exterior that is the heart of the operations of an interior.
In other words, the living organism is a transductive mediation of different degrees and forms of exteriority and interiority, from their absolute
separation (with the evolutionary eruption of life) to their ever-mediated
cooperation (in technologies). Living individuations occur topologically
rather than geometrically, through the folding of organs, organic processes, and the movements of reticulated foldings that constitute the
brain, leading to greater and more minute mediations of interiority and

exteriority, converting Euclidean space into topological space. This is a point of convergence in the writings of Simondon and Ruyer—the claim that in life, in consciousness in its broadest sense, there is a replacement or overlaying of geometrical with topological surfaces.

If the physical individual is produced historically but carries within itself no past other than that which formed it ("the past does not serve any purpose in its mass; it only plays the brute role of a support, it does not make available the informational signal: the successive time is not condensed"; *IGPB* 224), that is, if there no further virtuality in the inert object, the living being carries its past, all the becomings that created it, in its interiority, in the present. It is the echo of the past in the present that enables an internal resonance and the topological capacity of any interior space to be in contact with all of itself. "There is in effect no distance in topology; the entire mass of living matter which is in the interior space is actively present to the exterior world at the limit of the living being; all the products of the past individuations are present without distance and without delay." (*IGPB* 225).

Accompanying the transformation of the Euclidean space of physical things into the topological space of lived interiority is a conversion of the physicist's conception of time into lived chronology, a time without quantity, a time intimately inseparable from topological transformations.[21] Life transforms the continuity of temporality, the time of physics, into forms of condensation, contraction, succession, chronologies not only of continuity but also of discontinuity and envelopment. All of the past is condensed into the present existence of forms of life, every moment of lived time is connected to all other lived moments "thus for the living substance, the fact of being on the interior of the selective polarized membrane means that this substance has taken into itself the condensed past. The fact that a substance is in the milieu of exteriority means that this substance can come forth, be proposed for assimilation, or wound, the living individual" (*IGPB* 225).

In other words, the polarized membrane that constitutes the interior of an organism contains not only the topological relations that constitute its biological cohesion but also the chronogenetic relations that enable it to negotiate its (temporal) place in its milieu. The membrane is where "the interior past and the exterior future face one another" (*IGPB* 225). The present can be understood as a movement of metastability between interior and exterior, between the past that constitutes the interior and the future which beckons from outside, in which the past helps select those elements of the future that may assist in the regulation of its present and the provision for future actions and relations. For Simondon, the future lies on the exterior of the membrane, the past on the interior of the membrane, and the living being is a manner of regulation of the interaction of the multiple points of the past with the impending actions of the future. Life is the entwinement of topological and chronogenetic transformations, cohering only to the extent that the membrane can retain the disparation of exterior and interior and can produce a self-maintaining metastability in its relations between these different orders. This is why, like the physical or chemical individual, the living individual is "both more and less than unity, carries *inner problems and can enter as an element into a problematic that is larger than its own being*. Participation, for the individual, is *the fact of being an element in a greater individuation*, via the intermediary of the charge of *preindividual reality that the individual contains*, that is, *via* the potentials that the individual contains" (PPO 8). Every individual is more than itself. This means that every individual is open to becoming more, to further orders or dimensions of self-complication. The biological individual contains the potential, a charge from the preindividual, that makes both material and ideal possible not only for bodily but also for psychic and collective existence, for a life of concepts and inventions.

PSYCHIC AND COLLECTIVE LIFE

Simondon's concept of the emergence of psychic life from various orders of complexity of biological life elaborates the notion, shared by Spinoza and Bergson, that all "things" have a degree of consciousness, precisely the degree of consciousness linked to the complexity of the movements of the body. But, unlike his predecessors, Simondon claims that consciousness or psychic life is a property not coextensive with all materiality, but only with the forces of the preindividual from which all forms of identity and becoming are drawn and with particular configurations and orders of materiality, for example, those kinds of material organization that are required to address problems of interiority through perception and affect, the two integral dimensions of psychic life. These two orientations, one directed outward, the other inward, require a new operation and reorganization of biological being to intervene into and regulate its access, through successive individuations, to ever greater elements of preindividual potential.[22] The psychic emerges as a way of addressing problems of living—problems of perceiving and acting in an exterior milieu and problems of affect and feeling in an interior milieu— while developing a mode of acting that addresses how these two different and potentially incompatible orders communicate to function more effectively as perception and affect. The psychic—differentiated thought and affect—emerges but does not separate from biological cohesions, the organizations of organs; it coexists with them, forming as part of a living interior, thinking itself, and the affective energies by which thought engages with biological and natural life. As Bergson understood, life tends to thought, to psychic elaboration. The psychic—thought, the idea, consciousness, the unconscious—emerges to address the unstable relations between the (biological and psychic) interior and the external milieu through which the living being must sustain itself.[23] The interior functions through an internal resonance that folds into the present the force of the past and the structures and forces of the (external) milieu to which it directs itself.

To the extent that the living being is differentiated from but conditioned by its milieu, it creates not one but several orders of milieu and modes of differentiation as it develops a more complex relation across the membrane that distributes life between interior and exterior milieus. Simondon suggests that, to the degree that the body is defined by its relation to an external milieu, psychic operations require not only the body's external milieu but also create an internal milieu (or several) of their own. The psychic must be grounded in its own way as a biological being is grounded in its milieu: thoughts, like the body itself, must participate 'in a ground which gives them direction, a homeostatic unity, and which conveys informed energy from one to the other and from all to each. . . . Without the ground of thought, there would be no thinking being, but only a series of discontinuous representations without linkage. The ground is the associated mental milieu of forms. It is the middle term between life and conscious thought."[24] Thought is grounded, not in reason, which is to say in itself, but in the tensional relations and orientations interior to living beings between affect and perception. Thought emerges through disparation, through entering the zone of a problematic and devising a higher-order solution to spread informed energy with less impact on the living being. Thought is one such solution, a solution that, while it emerges from psychic individuals, also surpasses them in its collective and transindividual impact. One of the developed orders of invention of the preindividual, thought is carried within and produced by living beings through the differentiation of an interior milieu in which it can maintain and elaborate its consistency, in which it is subject to relations with other thoughts, where it is never unconnected from a living body but capable of addressing bodies beyond their inventor.

Affect and perception, capacities or abilities of complex organisms, are the ways in which life capitalizes on the dual orientations of matter/ideality as the preindividual conditions of all things. Perception directs itself to the external milieu. Not to its forms, its images, its commonality (which must be constructed later), but by orienting the living body to a place and things located in it, as a living being in a milieu constituted of vast ensembles of objects. Located on the very rim which distinguished its inside from its outside, perception orients this rim to locate itself, to act, to invent, in its milieu. Perception enables not only the recognition of forms but above all of orientations, movements, gradients, postures—it outlines, not forms, but actions. In a Bergsonian vein, for Simondon, perception removes from the objects of perception what they are in themselves in order to accommodate life's use of them. Perception is a provisional and not always unproblematic mode of resolution for the problem of differentials between its external location and its internal needs.

Affects, internal resonances, and consistencies are never fully separable from perceptions, nor perceptions from affects, because it is through affects, which psychic beings cannot but experience, that perceptions become tinged with the interest of living beings, the living being becomes involved in the objects it perceives, a way of resolving tensions or incompatibilities within and between an interior and its exterior. A new type of living being results, one that not only organizes an interior milieu, as all vital individuations require, but structures itself in two different directions, psychic and somatic, addressing a new order of incompatibility or problem, a new complexity in which the psychic can both amplify or diminish the somatic.

For Simondon, psychic and collective life do not precede each other but mutually condition and require each other: "Psychology and the theory of the collective are therefore linked: it is ontogenesis that shows what participation in the collective and what the psychic operation that is conceived of as the resolution of a problematic area" (PPO 9). He thinks of these as two individuations that are "in reciprocal relation to one another" (IPC 19): the psychic individuates the interior of the living being, and the collective individuates the exterior, the two poles of living existence that continually individuate themselves, each in their own directions, though not without affecting each other. The psychic is the condition for the emergence of the collective and always accompanies collective life, and the collective opens out and complexifies psychic life. Neither the psyche nor the collective can be considered substances or things any more than chemical or physical individuations can: they are ever-elaborating processes, continually in danger from psychologism and sociologism of being reified into entities or substances. They are individuations that continue, and sustain, vital individuations. They are "individualizations," the continuing individuation of a living being, the means by which it resolves new orders of problems in its milieu, both interior and exterior, by individualizing, that is, creating a never self-identical "individual."

The perceptual side of psychic individuation connects the interior of the living being to a series of relations with its exterior milieu, generating problems that it and the sciences human subjects create through the technical magnification of perceptual capacities elaborate; the affective/emotive side of psychic individuation, while it arises internally, and is affected by the impact of the past that also resides there, also orients us to the exterior, where we experience its impact (we do not feel anger or love "in us" but "to" something or someone). Neither perception nor affection are exterior or interior in themselves. They are modes of connection between an interior and an exterior whose relation is never purely internal or external. Perception orients us to a world by enabling us to act in it, preparing bodies for action; affection also orients us to a world by enabling us to feel it, to draw it into emotions that also bring us outside ourselves. If the interior is in touch with its exterior and the exterior with its interior, then perceptions and affects restore some of the preindividual connections that physical and vital individuations have not yet incorporated: "Each thought, each conceptual discovery, each surge of affection reprises the first individuation: thought develops as a reprise of this schema of the first individuation, of which it is a distant rebirth, partial but faithful" (*IPC* 127). The psyche is a continuously recalibrating difference of orders of disparation between interior and exterior, a mode of addressing problems, taking into its operations ever more of the open possibilities of the preindividual.

However, the tension, or orders of incompatibility, within psychic life between the never fully integrated poles of perception and affection and the ongoing yet uncontrollable relations of the nascent subject (animal as well as human—for they are different only by degrees) to its associated milieu remain problems to be resolved, and it is the function of psychic life to address these tensions and to invent ontogenetic solutions that lift it to a new level. The individualizing being is itself a problem, as it is produced from two different orders in a never fully completed or integrated process. This problem of the cohesion and agency of the subject relative to itself (and its own immanent processes) and its external milieu generates anxiety for the subject, anxiety that can both block the processes of becoming or generate inventions for overcoming blockages. As a being never identical with itself, a psychic being is a problem for itself: "the subject feels existence as a problem posed to itself, that is, to the subject" (ILFI 244). The subject bears in itself not only its history, interiority, genealogy but also the preindividual that remains unexhausted by individuation. The subject does not coincide with itself, for something, the preindividual, remains within it that cannot be self-identical (see *IPC* 253).

The subject is unable to resolve this problem in itself: indeed, it *is* this problem. Anxiety is the consequence not only of the impossibility of fully coordinating the outside with the inside, and the impossibility of fully identifying itself as a subject, but also the impossibility of the subject as individual. It leads the subject, never fully individuated and always carrying a (changing) residue of the preindividual within and around it, to a fruitless attempt to individuate the preindividual, to identify and master its milieu, to protect itself from the random, outside intrusions of order that it cannot control. Anxiety produces a strange expansion of the individual subject, a being whose every element and experience touches the furthest reaches of the universe and that now pose for it a danger or a deranging disorder. If Simondon has been charged with mysticism, it is because the intimate relation between the psychic individual and collective existence involves something of an acknowledgment of the preindividual within a part of nature, one's own nature, one's place within collective existence and within external nature, of something that has no identity but potentials for the production and dissolution of all identities: "The anxious being dissolves into the universe in order to find another subjectivity; it is exchanged for the universe, submerged in its dimensions" (ILFI 256).

The anxious being is the one who is ready to shake off something of the subject it has become in order to exceed the individual limits of subjectivity. The subject expands to touch the universe and in so doing brings to a new life something of the preindividual, of nature, that it always carried with it. In opening out onto another subjectivity, in finding a place in collective existence, the individual psychic subject must contract the structures of individuality. It must renounce a certain sense of self-containment within a world of uncontrollable events—the very sense that leads to anxiety—in order to move beyond subjectivity:

"Anxiety is the renunciation of the individuated being and that being agrees to traverse the destruction of individuality in order to pass to another unknown individuation" (ILFI 257), the desire to move beyond itself, to annihilate its yearning for self-containment in exchange for a new opening to a different kind of becoming: "Anxiety already bears the presentiment of this new birth of the individuated being on the basis of the chaos, with which it is in accord; . . . but in order for this new birth to be possible, the dissolution of the previous structures and their reduction in potential must be complete, in an acquiescence to the annihilation of the individuated being" (ILFI 265).

The individuated subject is "invaded" by the preindividual: as solitary subject, it cannot evade anxiety, which can only intensify. Anxiety is an "operation with no action, a permanent emotion that is not able to resolve affectivity" (PPO 9). The solitary subject, the disaffected being, is destined to anxiety if it is cut off from an order of collective being through which it can address its anxiety and enter a new kind of relation in which it can again invent new ways of living in a world that it cannot control.[25] Alone or isolated, the subject as individual is left to anxiety, the insecurity of a being cut off from its milieu; but collective existence provides a "much vaster" place, or many, by which the subject can overcome itself and enter into new relations, not only with other subjects in collective social and political life but also with the preindividual, the universe it touches in the process of its traumatic, anxious dissolution and reconfiguration. Psychic individuations become events in the process of a bigger, more encompassing collective individuation, which is not simply the social mingling of psychic individuals but the order of the elevation of psychic individuals, individuals prone to anxiety, into collective beings, where new kinds and orders of individuation become possible.

Collective individuations resolve some of the tensions generated within the individual expressed in anxiety. Collective life is not cut off from the possibilities of acting; it does not simply feel itself: it acts, invents at a different order. It is able to restore connections between perception and affection that are polarized in an individualized subject. The collective provides a number of ways in which the perceptual and the affective can be restored: it becomes the milieu in which they may come together. For an individuated being, the collective "is the mixed and stable home in which emotions are perceptual points of view, and points of view are possible emotions" (ILFI 261): it is a solution to how perception and emotion can be lived as such. Collective existence enables an individuated psychic being to go beyond itself, to produce a relative context in which to position itself, even to disindividuate itself, to generate a transindividual relation, one that is made possible only through collective existence, even as it remains a kind of excess of collective life. The collective itself is individuated, a second-order operation of the individuation of individuals, one that enables signification and language to be possible and a common existence through sharing the nondiminishing charge of nature in each individual. Individuals have relations with each other only because of a shared collective individuation, a shared charge of the potentials of the preindividual that are distributed through individuals rather than exist as such collectively.

A psychic individual may find itself at home in collective existence; but it is also capable of undergoing further transductions that give it access to even more of the preindividual—the transindividual—but only at the cost of its cohesion as an individual in the collective. As Combes puts it: "a subject cannot encounter transindividual without undergoing an ordeal, that of solitude."[26] The transindividual, as the collective resolution of the tensions of the psychic individual and its responses to its own preindividual conditions through collective life, brings into existence a new order of creation that binds the very processes of individuation with a new mode of knowledge by which we can understand processes and relations beyond individuals of whatever order of complexity. The transindividual erupts, through a kind of Bergsonian leap, through ongoing individuations that carry within them all the prior individuations that made them possible. The transindividual is the preindividual in touch with its own potentials for creation and thus with the potentials for new kinds of psychic and collective life, as well as the creation of new kinds of ethics and new forms of aesthetics.

THE TRANSINDIVIDUAL

The transindividual cannot be identified with collective existence. There are many competing philosophical conceptions of collective existence, "the people," the multitude, the community, whether joined through the social contract or through some other voluntary compact, the collectivity of men. Collective existence for Simondon represents, say, the life of a factory, a farm, a hospital, a school, small- and large-scale institutions and sites of collective production, where many people work together (happily or not) to produce things that could not have been made without social life and that, in turn, constitute the possibilities for a social existence, a life in which individuals may participate with others. Collective life solves the problem of anxiety by resolving the intrasubjective tension that marks individualized life, by bringing others into relation with the subject's self-conception, but not without generating its own loci of tension and its own forms of overcoming. Collective existence gives individualized subjects other subjects to recognize them and to work with, through which a subject can define its social activities and capacities. To the extent that it lives a collective life, it is life that participates in, benefits from, and is limited by the lives of other humans. Simondon is not suggesting that collective life comes "after" individual life, for they remain necessarily coextensive but function at different orders of complexity.

The transindividual, which conditions the social, however, can only begin its own processes of individuation, its own collective individuations, to the extent that the individual, the subject, identity, even collectivity are stripped from the subject and are themselves subjected to the tensional disparation through which becomings occur. The collective, the collection of individuals, an interindividual relation, is one of the ontogenetic transformations the individuated being undergoes, and it requires something different than what individuated beings bring with them to social life. So while the solitary subject finds its place in the collective, and while collective existence enables the invention of the most powerful mediators between natural and biological life through the creation of

language and various sign systems—tools, machines, and technical apparatuses; sciences, arts, philosophy—there is nevertheless a leap between
the individual and the collective which makes possible the emergence of
the transindividual and the rupturing of collective existence.

The transindividual occurs through the collapse of an "identity" or
individuality that enters the social relation, the moment Deleuze discusses
as "a life" hovering between life and death, a life of singularity without
identity, when life is stripped bare of its identity but is capable of provok-
ing the sympathy of strangers. While the transindividual may be identified in the unknown scoundrel in Charles Dickens's novel or in Bartleby,
Simondon seems drawn to the figure of the tightrope walker in Nietzsche's
Thus Spoke Zarathustra.[27] Zarathustra returns to the town to announce the
overman to an incredulous and mocking group: "Behold, I teach you the
overman: he is this lightning, he is this frenzy." Only a tightrope walker
among all the people gathered believed him, and he thus begins his tightrope performance. Zarathustra understood, as only he could, that man is
himself the tightrope that must be walked over to bridge the gulf between
man and the overman: "Man is a rope, tied between beast and overman—
a rope over an abyss. . . . What is great in man is that he is a bridge, and
not an end: what can be loved in man is that he is an overture, and a *going
under*." As the tightrope walker begins his perilous walk between two
towers, a jester jumps out and over him, causing him to fall, shattered, to
the ground, not yet dead, but not able to live. The tightrope walker speaks
about the devil, who tripped him up. Zarathustra affirms the nonexistence
of hell, the afterlife, and the devil to him:

> "The man looked up suspiciously. "If you speak the truth," he said, "I
> lose nothing when I lose my life. I am not much more than a beast that
> has been taught to dance by blows and a few meager morsels."
>
> "By no means," said Zarathustra. "You have made danger your voca-
> tion; there is nothing contemptible in that. Now you perish of your
> vocation: for that I will bury you with my own hands."
>
> When Zarathustra had said this, the dying man answered no more;
> but he moved his hand as if he sought Zarathustra's hand in thanks."
>
> ("Zarathustra's Prologue," Z #4–6)

Between life and death, the tightrope walker learns there is only this life, a life he is about to lose, a life he may have lived in order to live another life, but a life with no less meaning and value because it can only be lived once (and this is why this one life, no other, must be affirmed to eternity). His dangerous vocation is his will to power, his will to overcome himself, risk himself, and for this Zarathustra honors and celebrates him. This episode entranced Simondon. The tightrope walker at the point of death opens up something of the transindividual that collective existence hides. Dickens's scoundrel, Zarathustra's tightrope walker, Bartleby, at the point of their deaths, renounce something of their identity, not everything, but all the marks of personality, all capacities and distinctive qualities—all that counts in social and collective life. There must be a kind of *disindividuation*, a disssociation, for the individual to undo enough of itself to partake in the transindividual, a different kind of becoming that underlies, but sometimes also escapes, the collective and may be capable of reorienting it.

Disindividuation, the withdrawal from collective existence, is not the same as anxiety—on the contrary, it is its overcoming, its "solution" and reconfiguring at a higher level of information and energy. It is an expansion without anxiety, without the fear of being swallowed up by the preindividual carried within individuality that threatens the interior with the exterior milieu's capacity to annihilate it. This is an expansion of the preindividual reality that made individual and collective life possible but that collective existence tends to contain and limit, to regulate and habituate, and that threatens social life in collective practices and rituals. It is always a contingency—like the tightrope walker's death—an event, one that both brings together individuals in a collectivity (even if only momentarily) that enables the transindividual to erupt. The transindividual is possible only through an involuntary, disindividuating, and isolating movement, a disrupting event, in which an individuated subject is subtracted from the collectivity. The tightrope walker is overtaken by an event (an event not outside him, but beyond his control) that removes him from collective existence and, momentarily, brings to him a divine insight, an instant when he understands his place in all eternity, Spinoza's third kind of knowledge, one that can be shared.

This is Zarathustra's gift to the tightrope walker, a friendship that not only honors him with burial but above all gives to him the knowledge of the joy of his eternal return, not as anything other than what he is and has been, but through the events that have occurred to him and how he has lived up to them and become worthy of them. Zarathustra, who must live away from other humans alongside his animal companions, is his friend because, of all the villagers, only the tightrope walker heard him, believed him, and affirmed the will to power. Zarathustra sees in the tightrope walker a companion, someone who also undertakes risk, even death, for what he must do. Together only for a few moments, nevertheless they share something neither alone can accomplish, for even Zarathustra requires companions in order to create, in order to invent new thought, a new morality, new art, and a new kind of life. Together for a moment, each is subtracted from the social—Zarathustra self-consciously, the tightrope walker through an event, the fate which befalls him. Only then does the transindividual emerge, not above or through them, but through a tension between the random but significant, indeed overpowering, event that befalls an individual and the collective to which he or she belongs: that is, through the dissociation of something in the individual from the collective that subsides beyond the social roles and common linkages that contribute to the collective.

Zarathustra's solitude, and the rare moment he shares with the tightrope walker, mocked by the community, only occur away from the collective and outside its norms. Between them, a "rope" is constructed to the future: through the solitude of each, through undergoing the ordeal that the transindividual poses for the individual in the event that strips the individual of his or her subjectivity, the individual, or rather, something in the individual that exceeds identity enters a new milieu, populated not only by natural and social relations but also by incorporeals, ideas, practices that wrench the social and yield from it new work, beyond the horizon of the present. Two such beings, Zarathustra and his unnamed brief friend, in their solitude and isolation, in coming together, can produce a more-than-individual and more-than-collective relation, new thought, new art, a new relation that can create a bridge to the future. What is produced in this rare relation is a new kind of subject, as self-produced as any individuality through disparation, a new milieu, a new closeness to and proximity with an outside, and a new exploration of the preindividual.

The transindividual subsists, as the Stoics say, in the interstices between the individual and the collective and in a rupture between immanence and transcendence[28]: "The transindividual is not external to the individual, and yet it is detached to a certain degree from it: further-more, this transcendence which takes root in interiority, or rather, at the limit between the exterior and the interior, does not belong to an exteri-ority, but to the movement which exceeds the dimension of the individ-ual" (*IPC* 281). The transindividual returns to the preindividual "as the reality which grounds transindividuality" (*IPC* 317), and to its creative tensions, those which threaten the individuated being. It takes these ten-sions as the spur or challenge of engendering further and higher-order individuations, "ulterior individuations" (*IPC* 315) which can only take place *through* constituted subjects and their ordeal of detachment or isolation from the social. The transindividual—an impersonality that can exist between individuals—rejoins the force of the preindividual to generate what cannot be collectively produced (but which collective life admires, values, and requires—at least at times): art, literature, philos-ophy, science, inventions, creations made by individuals to have a life of their own, a collective life, that subsists and transforms collective life from within. The transindividual yields not art at its most typical, a recognizable style, to take just one example, but art at that moment when new kinds of art are produced that transform the ways in which art is understood and undertaken.

The transindividual is "something other than a superior individual, more extensive, but still as individual as that of the human being" (*IPC* 161). Simondon often speaks of the transindividual in semireligious terms (although in terms of a negative theology). But, as with Spinoza, his religious language can be understood in terms of this one world in all its complexity and not a being (or becoming) beyond it. With the tran-sindividual, individuals, through a subtraction of much of their identity and their social existence, can touch, can raise into existence, something of the preindividual, the forces of the real, with a new creativity that is able to invent ways to explore those forces, perhaps not so "useful" to collective life, which yet enhance and produce new forms of collective existence, higher possibilities for creation. The transindividual is what in the individual exceeds individuality and subjectivity yet subsists in the individual and the collective as "a charge of nature," a second out-flowing of and connection with the preindividual that is no longer *a* phase of being, but many phases, oriented in many directions.[29] Individuality is not undone but undergoes a new kind of becoming with its newly constituted milieu, a milieu of cultural and collective objects, technical apparatuses, art institutions, and political practices as well as the (divine) nature of the real from which it sprang.

Insofar as we may be able to survive the severing event of detachment that provides the (provisional yet ongoing) solitude necessary for the eruption of the new, we must maintain prior individuations to be able to add something to them. It is only through returning to the preindividual, from which one has never departed, that new problematics, new tensions, can be addressed in a new order of invention. The transindividual, as that which all individualizations share underneath their various forms of individuality, is what connects the collective through the work of a solitary subject—one such as Spinoza or Nietzsche, who had to withdraw from much of civic life in order to undertake a kind of philosophy capable of sweeping dominant philosophical orders aside—to the preindividual in order to expand it, to bring new forces to it, to make it reticulate new fields, new works, new philosophies. The disindividuated subject becomes less an agent of change than the disrupting germ in a new order of transductions and becomings, this time with social and collective resonance involving a kind of return to what has been left behind, a retrieval of the remainder that is either disposed of or unconsidered in any dialectical operation.

The transindividual subject—the inventor, the technician, the artist, the philosopher—subtracts him- or herself from the social through the mediation of the machine, technical apparatuses, the regimen of practices of the artist, the institutions, modes of operation, and habits of writing—through, that is, a return to and a restructuring of the forces and orders of energy and information that render social and collective life possible. This break is fundamentally different from the anxiety of the single individual, for it is a generative and productive break; it finds a way to create a relation between disparities as anxiety does not. It enables not only a creative destabilization of the individual's capacity to invent but perhaps above all a kind of counter to the normative and collective forces of social life, a new way of being.[30] It may be understood as the condition under which social revolutions, epistemological ruptures, and new kinds of practices can be invented.

While Simondon focuses primarily on technical invention and the production of technical objects and ensembles, some of his claims about technical invention apply equally well to other kinds of invention. He understands technologies, from artisanal tools to complex technical objects (cars, planes), networked apparatuses (diodes and triodes, engines, machines, power production plants, computer networks), and technical ensembles (the car or aircraft factory, the scientific laboratory and so on) as modes of human (and animal) mediation of nature that still carry a part of their preindividual charge within them, thus still containing potential for "evolution" or elaboration, as do all modes of creative invention addressing disparations. In many ways, Simondon regards the technical object as paradigmatic of all human invention, particularly insofar as human creativity relies on the potentialities latent in nature in every act it undertakes, and the more complex its acts, the more they require technical mediation.

If art represents humanity's noblest achievements, Simondon makes it clear that machines too are social accomplishments that produce the lived reality of humans. The machine is no more alien to the human than its own art products. The human becomes human through the organizations of nature, technology, concepts, arts, and politics it accomplishes. The transindividual can be addressed, however, only when a disruptive event propels some individuals to construct, from the preindividual, a transindividual relation that can subtend and transform social, cultural, and political life. It is to questions of art and ethics, strangely part of Simondon's philosophical model of technology, that we will now turn.

ART, ETHICS, AND PHILOSOPHY

Simondon presents a rich understanding of the ongoing relations between living beings, particularly human beings, and the world. The world, through its preindividual forces, is the open-ended, pliable, and transformable source that cannot be used up but, in elaborating itself, makes possible individuals of various orders and complexities, individuals who carry within themselves the increasingly elaborated preceding orders of complexity. In explaining the ontogenesis of beings of all kinds through the growing transformations and orders of complexity that metastable systems make possible, where there is no moment or phase of stability or self-identity and where the capacity for transformation is unceasing, there is nevertheless a directionality, an orientation, a broad trajectory of becomings. Becomings are elaborations, developments, and changes that occur when individuated beings are subjected to the relentless forces of events, encounters, and results from the transformations they induce.

Mediation is required to restore the human to a place in the world from which it is distinguished, and this is largely provided in contrary directions, on the one hand, through technics, man's attempt to objectively organize and regulate the world, and, on the other, religion, man's attempt to subjectively address and find a meaning in the world. Our relation to the world is thus divided in two directions, one technical, the other religious, one oriented to a practical life and the other to a reflective and collective life, one projected outward and the other inward. Between technics and religion, Simondon situates both science and, more unusually but significantly, aesthetics. The ethical direction of our currently technical, religious, and aesthetic impulses are, perhaps without our clear comprehension, oriented to a new concretizing relation to the whole, the relation between man and world, restored to some of the magical cohesion that held it together in its preindividual undifferentiated force.[31]

Religion and technics are parallel and symmetrical relations between the two orders of invention generated by the primordial consistency of the preindividual. If religion organizes the relation between human

and the world through a divine narrative and meaning, technics organizes this relation through "the efficiency of action on singular sites," the
capacity to invent tactics to accomplish a goal using what is available.[32]
Technics and religion, the results of a primary magical division of the
world, require each other and other orders of social life to complete what
is left out of the magical world in its division. They are complements
rather than competitors.

It is between technics and religion, as the two poles that order the
division of man and world from two different directions, that Simondon
understands ethics and aesthetics are positioned, for neither functions
to direct the man-world relation. Each is an attempt to immerse human
practices in the orders of the world, somehow more directly and with
more impact than religion and technics, although by incorporating their
own inventions and by addressing the gulf that separates them. Aesthetics and ethics (and, more conceptually, philosophy and the sciences) aim
to restore continuities and connections that were severed through the
processes of the various orders of individuation, not aiming at somehow
totalizing them (this is the impossible goal of religion, which, even if it
may totalize humanity as one under God, is not able to bring this about
as a fact—on the contrary, it has been a greater force than any other
in the production of many intractable and murderous divisions within
humanity!) but at enabling them to become more, to elaborate their own
becomings and key points beyond the magical order. Aesthetics aims to
reconstitute the reticular universe, the universe before its magical division, the potentials of its preindividual openness through the transindividual opened up by psychical and collective existence. Aesthetics, and
art production, are not "of a limited domain nor a determined species,
but only of a tendency,"[33] a tendency not only of the human, but primarily of the human (180). It is a tendency that the human has toward
the qualities and properties of matter, toward exploring and enhancing,
using organized matter to structure its relations to the world. There is a
becoming-aesthetics not only of the tool but also of the tool user and the
objects on which the tool can be used.

When art is produced, when it is thought or even recognized, it
returns us to something of the intensity, and chaos, of the preindividual

that is both within us and in the world, which we share with the world. Art is one mode of celebration of the capacity of the human to outstrip the collective; I would suggest that philosophy is another. By "returning" to the preindividual by means of the transindividual, a fragment of the world and of the living being come together, something collective is activated, even if by noncollective, that is, singular, means. There is no special object or form that characterizes art. Indeed, for Simondon, there is a certain art that accompanies the simplest technical objects. Art appears not before or outside technics or religion but through them and by appropriating their means of organizing the relations of figure and ground. Art relies on both technics and religion, but it is capable of amplifying each and removing them from their "proper" circuits of operation, technics directed to the order of the milieu and religion to the order of the psychic interior.

Technics has its own kind of beauty, its own economies of invention, style, and use (though Simondon himself seems to prefer a largely functional understanding of the beauty of machines: those machines which bring into their interior as many external factors as possible have a certain beauty or technical elegance in the ingenuity of their design. This marks, for example, his preference for the turbine over the combustion engine, for the triode over the diode, and for the functional car over the car designed for advertising),[34] just as religion relies on the mustering up and harnessing of affects of belonging, community, and universe that are also very common objects of aesthetic production. Under certain conditions of intensification, no object is immune to a kind of aestheticization, that is, to the capacity to reveal a part of the universe from which it comes. Aesthetics refers in Simondon to a process, a relation, and not an object (191). Aesthetics uses an art object to address an impression or expression of the real that the object supports or indicates, but that is part of the real. The art object is the vehicle for the transportation of qualities, elements, or forces that abide in the transindividual: "the real aesthetic impression cannot be subjugated to an object: the construction of an aesthetic object is only a necessarily vain effort for regaining a magic that has been forgotten" (192). The art object is "what prepares, develops, entertains the natural aesthetic impression" (194).

This aestheticization is the process of rendering a material organization most efficiently, a beauty not only of use but above all of organization, not only a fit between form and function—his attraction to Le Corbusier's architecture is explicit—but a fit between present and future, the opening up of objects, qualities, and sensations elsewhere.[35] Any object, act, process, place, or moment can become aesthetic to the extent that it can reticulate—that is, magnify, connect, transform—a relation between a living being and the universe. Every technical object has its own sensory qualities, the sensations that are generated when it is put to use; these sensations are continuous with (and perhaps a condition for) the art work, which can extend them as qualities and give them new resonance and new life in an art work that brings together the subject and world in its own way.[36]

Art continues with greater intensity the process of intuitive sensation that technics enables and that religion also harnesses and directs beyond this world. These are precisely sensations of qualities of this world: "moving more or less continuously to the sensations that artistic instruments give to those who play them: the touch of a piano, feeling the vibration and tension of strings of a harp, the snapping off the strings on the hurdy-gurdy on the cylinder covered with rosin—it's a register that's almost inexhaustible. Art is not only the object of contemplation; for those who practice it, it is a form of action that is a little like practicing sports. Painters feel the stickiness of the paint they are mixing on the palette or spreading on the canvas."[37] Art brings the transindividual directly back to the preindividual and then to the collective. The collective is touched, perhaps even transformed, by this work that recalls and reframes something that is shared only through each individuation. At its best, art is able to return something of the force, that is, the energy-information, of the preindividual back into collective relations. It is capable of reinserting the *apeiron*, a limitless "charge of indeterminacy," to already individuated collective subjects through the creative return of the subject to an immersion in the world.[38]

Artistic (no less than scientific or philosophical) invention makes parts of the cultural and collective world key points through which to collectively navigate through social, political, and natural crises, to aim again at the restoration of a preindividual, less and less divided into figure and ground, more restored to its metastable order. Art resituates metastability within and between social and collective existence, returning to collective life what it has left behind of qualities, relations, sensations. Art enables us to feel something of the more-than-unity from which we came, passions and affects the ancients sought to diminish in us to make us more amenable to the universe's rational order. Simondon outlines, even if briefly, an aesthetics that represents life's affective relations to the world; he will also aim to develop the possibility of a new kind of ethics that addresses nature, that is, the relations between the forces of human subjects, in social and collective life, and the forces of the world, that addresses the earliest phases of individuation and their social consequences: "Nature is not the contrary of the Human but the first phase of being" (*IPC* 196), the first phase that never abides but transforms itself continually through physical, biological, psychic, and collective transductions. If art comes from the individual's immersion in a transindividual that can address what a collective shares, it also directs itself, above all, to the future that the object aims to bring into being: "every inventor in the matter of art is futurist to a certain extent, which means that he exceeds the *hic et nunc* of needs and ends by enlisting in the created object sources of effects that live and multiply themselves in the work: the creator is sensitive to the virtual, to what demands from the ground of time and in the tightly situated humbleness of a place, the process of the future and the amplitude of the world as a place of manifestation" (*IPC* 182).

To the extent that humans can return to the preindividual forces that make all identities provisional, in art, in thought, in technics and other social practices, it is because the preindividual is both material and ideal without distinction, both identity and the undoing of identity, being only through continuous becoming. This is true not only for subjects and collectives but also for all the products of subjects and collectives—art works, technical objects and ensembles, social and cultural practices—that reticulate the preindividual forces from which they are formed into objects, practices, individuals, and collectives capable of bringing some kind of life to the preindividual that the transindividual bears.

Ethics, for Simondon, is part of this movement of temporal and spatial looping—where the being "returns" without ever leaving them to the forces that made it possible in order to constitute for a collective a new field of resonances and amplifications in which more inclusive acts are possible. Acts are more inclusive in the sense that they bring to use, and change, preindividual forces that have been left aside in earlier geneses and in the sense that, radiating from a particular point, more and more individuals within a society become capable of generating inventions of their own. These acts need not be inclusive of more subjects but of more of the transindividual, of what is subtracted from the individual as subject yet shared by all subjects. Ethics is not a morality of actions but Spinozan affirmation of the powers of acting (and being acted on) that are enhanced and amplified by the renewal of the forces from which all individuality and collectivity come. Like aesthetics, ethics is not comprised of ethical objects (whether acts, attitudes, beliefs, norms) but a capacity to bring ways of living into being, to enable ways of living to transform themselves, to address their tensions and invent other, more inclusive, ways of living: in ethics he seeks the "the preindividual of norms" (*IGPB* 244), the ability of norms to transform themselves, to undertake transductions, structural and historical becomings that address the human's (individual and collective) ongoing and ever-changing, ever-complexifying relations to the problem-generating world it occupies.

Ethics is the power of the amplification of acts that may connect individuals outside of and beyond their place within society, the power of affirming a "singular point in an open infinity of relations" (*IPC* 506), which connects to the singularity of each subject in a field of relations with others.[39] Like aesthetics, ethics is the capacity to make the preindividual resonate into higher orders of energy/information so that it may touch and set off new becomings in the processes of (endless) individuation. As a mode of valuing acts, ethics is a reflective understanding that "the value of an act is its amplitude, its capacity for transductive spacing" (*IPC* 334n6), that is, an act has value to the extent that it affects and amplifies other acts. Ethics is nothing other than the affirmation of the inventions of life in all its forms, the setting into resonance of their differences, the reactivation of the openness of the preindividual and the creation of new solutions to tensions, which generate new forms of living.[40]

Like the tradition that precedes him, Simondon proposes a special place for philosophy within the schema of endless individuations and their potential for further individuations, mediating with ever finer, more porous, and nuanced borders between interior milieu and exterior milieu. Philosophy, the discipline of reflexive thinking—Deleuze's construction of concepts and the plane of immanence they populate—founds and accompanies the divisions the preindividual continually traverses and complicates—inside/outside, form/matter, subject/object, even technics/religion—and aims to reunite them with the order that formed them, to restore to them the power of their genesis.[41]

Philosophy, the thinking that accompanies the most primordial divisions of the real, is made possible by the preindividual as much as any other individuated practice, and contains within itself the power of thought, a power that can, by degrees, be refined, as Spinoza understood, by comprehending and reflecting on the place of the singular in the orders of ontogenesis. The power of thinking is as much the result of an ontogenesis as its objects of reflection—indeed, this is why thought is as transductive as its investigative objects. If technics and religion elaborate human life in two different directions, and science and ethics attempt to provide more general knowledge of the localized formations of the history of technics and the history of religion, it is philosophy, the capacity for rigorous and self-reflective thought, the orientation and ordering of sense, the forward and open direction of concepts, that enables, if not the perfection of technics and religion—an infinite task—then at least a knowledge of "the real meaning of these two geneses" (*IPC* 334) made possible by the capacity, not of the human, but of the preindividual, to make thought address the division between interior and exterior, figure and ground. Philosophy *is* an ethics, a way of thinking the genesis and fundamental potential for integration (through transformation) of these divisions:

> Reflexive thinking has a mission to redress and refine the successive waves of genesis by which the primitive unity of the relation of man to the world becomes divided and comes to sustain science and ethics

through technics and religion, between which aesthetic thinking develops. In these successive divisions, primitive unity would be lost if science and ethics were not able to come together at the end of the genesis;
philosophical thinking is inserted between theoretical thinking and
practical thinking, in the extension of aesthetic thinking and of the
original magical unity.

(*IPC* 409)

Philosophy, in other words, a "transfer without loss,"[42] extends the
aesthetic work of expanding qualities and intensities, the scientific work
of ordering principles and regularities, the technical labor of inventing
machines and the networks they require, and the ethical function of
touching and transforming individuals and collectives. It is the conceptual accompaniment of the individuation of each of these orders and its
own genesis recapitulates that of every other individuation. But its project is also synthetic: to bring together disparate domains not through
reduction but through understanding the orders of complexity that
make philosophy itself, reflective thought of the world, possible. It is
a "transcategorical knowledge, which supposes a theory of knowledge
that would be a close kin of a truly realist idealism."[43] Philosophy must
be understood, in Simondon's terms (rather than my own) as a "realist
idealism" that restores both the force of reality and its ideality to the
geneses of orders of being. As such, philosophy, as much as technics and
religion, participates in a movement that is both ethical and aesthetic,
that opens life out onto the real from which it is drawn. In Simondon's
words, which conclude his remarkable text on the transformation of
ontology into ontogenesis, *L'individu et sa genèse physico-biologique*, he
claims that ethics is precisely the affirmation of this movement of individuation, and it is the affirmation of acts that amplify and reticulate
the preindividual and its forces most directly through the inventions of
life: "Ethics expresses the sense of perpetual individuation, the stability
of becoming which is that of being as preindividual, individuating itself
and tending toward the continuity which reconstructs under a form of
organized communication a reality as vast as the preindividual system.
Through the individual, amplicatory transfer [perhaps like a tightrope
or bridge?] coming from Nature, societies become a World" (247).

6

RUYER AND AN EMBRYOGENESIS
OF THE WORLD

*Memory is not the property of bodies. Bodies, or what
appear as "bodies" are the property of memory.*

—RAYMOND RUYER, "THERE IS NO SUBCONSCIOUS:
EMBRYOGENESIS AND MEMORY"

long with the writings of Simondon, Raymond Ruyer (1902–
1987) is one of the key figures in a genealogy of the incorporeal
that I have explored in this book. His work is not widely known
outside France, and even there it has generated only a few monographs
and scholarly papers,[1] all published in the wake of Deleuze's work,
particularly the publication of *What Is Philosophy?*[2] Ruyer published over
twenty books, on the philosophy of biology, cybernetics, technology and
information, religion and conceptions of God, and on psychic, ethical,
and political life. His works are extraordinarily difficult, aphoristic, and
cryptically allusive, based on numerous detailed and sometimes paradoxical examples. While his reception in Anglophone philosophy is
thus far limited, here too it is primarily the translations of Deleuze and
Guattari's work that have stimulated the publication of a few short introductions.[3] In this chapter I will not develop a systematic or thorough
reading of his writings but will focus only on his concept of the mnemic
theme, goals or ideals, ends that form material objects and relations, the
concept of finality that marks every consciousness, every primary form,
every mode of materiality with a sense, direction, or orientation that we
can understand as ideal.

Ideas are not, for Ruyer, any more than they are for all the others addressed here, independent of or separable from the alignments of material forces; values and ideals are directly connected to the ways the world is and our various capacities to act in it. Ideals subsist in and provide sense or direction, less than a telos but more than randomness, for the movements of becoming, the increasing orders of organization that mark material existence from subatomic, atomic, molecular as well as to organic, human, and extraorganic orders. They are immanent in materiality and its orders of complexity. Ruyer does not seek a "subjective idealism" that marks the philosophical tradition from Kant to Sartre and beyond ("There Is No Subconscious," 30), in which the idea as the subject apprehends it orders reality through representations it imposes on the world. Instead he claims he is searching for an "objective idealism," or, as I described it, for incorporeals, in which it is the world itself that generates idea(l)s and indeed generates consciousnesses of many different kinds, including but not limited to the human subject. Ruyer seeks an ontology adequate to the complexities of the world of material objects as understood through the natural sciences, as well as an ontology with cosmological reach, which brings with it a conception of an ethics and aesthetics of existence, ways to live and enhance material existence, together with a concept of the divine that inheres in the orders of this one world.[4]

Before there can be an individual consciousness, particularly a human consciousness, Ruyer claims, there must already be a field in which the individual comes to be constituted: "the individualized field as 'absolute surface' precedes, in formation, the individual who will say 'I' of himself, or who will believe, without saying so, that he is acting like an 'I.'"[5] Consciousness characterizes all primary forms, and the purposiveness and directionality of primary forms. For Ruyer, the Stoics develop a model of how philosophy, in contemplating and coming to understand the complexities and order of the world, enables us to achieve inner goals and directions even amid social upheaval: "The Stoic is free in bondage. Collective happiness or unhappiness is an indifferent framework in which the individual makes his personal embroideries, accomplished or not according to his talents."[6] The Stoic realizes a kind of path to self-satisfaction, a way of being, a *Tao*. Instead of a Person-God, God as the superhuman projection and fulfillment of human identification, Ruyer is more interested what he calls a Tao-God, a path, indistinguishably material and spiritual, a way to understand, participate in, and help constitute a larger order.[7]

Ruyer's God, like Spinoza's, is not separate from the world but coextensive with it, for the world is "in" God as much as God is "in" the world, not as presence but as a virtual, potential, or future. Consciousness, prepersonal or impersonal, before and beyond the human as well as comprising it, characterizes the directionality, the capacity for complexity and even life, carried in the atom, its subatomic ingredients, and molecular connections. Ruyer is interested in an order that runs through all existence, an order that could be understood as divine, but whose divinity resides in its terrestrial form-producing capacities. For Ruyer, God cannot be understood outside creation but is the name for an order, a regularity, and a form, a direction, a pull of the future on the present that the creativity of the world expresses: "Man acts, thinks and creates validly, veraciously, aesthetically without aiming at a 'substantive' value (such as Beauty, Goodness, Truth)—which would be very awkward and at the same very pedantic, and would risk making his efforts sterile. In the same way, God (so-called and otherwise) exists only by participation without observation."[8]

This idea of "participation without observation," immersion without a separate position to provide perspective—*survol*, overflight, self-survey without distance—is the very center of Ruyer's conception of being, life, and the divine. Ruyer aspires to an ontoethics and ontoaesthetics that addresses the creativity of the world and the openness of the future. The call of the future, the call to make a future according to forms and patterns that do not annihilate us, and that enhance and create themselves, is the center of his ethics and his conception of religion. He understands the ontological implication of any ethology and the fact that any ethology, any ethics of life's self-regulations, any axiology also entails an aesthetics of existence. And such an ethical and aesthetic orientation is itself the expression and creation of values, both mundane, organized by cultural and social life, and divine, of a natural and cosmological order.

Like Nietzsche, Ruyer also understands a will to power, a spark of the divine, that marks not only the operations of subjects in relation to each other, social and cultural life, but of every organ, cell, and biological system as much as it does every atom, molecule, and material object or process. For Nietzsche, the will to power is the force that takes a thing as far as it can go, that wills its own self-expansion and intensification. This will to power, which seeks to command (itself) in its indifference to and separation from all other competing wills, always has a direction, the opposite of Newton's law of the conservation of energy, the law of death. The will to power seeks to expand itself to the maximum. This directionality—further, always more—is the affirmation of its being as becoming. This directionality is the object of Ruyer's philosophical speculations: to what is it directed, what does it aim in the future to do? This is precisely what finalism articulates—not a final state or stage, an end or telos but a trajectory of continuing elaboration/transformation, not *to* something, an ideal, but *from* something, that is, a becoming. Following Uexküll's understanding of the contrapuntal relations between a living being and its *Umwelt*, Ruyer also sees this ideal in terms of a harmonic melody, a musical variation upon an environmentally oriented melody, a mnemic theme.[9]

Deleuze describes Ruyer as "the latest of Leibniz's great disciples,"[10] a thinker of the monad, which can no longer be considered a self-contained and self-enclosed unit, but rather one composed entirely of windows and doors, of openings, a being that enfolds into its inside what is outside. Deleuze is fascinated by Ruyer's conception of the self-forming properties of "primary forms," which range from the most elementary forms of matter, the atom and its subatomic ingredients, to the most complex forms of self-production that characterize all forms of life. There is something that links all of materiality to the entirety of ideality, an order and organization, an orientation forward. Thought, consciousness, perception, the orders of internal resonance, cannot simply appear ex nihilo, nor can consciousness be an emergent property or quality supervening on a certain order of complexity in the organization of matter. Mechanism, the conceptualization of matter as composed of passive determinable and separable units regulated by external causes, can never explain the eruption of consciousness, subjectivity, or life.[11] Moreover, it *reduces* consciousness to the cognitively calculable, subjectivity to behavior, and life to its genetic code. It treats consciousness as if it can only be understood from outside itself, as an object of reflection or speculation rather than the very condition for its own self-organization and self-questioning.

Writing at the time of the first emergence of general systems theory, cybernetics, and robotics in the 1940s, Ruyer argues that there is an irreducible directionality to the operations of primary form that, while composed entirely of materiality in its various configurations, exhibits an orientation that belies the order of external determinations and can be understood only without distance, without external observation, in an immediacy. Primary forms are not externally determined but are the conditions under which any determination can have effects, the order of implication that causes set off in consciousness. Rather than an anthropomorphic projection of human consciousness onto the realms of the inorganic and the organic, Ruyer seeks a common quality, sense, or orientedness as the condition of every consciousness, including those before and beyond the human. Consciousness, in Ruyer's sense, is what responds rather than is an effect of the order of causes: it is the capacity to make causes its own and to use them as a mode of self-creation. Nietzsche understands this as a "style," a way of living. The brain, the embryo, and all the organs capable of forming themselves—also conditions of the most elementary forms of life—must continue a trajectory that is already virtual in the constituents of its most elementary ingredients, from the atom and its constituents to the creation of cells, organs, circulatory systems, and living bodies. If mind or consciousness occurs at the higher levels of organic functioning, it must also characterize its most elementary, non- or preorganic conditions.

Ruyer is interested in the genesis of living forms, the conditions under which self-formation is possible, the organic and inorganic conditions under which consciousness, or immediate self-proximity, can occur. Like Simondon, Ruyer is interested in the processes and orders by which life emerges from and maintains a continuity with the material forces that compose it. Ruyer too is concerned with

technologies, automation, machines, and mechanistic functioning—
and the limits of automatism—that characterize a rigidly conceived
and reductive materialism, determinism, the automatic operation of
mechanical principles. Materialism needs reconsideration to be rendered more complex, provided with an orientation to the future and
some kind of energetic forming force from the past that enables things
to maintain a cohesion over time. Like Simondon, Ruyer is interested
in understanding material things, processes, and living beings as sites
as well for ideal or conceptual self-production. The emergence of life is
not the wild deterritorialization of elementary matter but the magnification and intensification of open-ended, self-forming principles that
also regulate material events.

Life cannot be understood mechanistically; instead it must be understood axiologically. The *axiological cogito*, the cogito that values rather
than knows, is foundational for Ruyer; this cogito is fundamentally
free insofar as it searches for values, even in arguing, as the determinist
does, that we are entirely caused.[12] In displacing Descartes's epistemological cogito, the axiological cogito resolves the problems of solipsism,
dualism, mechanism, and deism that Cartesianism entails, to ground
the reasoning cogito in a world, provided with an inner cohesion that
accomplishes the connections with everything beyond the cogito.[13] The
axiological I, in seeking values, grounds itself in a world that always
already has value, in which values are the theme to which life must
respond. Moreover, what the cogito demonstrates is not an "I" that
knows itself, but something fundamentally impersonal, "the Agent, or
the Acting,"[14] that is, an acting, an agency well below the level of the "I,"
a doubting, a knowing, a believing, a valuing that acts, each a kind of
self-creating consciousness.

In what follows I focus on a few keys concepts in Ruyer's work that
indicate his own unique version of the concept of the incorporeal—
primary form, immediate self-proximity, and embryogenesis—by exploring one strand of his thought, that of the self-constitution of primary
form that also helps to explain the self-production of the embryo and
the brain.

PRIMARY OR TRUE FORM

Ruyer's understanding of form is decidedly anti-Platonic. Forms or Ideas are never perfect, nor are they separable from the material, the actions and processes that materialize them. Forms do not produce an unformed matter; for Ruyer there is no such thing as unformed or pure matter, just matter in its various forms and under particular conditions, with its own potentials for change. Ruyer is interested in the sense of things and events, the themes to which things, primary forms, tend.

We can distinguish between two kinds of forms. There are forms that exist in material equilibrium. Whether natural or cultural, they are an aggregation of material elements brought together into a composite structure. A house, a car, a bridge are all planned structures, aggregates, or composites, subjected to wearing and decay, surviving as long as they do largely due to inertia or external intervention (maintenance, repairs). They constitute the material needed for the operation of a system in broad equilibrium. They are composed by the accumulation of parts integrated together piece by piece, each part more or less self-contained before the construction of the aggregate. Some parts might wear out more quickly than others. Eventually, because these composites are not self-repairing, they will fall apart. Composites, aggregates, or, more broadly, secondary forms, are capable of mechanical composition and thus either decomposition or recomposition.

There are also dynamic structures, primary or true forms, that can never be produced by the accumulation of parts or mechanically, but must always produce themselves before anything can be produced with or from them. Such forms are no longer composites, with parts existing side by side (*partes extra partes*), but a unity or cohesion of forces, a form, that is a structuring activity, one which can be understood but not decomposed. Dynamic forms are self-structuring, that is, they maintain and "repair" themselves, they maintain a consistency and an orientation in the processes by which they continually create themselves. True form is a consciousness that is both a form to be accomplished, a mnemic theme that is transpatial, a future conditional and a bodily integration that enables action in a spatiotemporal world directed toward mnemic themes and the values by which they are embodied. Primary forms are composed of relations that can be inferred but not observed, or at least are not capable of being observed from an external position. Primary forms can be attributed both a "life" and a "consciousness," even though they cannot be understood on the models of life and consciousness that we attribute to ourselves. Far from being anthropomorphic, consciousness constitutes the conditions under which human life and human consciousness become possible, the dynamic forces of self-perpetuation that preexist life and make it possible and that each type of life develops in its own way.

The dynamic, form-giving nature of such primary forms persists even in a continually changing organism. Every living thing is subjected to constant changes from its milieu and from its own ever-changing morphology, processes of development, and aging. If living things are never stable forms, always undergoing change, nevertheless there is something that subsists in these changes: not anything bodily—for every cell and organ is in the process of self-regeneration or self-replacement—but what Ruyer understands as a melodic or mnemic theme, not locatable in space or time but that subsists and accompanies life, and all primary forms, through its processes of autoaffection. The theme that each living being performs is its potential (or, in Bergson's terms, its virtuality, in Simondon's its preindividual charge), the form-bestowing heritage it must use to make itself. This is a reserve of dynamism, a direction for growth, the orientation to which each individual body and its immediate self-proximity—its form, consciousness, psyche, or even soul—is directed as it creates itself, according to the theme it plays and that it will continue to play in spite of accidents, mutilations, and other contingencies. Consciousness is not a separate organ added to life at a certain stage of its growing complexity; rather, it is the condition for the dynamic unity of an organism, an organism's capacity to survive, to act in its environment, in short, to enjoy itself, to experience autoaffection, immediate self-enjoyment.[15] This capacity for self-proximity, a relation to oneself that occurs without distance or perspective, is the defining condition for any primary form. It characterizes life long before the evolutionary emergence of man, long before the development of a central nervous system and brain: even the most simple and primitive organisms—and the atomic and molecular structures they make in the process of their self-formation and self-enjoyment—function and make themselves through autoaffection.

It is the capacity for *survol*, absolute survey, immediate self-proximity, "surview" or "overflight," that connects Ruyer's concept of consciousness to organic form. Consciousness is that which is in immediate contact with all of itself at once. Consciousness is the unity and direction of the organism and its material conditions. Its consciousness is not separate from or other than a living body, or a primary form, but is its capacity to remain in touch with all of itself without distance.[16] Consciousness, psychic life at its most simple, is directed to a living engagement with its milieu and provides a kind of finality—a neo- or quasi finalism that is less a teleology, a definite goal or end, than a continually renewed direction, a sense, not unlike Spinoza's concept of conatus or Nietzsche's will to power.[17] Consciousness is not the result of absolute self-survey; it *is* this process. Primary forms cannot be understood part by part. Instead they require some understanding of the forces of cohesion that draw all "parts" or elements into a totality where they can no longer function as determinable parts. The minerals and nutrients that we require for our living being are transformed ("blended") into the body's operations without us being capable of restoring the parts that compose it.

A primary form, consciousness, however, commonly mistakes itself for an object, while ignoring the qualities of autoaffection that characterize its operations. This explains the tendency to reductionism in the sciences of consciousness—psychology in its behaviorist, psychoanalytic, and gestaltist forms—where each reduces the subject to a repository of the meaning, significance, or impact of external objects. In its Ruyerian sense, consciousness is the condition for a self-proximity that confuses itself with objectivity, a consciousness transparent to itself, through which a being accesses a world while engaging and elaborating the mnemic themes, the bodily and psychic styles, that direct it to the future:

> Consciousness seems to be a sort of invisible medium which offers us objects on which we may exercize [sic] our ability to act. It is self-forgetting. The manner in which its acts on these objects, like the manner in which it perceives them, escapes its notice. It will only consider the object, which it knows and on which it acts. A child will forget to count himself when he is counting the playmates of his band. It is easier for him to recognize his brother as his brother, than himself as the brother to his brother. Furthermore, when consciousness recognizes its own existence, it gives itself the status of mere object. It refers to itself as a being with permanent properties, independent of its action.[18]

Ruyer claims that as consciousness comes into contact with the materials it disappears into the surface it works on, becoming an absolute surface even though the object may exist as an aggregate or composition of elements. As work for the craftsman, in which he or she is intensely engaged, consciousness of self disappears, to be replaced by the objects "in" consciousness: "The craftsman is lost in his work in progress. Not lost, but he identifies himself intensely with the form of this work being transformed by his hands and therefore his eyes. The work in progress is an 'absolute surface' and not a series of points, of isolated parts functioning together progressively. The hand and the eye are not essential for the essence of consciousness that is 'subjectivity,' the 'for itself' of every 'absolute surface.'"[19]

If we take Ruyer's example of the visual perception of an old-style checkered tablecloth,[20] we can distinguish between *vision*, the perception that connects the eye to an object, and the sensation of *seeing* it generates in consciousness. They closely resemble each other, they are perhaps two phases or stages of the elaboration of sensation or self-enjoyment, but with a crucial difference that explains the nature of this immediate self-contact that marks all forms of consciousness, from the atom to the brain. Ruyer imagines himself seated at a table with a patterned tablecloth. In theories of perception, especially those issuing from Descartes's conception of the cogito, the eye is normally understood as the organ that sees the tablecloth and presents it to the brain or mind to confirm. But if the eye is the disembodied observer of the table, then we need to invoke another eye to confirm the existence of the eye that sees over the table. Ruyer suggests that, in claiming the organ sees in itself and that consciousness is somehow a supplementary dimension added to perception, a place where perception is registered or cognized, we misunderstand the fundamentally autoaffective nature of consciousness. Like Descartes, we reduce consciousness to a substance added to perception to confirm or question it. For Ruyer, when we perceive the table's surface, it is not a mediated perception in which the mind confirms what the body presents to it; rather, in perception, consciousness and its objects are one, without clear division, without separation or distance.[21] Perception does not resemble the photograph except in the most superficial ways (the camera remains a means of mechanical reproduction that always requires both distance and perspective, that changes its representational objects according to where, outside those objects, it is located; moreover, each photograph has edges). While the seated subject requires distance in order to see the tablecloth, it becomes conscious of the tablecloth without distance. The tablecloth in our perception is an object of self-conscious autoaffection or self-enjoyment, as internal and without external perspective as tastes and smells and other perceptions are in consciousness. I do not access my consciousness from another consciousness: likewise I do not access the objects I perceive and act on from the outside. To the extent that I engage with and work on such objects, they are presented not to me so much *as* me. I participate in an overflight of their qualities.

Each checkered square on the tablecloth covering the table exists in contiguity with and in a spatial relation to all the others, capable of being separated and focused on alone (*partes extra partes*, outside each other); in consciousness all the squares are grasped together as a single unit, without, however, ignoring the qualities of each particular square. In consciousness there is no vertical or perpendicular perspective from which to provide an overview, for access is always on the surface, the metaphysical or topological surface that joins the object to consciousness. Consciousness does not perceive by internalization but by immediate or direct overflight, direct contact with the unity of the object without observing itself. Action without external observation, "participation without observation," indicates an immanence of things in consciousness and of consciousness in things. Consciousness, in other words, makes its objects internal to its actions at the cost of being unable to access itself except as an object, subjecting itself to the error that sees the object in front of a consciousness rather than as part of consciousness.[22] This is the difficulty of introspection, which always tends to objects rather than to consciousness itself, which cannot know itself as an object, cannot distance itself from itself. Consciousness brings into itself what it accesses and cognizes while nullifying its own internality: "Introspection is difficult because an object tends to obliterate the consciousness of the action which defines that object."[23]

The tablecloth is a composite of interconnected parts without a form to bind it; it lacks the qualities that would classify it as a primary form. The tablecloth is laid out on a physical surface. But the tablecloth in consciousness, as it is perceived, is a form, interconnected and interdependent elements, a metaphysical or absolute surface. The tablecloth as it occupies the metaphysical surface is a unity, a whole, that is, an activity, a cohesion. If perception as a physical and physiological process requires perspective and outsideness, visual and other sensations are of the order of consciousness itself; they follow the principles of autoaffection, of immediate self-contact without distance. The table, as seen, does not obey the laws of geometry, the requirement of a supplementary or perpendicular, external viewpoint; it obeys the principles of perspective without distance: "It is a surface seized in all its details, without a third dimension. It is an 'absolute surface,' which is not relative to any view external to it, which knows itself without observing itself."[24]

A visual sensation is topological, flat, without third dimension, without verticality or height. Consciousness "has" a visual sensation only to the extent that the sensation occupies consciousness without distance; consciousness becomes coextensive with the sensation without residue or leftover, and, unlike a perception, the sensation ceases to have edges or borders, being fully submerged in consciousness. Such a consciousness has no location, indeed its location is infinitely extendable to the degree that it senses, conceives, affects, and is affected by its objects and co-occupies the object. The sensation is "true form" as much as consciousness itself is "true form." This consciousness is ubiquitous, not able to be located in one place, existing without distance from itself. In this, consciousness remains, surprisingly, rather close to the peculiar non-localizable true form of subatomic particles, a consciousness before or without subjectivity, "subjectless subjectivity" as Bains describes it, a consciousness that makes human subjectivity possible and undermines its aspiration to the position of outside observer, knower.

MNEMIC THEMES

It is significant that Ruyer does not locate consciousness in a human subject or identify it with the brain's cognitive abilities, nor does he see it as a unique accomplishment of the highest forms of life. Consciousness in his specific sense—self-proximity, autoaffection—must already exist in the world, and especially in its most elementary particles insofar as consciousness exists in the world now. It does not appear magically, an emergent property of a certain degree of complexity in the organization of matter. This is the continuity in nature that Ruyer seeks, a continuity that links the most elementary material relations to the logic of sense, the order of values, and the domain of the future. Elementary particles, the atom, its subatomic constituents, and its relations with other atoms in the molecule, condition and make possible consciousness in its more recognizable forms. The atom and its constituents share with embryos and brains the capacity for immediate auto-overflight or self-survey. Atoms must be considered primary or true forms in continuous touch with their constituents, as must subatomic particles and quantum fields. These are forms, that is to say, structuring activities rather than passive or inert matter structured by something outside.

It is easy to see how Ruyer might be understood as a subjective idealist, one who projects the qualities of human consciousness onto the nonliving world. This is indeed how his work has been commonly dismissed. But, given his interest in post-Einsteinian and subatomic physics, it is difficult to accuse him convincingly of mistaking what is material for what is ideal. The ideal is not separate from materiality but materiality in its primary form. Life itself could not be possible without the self-forming and self-orienting properties of matter at its most elementary. The atom is Spinozan—it perseveres in its being and its activities adhere to a "norm" or a direction, the possibility of certain liaisons with other atoms or its own self-regulated activities. It performs itself, its identity or consciousness such that it directs the atom's actions. The atom is what it does, and what it does is to maintain a certain cohesion and consistency, a distinctive "style" in its actions and in its potential and actual relations with other atoms. It acts according to an ideal, and when its actions are interfered with or perturbed from outside, as in scientific experiments, it attempts to restore its own natural orientation. In this sense, we can understand that even the atom is free—it acts according to its own modes of self-regulation, according to its own ends, which even the most advanced physicists are only now beginning to understand. This is not "free will," the capacity to make a different choice under the same circumstances, but acting in accordance with what is self-regulated, according to a self-generated, self-affecting ideal.[25] An atom and all its constituents continuously form themselves into an autoaffecting form. They are not composed or decomposable mechanically. Indeed, for Ruyer, the atom is constituted by the cohesion of quantum fields, forces that are self-generating and immensely difficult to detangle or unravel from their constitutive interactions. The electron, for example, must be in continuous touch with all of the quantum field at any time. Wherever it occupies one location in a quantum field, it occupies all locations.[26]

We can say, as long as it is clear that we are not attributing a human version to the atom and its molecular combinations, that the atom has purpose and direction, has its own orientations and thus its own consciousness, one precisely as complicated as the actions it can accomplish.

Its consciousness *is* the activity of these actions. As primary form, the atom is free, not in the sense that it can do anything, but in the sense that its own characteristics, its own internal constituents regulate themselves according to a path that has become relatively predictable to science, that is, which exhibit their own order, manner of acting, and modes of connection with other atoms. An atom "knows" what it is capable of, more than we are capable of understanding. This knowledge is not mechanical, *partes extra partes*, but internal, from within the atom, the electron and proton in their relations, in a quantum field. Bergson understands that there is what he calls "a spark of indeterminacy" at the atomic and subatomic level, but Ruyer enables this concept to be more carefully articulated.[27] It is not that there is an indeterminacy at the level of the atom (or below this level, with its subatomic ingredients); it is that the atom has its own qualities of "consciousness" that we can come to know at first mechanically and only later, with the development of more nuanced sciences, can we see that the atom must be as much in self-contact, have as much autoaffection or self-enjoyment, as those complexes that are created from atoms—molecules, macromolecules, living cells, organs, embryos, brains, and living beings.

Primary forms cannot be understood as such from any external viewpoint. They exhibit the characteristics of a field that brings into being connections that are regulated internally rather than added together externally, and whose internal bonds, while "invisible," are always in immediate contact with each other. Molecules are created by the self-forming properties of interacting atoms, as atoms are themselves self-forming properties of interacting subatomic particles that do not provide them with a coherent identity so much as with a coherent behavior, a behavior or movement regulated from within, a pattern of actions, the connections it can make. When atoms combine to form a molecule, "the connecting and interacting electrons are not localizable."[28] Molecules are not "made" or do not make themselves through the side-by-side placement of atoms: it is only to the extent that atoms of different kinds are capable of transforming themselves through the molecular bonds they form that a new kind of being is created, beyond its constituents, with different properties and qualities.

Ruyer develops his understanding of the qualities of living beings, individuals in the process of individuation, from microphysics.

> The fundamental paradox, which is the origin of all the others, is that a domain of primary consciousness is in "absolute survey"—that is to say without any need of an external scanning—that it possesses a kind of *autovision without gaze*. This character has no analogy in classical physics, but it does in microphysics because the domains of consciousness come directly from microphysics, which are already in autosurvey. . . . In order to "speak" of primary consciousness, to evoke it, we must use expressions like "form perceiving itself," a "form that sees itself without eyes." . . . It is very difficult to admit that a protoplasm, a molecular edifice, an embryo, an organic tissue or a cortex, are conscious of themselves (possess their own form) before becoming, by added modulation, conscious of the form of other beings, and without being obliged to pass by this detour.[29]

Subatomic particles, atoms, molecules are the lowest levels of "agent," or "consciousness," the most elementary patterns of action without external supervision or observation, purposive action that has a self-given direction. They are centers of finalist activity. The atom, molecule, and their ingredients have the absolute overflight of form, which is to say that their actions are the forces of connection: they form themselves. While aggregates—molar relations, structures, mechanisms composed piece by piece—are the objects of Newtonian physics which views even atoms and their ingredients as passive solids, it is "microphysics," the exploration of the subatomic realm, that reveals the operations of true form at its most elementary. All such primary beings—continuously in touch with all of themselves without distance, in autoaffection—can be distinguished from aggregates, which can be understood by the decomposition of their parts. Primary beings, by contrast, have parts only abstractly, and any decomposition results in their destruction. Primary forms are self-forming forms in auto-overflight, continuously in touch with all of themselves without distance or external perspective. They are virtual forms, capable of actualization in numerous, but constrained, directions.

CELLS, ORGANS, BRAINS

There is a direct connection between the inorganic world, which consists in both primary forms and aggregates of various kinds, and the organic world. If primary forms are always in immediate self-proximity, in absolute overflight, and aggregates or structures exist with parts side by side without forming organic or internal connections, then, as Spinoza, Nietzsche, Deleuze, and Simondon affirm, there is an order that connects the most elementary (and dynamic) forms of matter to the operations of all forms of life, all forms of consciousness. In Ruyer's understanding, materialists have misunderstood the complexity of materiality to the extent that they conceive of matter as passive, receptive, or reactive. Matter is self-forming, either through its own internal forms and forces or through the operation of external forces that shape it into aggregates and structures, such as a rock, a cloud, a group, which exists by addition and can be analyzed by decomposition or calculation. To the extent that it is self-forming, the direction of primary forms is never random—this is Ruyer's objection to a Darwinism that sees the organism as mere responses to external or chance events or to a preformed (and eventually readable) but randomly mixed genetic code. Seeing life as the result of a random arrangement of genes, or as a response to the contingency of random events that serve to remove the less fit and distinguish them from the more fit (natural selection), can never explain how life arises or the coherent and operational forms it has always taken. Such an explanation ignores the orientedness of the biological body to its environment and the fact that, to the extent random events occur, they occur within a frame to which the living being is already oriented. Evolutionary evidence does not show creatures half formed or partially formed—every living being has a cohesion, a consistency, a speed, a mode of engaging with its milieu.

Ruyer talks of an "invisible world" of unseen and unseeable interactions that we sometimes mistakenly, through faith or superstition, attribute to God. He claims that this world is not divinely ordained, but makes itself, in all its levels and orders of complexity, according to principles that are transpatial, imposed by the forces of time and the nature of bodies in their self-forming capacities. He understands that atoms, molecules, cells, organs do not form randomly, by accretion or external connection, but only when there is a capacity to bring inside primary form all the conditions that enable it to make itself, even as it is capable of great variation: "To take on a certain task implies accepting a certain obligatory itinerary."[30] Ruyer calls these "mnemic" or "transpatial" themes, not eternal or a priori necessities, neither Platonic nor Aristotelian forms separated from matter, but patterns or melodies, cohesions or consistencies through which primary forms develop themselves according to their nature, forms that generate that nature.[31]

The invisible world of transpatial or mnemic themes is a world in which the energy and direction of consciousness must come before there can be a cohesive thing, in which a thing comes into existence only because of the self-forming properties of material connections that function according to these themes. The transpatial theme pervades all of time, to the extent that it constitutes the melody, the rhythm, through which each thing forms itself. Primary form appropriates themes that have already been laid out for it in advance, not a priori like a command, but more like the musical performance of a score, which preexists and to some extent directs but does not determine each performance. Ruyer understands the mnemic theme as the inherited potential of each form of material organization; it can be understood in terms of the bonds of connection or patterns that enable atoms with particular qualities to connect with others in their own particular way—a mnemic theme housed in the orders of chemical connection according to which the world organizes itself. Species can also be understood in this way, each form producing itself, amid great variation or improvisation, in space and time according to a pattern or form which directs it to the future.[32] Such themes are not norms but modes of self-formation according to a form which precedes the individuals and collectives it forms and which explains the family resemblances generated by both chemical reactions and evolutionary changes.[33]

Ruyer understands the mnemic theme as transpatial in the sense that, as atomic, molecular, and organic primary forms are individuals with a certain degree of chemical and living cohesion, with a finite existence, they come and go. What survives is the mnemic theme, which is a pattern of possible connections that constitute and enable primary forms. They are not transpatial in the sense that they are unchanging or fixed, but in the sense that these patterns of internal alignment and organization preexist and postdate the organization of any particular individual, directing not only forms we already know but also the modifications and transformations—the potential—they contain. It is by means of the mnemic theme that values are imbued to organic forms, a direction is provided in their bodily growth and organization: "Nature (*sive Deus*) is never, apparently, overly concerned with the exact number of individuals: birch trees, herrings or men. The exact number of units is apparently unimportant. It only prefers large numbers as a precaution, to maintain the species. The same is not true for the theme that can be represented as external to the self-conscious subjective tableau present and actual, extended in a spatial field, whether it be the theme-form (in the case of the unicellular entity or young embryo) or of a theme-image or idea (in the case of a second order cerebral consciousness)."[34]

Values do not emerge directly from primary forms, but from the relations between bodily organization and the themes they are to actualize, the directions to which they are internally oriented. Primary forms bring themselves into being only to the extent that they can mutate this mnemic theme into a spatial and temporal organization, bringing the transpatial or the "eternal form" into existence in self-created individuals and directing individuals, through their morphology, to move in a determinate corporeal manner. The structure of an organism, the layout and interaction of its organs relative to each other, is the means by which the mnemic theme is concretized in space and time, in and as a particular being. The mnemic theme provides an iterable form through which a being can create itself and to which the organization of its organs tends.

Ruyer develops his account of the priority and precedence of memory over being, consciousness over biology, both utilizing and moving beyond Bergson's understanding of the place of memory in human consciousness. Bergson is indebted to the understanding of habit and memory in the work of Félix Ravaisson.[35] Bergson carefully distinguishes habit-memory, memory that is induced by the repetition and contraction of similar actions, such as learning a poem by rote, from what he calls "memory-proper," the concrete remembrance of a specific event which can be accessed only by a "leap" into the virtuality of the past. Habit-memory is bodily, stored in the body's behavior and triggered by a signal that begins the body's mechanical or habitual response; while memory-proper is imagistic, though not located in the mind but in the past itself, to which memory directs us. For Ruyer, it is incorrect to associate memory-proper with a spiritual order while habit-memory is characterized within a mechanical order, an order of automatism. For him, habit-memory, whether instinctive or acquired, is thematic, immaterial, a potential that cannot be localized; while, paradoxically, memory-proper or recollection, which for Bergson requires a detachment from the immediacy of the present in order that the subject access a memory where it is, in the past, is, in Ruyer's view, localized, more like an image as photography or cinema renders it.[36] Our habits demonstrate a mnemic theme, one that is most clear when our habitual relations break down. Only then, when habits fail us, must we try to figure out consciously what the habit performs: "In cerebral psychological life, habitual behavior is only apparently automatic and mechanical. When habits break down, the theme is generally more solid than the details of its realization."[37]

Ruyer claims, in the epigram that opens this chapter, that memory is not a property of bodies but that bodies are properties of memory; bodies form themselves according to a theme that preexists them and which they bring into actuality and locate in space and time. Mnemic themes precede and structure all primary forms, providing them with their orientation, rationale, or conatus:

> It must thus be emphasized that habitual memory is not a property of the present material medium to which it is applied. It forms this medium, it is not derived from it. It is potential not actual, unlike the organized bodies (of all types) through which it is actualized. It is a potential theme outside of space, or rather, transpatial, occupying all

of space insofar as that theme can actualize, a potential that passes into space by using the small spatial domain that serves as its permanent *pied-à-terre*, but which does not contain it, which is only a starting point, an initial field of application for its full deployment. . . . Mnemic potential, outside of space, does not appear, does not arrive in this *pied-à-terre* like some sort of extra-terrestrial creature landing. It is always in this *pied-à-terre* that it actively maintains, like the flame of a pilot light constantly maintains the possibility of lighting the gas of a heater. If an accident should destroy the *pied-à-terre*, the mnemic potential can no longer pass into space.[38]

The mnemic theme is not laid out as pure model, the way Platonic forms function as models; rather it constitutes the field in which all possible configurations may come into being, the virtual order from which varying actualizations make themselves. Like the score whose performance is infinitely variable but nevertheless recognizable in its unity as performances of this and no other score.[39] Ruyer proposes that mnemic themes order the self-creation of primary forms, such as the atom and its subatomic constituents, the self-formation of all living things, and even the self-creating, autoaffecting properties of the universe itself. These forms do not lie dormant waiting for actualization; rather, they are the principles through which all primary forms create and sustain themselves; they exist as transpatial only to the extent that they can be and have been actualized.

For Ruyer, even God must be understood, not as a divine being separate from the world, but as an acting, a mode of self-creation according to an internal ideal.[40] All primary forms are both agent and ideal: both an agent, or many, that acts first of all to form and maintain itself before and as it acts in the world, and an ideal, a form directed to goals, those that are required for its self-formation and action in a particular manner. These are two orientations or directions for each being—the finality represented by the ideals, the mnemic themes which regulate form, and the modes of materialization by which forms come into the world and act in it. The atom and its elementary particles are the smallest domain of consciousness or autoaffection before what Ruyer calls "the last domains,"

domains that are pure activities with no agent, perhaps the very forces that cohere the universe—forces such as gravity and electromagnetism. The atom's being coincides with its capacities for acting.

Ruyer distinguishes between three orders of self-survey or three broad types of form or mnemic theme in *La Genèse des formes vivantes*. He claims that Form I, primary consciousness, is composed of atoms, the molecular relations between atoms, and the most elementary organisms, such as protozoa. Such forms function by self-survey or overflight. Form II, secondary consciousness, is a development or elaboration of Form I. Here he places most of the higher animals with a representational consciousness and the separation of the organs of perception from the organs of motor action. Form III is the human capacity not only for consciousness but for self-consciousness, however much such self-consciousness considers itself as transparent, a cogito, a thing. Each form masters a larger domain of space and time and generates a broader field of influences and effects. Form I develops itself in broader and more open ways in its Form II and Form III elaborations, each order operating according to increasing complex mnemic themes with increasingly wider capacities for acting. As each order develops, it elaborates more complex mnemic themes and addresses and operates within an Umwelt. If the internal unity of such forms comes from their conformity to an ideal, a mnemic theme, that is, from their performance of transpatial themes with increasing complexity and organization, forms also come to address, through their contrapuntal relations with an Umwelt, their belonging in a world and to engage with the details of that world in their own ways. Following Uexküll, Ruyer understands increasing orders of complexity in a being's world with an increasing complexity of internal organization. The more refined and developed is the distinction between perception and motor action, the more complex the being's immersion in its Umwelt, the more open and inventive the being becomes.[41]

We will turn in the next section to how Forms II and III are capable of forming themselves through their autoaffective, surviewing self-production, and, in the process, Ruyer will provide us a (sort of) resolution to the chicken/egg conundrum. An egg must produce the chicken well before a chicken can lay an egg. It is because of the self-creative capacities of the embryo or egg (and, in its own way, the brain) that embryogenesis itself best represents the autoproduction of all forms.

THE EMBRYO

Probably the most convincing and developed claims Ruyer makes are those where he discusses the autoaffective qualities of the embryo's self-genesis and the brain's ongoing embryonic qualities. Ruyer suggests that the brain is an ongoing embryo in an increasingly aging body. Both the brain and the embryo are primary forms, in immediate overflight or surview, and both make clear the qualities and characteristics of auto-creation and autoaffection.

Ruyer refers to the work of his predecessors in philosophical biology, Hans Driesch, whose experiments on grafting frog cells onto the mouth of the triton larva were so intriguing to Uexküll as well, and Hans Spemann, whose experiments in embryological development provided a decisive blow to mechanistic or reductive materialist accounts of growth and form.[42] Driesch performed various experiments on the embryos of sea urchins, dividing blastocytes, the earliest undifferentiated embryonic cells, at the stage of only eight cells into four cell units. Each of the divided units then continued to divide and to produce an organism rather than, as was expected, creating two half-organisms. Driesch induced the creation of two different organism, each smaller than usual, but fully functional.[43] From this he deduced that embryonic development cannot occur mechanically, through the additional creation of limbs, organs, etc., during development, but occurs through what he called the pluripotentiality or the monadlike properties of each cell, that is, an embryonic cell's capacity to take over the functions of any other cell, today also called equipotentiality. Each embryonic cell can deputize for any other. Driesch observed that even producing lesions in the egg or moving cells from one location to another seemed to have little effect on the developing embryo. This demonstrated that a mechanical or piece-by-piece model for the development of organisms cannot explain what otherwise appear to be the magical properties of damaged embryos. If embryonic regions are localized, then damage to cells of the embryo should produce corresponding damage in the living individual. Because embryonic cells can deputize for each other, they do not function according to mechanical principles. This is a regenerative capacity that fully formed beings generally lose, but that occurs with great reliability with germinal or embryonic cells: "Even two adult humans cannot reproduce by amalgamating or dividing in two like phantoms. Only their germinal cells can do this, because they are not machines. An adult with organs which are developed functionally can no more split into two than a belltower clock or a steam engine. Whereas a germinal cell, apparently, is sufficiently close to the microphysical order to be able to do so, by following the laws pertaining to fields in 'absolute surface,' which are within the domain of contemporary physics."[44]

Spemann's experimental work on the embryological development of amphibian animals further confirmed a number of the insights elaborated by Driesch. Spemann claimed that the embryo could be divided in such a way that two individuals may form where originally there was one, each with a fully functional bodily form—a matter of considerable contention, given the conflicts in biological theory between preformism, the dominant view,[45] and epigenesis, the position it challenged,[46] wrought by Driesch—but he demonstrated that this was possible only if the division occurs in a precise way, according to a specific plane, and only in the very early gastrula stage of the embryo's development. By tightly binding cells in the young embryo, he could induce two individuals, sometimes conjoined, where the constraint did not fully separate cells, and sometimes separate. Depending on the plane constricted, its angle, direction, and placement, he could generate quite specific effects on the embryo, showing that some cells—dorsal cells of the blastopore—more readily form a complete individual than ventral cells. From this insight, he understood that the embryonic region is differentiated and, using certain directions or orientations for surgical intervention, he could induce the development of the whole embryo, a head, or a particular part, depending on whether he manipulated the dorsal or ventral sides. If one transplants the dorsal side of a blastopore into the ventral region of another species' embryo, one can induce specific organ development, even if it is that of another species. These specific dorsal qualities came to be understood as organizers or inducers which can influence the development of other cells, even those in a different region of the organism, and especially in ventral sites, that is, one could more easily induce organs, limbs, and forms from the upper half of the body onto the lower half of the body than the reverse.

Spemann transplanted the dorsal lips of the blastopore onto the embryonic cells of another species of light and dark tritons (a species of newt). He produced remarkable visible internal and external changes to the host embryo, which varied considerably depending on where they were grafted. Ruyer understands these early experiments in embryogenesis as demonstrating the force of the mnemic theme in directing embryonic development long before there is a subject or even a body to be directed. The transplanted blastopores were still living elements or fragments that invoke a mnemic theme other than that which regulates the host species, bringing into being a chimera that nevertheless obeys the overall form of the host.[47] When such grafts are performed early in embryonic development, they can introduce a new or additional theme to the unfolding or self-creation of the embryo, which nevertheless continues to elaborate its own themes as well as it can in spite of the external intervention of an alien theme. For example, he could induce the formation of primitive eyes in the abdomen of the triton through grafting:

> The experimenter, we have seen, can easily multiply organs or even organisms by grafting anlagen outside their original locations in the embryo. He can make a dorsal cord appear on the ventral section, make an eye appear (or an optic vesicle with crystalline lens anlage) outside its natural place, or a tail or a head (incomplete) in the ventral region of a Triton. But the experimenter cannot change the specific mnemic potentialities of a graft. The graft is plastic (before determination) with regard to the organ it develops in the individual on which it is grafted. It harmonizes its development with the site on the host where it is grafted.

But it is not plastic with regard to the specific character that it sup-
plies. . . . The local inductors say to the graft, "Form adhesive organs";
they leave it to the graft to decide "how to go about doing it," depending
on its own memory.[48]

The embryonic host performs its melodic theme: the graft, while now
located in the embryonic host, continues to play its own melody, create
its own form according to its theme, even as the embryo continues to
play its own mnemic theme, with which the graft must now, in its own
way and through its own inventiveness, harmonize.

In other words, the embryonic surface cannot be understood in
physical or geometrical terms. When it is subjected to lesions, interferences, or transplants, it is capable of addressing and responding to
them, correcting and even eliminating their effects. It aims, insofar as
it can, to correct or repair such damage and it functions throughout
its organic constitution to compensate for it. The embryo exhibits the
characteristics of pure form, absolute self-proximity without external
observation, an internal means for self-organization; and it seems to
be directed by a mnemic theme, a bodily order with which it attempts
to cohere, and correct, so that it conforms as much as possible to, and
it improvises in its own way with, this theme. The theme orders the
embryonic cells to function in a particular way according to their local-
ity and function. Cells can be induced to operate in different ways,
depending on how they are directed by so-called inductor cells. A triton stomach can interrupt its digestive melody through the thematic
intervention of an eye from another species that is built according to its
own optical melody. The equipotentiality of embryonic cells is a kind
of biological expression of immediate self-proximity: the embryo can
develop in space and time as a material being only to the extent that it
conforms, to some degree, to the mnemic themes that organize it and
that it actualizes.

The embryo invents the means by which it actualizes the mnemic
themes that mark its potentials, and in this process it actualizes these
themes in a particular bodily and behavioral form, bringing the transpatial theme into a finite and material existence for as many individuals

and species as have existed and will exist. These mnemic themes exist as incorporeal, eternal though not fixed, even if they are not (yet) instantiated in space. A mnemic theme is reproduced, improvised on, by beings as they produce themselves. A being produces itself only to the extent that it has no external plan, no blueprint by which to make itself: " 'To reproduce itself' designates an action, inconceivable outside of a field in 'absolute surface' in which the forms 'read themselves' and can consequently 'read' the possible resemblance between things themselves and their own limbs (that is, an analogous 'self' within their own numerical 'self'). When a gene or a virus reproduces itself, in seeming to induce at a distance the formation of a proteinic chain resembling it, this 'at a distance' must be the quasi-distance analogous to that of the details of a field of vision, rather than a true distance of ordinary physics."[49]

In the process of producing itself, an embryo follows the species theme of the mnemic order which directs its growth transpatially and invents a way of bringing about its material and organic operations in a spatial and temporal order. The mnemic theme functions vertically while accompanying and directing the horizontal structure of organic/spatial/corporeal development. The more the mnemic theme is actualized in a living body of a certain form or configuration, the more it becomes materialized. Equipotentiality generates beings in space from mnemic themes that are transpatial. Development transforms equipotentiality into highly specified bodily themes, an eye, a leg, a mouth, and makes the theme increasingly concrete or actualized. While adult cells still contain some of the equipotentiality that regulated their earliest embryonic stages, the more formed organs and limbs, the more habituated they are for use in a particular manner—a gait, a walking style, a way of looking—the more they lose openness to change: "Primitive embryonic equipotentiality thus disappears progressively; it is distributed in more and more limited areas. The theme of the organs, by taking shape, ceases to be a theme to become a structure."[50] If every region of the embryo contains equipotentiality, and each equipotential cell can be understood as a form of primary consciousness, an internal unity incapable of external observation but accessible to absolute overflight, then every living being, including humans, is composed of many microsubjectivities or consciousnesses well beyond the knowledge of the Cartesian thinking "I."

The unicellular organism remains identical with its own embryo, capable of making itself, and, as the simplest forms of life, of eventually making the organs that will enable new species to emerge. Infusoria (simple, often unicellular, inhabitants of freshwater ponds), for example, make themselves not by mechanism or automatism but through direct self-survey that not even the most advanced forms of science have been able to replicate:

> Nothing prevents the assumption that if the Infusorium animates the mechanism, the mechanism and its functioning would develop on its part the consciousness (or primary subjectivity) of the Infusorium. It is known that a unicellular organism is capable of habituation and learning. Receiving more numerous information coming from farther away, its subjectivity will become a genuine consciousness with the appearance in image of exterior objects in its own field. For although it is absurd to pretend to manufacture a subjectivity, it is completely possible to develop a primary consciousness into a secondary consciousness, that is, into a consciousness that perceives and animates a vast annex field.[51]

The most elementary organisms function as a continuously self-forming embryo, making and repairing themselves, acting upon themselves and through their internal relations on a small fragment of their *Umwelten*.[52] Unicellular beings act like eggs or the earliest developments of the embryo: they are conscious only of what they do, not of what they are. They are fully focused on making themselves, like organs, atoms, and all forms of immediate self-proximity or overflight.[53]

There are limits to any piece by piece or mechanistic approach to primary forms. Automatism, the mechanical production of other machines, reaches its limit with the most elementary forms of life. The machine is unable to provide the force of a direction for the use of limbs and bodily organs, even as we can produce very worthy prostheses, artificial limbs, that can replace living ones. Without the mnemic form, no limb could function organically, could act as fundamentally in tune with all the other organs that comprise a living body. No artificial limb can provide this orientation—rather, as the phantom limb attests, limbs are always already, insofar as they are developed, oriented to certain potential or possible habits, ways of acting:

> There are two limits to automatism, the conscious behavior on the one hand, with self-guidance, and reproduction on the other. It is remarkable that at these two limits one discovers the same reality: some living cells, either in the form of nerve cells or in the form of embryonic cells. In the young embryo everything is as yet undifferentiated, as in a unicellular organism: the cells are at the same time capable of reproduction and of self-guidance. In the same way, in a single cell is entirely its own brain, it is entirely gamete of itself. It is also its own body (in the sense of "the whole of its auxiliary organs"). The same is true for the young embryo, with the difference of the protozoan, knows how to manufacture itself by making use of itself, of its massive organs of behavior as well as of its massive organs of reproduction, utilizable by those of its own cells that are kept at its disposal for improvisations in "absolute surface."[54]

The embryo makes itself in the dark milieu—eggshell, placenta—not subjected to the laws of physics, but to the laws of absolute surface. It functions as a *dark consciousness*, so absorbed in its labor of self-production that it remains uninterrupted in its task even if there are interferences from outside. It is conscious of what it does without being external to this process of doing, perfectly self-absorbed. Tools, machines, and technologies enhance living bodies but are incapable of the most elementary properties of life. In this sense, the tool or factory, as prosthesis or bodily extension, is a form of complication and mastery over greater distances that augments and adds to the body. But the body, especially the embryo, is already a series of tools and a factory that runs without mechanization.[55]

Technology opens the world to new meanings and values by expanding and changing how humans live in the world. Technologies are what living beings devise and construct according to the needs and capacities of their own bodies. We can even consider that biological processes internalize and augment themselves technologically, though not without social and political implications well beyond technology: "biological evolution is a technical evolution of internal circuitry. . . . The airplane had been sought in order to realise an old human dream. But once invented, it allowed a new political equilibrium and a new geography, a new vision and a new usage: it opened a new world in all orders, political, strategic, moral, aesthetic; it revealed a new terror and a new courage."[56] While numerous, indeed increasingly more, organs and limbs can be artificially produced—from bionic eyes and ears to robotic limbs and even exoskeletal propulsion machines—they only function according to the mnemic theme that directs the body's self-creation. To the extent that these prostheses can be incorporated into the biologico-cultural body, prostheses function according to a mnemic theme.[57]

The embryo that makes itself also makes a world: not just an organic world but also a world of technologies and cultures, an extraorganic world in making itself a living, quasi-autonomous being. The first and abiding task of the embryo is to realize, that is, materialize in space (and time), a primary form that brings the mnemic themes it relies on into bodily existence. It makes a body for itself. Embryogenesis brings specific "improvisations" of that theme into existence, even in the case of lesions, transplants, and grafts that interfere with its regular operations. The embryo, like the living being, will attempt to return to or replace the damaged or transformed relation between its body and its Umwelt through the reorientation of the regular use of its organs.

It embodies, builds a body, according to a theme, which is capable of being oriented in the future to actions that enhance it or bring value to its life. Through the body and its organs, it is a being that produces and uses tools and technologies as if these were part of its organic structure, adding the extraorganic to its organic operations. Each complex organic body is composed of a multiplicity of subjects or consciousnesses, a multiplicity of organs that, like musical instruments, function in harmony with the body's mnemic themes: "each organ is a small organism within an organism. And this is true at all levels—molecular, cellular, tissue, organic, in a literal sense. There is no reason to favor the molecular level."[58]

Significantly, it is also the embryo that, according to its species, is capable of constructing a brain, a nervous system, perceptual and motor capacities, organs and limbs for itself. The embryo, in its self-forming capacities, always in touch with itself in direct overflight, can be extended not only to every bodily organ and limb but above all to the brain, which remains, for Ruyer, the only embryonic organ that persists for the duration of a mature adult's life. The brain remains embryonic, self-forming, self-constituting, and connecting the body to an ever wider and more open world: "the brain is an embryo that has not completed its growth. The embryo is a brain, which begins to organize itself before organizing the external world."[59]

THE BRAIN

Embryos construct brains that are capable of coming to knowledge, however limited, of embryos and thus of themselves. Embryos, as they mature, are born, become babies, children, and then adults, lose most of the pluripotentiality that characterized their earliest existence. However, the brain continues to learn, to understand, being marked by a plasticity such that one part can deputize for another that has been disabled, damaged, or even removed. Like the embryo or egg, the brain is an organ of autoaffection that, unlike the embryo, is also directed to the world, a world not only composed of visible and mechanical things but also of mnemic themes, ideas and ideals, located nowhere in space but exerting an influence on the future direction of the living being. If mnemic themes provide a kind of recapitulated ontogenesis of all previous species from which an individual and species are drawn, they also provide the horizon of a future direction, a finality, a goal (or many) to action and reflection, whose distinction is made possible by the increasing elaboration and development of the brain. Hovering over a horizontal or linear development that coheres as bodily beings who develop, age, and die (what Ruyer has termed "a black board as absolute surface") is a vertical dimension ("a mnemic theme or a problem theme . . . arriving from a region 'perpendicular' to this blackboard")[60] that provides trans-patial and incorporeal values, directions, orientations—a field of possible actions—latent in the mnemic themes which give rise to our forms of embodiment and provide a potential for more and other conceptual and bodily possibilities than we have utilized.[61]

The brain is the point of connection or the junction between the autoaffective and mnemically ordered absolute surface, on the one side, and, on the other, the teeming, chaotic forces of a world that provide the living being with the means for its ongoing existence, a border or barrier between the internal self-regulation of the organism and the ordering and understanding of external forces which enable it to act. The sense or orientation that directs the embryo is the same sense or orientation that directs the brain to regulate bodily processes such as circulation and res-piration, to think and act in its own ways, for there is a direct continuity between the fertilized egg and the mature adult it becomes, a continuity that even exceeds the boundaries of life, for it begins with it processes of materialization at the subatomic and atomic level. The brain is the point at which internal circuits, those marking primary and secondary form, expand themselves to connect with and forge external circuits, enabled by the increasing development and elaboration of the nervous system, by which we access the external world, and, in the process, enabling the internal circuits to exceed auto-affection and expand the space and range of accomplishments that modify and extend these internal cir-cuits. The nervous system allows the organism to widen its scope of action and influence in order to apprehend instinctive behavior through wider transformations and complications. The brain converts such per-ceptions into self-reflective conduct and enables the internal unity that constitutes life to elaborate a "self," an "I" that does not just know itself, as Descartes claims, but knows and acts by establishing values, tasks to be undertaken, activities that enhance our extraorganic existence. Autoaffection is augmented and expanded by perception, which gives to the objects of perception a potential value in seeking ways for material living beings to materialize transpatial themes in their actions.

The brain is neither the organ for images, or the location of representational thought, nor the organ through which thought is possible: it is the organ that enables the expansion of the organism not only conceptually but also by its capacity to intensify affect through perception and action, through the invention of tools, technologies, societies, institutions, all aggregates or composites, multitudes, brought together and capable of falling apart. The more indirect or circuitous the path of the external circuit, the wider the scope of liaisons and relations and the wider the sphere of influence on the actions of a being with a brain. The wider the connections, the more urgently must the external circuits reconnect with internal circuits.

The brain does not create or enable thought, consciousness, or subjectivity, or indeed even intelligence, which every form of life expresses in its own way. It redirects life outside itself and, at the same time, introduces into the organism the forces and effects of its outside, its milieu. The brain is the organ through which autoaffection increasingly includes the objects, things, and processes in the world and, equally, the organ through which mnemic themes can be ever more effectively and creatively brought into existence, actualized. Life is the increasing actualization of form, whose own forms are enhanced, intensified, and augmented by its interactions in its world. The brain enables the body to live outside itself and for its perceptual objects to generate new forms of autoaffection internal to it. It enhances the body's capacity to engage and exchange with a world by protecting the body through cultural inventions (clothing, housing, social relations and institutions), by extending the body with machines it invents—cars, trains, planes, phones—and prosthetically transforming it with food, exercise, interpersonal relations. Perception, the extension of the organism beyond autoaffection, enables the accumulation of personal memory, extraorganic memory, from which to learn and by which we habituate ourselves to perceptual forms. Through memory, ever-widening external circuits can be directly linked to internal circuits, enabling the thinking of the counterfactual or the virtual and the other paths by which it may be actualized, to substitute one kind of action for another. As E. W. Tomlin explains, "From the embryo has grown the whole organic world. From the brain has grown the extra-organic world. But whereas the embryo has in a sense completed its task, the brain is an embryo of which the achievements are as yet 'embryonic.' "[62]

The brain is the meeting point or conjunction where the autoaffective qualities of the absolute surface and the physical properties of material things engage each other, the means by which each extends itself into the other, enabling the materialization not only of things but also the values they embody and the new uses they open up. The brain is a "converter," which has thus far best facilitated the materialization of transpatial themes or, as Ruyer understands them, values and their conversion into objects and tasks directed to goals and aims or ends. The conscious and reflective actions that the central nervous system and the brain enable expand the world of plants and invertebrate animals in which internal and external circuits cannot be clearly distinguished. We need not assume that man, with his developed brain, is the pinnacle accomplishment of evolution; man expresses one kind of brain-becoming, one kind of integration with and transpositions of the internal and the external, but we cannot assume man stands alone, outside an animal world, able to take it as object of reflection and mastery. Man is merely one expression, one mode of materialization for transpatial themes that are addressed in many organic ways and in the creation of all the extraorganic relations in which living beings engage. The brain enables a being to address problems, to figure out strategies that move beyond the reflexive, to seek meanings, significances, or, in Ruyer's terms, values or ends.

Like the embryo, the brain exhibits equipotentiality: cells can deputize for others, and functions that occur in one part of the brain can be taken over by another. The brain too is thus an absolute surface in immediate proximity with itself. Because the rest of the body's organs and limbs age, they lose much of their mnemic potential, but the brain remains a uniquely open organ that continues to engage with and be immersed in the invisible world of mnemic themes and values, of incorporeal forces, as well as to engage with the world of material forces that brings with it problems and questions that need to be addressed by the living being. It is a primary surface for the conversion of internal to external and external to internal circuits.[63]

VALUES: ETHICS AND AESTHETICS

Ruyer's particular conception of the incorporeal has been understood largely in religious or theological terms. For him, transpatial disembodied ideas—mnemic themes, the order of organization of true forms—produce forms, directions, means for the processes of materialization that, through autoaffection, create bodies, activities which, in their turn, create things, ensembles of things, relations between living and nonliving things. One *could* read his work as privileging a divine order that precedes and regulates the material order. One *could*, in other words, read his work as a form of Neoplatonism, as a mode of unrequited divine idealism. But Ruyer himself is quite clear in claiming that neither Platonic forms nor the concept of a transcendent Person-God, external creator of the world and of the laws that regulate it, adequately characterize dynamic forms that exist only in this world, unregulated from outside.[64] If there is a divine order, it is an order and force immanent in this world that can be understood through the processes that characterize this one world, the world that generates limitless Umwelten for all that live in it. If there is a divine order, it is less what the Greeks understand as an order regulated by gods and goddesses, or the Abrahamic religions for whom law is articulated by a fully transcendent and external God. It may be better understood, as Spinoza suggests, as a joy in understanding and finding one's place in the intimate and open connections not only between objects and subjects but also within subjects, provided in the orders of this one world.

Ruyer claims that just as there is a call to primary forms from the world itself to act, to respond, to create, a self-touching that requires an expanding relation to the world, so there is a call from an order of values, from ideals, the transpatial, which need not be considered to emanate from a divine being or from any thing external to this world. These ideals or values can come from and mingle with ideals we take up consciously—the struggle toward a political goal, the desire to make a work of art, the effort to address a problem, to act in a certain way—providing specific means by which we improvise transpatial themes.

Our behavior as living beings is goal directed from the beginning, from even before conception, in the very gametes that produce us and the atomic, molecular, and cellular forces that produce them. These goals, aims, directions, or orientations are not imposed from outside but act and are felt from within—they direct beings in how to survive, to eat, to move, to protect themselves, to grow, to connect with the world and with others, including other forms of life, to manage those consciousnesses (bacterial, microbial, viral, organic) within us in order that we have a certain form and can act in the particular ways our body is capable of.

We may experience the force of the transpatial themes most directly in the sense of incompleteness and failure we feel when a task we have set ourselves has not been accomplished, a task whose order and outlines we may discern but not complete—an experience that is likely to be familiar to every writer, artist, and scientist. To be drawn to a task is to feel the pull of the future, of an ideal to be accomplished or a goal or purpose to be attained, however much we are unable to achieve this goal.[65] Such ideals are not imposed on us from without, as moral precepts may be. They are given, not externally, but from within an order or end, a finality, that action directs or is directed to, which both extends materializations, becomings, while adhering to an ideal or, as Ruyer calls it, an invisible world of values. Values, in his sense, are both immanent and transcendent, they are immanent in all that is material and all that regulates its actions as material (its "laws" of possible action) and they are transcendent, not in the sense that they rise above and direct life, but only in the goals and purposes they aim to bring into being that might direct the becomings of material forms of whatever type. Ruyer understands these two poles or orientations not simply as material and ideal, organic and transpatial, but also in terms of an "Agent" and an "Ideal." These are not two orders, but the latent directionality, the belonging of the one, the Agent, to the order of the Ideal. What acts, not a subject but the consciousnesses within each subject, is not a self-directed agent, but an agent directed by an ideal, in other words, whose actions have a goal, an aim, a place in the future. Mnemic themes enable and direct all inventions insofar as they are inventions for the enhancement of life that are already virtual directions immanent in even the most simple primary forms.

Such mnemic themes are not fixed, able to be intuited or discerned; they are not measurable or calculable; neither faith nor reason brings us any closer to understanding them. They are virtuals, potentials, forming forces that can only be inferred from the regularities they create. They are not normative, fixed measurements against which we can calculate our performances: they are inferred from the regularity of the form-taking capacities of different orders or levels of material existence. It is because atoms of a particular type—oxygen, hydrogen, carbon—have behaviors, which are relatively open but also highly circumscribed, that we can say the form of each is what it is. All primary forms, from the atom and its constituents to the living cell and the simplest organisms, are open but highly circumscribed. The limits of its openness and its circumscription define the "nature" of the form. All living forms, secondary and tertiary forms, have a bodily organization that easily tolerates significant modifications and transformations but nevertheless retains its bodily capacity to act in a specific manner.

It is significant that, when evoking what he calls a "religious" order in our moral and creative actions, it is not to religion that Ruyer turns. He seems scathing about the naive superstitions and projections that mark religious rituals. Instead of discussing organized religions, Ruyer illustrates our adherence to a world of transpatial or mnemic themes with the figure of the artist struggling with art's materials: "The artist, scorning the subtle norms of aesthetic success, sees the work that he dreamed decomposing and contorting in his hands, has the difficult sentiment of a kind of indignity, of an offense to something which is not a pure thing. The painter who fails at a painting experiences a sort of revulsion which transforms itself in the dizziness of auto-destruction, and drives him close to suicide. The conditions of artistic failure are moreover analogous to the conditions of incrimination: fatigue, a kind of lazy nervousness, the envy in deceiving, then a 'pique' of self-esteem which diabolically perseveres in error."[66] Here it is the pull of an ideal, what the painter wants the painting to capture but feels has not been done adequately, that plunges the artist into despair, but perhaps also into rethinking how the work can be completed. The incompletion or failure of a work of art, like the inadequacy of an ethical act, attests even more clearly to the force of the ideal which waits for its actualization. This is not an ideal for anyone but the painter who feels inadequate to capture it in a work. But it is the ideal that directs the work and signals its success or failure as the materialization of that particular ideal and no other, just as it is an ideal, many ideals, that direct our morphological development and the mode of operation and goals of our acts. Even if the world as a totality exhibits nothing of a telos or finality, even if world history has no dialectical direction, nevertheless each act that constitutes the dynamism of the world exhibits its own finality. This is not to be confused with intentionality, the object of meaning, the phenomenological object, but rather with a task and the creation of a path, a Tao, to accomplish it. It is about the conversion of movement into action and the direction of action to a felicitous, often self-chosen aim. We do not develop legs in order to walk; we create legs for ourselves in utero that enable us to walk, that facilitate walking, running, climbing, swimming, and many other activities, some of which may have not been invented yet. This is neither preformist nor teleological, insofar as there is no end, no absolute finality, only the finality of the activities of primary forms and beyond.

The world of values Ruyer elaborates is a world to be made, not given, even though it often appears as a command to be obeyed according to a lawgiver who judges.[67] This is why Ruyer prefers, without offering a real discussion of it, the Tao, the way, the path that, without providence or miracles, elaborates the ramifying implications and effects of one's action, an understanding from the point of view of the universe, from the view of "God within us." This is why we may see the expressions or creations of the transpatial, the invisible world of values, as readily and far more directly in a work of art than in a church.[68] These values are not divine because a divine creator made them; they are divine only to the extent that they participate in an order, many orders, greater than each thing, the principle for the self-creation of things, an order that is the unity of all mnemic themes, the point at which all memories converge. We must understand, not a Person-God, a being outside us, a divine father, but, as Ruyer says, a "God in us," the complexity by which we create ourselves from other entities that have created themselves. This is a God who functions "by participation without observation,"[69] that is, God conceived as an ordered nature, as both *natura naturata* and *natura naturans*, whose complexities we don't adequately understand. It is only this kind of God that allows us to conceptualize the creativity of the artist, which is to say, the capacities for creativity and invention enabled by transpatial themes in place of a traditional God: "It is God who exists in each of us, as he subsists in each of the Ideals. We said that there was no free being, only free activities. We can now modify this formula and say: There is only one free being, God in us, and we exist only through creating, that is to say, through working according to the order of the ideal, which is also God in the ideals. . . . Our soul makes itself by making our body and the tools which prolong our body. But the soul of our soul, to speak like the mystics, never has to make itself, because it is eternal and produces time, like all the rest."[70] God is the name for the ordering force in agents and for the ideality of the Ideal through which agents act. For Ruyer, we participate in the divine, or in soul, to the extent that we further the self-creativity that is the work of the absolute or metaphysical surface by allowing it, in a transversal or perpendicular relation, to elaborate and modify, to create, living forms and their creative acts, both conceptual and corporeal. The material world is not endowed with extra values, with a divine, disembodied copy, an extra, heavenly, or ideal dimension, but is itself the experimentation in forms and in the materialization of things according to its own forms and deformations.

At his most enigmatic, Ruyer suggests, in place of any Person-God, or even a Tao-God, that the *future itself* may be the destination, the finality—ever deferred—of true form, what it directs its self-making toward. It may be the eternal flow of time, with the adherence of the past in the present, with the present directed always toward a future that is to be made rather than found, that best describes the work of mnemic themes, of transpatial melodies that direct our very being and the world it supposes:

> It is the future, in its virtual, but also constraining and dynamizing, necessity which is the only true guide for the only possible theology, just as it is the only true guide for all action. God, if we hold to this word, is the future itself, or rather the eternal reservoir beyond time and creating time, who constantly projects himself or pours himself into the present and who transforms the functioning of already created beings into sensible behavior and actions in order to cause the world to evolve in a living manner and not like a great machine which could only finish at a stable equilibrium or with irremediable wear and degradation. . . . God is imperceptible and apparently unpowerful, just like the future, whose dynamism seems quite weak beside the great masses blindly forced into brutal movements.[71]

The pull of the future, toward which all our acts are directed, is the invisible force, the world of values, to which primary form tends, a future connected thematically to the past but with the dynamic potential for divergence from the present. The material organization of things, particularly living things, tends to experimentation with the limits of form and with the possibilities of deformation and transformation: conatus, will to power, a people to come, the transindividual replace providence, divine judgment, and the future as given. In forming aggregates—machines, institutions, collectives, organizations, states, and so on—dynamic or self-sustaining forms, consciousnesses, especially human, enliven these as organic extensions, tools to better address (or be less able to address) how to invent ways to live, that better address (or don't) the future to come. This is precisely an ontoethics and an ontoaesthetics, joining the forces of the cosmos to the smallest of particles.

CONCLUSION

I have presented a schematic and highly selective, perhaps even idio-syncratic, history or genealogy of what I have called the incorporeal, a tradition latent and largely neglected in the present, but one capable of numerous revivals and new lives. This is a tradition that eschews dualism—any conception of the mind or ideality and body, or materiality, as separate substances—in order to develop a nonreductive monism or a paradoxical dualist monism. Materialism addresses the material reality of things, objects, relations, events; idealism addresses the conceptual, significatory, representational directionality, sense, or form by which matter materializes itself into things from its primary resources (subatomic, atomic, quantum fields, chemical bonds). Traditionally they have been construed as contradictory or at least contrary substances or relations, two different types of "thing," one mental (or psychological), the other material. But if they are two different substances then we can never explain their interactions, which are so readily apparent. This has been a continuing problem in the history of Western thought more or less since its earliest origins, and there is no real conclusion that can resolve the question of how best to conceive of ideality and materiality other than or beyond their representation in binarized forms.

I have attempted in this book to look at a series of philosophers who have aimed, each in his own way, to problematize and move beyond dualism without, however, resorting to the most common form of "resolution," that of reductionism, in which one term, usually ideality, is reduced to or explained by and as the other. I have aimed to elaborate neither dualism nor a reductionist monism, but have sought out thinkers who have addressed this question through their own, sometimes elaborate and always complex, reconsiderations of the extramateriality or the prematerial, or, as I have called it here, the incorporeal. By the incorporeal, I mean the direction or trajectory that orients a movement of concepts or thought, that constitutes the possibility of a process of understanding, that enables the creation of a philosophy or a work of art as an emergence from and an entwinement with a material order, planets, stars, constellations, nebulae, and so on, beyond us, and a world of objects, things, processes, and events that constitute materiality on earth, with the emergence and evolution of life in its growing complexity. The incorporeal is the dimension of ideality that suffuses all things, enabling them to signify and generate representations. I have claimed that there is always already something in the organization of matter—matter at its most elementary—that contains the smallest but perhaps most significant elements of ideality. Ideality, conceptuality, thought, does not simply erupt into existence from a mechanically regulated, thoroughly material world, no matter how complex. Nor are thoughts, ideas, or concepts simply the products of the human brain, which is itself only possible if all the brains, the prebrains, the bodies and bodily organization of earlier and contemporaneous forms of life that come before and did not carry ideality, one of the conditions for human thought, within them. They would be incapable of even the most elementary forms of organization and orientation, what Ruyer calls "true form," those exhibited by single-cell organisms that constitute the most primitive and earliest forms of life, if these elementary forms of life did not carry with them the ideality, the directionality, the mnemic themes of their material components, subatomic particles and fields, atoms and their molecular connections and composites, aggregates composed of the relations of molecules, if they themselves were not in some way composed of material-ideal relations. The chain of evolutionary emergence is unbroken not only materially but also conceptually. There are no unconditioned or mysterious eruptions of thought from matter. There must be the most elementary traces of ideality along with the materiality of the atom and its components, all the way down and up. These elementary traces are the conditions, at a much more primary level, of articulated, discursively preserved thought, whether animal or human, one of the subatomic world's uncontained and indirect effects.

In the preceding chapters I have explored—briefly and selectively—ancient, modern, and contemporary conceptions of the material-ideal relation with the aim of tracing a history of philosophical thought that runs contrary to mainstream philosophies (Platonism, Aristotelianism, Cartesianism, Hegelianism, and their contemporary inflections) and that coheres and binds together ideality and materiality, not through their identity, as monistic reductionism proposes, nor through their binarization, as dualism entails, but in terms of their thorough interplay and accompaniment, their transversal or perpendicular relations. Ideality and materiality are not two substances but two ways in which the real is distributed: ideality is not the shadow or ghost that accompanies materiality, but the spatial and temporal frame by which materiality comes to act as well as be acted on, the incorporeality that subtends matter, that makes materiality locatable, changeable, meaningful, and capable of being spoken about. Ideality is the capacity of materiality to represent and expand itself, its load of virtuality, its potential to be otherwise. Ideality informs materiality, not as form imposed on matter from outside, but as primary form, form always in touch with itself without external observation, internal and self-constituting form. Ideality enables materiality to be in touch with itself, to be autoaffective, which is the condition under which materiality can complexify itself, can give rise to life in its varied forms and to the technological and artistic inventions and transformation of matter that life enables.

Life is the increasing complexification of material relations, the creation or invention of a membrane or barrier and the emergence of an internal circuit to regulate the cell in its external milieu and complicate their relation. This complexification is also the increasing complexification of ideality or conceptuality, the emergence not only of orientation or direction but of sense, whose elaboration through language and

collective cultural and political practices is the condition of thought or
the concept. Ideality is not in another world, another dimension or order
than materiality; it shares this world by providing materiality with an
excess, a virtuality, that enables it to shape itself according to a direction
or a theme coming from within its configurations and always positioning
it within the rest of the world through different degrees of connection,
with a future in view, even if this is not our future, or our wished-for
goals and ends. To the extent that we understand our own materiality,
as well as that of things in the world, mechanically, in the light of Cartesianism, we cannot conceive of goals and ends; we cannot understand
how organic wholes, both molecular and living, are composed of "parts"
or components without external relations, we cannot understand how
activities are oriented to tasks, ends, and ideals that are invented, without a "thing," a separate consciousness, to invent these ends. The very
existence of our own goals and intentions, wishes and aims, enacted or
thwarted, makes clear in an incontestable manner that we ourselves are
oriented to the future in the aims and tasks by which we direct ourselves.
We should assume no less of our material components, the organs and
tissues, the molecular and atomic movements and processes that compose our bodies and continually connect them to the materials of our
world. Our conscious goals, as large or small as they may be, make it
clear that there can be a direction to our actions, a goal or finality. This is
possible not because the world has a final order, purpose, or direction—
the assumption made by most of the world's religions—but because each
thing, each material object is both identical with its constituents and
also an excess, an ideality, whether meaningful to us or not, that directs
and orients things, with or without a human frame or purpose. Sometimes we mistake this for divine being instead of seeing in it a kind of
terrestrial divinity of the orders and complexities, the self-forming
properties of this world and all its constituents. If religious terms
have long characterized the global order and its significances—now
increasingly occupied by possibilities for economic exploitation rather
than meaning-production or the creation of incalculable, innumerable
values—it is time to return to a history of immanent philosophies that

see beauty and joy in the natural and cultural world, in the capacities of life to enhance and complicate itself and its worlds.

I have called ideality an excess over materiality. This is true only insofar as materiality remains our object of investigation. Ideality is an attenuated or subsisting quality or attribute of materiality, whether a living consciousness addresses it or not. Ideality is the quality that makes things available for and changeable by various forms of life or through its own capacities. But, from the point of view of conceptuality or ideality, the material it frames, addresses, and makes capable of conceptualization and representation is not complete and in itself; ideality is not a supplement added to an already intact material object. Rather, material objects and their relations add complexity and the interchange and confrontation of ideas with each other for ideas to grow more complex, more multifaceted, the more they encounter each other. If materiality is not an excess of ideality, it is nevertheless the order through which ideality complexifies itself and the means by which ideas come to populate the plane of immanence and have an (eternal) existence independent of their means of material production. Just as material encounters transform materiality, so conceptual encounters, the clash or confirmation of concepts, transform ideality, each adding to and complicating the other. As the incorporeal frame of each thing (and the totality of all things), space, time, lekta, meaning, sense, direction, theme, or goal cohere, integrate, and connect material things together, in particular configurations or alliances, enabling patterns, an order, laws, to be discerned that permit events, provisional alignments, even identities, to emerge. As an incorporeal frame, the world of meaning or sense enables living beings and their chemical and biological constituents to orient themselves in relation to objects and each other, to direct their own actions, to give meaning and value to things, including themselves, and to develop languages and sign systems that refer to, address, signify, or express things, relations, events, and the universe they inhabit. The incorporeal is the condition under which language becomes more than material, more than breath and trace, the condition under which it connects the world of events to the life of reflection, thought.

As incorporeal direction or orientation, the world of values, whether the "invisible world" of mnemic themes or the more explicitly self-chosen goals by which individuals and groups aim to live their lives, beckons life, and matter in its primary forms, to self-generated goals and ends, to create improvisations of various themes that organize both material transformations and the directions toward which such forms are oriented. That is, as a future toward which actions and passions are directed, the incorporeal not only frames and makes meaning from materiality but also gives it a destination, one that we cannot discern or that is beyond us, the becomings to which things, both material and conceptual, tend. As I have stressed, these becomings are not dialectical: they do not leave a remainder in the dust of history. Rather, they are precisely becomings of virtuals that are unused by processes of actualization up to now, eruptions of substance, the will to power, the preindividual in its resource-laden potential, or primary form creating itself by itself. These virtuals are the directions, the future, to and by which things and ideas bring themselves into existence and orient themselves. These are not futures we can discern in the present but futures that are virtual, among many possible paths of actualization to which the present may lead.

I have sought out philosophers who not only focus on an interrogation and critique of dualisms and reductionisms: more positively, I have looked for positions and texts that address the intrication of ontology, a theory of what is, particularly a theory of becomings, whether material or immaterial, with ethics. The Stoics, Spinoza, and Nietzsche are well-known for their ethical works; it is perhaps less well-known that Deleuze and Guattari also provide at least the beginnings of an ethics. This interest in a nonnormative ethics is also a clear focus in the writings of both Simondon and Ruyer. Each in his own way, and in accordance with a lineage that entwines materiality and ideality beyond any binarized model, sees that forms of materiality, whether that understood by physics, by biology, or in everyday life, and concepts, ideas, or incorporeals are directed toward goals, ends, purposes, whether in accordance with the organization of information and energy in metastable systems or transpatial mnemic themes, which are the process of continually producing values. These are not, as I have argued throughout, transcendent values, nor need they be universal or even species-specific values. They are the orders of values by which one directs one's actions, the orders of intelligibility and affective commitment created by acting and interacting. Some of these values are given long before any particular human life can be lived, the values of self-proximity and self-formation and the modes of self-creation each primary form requires: others are given historically to living beings with a particular degree of social interaction, and these may be considered social, cultural, and political values that inform and direct social practices perhaps even before living beings are born; others are created by individuals and groups in the selection of tasks and activities, projects that are more self-consciously planned. These values are not so much moral rules or imperatives as "logics" of practice, the values or aims that emerge in undertaking the invention of the various protocols of different practices, which entail the invention of aims, goals, and ends.

To the extent that the orders of the world are immanent rather than transcendent, we must seek an immanent ethics to adequately address ways of living, styles of life, made possible in and of this world. Such an ethics is not a function of judgment, of moral right or law, but of action, of values not given but made. Like a politics, which directs such questions to collective social life and its forms of division and separation, it seeks ways to act and be acted upon in both collective life and its cultural and natural milieus. How can one live in the world, act in the world, make things and oneself, while also creating values that enhance oneself and one's milieu, not through preexisting values but through acting, making, and doing that generate new values? There is no single answer to this question, only ways or styles of living in their multiplicity. Each of the philosophers discussed here values a mode of reason, not given in advance, that emerges from one's understanding of and immersion in the things, events, and processes of the world and that is capable of changing itself to the extent that it understands more and more of the world and its principles of action. It is a reflective yet also intuitive immersion in the world that generates both understanding (or knowledge) and action at the same time. Values are to be made that come from the potential of things in the world to be otherwise, that is, to the extent that a living being, individually and collectively, participates in and harnesses for its own (singular and collective) uses the forces and powers of the real, the capacities for action and passion provided by its nature and that of the things in this world with which it interacts. Values are not made voluntaristically, according to choice or "free will," according to a subject's conscience; they are made according to immanent directions and forces coming at us beyond and outside of a "self"—from the orientations and capacities of the microselves or consciousnesses within and surrounding us. We conform to and improvise on these values in the process of self-consciously creating and living our lives.

The Stoics, Spinoza, and Nietzsche each claim, though in very different, not entirely consistent, ways that there is a touch of eternity in the constitution of an immanent ethics, an eternity commensurate with the order and organization of this world. Ethics does not create eternal values, but to the extent that values are created, they cannot be uncreated: they are, they come into being and abide forever, waiting activation or actualization, capable of directing action or of denunciation, critique, and transformation. They have the character of ideals, which, like concepts, always participate in an eternity. Values are eternal to the extent that they address not just personal and political life and social interactions but, beyond us, the life of the world, what comes before and makes us possible and also what follows us, what is to come. They are not eternal in the sense of unchanging but insofar as aims, orientations, goals, and directions cannot be undone but continue to generate effects and implications. It is only this larger perspective, in Spinoza's understanding, a perspective sub specie aeternitatis, or, for Nietzsche, the transvaluation generated by the eternal return, values provided by that given *in* a life—that can provide the basis for an ontoethics. Ethics is the affirmation of life and the nonliving forces that compose and frame it, forces that are directed to the future. Ethics is an attempt to live in accordance with the principles one has chosen for oneself by which to regulate one's life, according to goals and ideals that are also those life takes from the world, the directions or orientations already latent or virtual in the world. Ethics is the capacity for the enhancement of life and of materiality, an understanding of its implications and costs, and an awareness of its forces and their distribution.

Such an ethics, as Deleuze understood, is both an ontology and an ethology, or, rather, ethics can be construed as somewhere *between* ontology and ethology. Ethology as a disciplinary field is itself divided between the study of human character, through its evolution and history, and the study of animal behavior and character; that is, ethology may be capable of bridging a divide between the study of humans and the study of animals. As the study of the behavior and worlds of animals (the study of animals and their behavior is something that Uexküll, Lorenz, Karl von Frisch, Nikolaas Tinbergen, and others insisted included the worlds animals inhabit, their *Umwelten*), an ethology is an exploration of the creation and ever-changing constitution of a living being and its world, the changing relations of the inner and outer circuits that characterize life, the changing relations of self-modification that direct both life and its worlds according to tendencies or directions immanent in them. An ethology is a nonnormative description and analysis of the varying behaviors of animals (and the sense that these behaviors reveal) and their living "logics," the differences that constitute animal worlds. Ethology provides a model by which we can create a nonnormative ethics that seeks, not the evaluation of encounters one undergoes, but an acknowledgment of what they add to or subtract from our capacities for action and reflection, how they enhance not only our personal powers of action, and passion, but also the powers and capacities of our species. As Simondon and Ruyer suggest, there may be a direction immanent in the orders of engagement constituting nature before the emergence of life, provided by localized sites of metastability and self-organization and their orientation toward the solution of local "problems" through the invention of higher orders of metastability, or according to the requirements of mnemic themes; there is an added direction, or numerous directions, to the forces and forms of the natural world by the purposes, intentions, and acts of living beings who liberate and transform material relations through their reframing, systems of knowledge and representation, and material labor, including technology, and the concepts, affects, and sensations they induce and create.

This wayward or idiosyncratic tradition has directed itself to the question of invention or creation, whether in works of art, technological and scientific invention, or the creation of concepts, from at least the work of Nietzsche through to that of Deleuze. While art was considered medicinal, good for health and well-being for the Stoics, and appears to be largely neglected in the work of Spinoza, in the writings of Nietzsche, art is an affirmation of the powers of the false, the highest order of affirmation of the creative nature of all human production, even an affirmation of the fundamentally artistic (rather than truth-laden) nature of sciences that take themselves as unmediated truth. Art is not something human beings make for themselves out of nothing. Like sciences and technologies, art is a particular engagement of materiality and ideality that forms of life, particularly forms of human life, produce in their various ways as a play with an excess of ideality over materiality, and of materiality over ideality, for the purposes of enhancing sensations and affects, for intensifying how life feels itself and its world. The natural sciences are also the discerning of protocols, principles, and laws from the regularities of material conditions and the orders of sense they produce, which are carefully controlled in experiments and tests. Each is the ideal binding of material forms in new representational orders that are themselves both material and ideal. While this does not provide an adequate analysis of the ways that art works, sciences, and technologies are produced from the ordered and ideal directions of material existence and its potential to be otherwise—this would entail a different project—the ontoethics I have aimed to explore here requires changes in the ways in which we view human and animal creations, forms or orders of organization, that direct life to inventive production that enhances and transforms lived milieus.

Art, science, and philosophy are human productions that elaborate, complicate, and direct, through higher orders of complexity, the same orders of materiality and ideality that order the world itself. Art, science, and technology are not frames we impose on matter and ideality but explorations and inventions through the framing that incorporeals provide for our ongoing explorations of matter. They are contingent, contested elaborations of the world's qualities and processes. Art, science, and technology, not to mention the creation of economic and political systems, do not impose themselves from the outside on brute matter—although they may and do involve the social impositions of some privileged, rather than other minoritized, practices of creation and destruction and the subjects who bare the brunt of such practices—but are rather the elaborations, in potentially infinite directions, of trajectories, lines of development, that are already there, immanent, in the prehuman and nonhuman world. It is to the prehuman, the inhuman, the organic and the inorganic, that we must direct our efforts, and which provide us with human ways to invent, to create ourselves and what comes beyond us.

To say that these directions are immanent is not to suggest that they must be elaborated in a particular manner but only that they can be. We have attributed a great deal of responsibility and recognition for artistic, scientific, and technological creations and social, political, and economic relations to human inventiveness, creativity, intelligence, or ingenuity; while I do not want to deny a great facility for creativity and invention, as should be clear by now, this is an inventive capitalization on forces that are primarily non- and prehuman, forces that precede and make the human possible. I am not suggesting that human inventiveness is a fiction: on the contrary, such inventiveness exists only to the extent that human inventiveness seeks out and relies on properties and qualities of the real that it can comprehend, through experimentation and usage, through intuition and attunement, if not through a complete understanding. Simondon and Ruyer have elaborated the strange processes of technical and artistic invention and scientific discovery, which are often far more "artistic" or intuitive than the common self-representation of the scientist or technician as rational, directed by "facts" and the hard labor of testing, perfecting, and redesigning initial findings. The constitution of arts and sciences, and of the religions and technologies that are to transform and organize human life in particular directions according to the whole or totality of the world, and to its particular terrestrial configurations, respectively, are ways of mediating between life and the inorganic world, ways of inventing and elaborating potentialities of each to be more and otherwise. Arts, sciences, and philosophy, all forms of human knowledge and creativity, are the extension of the forces of the world in directions and through tangents that are already there, virtually, in the resources that make and locate the human. The human protracts and uses what the natural world allows and enables.

Considering life in general and the human species in particular not in opposition to the world but as a fold within it, in which are also enfolded elements and features from the world, and which unfold into the world new connections, new relations between things and ideas, life is of the world, made of the same "substance," the same materiality and ideality that composes the world, though now directed through the specificity of its bodily morphology and its particular internal circuits and their manners of connection with external circuits. It thus adds to the non-living world the connections between things, and between ideas, new connections and networks, new capacities to affect and be affected that are latent or virtual but can be developed in many other directions as yet unimagined or thus far considered impossible.

The ontologies and ethics I have explored in this volume would remain external to each other if ontology is understood in its more conventional sense, as an ontology of what is, an ontology of individuated beings. If, however, we following the Stoics in understanding ontology in terms of "something," rather than "being," ontology ceases to direct us only to things and their relations, whether things are understood materially or in conceptual terms, and shows us the processes of becoming, the processes of individuation, that underlie and complicate how being can be understood. If being is, at best, a stage of becoming, or a tendency to which becomings may be directed, a momentary and abstract fixing of what is always changing, then in place of an ontology we must develop an ontogenesis, even an embryogenesis, if we consider primary or true form, an understanding of the processes of coming into being, the processes that engender becomings and ensure that being cannot be identical to itself (over time): a being is always more than itself insofar as it is also the site of becomings without end, becomings that keep it "alive" in whatever sense, that keep a being from remaining the same as itself.

At their most consistent and unchanging, beings are nevertheless points of convergence for an infinity of relations that ensure the entire system of things, the universe, is always changing, becoming. Any stability or foundation is itself only relative to the instability and interactivity that mark the broader and further-reaching environment, the infinite connections between all things and all processes. If ethics is the reasoned reflection on the conditions under which living beings and their milieus of becomings can be understood and made otherwise, can have new directions and energies liberated from beings and their infinite connections in relation to all that is "something," then ethics is not just embedded in and relies upon an ontology: it requires an ontogenesis, a thinking of the processes that engender all kinds of becomings, within which values, mnemic themes, goals are themselves in the process of becoming and may be able to direct some of becomings in material, natural, and social directions that facilitate more and greater reasoning and more and greater connections.

This is an ethics without norms, without prescriptions, but with an orientation to the future, the force of conatus, the will to power, planes of immanence, of the preindividual and immediate self-survey, all directing themselves toward the pull of the infinite, the infinity of future material and conceptual forms. The pull of our material practices and productions is precisely to the incorporeal world of sense and values, the order or direction of immanence, that are to be made or make themselves rather than be found outside. Art is the celebration of this pull of the future; science is aimed at the ordering and knowledge of its regularizations and the creation of orders of predictability; philosophy provides us with forms of self-reflection that addresses the whole of existence in its complexity, not as a thing but as future orientation. Ethics at its most radical can be understood as the capacity to live with and enhance oneself and one's fellow life forms in an immersion in (fragments or Umwelten of) the world as we can come to understand it, and, as such, ethics is the enhancement of a life of and as becoming through the acknowledgment of its interrelations, less and less direct, with wider and wider circuits of the universe. Ethics can borrow something of the artistic in its celebrations of life, materiality, and their excesses; it can also borrow something of the sciences in seeking a knowledge of and direct familiarity with the many, sometimes contrary, ways in which the world works.

Yet it remains embedded in and part of philosophy, a part that perhaps most directly connects philosophy to what is outside it, which aims at an understanding of the orders of the world and its populations—things, living beings, nations, peoples, as well as ideas and concepts—so that they may enhance themselves and be enhanced in their encounters with other things and with events. The fate to which the Stoics and Nietzsche direct us is nothing but this—to become what one is and to be what one becomes—to become with and in the world with its forces, resources, resistances and to affirm their forces of becoming-otherwise.

NOTES

INTRODUCTION

1. See, for example, Emmanuel Levinas, *Totality and Infinity. An Essay on Exteriority* (Pittsburgh: Dusquesne University Press, 1969). Even among those philosophers who have a deep interest in ethical questions, such as Sartre or Beauvoir, ethics is linked primarily to epistemic rather than ontological concerns.

2. For further details on Bergson's conception of the relations between mind and matter, see Elizabeth Grosz, *The Nick of Time: Politics, Evolution, and the Untimely* (Durham: Duke University Press, 2004), *Time Travels: Feminism, Nature, Power* (Durham: Duke University Press, 2008), and *Becoming Undone: Darwinian Reflections on Life, Art, and Politics* (Durham: Duke University Press, 2011).

3. There are deep discontinuities and disputes between the figures I have brought together here—they each follow a meandering line. And they are not the only philosophers who have sought out a concept that is both ideal and material. Not only Schelling and Hegel, for whom the ideal orders the material, but most particularly Charles Sanders Peirce and Alfred North Whitehead. Many of the figures who make up the so-called new materialism address the intimate engagement of living with nonliving materialities. There is no doubt an affinity between these projects and my own, and I am indebted to new feminist materialisms in the works of Stacy Alaimo, Rosi Braidotti, Claire Colebrook, Diana Coole, and Rebecca Hill. However, I believe that the increasing emphasis on an ever more open materiality must address what this entails for ideality—for ideas, concepts, for space and time, for language and its capacities to represent, signify, and express.

4. Deleuze is commonly understood as a materialist—in, for example, the careful readings of his work undertaken by John Protevi, Daniel W. Smith, Todd May, as well as, in another direction, Manuel de Landa. Slavoj Žižek, in *Organs Without Bodies:*

On Deleuze and Consequences (London: Routledge, 2003), suggests that Deleuze vacillates between materialism and idealism, seeing this as criticism rather than as one of Deleuze's great strengths.

1. THE STOICS, MATERIALISM, AND THE INCORPOREAL

1. In Descartes this was posited through the operations of the pineal gland, a bodily organ that somehow mysteriously enables thought to address and impress the body and the body to express its needs, wishes, and activities to the mind.

2. From Annette Kuhn and AnnMarieWolpe, eds., *Feminism and Materialism* (London: Routledge, 1988); through to Rosi Braidotti, *Metamorphoses: Towards a Materialist Theory of Becoming* (London: Polity, 2002) and *The Posthuman* (London: Polity, 2013), materialism has been a dominant orientation of feminist philosophy; see also Diana Coole and Samantha Frost, eds., *New Materialisms: Ontology, Agency, and Politics* (Durham: Duke University Press, 2010); Stacy Alaimo and Susan Hekman, eds., *Material Feminisms* (Bloomington: Indiana University Press, 2008); Jane Bennett, *Vibrant Matter: A Political Ecology of Things* (Durham: Duke University Press, 2010).

3. For example, object-oriented ontology and speculative realism. See Quentin Mellasioux, *After Finitude. An Essay on the Necessity of Contingency. An Essay on the Necessity of Contingency*, trans. Ray Brassier (London: Bloomsbury Academic, 2010); Ian Bogost, *Alien Phenomenology, or What It's Like to Be a Thing* (Minneapolis: University of Minnesota Press, 2012); and Levi Bryant, Nick Srnicek, and Graham Harman, eds., *The Speculative Turn: Continental Materialism and Realism* (Melbourne: Re.press, 2011).

4. This is perhaps most clearly articulated in Jacques Derrida, *Positions*, trans. Alan Bass (Chicago: University of Chicago Press, 1982).

5. Émile Bréhier, *The History of Philosophy: The Hellenistic and Roman Age*, trans. Wade Baskin (Chicago: University of Chicago Press, 1971), 25.

6. This Zeno, the founder of the Stoa, is not to be confused with Zeno of Elea, who elaborated the famous paradoxes.

7. See Benson Mates, *Stoic Logic* (Berkeley: University of California Press, 1953), 5.

8. There are primarily three sources who cite the works of Zeno, Cleanthes, and Chrisyppus: Diogenes Laërtius, the Augustan; Arius Didymus; and the Byzantine, Stobaeus. See Malcolm Schofield, "Stoic Ethics," in Brad Inwood, ed., *The Cambridge Companion to the Stoics* (Cambridge: Cambridge University Press, 2003), 236. These, and the other Stoic source texts are all are translated and published in A. A. Long and D. N. Sedley, *The Hellenistic Philosophers*, vol. 1: *Translations of the Principal Sources, with Philosophical Commentary* (Cambridge: Cambridge University Press, 1987).

9. Plutarch wrote texts with titles such as *Against the Stoics* and *On the Contradiction of the Stoics*. Bréhier notes that "these treatises, which are either mutilated or malicious, are all that we have except for one valuable source, the summary of Stoic logic which

Diogenes Laërtius copied." Émile Bréhier, *The History of Philosophy: The Hellenistic and Roman Age*, trans. Wade Baskin (Chicago: University of Chicago Press, 1971), 30.

10. Gilles Deleuze, *The Logic of Sense*, trans. Mark Lester (New York: Columbia University Press, 1990), 127, hereafter *LS*.

11. It is perhaps the Semitic tinge that foreign philosophers brought with them that transforms the Stoics into those who believe in both fate and freedom, the freedom to be worthy of the fate which the cosmos has deemed.

12. As Lossky argues: "The Stoics insist throughout that Cosmic Reason is *corporeal*. It is the Fire . . . that penetrates the universe. To distinguish it from ordinary fire they often call it . . . a creative fire, or ether, and . . . the breath of fire. They definitively say that this principle is a *body*, the purest and finest conceivable. This body is God . . . and all other bodies and the world as a whole proceed from it." N. Lossky, "The Metaphysics of the Stoics," *Journal of Philosophical Studies* 4, no. 16 (1929): 481.

13. Ibid., 482.

14. A. A. Long and D. N. Sedley, eds. and trans., *The Hellenistic Philosophers* (Cambridge: Cambridge University Press, 1987), 1:51.

15. Lossky, "The Metaphysics of the Stoics," 482.

16. Contemporary physics has addressed the idea of the inflationary universe, a universe born in a big bang and that ends with the energetic exhaustion of matter, inflating or deflating itself endlessly—precisely the Stoic concept of the eternal return of the universe. See Alan Guth, *The Inflationary Universe: The Quest for a New Theory of Cosmic Origins* (New York: Basic Books, 1998); and João Magueijo and Lee Smolin, "Gravity's Rainbow," *Classical and Quantum Gravity* 21 (2013): 1725–36.

17. A soul is a body insofar as it has causal agency (just as our character or psychology does): according to Nemesius, Cleanthes said that "nothing incorporeal shares an experience with the body, nor does a body with an incorporeal: but the soul suffers with the body when it is ill and when it is cut, and the body [suffers] with the soul—at any rate when [the soul] is ashamed if [the body] turns red, and pale when [the soul] is frightened: therefore, the soul is a body." Brad Inwood and Lloyd Gerson, eds., *The Stoics Reader: Selected Writings and Testimonia* (Indianapolis: Hackett, 2008), 99.

18. As Long and Sedley suggest, "it is not with the existent but with the prior notion of 'something' that the Stoic ontological scheme starts" (*The Hellenistic Philosophers*, 163). The existent, a being, must be endowed with qualities and properties; where a "something" remains indeterminate and in no need of further determination.

19. Quoted in Lossky, "The Metaphysics of the Stoics," 481.

20. Bréhier argues that "reason is a body because it acts, and the thing that is subjected to its actions or is acted upon is also a body and is called matter. An agent (reason or God) and a patient (brute matter that submits docilely to divine action) or, putting it another way, an active body that always acts and is never acted upon together with matter that is acted upon but never acts, such are the two principles posited by the Stoics" (*The History of Philosophy*, 45).

21. *On Fate*, quoted by Sean Bowden, *The Priority of Events: Deleuze's Logic of Sense* (Edinburgh: Edinburgh University Press, 2011), 20.

22. Dorothea Frede explains: "The term 'cause' applies only to a body that is actively engaged in some process or responsible for some fate." Dorothea Frede, "Stoic Determinism," in Inwood, *The Cambridge Companion to the Stoics*, 189.

23. Long and Sedley, *The Hellenistic Philosophers*, 333.

24. Dorothea Frede, "Stoic Determinism," in Inwood, *The Cambridge Companion to the Stoics*, 189.

25. Vanessa de Harven claims that "nothing" is not the same as a not-something. See Vanessa de Harven, "How Nothing Can Be Something: The Stoic Theory of the Void," in "The Coherence of Stoic Ontology" (PhD diss., University of California, Berkeley, 2012). The not-something is not-something-in-particular, but the condition for the appearance of something.

26. See, for example, Alexander's *On Aristotle's Topics*, 301, 19–25: "This is how you could show the impropriety of the Stoics' making 'something' the genus to which the existent belongs: if it is something it is obviously also existent, and if existent it would receive the definition of the existent. But they would escape the difficulty by legislating for themselves that 'existent' is said only of bodies; for on this ground they say that 'something' is more generic than it, being predicated not only of bodies but also of incorporeals" (Long and Sedley, *The Hellenistic Philosophers*, 162).

27. On this point, see John Sellars, *Stoicism* (Los Angeles: University of California Press, 2006), 88–89.

28. Sextus Empiricus, *Against the Professors*, in Long and Sedley, *The Hellenistic Philosophers*, 333.

29. Ibid., 333–34.

30. As Sextus Empiricus claims, "They [the Stoics] say that of somethings some are bodies, others incorporeals, and they list for species of the incorporeals—sayable (*lekton*), void, place, and time" (ibid., 162).

31. This is the position of Marcelo D. Boeri, "The Stoics on Bodies and Incorporeals," *Review of Metaphysics* 54 (2001): 723–52.

32. Jacques Brunschwig, "Stoic Metaphysics," in Inwood, *The Cambridge Companion to the Stoics*, 213. Brunschwig uses a passage from Cleomedes to confirm his claim: "The notion of it is very simple since it is incorporeal and without contact neither has shape nor takes on shape, neither is acted upon in any respect nor acts, but *is* simply capable of receiving the body" (Long and Sedley, *The Hellenistic Philosophers*, 294).

33. Ibid.

34. Brunschwig, "Stoic Metaphysics," 213.

35. Cleomedes describes the void as that which encompasses things, including the whole of the cosmos itself: "Void is not scattered among bodies but encompasses them, and void is something outside the heavens *per se*, just as the impression of many people exceedingly holds, considering void to be something infinite outside the heavens" (quoted in Harven, "How Nothing Can Be Something," 4). Deleuze understands the void not so much as a model of extension but as the site of the intensive. But in the

writings of the Stoics themselves, while void is not the model for space, void and space share the three-dimensional extensity, a capacity to be occupied by bodies.

36. Zeno, quoted in Simplicitus, *On Aristotle's Categories* (Long and Sedley, *The Hellenistic Philosophers*, 304).

37. Apollodorus understands that 'the whole of time is present, as we say that the year is present on a larger compass" (Stobaeus, in Long and Sedley, *The Hellenistic Philosophers*, 304).

38. See, for example, Henri Bergson, *Matter and Memory*, trans. N. M. Paul and W. S. Palmer (New York: Zone, 1988). For Bergson, the past and the future are virtual, while only the present is actual.

39. Stobaeus, in Long and Sedley, *The Hellenistic Philosophers*, 305.

40. Frede provides a convincing explanation of the ways in which Stoic concepts of freedom or human responsibility do not necessarily contradict the idea of a causally determined universe (Inwood, *The Cambridge Companion to the Stoics*, 192–93).

41. It is important not to conflate lekta with Platonic ideas or Cartesian consciousness: the sense they have is not detachable from the bodies to which they adhere.

42. Long and Sedley, *The Hellenistic Philosophers*, 33.

43. Diogenes Laërtius says: "An animal's utterance is air that has been struck by an impulse, but that of man is articulated and issues from thought, as Diogenes [of Babylon] says, and is perfected at the age of fourteen . . . for everything that acts is a body: and utterance acts when it travels from those who utter it to those who hear it" (Long and Sedley, *The Hellenistic Philosophers*, 185).

44. In the briefest terms, Stoic arguments are not developed out of terms, as in Aristotelian logic, but out of assertables or propositions that provide information about the world. In the classical Aristotelian syllogism "All men are mortal, Socrates is a man, therefore Socrates is mortal," the first or major premise already contains the conclusion. The Stoics invented five main types of syllogism that are indemonstrable or axiomatic (developing *modus ponens* and *modus tollens* forms), such as the following:

   1. The conditional: "If it is light, it is day."
   2. The conjunctive: "It is light and it is day."
   3. The disjunctive: "Either it is light or it is day."
   4. The causal: "It is light because it is day."
   5. The likely: "It is more likely that it is day than that it is night."

   These kinds of arguments provide us with the possibility of knowing something new, transient, nontautological, beyond the major premise. For further details, see John Sellars, *Stoicism* (Los Angeles: University of California Press, 2006), 58–60; and Susanne Bobzien, "Logic," in Inwood, *The Cambridge Companion to the Stoics*, 85–123.

45. Diogenes Laërtius, in Long and Sedley, *The Hellenistic Philosophers*, 202.

46. Quoted in de Harven, "How Nothing Can Be Something," 41.

47. The concept of impressions and the ways in which perceptions mark the mind and enable the creation of propositions is central to Stoic epistemology, psychology, and logic. See Sellars, *Stoicism*, 70–74.

48. For example, Frede, "Stoic Determinism"; and Jacques Brunschwig, "Stoic Metaphysics," also in Inwood, *The Cambridge Companion to the Stoics*, 206–32.

49. Long and Sedley, *The Hellenistic Philosophers*, 340.

50. Deleuze, in *LS*, 5, claims that the incorporeal is a *way of being* rather than a being.

51. Foucault's last two books *A History of Sexuality*, vol. 3: *The Care of the Self*, trans. Robert Hurley (New York: Vintage, 1988) and *A History of Sexuality*, vol. 2: *The Use of Pleasure*, trans. Robert Hurley (New York: Vintage, 1990), were strongly influenced by Stoic ethics.

52. Marcus Aurelius, *The Meditations*, trans. G. M. A. Grube (Indianapolis: Hackett, 1988), 28, book 4, 14.

53. Epictetus, *The Handbook*, trans. Nicholas P. White (Indianapolis: Hackett, 1983), 49.

54. Diogenes Laërtius claims that there are eight topics (it is not clear if this is a systematic or comprehensive list, or an order for the discussion of ethics) of "the ethical part of philosophy," which the Stoics divide into "A] the topic of impulse; B] the topic of goods and bads; C] the topic of passions, D] of virtue, E] of the goal, F] of primary value and actions, G] of appropriate functions, H] of persuasions and dissuasions" (cited in Schofield, "Stoic Ethics," 237; see also Long and Sedley, *The Hellenistic Philosophers*, 112 for a different translation).

55. Marcus Aurelius, *The Meditations*, 34, book 4, 41.

56. Cited in Schofield, "Stoic Ethics," 244.

57. Stobaeus, in Inwood and Gerson, *The Stoics Reader*, 128.

58. Ibid., 126.

59. Diogenes Laërtius, in Long and Sedley, *The Hellenistic Philosophers*, 346.

60. Epictetus. *The Handbook*, trans. Nicholas P. White (Indianapolis: Hackett, 1983), 1, book 1.

61. Stobaeus, in Long and Sedley, *The Hellenistic Philosophers*, 355.

62. Ibid., 356.

63. For the Stoics, as Stobaeus represents them, sexual love (with women and boys, for men) is not a degradation of ethics, but one of the preferred indifferents and indeed, conditions of life: "Being worthy of sexual love means the same as being worthy of friendship, and not the same as being worthy of being enjoyed; for he who is worthy of virtuous sexual love is properly worthy of sexual love. . . . And sexual activity just by itself is an indifferent since at times it also occurs among base men. But sexual love is not desire nor is it directed at any base object but is an effort to gain friendship resulting from the appearance of beauty" (Inwood and Gerson, *The Stoics Reader*, 128). Strangely enough, Deleuze also address the question of sexuality and its relations not only to ethics but to the constitution of both bodies and sense: "It is certain that the sexual organization is a prefiguration of the organization of language, just as the physical surface was a preparation for the metaphysical surface. The phallus plays an important role in the stages of the conflict between mouth and brain. Sexuality is in between eating and speaking, and, at the same time that the sexual drives are detached from the destructive alimentary drives, they inspire the first words made up of phonemes, morphemes, and semantemes. Sexual organization already presents us with an entire point-line-surface system" (*LS* 242). This may explain Deleuze's well-known but

puzzling affirmation of the girl's special relation to Stoicism: "As a general rule, only little girls understand Stoicism; they have a sense of the event and release an incorporeal double. But it sometimes happens that a little boy is a stutterer and left-handed, and thus conquers sense as the double sense or direction of the surface" (*LS* 10). It also explains why the boy, as a left-handed stutterer, as someone who wants to retain both the phallus and the mother, may have some access to it as well. The children who refuse the oedipal injunction, who resist phallocentrism, may come to know something of a universe beyond the self and its desires.

64. Diogenes, translated in Julia Annas, "Ethics in Stoic Philosophy," *Phronesis* 52 (2007): 74.

2. SPINOZA, SUBSTANCE, AND ATTRIBUTES

1. Gilles Deleuze and Félix Guattari, *What Is Philosophy?* trans. Hugh Tomlinson and Graham Burchill (New York: Columbia University Press), 60, hereafter *WIP*.

2. Deleuze and Guattari represent the culmination of a French philosophical obsession with Spinoza over the last seventy years that redresses the privileging of Cartesianism in French thought for the previous three centuries by returning to the disturbing and effective alternative to dualism that Spinoza developed, a fascination that marks the writings of Louis Althusser in *Reading Capital,* trans. Ben Brewster (London: New Left, 1977); Etienne Balibar, "Spinoza: From Individuality to Transindividuality," *Mededelingen vanwege het Spinozahuis* (1997): 11–59, http://www.ciepfc.fr/spip.php?article236); Luce Irigaray, *An Ethics of Sexual Difference,* trans. Caroyn Burke and Gillian C. Gill (Ithaca: Cornell University Press), not to mention Pierre Macheray and Antonio Negri. It is largely Deleuze's frequent discussions of Spinoza that have served to introduce a new generation of thinkers to Spinoza's revivification of immanence in feminist and queer theory and ecopolitics. See, for example, Hasana Sharp, *Spinoza and the Politics of Renaturalization* (Chicago: University of Chicago Press, 2011); and Genevieve Lloyd and Moira Gatens, *Collective Imaginings: Spinoza Past and Present* (London: Routledge, 1999).

3. See, for example, Aurelia Armstrong, "The Passions, Power, and Practical Philosophy: Spinoza and Nietzsche Contra the Stoics," *Journal of Nietzsche Studies* 44, no. 1 (2013): 6–24; and Fermin DeBrabander, *Spinoza and the Stoics: Power, Politics, and the Passions* (London: Continuum, 2007).

4. Such as Amélie Oksenberg Rorty, "The Two Faces of Spinoza," *Review of Metaphysics* 41 (1987): 299–316; Jon Miller, "Spinoza and the Stoics on Substance Monism," in Olli Koistinen, ed., *The Cambridge Companion to Spinoza's Ethics* (Cambridge: Cambridge University Press, 2012), 99–117; and Alexandre Matheron, "Ideas of Ideas and Certainty in the *Tractatus de Intellectus Emendatione* and in the *Ethics*," trans. Jonathan Bennett, in Yirmiyahu Yovel, ed., *Spinoza on Knowledge and the Human Mind* (Leiden: Brill, 1994).

5. See Leibniz, "Two Sects of Naturalists," 282; Leibniz also wrote a paper in 1707 specifically directed at Spinoza's writings, "Comments on Spinoza's Philosophy," both published in *G. W. Leibniz: Philosophical Essays,* ed. and trans. Roger Ariew and Daniel Garber (Indianapolis: Hackett, 1989).

6.   "The Stoics thought that [reason's dominion over affects] depend entirely on the will, and that we can command them absolutely. But experience cries out against this, and has forced them, in spite of their principles, to confess that much practice and application are required to restrain and modify [the affects]." Spinoza, *Ethics*, V, preface (II/276), hereafter *E*. Throughout this chapter I will use the traditional way of referring to Spinoza's *Ethics*, by book, definition, axiom, proposition, corollary, scholia, rather than page number. References are to the Curley translation unless noted otherwise. See Curley's abbreviations for the text in the frontmatter. While Spinoza is correct to distinguish between the Stoics' conception of will and his own understand of the will's nonexistence and its replacement by the order of causes, there is still a great deal that connects them, far more than Spinoza recognizes. Their ontologies resonate, and although each derives an ethics on the basis of a reasoned knowledge of the real, or God, they come to different understandings of what that ethics consists in.

7.   This is broadly Fermin DeBrabander's argument in *Spinoza and the Stoics: Power, Politics and the Passions* (London: Continuum, 2007), 2.

8.   Spinoza here clearly differs from the Stoics. Effects for him are as material as causes; they cannot be considered ideas; or lekta. Moreover, Spinoza affirms that these causal relations, including the network of effects, are a matter of great significance to living beings, who make themselves through these relations. For Spinoza, there is a direction to causal action, ends and goals, aims and purposes, but no higher purpose, no preordained direction.

9.   In his analysis of the Stoics, Spinoza, and Nietzsche, Donald Rutherford argues that Spinoza goes beyond the Stoics in two primary ways—his rejection of the Stoics' teleological structuring of nature (something, however, that Nietzsche returns to in his understanding of the eternal return) and his rejection of a providential God, or gods, intimately involved with and concerned about human affairs. However, what they share is a concept of freedom. Donald Rutherford, "Freedom as a Philosophical Ideal: Nietzsche and His Antecedents," *Inquiry* 54, no. 5 (2011): 519.

10.   See Aurelia Armstrong, "The Passions, Power, and Practical Philosophy: Spinoza and Nietzsche Contra the Stoics," *Journal of Nietzsche Studies*, 44, no. 1 (2013): 7–8.

11.   Jon Miller argues that, while there are nuanced differences between Stoic and Spinozist conceptions of substance, nevertheless there is an underlying shared concept of nature. Jon Miller, "Spinoza and the Stoics on Substance Monism," in Olli Koistinen, ed., *The Cambridge Companion to Spinoza's Ethics* (Cambridge: Cambridge University Press, 2012), 105.

12.   Spinoza's surviving correspondence is testimony to the growing hostility to his work, even among those with some friendly allegiance to him. See, for example, Letter 34 to Blyenbergh, in *Works of Spinoza. On the Improvement of Human Intellect; The Ethics; Selected Letters,* trans. R. H. M. Elwes (New York: Dover, 1951), 336–44.

13.   Errol E. Harris, *The Substance of Spinoza* (Atlantic Highlands, NJ: Humanities International, 1995), 13.

14.   Benedict de Spinoza, *Ethics*, trans. Edwin Curley (London: Penguin, 1996), ID6, hereafter *E*.

15. His opponents, who believe in the divisibility of substance and use it to claim that substance cannot be divine, "wish to infer that extended substance is finite. . . . They suppose an infinite quantity to be measurable and composed of finite parts. . . . So also others, after they feign that a line is composed of points, know how to invent many arguments, by which they show that a line cannot be divided to infinity. And indeed it is no less absurd to assert that corporeal substance is composed of bodies, or parts, than that a body is composed of surfaces, the surfaces of lines, and the lines, finally, of points" (*E* IP15, SIV).

16. Deleuze understands the force of an incalculable infinite in part from his reading of Bergson's writings on the qualitative character of duration, which distinguishes it from the numerical, designatable character of space. Gilles Deleuze, *Expressionism in Philosophy: Spinoza,* trans. Martin Joughin (New York: Zone, 1990), 33.

17. Spinoza, Letter 72 in *Works of Spinoza,* 409. For Spinoza, in other words, extension per se, the mere principle of taking up space, of three dimensionality, is the barest understanding of materiality, which is composed of relations between things, relations that necessarily occupy space. For him, materiality is a positive engagement of at least two, although, in fact, very large numbers of things, in relation to each other. "Extension" serves as his shorthand for the relation of extended material things to each other.

18. Spinoza clearly differentiates conception from perception, which he defines in relation to the active power of the mind to produce and the mind's passive position in relation to perception (*E* IID3, E). If the concept is active, perception is passive, the result of the mind being acted upon.

19. Pierre Macherey argues that Spinoza does not, contrary to Hegel's interpretation of him, elaborate a new kind of idealism, in which attributes are understood as subjective projections rather than parts or aspects under which we can understand something of the real qualities and forces of the attributes. See Pierre Macherey, "The Problem of Attributes," in W. Montag and T. Stolze, eds., *The New Spinoza* (Minneapolis: University of Minnesota Press, 1997), 73.

20. Ibid., 79.

21. Ibid., 79–80.

22. Macherey argues that number is a projection of the imagination, perhaps even a productive projection, but one that reduces substance to Being: "By himself, God is not 'one,' any more than he is two or three, or he is beautiful or ugly. Contrary to a tenacious tradition, it must be said that Spinoza was no more a monist than he was a dualist, or a representative of any number that one wants to assign to this fiction, a number all the better for the ignorant or the slave" (ibid., 88).

23. Gilles Deleuze, *Expressionism in Philosophy: Spinoza,* trans. Martin Joughin (New York: Zone, 1990), 13.

24. As Deleuze elaborates, in arguing that expressionism is Spinoza's way of addressing immanence: "To explicate is to evolve, to involve is to implicate. Yet the two terms are not opposites: they simply mark two aspects of expression. Expression is on the one hand an explication, an unfolding of what expresses itself, the One manifesting itself in the Many (substance manifesting itself in its attributes, and these attributes

manifesting themselves in their modes). Its multiple expression, on the other hand, involves Unity" (ibid., 16).

25. Spinoza reserves a special place of scorn for Descartes's "solution" to the division between mind and body, the pineal gland: "Descartes . . . maintained that the soul, or mind, was especially united to a certain part of the brain, called the pineal gland, by whose aid the mind is aware of all the motions aroused in the body and of external objects, and which the mind can move in various ways simply by willing. . . . For example, if someone has a will to look at a distant object, this will brings it about that the pupil is dilated" (*E* V, Preface). Spinoza also directs his incredulity to Descartes's recourse to the concept of a benevolent God who guarantees the correspondence of our (mental) ideas with their (material) objects.

26. While Irigaray accuses Spinoza of participating in the phallocentric exclusion of woman (*An Ethics of Sexual Difference*, 88), she also acknowledges that Spinoza may provide a way to think sexual difference as a relation between (at least) two: "If man and woman are both body and thought, they provide each other with finiteness, limit and the possibility of access to the divine thought through the development of envelopes. Greater and greater envelopes, vaster and vaster horizons, but above all, envelopes that are qualitatively more and more necessary and different. But always *overflowing*; with the female one becoming a cause of the other by providing him with self-cause. The set-up must always be open for this to occur. It must also afford *qualitative* difference. Essence must never be completely realized in existence—as Spinoza might say?" (86).

27. See Deleuze, *Expressionism in Philosophy*, 35–36.

28. Spinoza affirms: "Therefore, God has the idea of the human body, *or* knows the human body, insofar as he is affected by a great many other ideas, and not insofar as he constitutes the nature of the human mind, that is, the human mind does not know the human body" (*E* IIP19D).

29. Harris, *The Substance of Spinoza*, 26.

30. Effects are just as real as causes for Spinoza. See Gilles Deleuze, *Spinoza: Practical Philosophy*, trans. Robert Hurley (San Francisco: City Lights, 1988), 91.

31. Deleuze argues that there is a parallel between the conceptual and the material that mirrors or expresses an ontological relation (ibid.).

32. This is Edwin Curley's argument, in *Beyond the Geometrical Method: A Reading of Spinoza's Ethics* (Princeton: Princeton University Press, 1988), that modes are causally connected to substance and actual things can be deduced from causal or natural laws alone. Bennett claims that the inherence of modes in substance must include more than causality. Harris claims that the reduction of things to expressions of the laws of nature, as Curley attempts, is a confused idea (for it leaves aside the mediation between the laws of nature that leads to the existence of actual things). See Errol Harris, *The Substance of Spinoza* (Atlantic Highlands, NJ: Humanities International Press, 1995), 31.

33. An essence is perfectly capable of expressing God without existence. Its essence is "in" God; existence is determined by causal chains. God generates, in extension, causal chains, as he generates, in thought, essences (*E* I, EP24C).

34. See www.webdeleuze.com/php/sommaire.html, as well as Deleuze, *Expressionism in Philosophy* and *Spinoza: Practical Philosophy*.

35. To mention just a few such examples, Brian Massumi, in *Parables for the Virtual 1: Movement, Affect, Sensation* (Durham: Duke University Press, 2010); Patricia Clough and Jean Halley, eds., *The Affective Turn: Theorizing the Social* (Durham: Duke University Press, 2007); Melissa Gregg and Gregory Seigworth, ed., *The Affect Theory Reader* (Durham: Duke University Press, 2010); and Elizabeth Wilson, *Affect and Artificial Intelligence* (Seattle: University of Washington Press, 2010).

36. Gilles Deleuze, "Lecture Transcripts on Spinoza's Concept of Affect" (1978, http:www.webdeleuze.com/php/sommaire.html), paragraph 5.

37. Letter 32 in *Works of Spinoza*, 291–92.

38. Ibid., 292.

39. Letter 62 to Anon (G. H. Schaller), ibid., 390.

40. Spinoza discusses this briefly in *E* IV, Appendix 19–20.

41. "Man's lack of power to moderate and restrain the affects I call bondage. For man who is subject to affects is under the control, not of himself, but of fortune, in whose power he so greatly is that often, though he sees the better for himself, he is still forced to follow the worse" (*E* IV preface).

42. As Spinoza understands these terms, *will* refers to the mind's strivings, while *appetite* refers to the body's. Yet, these are two angles on the same thing (*E* IIIP9S).

43. Spinoza's reading of the story in the creation claims that the angel warns Adam not to eat the forbidden fruit, not because it is a commandment from God, but because it disagrees with his nature. It will make him sick. We have misinterpreted this story as a moral injunction rather than a therapeutic prescription. The apple is not morally forbidden, it is a conjunction, a bad encounter, that disagrees with Adam's nature. See Spinoza's letter to Blyenbergh, Letter 32, in *Works of Spinoza*, 334–35. For further discussion, see Deleuze, *Spinoza: Practical Philosophy*, 22, and *Expressionism in Philosophy*, 247.

44. Spinoza describes friendship as a self-evident good, insofar as man thrives better in the company of other men (*E* IV, P37S1 (II/236)).

3. NIETZSCHE AND *AMOR FATI*

1. Nietzsche considers consciousness the result of the turning inward of instincts that are directed outward in animals, the taming of body and thought. Nietzsche, *The Gay Science*, trans. Walter Kaufmann (New York: Vintage, 1974), #333, hereafter *GS*. Not only is consciousness the least interesting part of thought, it is also its most conservative director (*GS* #354). As is common in Nietzsche scholarship, I will refer to numbered paragraphs or sections in Nietzsche's texts rather than page numbers, as this enables any translation to be useful.

2. Yirmiyahu Yovel, *Spinoza and Other Heretics: The Adventures of Immanence* (Princeton: Princeton University Press, 1989), 111.

3. *GS* #10.

4. His paper, "De Laertii Diogenis fontibus. I–IV" was published in *Rheinisches Museaum für Phililogie*, vols. 33–34 (1868–69). For further detail on the influence of Diogenes and his compilation of a history that Nietzsche also identified as part of his task as a philosopher of the future, see Jonathan Barnes's analysis of their relations, "Nietzsche and Diogenes Laertius," in Anthony Jensen and Helmut Heit, eds., *Nietzsche as a Scholar of Antiquity* (London: Bloomsbury, 2014), 115–38. See also Nietzsche's *The Pre-Platonic Philosophers*, ed. and trans. Greg Whitlock (Chicago: University of Illinois Press, 2006).

5. This relation to Stoic therapeutics is perhaps most striking in Nietzsche, *Human, All Too Human: A Book for Free Spirits*, trans. R. J. Hollingdale (Cambridge: Cambridge University Press, 1988); by the time Nietzsche publishes *The Gay Science*, his relation to the Stoics and their conception of the overcoming of passions becomes more critical. For a more detailed analysis of this development in Nietzsche's writings, see Michael Ure, "Nietzsche's Free Spirit Trilogy and Stoic Therapy," *Journal of Nietzsche Studies* 38 (2009): 60–84; and Aurelia Armstrong, "The Passions, Power, and Practical Philosophy: Spinoza and Nietzsche Contra the Stoics," *Journal of Nietzsche Studies* 44, no. 1 (2013): 6–24.

6. Although often associated with pleasure seeking, Epicurus of Samos (341–270 bce) sought a life free from the debilitations of pain and directed by a tranquillity that is lifelong, rather than momentary pleasures.

7. For a more detailed discussion of the relation between Nietzsche's understanding of fate and that of the Stoics, see Donald Rutherford, "Freedom as a Philosophical Ideal: Nietzsche and His Antecedents," *Inquiry* 54, no. 5 (2011): 512–40.

8. Nietzsche, "Why I Write Such Great Books," #1, in *Ecce Homo*, in *On the Genealogy of Morals; and Ecce Homo*, trans. Walter Kauffman (New York: Vintage, 1969), hereafter *EH*.

9. Nietzsche invokes such an audience for those readers of Zarathustra who may really understand him in his final text: "This book belongs to the most rare of men. Perhaps not one of them is yet alive. It is possible that they may be among those who understand my *Zarathustra*: how *could* I confound myself with those who are now sprouting ears?—First the day after tomorrow must come for me. Some men are born posthumously." Nietzsche, "Preface," *The Anti-Christ*, in *Twilight of the Idols; and The Anti-Christ*, trans. R. J. Hollingdale (London: Penguin, 1972).

10. As Yovel argues in his analysis of Nietzsche, "Nietzsche and Spinoza: *Amor Fati* and *Amor Dei*," in Yirmiyahu Yovel, ed., *Nietzsche as Affirmative Thinker* (The Hague: Martinus Nijhoff, 1986):

    > The pair *amor dei* and *amor fati* can provide an adequate verbal representation of the complex relationship between Nietzsche and Spinoza, the two enemy-brothers of modern philosophy. Perhaps no two philosophers are as akin as Spinoza and Nietzsche, yet no two others are as opposed as they are. If Spinoza started the modern philosophy of immanence and underlies it throughout, then Nietzsche brings it to its most radical conclusion—and . . . turns this conclusion against Spinoza himself. Nietzsche explicitly recognizes his debt and kinship to

Spinoza. Speaking of his "ancestors," Nietzsche at various times gives several lists, but he always mentions Spinoza.

(183)

11. Spinoza's *Theological-Political Treatise* (I, #4), trans. Michael Silverhorn and Jonathon Israel (Cambridge: Cambridge University Press, 2007).

12. For all Nietzsche's admiration for the natural sciences, he remains critical of the assumptions of its practitioners (and readers) that science simply states the truth. In a passage that closely anticipates the work of Thomas Kuhn, Nietzsche affirms the necessarily unscientific origins of science that always leave their trace in contemporary science: "*To make it possible for this discipline to begin*, must there not be some prior conviction—even one that is so commanding and unconditional that it sacrifices all other convictions to itself? We see that science also rests on a faith; there simply is no science 'without presuppositions'" (*GS* #344).

13. Nietzsche is here probably closer to the Stoics than Spinoza: for him, causation, the model that conceives cause as distinct from effect, is fictional insofar as it separates out elements, cause and effect, from a continuum and identifies in them causal agency and passive effect when we should direct ourselves more carefully to the continuum from which they are arbitrarily cut.

14. On the question of why there is little to no discussion of art in Spinoza's works, see James C Morrison, "Why Spinoza Had No Aesthetics," *Journal of Aesthetics and Art Criticism* 47, no. 4 (1989): 359–65.

15. In a section of *The Gay Science* called "Our Ultimate Gratitude to Art" (#107), Nietzsche affirms that art is the condition of untruth that makes the truth of science possible: "If we had not welcomed the arts and invented this kind of cult of the untrue, then the realization of the general untruth and mendaciousness that now comes to us through science—the realization that delusion and error are conditions of human knowledge and sensation—would be utterly unbearable. *Honesty* would lead to nausea and suicide. . . . As an aesthetic phenomenon existence is still *bearable* for us, art furnishes us with eyes and hands and above all the good conscience to be *able* to turn ourselves into such a phenomenon."

16. If God is dead and we are responsible for this killing, then the divine is error itself (*GS* #344). Even given the central place he accords to art in the development of the gay science, he differentiates between the arts: music, more than theater, enhances life. Theater remains directed to the most coarse and common impulses, to which some or most music tends too, including Wagner's, while music has the capacity to enhance sorrow and melancholy as much as joy (its strength). See *GS* #368, where he explains that his objection to Wagner's music is its theatricality.

17. The "higher" human is not the brightest or the bravest but the one most open to being affected, the most passionate, the one who can convert the intensity of senses into an affirmation of the world and thus an affirmation of itself (*GS* #301).

18. As much as Nietzsche expresses his admiration for the pre-Socratics, he also expresses his disdain for those that come after, the Platonists who prepare for Christianity. It is only the Romans who make the Greeks legible: "I have received absolutely no such

strong impressions from the Greeks; and, not to mince words, they *cannot* be to us what the Romans are. One does not *learn* from the Greeks—their manner is too strange, it is also too fluid to produce an imperative, a 'classical' effect. Who would ever have learned to write from a Greek! Who would ever have learned it *without* the Romans! . . . Plato is boring. —Ultimately my mistrust of Plato extends to the very bottom of him: I find him deviated so far from all the fundamental instincts of the Hellenes, so morally infected, so much an antecedent Christian" ("What I Owe to the Ancients," in *Twilight of the Idols*, #2 hereafter *TI*).

19.   *TI* #4.

20.   Nietzsche, *The Anti-Christ*, #7.

21.   Nietzsche argues strongly in a number of texts that the mechanistic understanding of the world suits the scientist, perhaps, but does not represent the real. Nietzsche addresses scientists themselves "That the only justifiable interpretation of the world should be one in which *you* are justified because one can continue to do work and do research scientifically in *your* sense (you really mean mechanistically?)—an interpretation that permits counting, calculating, weighing, seeing and touching, and nothing more—that is crudity and naiveté, assuming it is not a mental illness, an idiocy" (*GS* #373).

22.   Nietzsche, *The Will to Power,* trans. Walter Kauffman and R. J. Hollingdale (New York: Vintage, 1968), hereafter *WP*.

23.   Nietzsche claims that the Dionysian does not rise above the human but intensifies it ("What I Owe the Ancients," *TI* #5).

24.   "For a typically healthy person . . . being sick can even become an energetic *stimulus* for life, for living *more*. This, in fact, is how that long period of sickness appears to me *now*: as it were, I discovered life anew, including myself; I tasted all good and even little things, as others cannot taste them—I turned my will to health, for *life*, into a philosophy." "Why I Am So Wise," *EH*.

25.   *EH* # 2.

26.   It is clear that for Nietzsche the primary conditions for self-overcoming are not collective, social, interpersonal, but primarily solitary, a matter of the rare individual actively confronting his (or her) own limits, with no concern for others, for those understood as weak, unhealthy, downtrodden, or part of the herd. Nietzsche has long been recognized as an imperial thinker, one indifferent or actively hostile to collectively ordered and measured social change. This is perhaps the reason for a common feminist nervousness in using his works to address social and political questions central to feminism or to other philosophies directed to questions of oppression and resistance.

27.   Among current competing accounts of the origins of the universe in post-Einsteinian cosmology, there are a number that seem to support Nietzsche's hypothesis of the eternal return and question the dominant present assumption of a single big bang. The idea that there is no big bang, no single moment of origin for the universe, is developed in the work of João Magueijo and Lee Smolin, "Gravity's Rainbow," *Classical and Quantum Gravity* 21 (2004): 1725–36; and in the work of Adel Awad, Ahmed Farag Ali, and Barun Majumder, "Nonsingular Rainbow Universes," *Journal of Cosmology*

and Astroparticle Physics 52 (2013), doi:10.1088/1475–7516/2013/10/052. On the theory of multiple inflationary universes, see Alan Guth, *The Inflationary Universe: The Quest for a New Theory of Cosmic Origins* (New York: Basic Books, 1998).

28. Nietzsche makes his most clear and explicit characterization of the eternal return in *WP* #1066:

> If the world may be thought of as a certain definite quantity of force, and as a certain definite number of centers of force—and every other representation remains indefinite and therefore useless—it follows that, in the great dice game of existence, it must pass through a calculable number of combinations. In infinite time, every possible combination would at some time or another be realized; more: it would be realized an infinite number of times. And since between every combination and its next recurrence all other possible combinations would have to take place, and each of these combinations conditions the entire sequence of combinations in the same series, a circular movement that has already repeated itself infinitely often and plays its game *in infinitum*.

29. As Nietzsche proclaims (*WP* #1062). In #1063 he announces: "The law of the conservation of energy demands *eternal recurrence*."

30. Nietzsche, *Thus Spoke Zarathustra: A Book for All and None*, trans. Walter Kauffman (New York: Modern Library, 1995), III, 13, hereafter *Z*.

31. Luce Irigaray, *Marine Lover: Of Friedrich Nietzsche*, trans. Gillian C Gill (New York: Columbia University Press, 1991), 26.

32. As Irigaray claims: "And, in the eternal recurrence, she [the mythical Ariadne, Nietzsche's greatest love] attends your wedding celebration, she takes part in it, but you yourself are bride and groom. She keeps hold of the thread, anchors the harmony, sings the tune. An accompaniment that is necessary to you while remaining fundamentally reactive as long as you do not allow her her self" (ibid., 26).

33. Ibid., 11.

34. For further detail on the relation of the dead father to the living mother, see Derrida's reading of Nietzsche in *The Ear of the Other: Otobiography, Transference, Translation*, trans. Peggy Kamuf (Lincoln: University of Nebraska Press, 1988).

35. See, for example, Brian Domino, "Nietzsche's Use of *Amor Fati* in *Ecce Homo*," *Journal of Nietzsche Studies* 43, no. 2 (2012): 283–302; and Robert Solomon, "Nietzsche on Fatalism and 'Free Will,'" *Journal of Nietzsche Studies* 23 (2002): 63–87, for the distinction between amor fati and determinism.

36. Nietzsche insists that, without satisfaction, one cannot but elaborate *ressentiment* (*GS* #290).

37. Even for the highest and strongest humans, there is a moment which, beyond the recognition of scientific laws and our own nature, "no matter how much we have faced up to the beautiful chaos of existence and denied it all providential reason and goodness, we have still to pass our hardest test. For it is only now that the idea of a personal providence confronts us with the most penetrating force, and the best advocate, the evidence of our eyes, speaks for it—now that we can see how palpably always everything that

happens to us turns out for the best. Every day and every hour, life seems to have no other wish that to prove this proposition again and again" (*GS* #269).

38. On the relation between Nietzsche and the Stoics with regard to the question of necessity, see Béatrice Han-Pile, "Nietzsche and *Amor Fati*," *European Journal of Philosophy* 19, no. 2 (2009), especially 229–35.

39. In Nietzsche, *Human, All Too Human. A Book for Free Spirits*, trans. R. J. Hollingdale (Cambridge: Cambridge University Press, 1988), #150, he conjectures that art has the ability to replace religious feelings, to provide a kind of sublimation of the tendency to worship.

4. DELEUZE AND THE PLANE OF IMMANENCE

1. Nietzsche, *Selected Letters of Friedrich Nietzsche*, trans. C. Middleton (Indianapolis: Hackett, 1996), 259.

2. In his study of the reception of Nietzsche's work in France before the First World War, *Zarathustra in Paris: The Nietzsche Vogue in France, 1891–1910* (DeKalb: North Illinios University Press, 2001), Christopher Forth claims that writers in the short-lived journal *Le Banquet* were responsible for Nietzsche's "avant-garde" reception in France. In addition, his reception by writers such as Proust, Flaubert, France, and Baudelaire substantially contributed to Nietzsche's strange becoming-French.

3. Gaultier, quoted in Ali Nematollohay, "Nietzsche in France, 1890–1914," trans. Sheldon Huggins, *Philosophical Forum* 40 (2009): 172. For further on the differences between Nietzsche's French and German receptions, see Henri Lichtenberger, "France and Germany Judged by Nietzsche," *Philosophical Forum* 40 (2009): 211–27.

4. Gilles Deleuze and Félix Guattari, *Anti-Oedipus. Capitalism and Schizophrenia*, vol. 1, trans. Robert Hurley, Mark Seem, and Helen R. Lane (London: Athlone, 1983).

5. Gilles Deleuze, *Empiricism and Subjectivity*, trans. Constantine Boundas (New York: Columbia University Press, 1991).

6. Daniel W. Smith, in "Deleuze and the Question of Desire: Toward an Immanent Theory of Ethics," *Parrhesia* 2 (2007): 66–67, articulates the distinction between morality and ethics: "Deleuze . . . uses the term 'morality' to define, in very general terms, any set of 'constraining' rules, such as a moral code, that consists in judging actions and intentions by relating them to transcendent or universal values. . . . What he calls 'ethics' is, on the contrary, a set of 'facilitative' rules that evaluate what we do, say or think according to an immanent mode of existence that implies this. One says or does this, thinks or feels that: what mode of existence does it imply?" I agree with Smith's distinction, even though, throughout this text, I have used the terminology of the particular philosophers themselves (hence Nietzsche's concept is *morals* or *morality* rather than my preferred term *ethics*).

7. Critics from the time of the publication of *The Logic of Sense* and *Difference and Repetition* have accused Deleuze of amoralism and apoliticism, without understanding that his project is the transfiguration of ethics and politics as we currently understand them

and their replacement by an immanentist ontology. Gilles Deleuze, *The Logic of Sense*, trans. Mark Lester (New York: Columbia University Press, 1990), hereafter *LS; Difference and Repetition*, trans. Paul Patton (New York: Columbia University Press, 1994), hereafter *DR*. Gayatri Spivak, in "Can the Subaltern Speak?" in Cary Nelson and Lawrence Grossberg, eds., *Marxism and the Interpretation of Culture* (Chicago: University of Illinois Press, 1988), especially 273–75; along with Alice Jardine, in *Gynesis: Configurations of Woman and Modernity* (Ithaca: Cornell University Press, 1986); and Rosi Braidotti, in her earliest writings, especially *Patterns of Dissonance* (Cambridge: Polity, 1991), make these charges against Deleuze. See Alain Badiou, *Deleuze: The Clamour of Being*, trans. Louise Burchill (Minneapolis: University of Minnesota Press, 2000); and Peter Hallward, *Out of this World: Deleuze and the Philosophy of Creation* (London: Verso, 2006) for more detailed critiques of his ontological politics.

8.   I am reluctant to put Foucault into this category of philosophers, though it is clear that he shares many concerns with Deleuze, because Foucault comes to regard his work explicitly as an ethics, and, although both the Stoics and Nietzsche are powerful influences for him, his concern with the ethics of self-regulation seems indifferent to questions of ontology and the distinction between material and ideal.

9.   See Alberto Toscano, *The Theatre of Individuation: Philosophy and Individuation Between Kant and Deleuze* (London: Palgrave Macmillan, 2006), for an analysis of Deleuze's attempts to derive a quite different conception of ethics from Kant.

10. Gilles Deleuze, "Life as a Work of Art," in *Negotiations, 1972–1990*, trans. Martin Joughin (New York: Columbia University Press, 1995), 100.

11. Ibid.

12. Deleuze understood this entwinement of ethics and ontology most explicitly in relation to Spinoza: "Spinoza didn't entitle his book Ontology, he's too shrewd for that, he entitles it Ethics. Which is a way of saying that, whatever the importance of my speculative propositions may be, you can only judge them at the level of the ethics that they envelope or imply." Deleuze, "Lecture Transcripts on Spinoza's Concept of Affect," http:www.webdeleuze.com/php/sommaire.html.

13. Bogue identifies Deleuze's "ethic of the event" explicitly with Nietzsche's amor fati, with Spinoza's ethics, and with the Stoic concept of the incorporeal event. See Ronald Bogue, *Deleuze's Way: Essays in Transverse Ethics and Aesthetics* (Burlington, VT: Ashgate, 2007), 7–8.

14. This seems to be the tenor of criticisms inspired by Badiou's reading of Deleuze as a philosopher of "the one." See Badiou, *Deleuze*; and Miguel de Beistegui, "The Vertigo of Immanence: Deleuze's Spinozism," *Research in Phenomenology* 35 (2005): 77–100.

15. For a rare exception, see Eric Alliez, *The Signature of the World: What Is Deleuze and Guattari's Philosophy?* trans. Eliot Ross Albert and Alberto Toscano (London: Continuum, 2004).

16. Deleuze provides much less detail regarding the plane of reference than the planes of immanence and composition. In *What Is Philosophy?* trans. Hugh Tomlinson and Graham Burchill (New York: Columbia University Press), hereafter *WIP*, and in "What Is a Creative Act?" he suggests that the scientist too must throw a plane over chaos in order

to slow it down and make it capable of supporting calculations, sets. Gilles Deleuze, "What Is a Creative Act?" in *Two Regimes of Madness: Texts and Interviews, 1975–1995*, trans. Ames Hodges and Mike Taormina (New York: Semiotext(e), 2006), 314.

17. Deleuze, "What Is a Creative Act?" 313.

18. De Beistegui argues that the plane of immanence must exist without concept insofar as it is the unthought condition of concepts ("The Vertigo of Immanence," 84). But Deleuze and Guattari do *not* deny that the plane of immanence or consistency is a concept, but only that it cannot be thought as such. It is a concept, albeit a very complex one, that clearly marks the writings of Deleuze, and Deleuze and Guattari, with the originality that marks any philosophical concept. The plane of immanence is not the concept of concepts, or the unthinkable or prephilosophical condition of concepts, the horizon of concepts: rather, it is a new concept, one that addresses the modes of encounter between concepts.

19. Gilles Deleuze and Félix Guattari, *A Thousand Plateaus. Capitalism and Schizophrenia*, vol. 2, trans. Brian Massumi (Minneapolis: University of Minnesota Press, 1987), hereafter *ATP*.

20. No concept can work beyond its historical production without acquiring a new force to keep it active. Concepts can be remobilized through their capacity to contest or align with other concepts: "a concept always has the components that can prevent the appearance of another concept or, on the contrary, that can themselves appear only at the cost of the disappearance of other concepts" (*WIP* 31).

21. They suggest confusing concepts with propositions results in an impoverished logic governed by the laws of contradiction that regulate propositions rather than the work of the concept (*WIP* 22).

22. This irreducible trace of ideality enables Badiou, in *Deleuze*, to assert that Deleuze submerges the multiplicity into the One. But Badiou implies that idealism *can* be thoroughly removed from thought. What then would the character of thought be? How could concepts even exist?

23. *WIP* 40–41.

24. This outside, the outside that generates events and problems, is not to be confused with the "'inside' outside" that Deleuze articulates in *The Fold: Leibniz and the Baroque*, trans. Tom Conley (Minneapolis: University of Minnesota Press, 1993). For Leibniz, the monad represents on its inside what is "outside," a relative outside already folding into the inside in the monad; however, Deleuze and Guattari invoke the Bergsonian sense of outside as that which poses problems that must somehow be addressed, an absolute outside.

25. In *LS* (121) Deleuze is quite scathing about those who propose philosophy, or even science, as answers to problems which thereby eliminate the problem.

26. Deleuze and Guattari suggest that Bergsonian intuition is perhaps the only true heir of Spinoza's rigorous refusal of transcendence and his commitment to seek out immanence wherever that is possible (*WIP* 49).

27. Deleuze and Guattari (*WIP* 64) claim that the conceptual personae that populate philosophical texts (like the aesthetic figures that occupy artistic space and the scientific

demons that exemplify scientific practice) do not represent but stand in place of the philosopher: the figure *in* the philosopher that enables her to think a new thought.

28. Gilles Deleuze, *Pure Immanence: Essays on a Life*, trans. Anne Boyman (New York: Columbia University Press, 2001), 27, hereafter *PI*.

29. Deleuze refers to the wicked rogue in Dickens's *Our Mutual Friend*, around whose dying body strangers find a respect for what remains of life in him only as he dies, not as he struggles to live. At this moment between life and death, something singular— Deleuze calls it "a life"—impersonal life, emerges.

30. Bergson claims that memory, our mode of access to the past, is motivated by the impending future; only in this way can past recollections become useful. See Henri Bergson, *Matter and Memory*, trans. N. M. Paul and W. S. Palmer (New York: Zone, 1988), 140.

31. These are the objects of analysis in Jane Bennett's *Vibrant Matter: A Political Ecology of Things* (Durham: Duke University Press, 2010).

32. Jakob von Uexküll's work on the contrapuntal relations between a living being and its environment or milieu has been a powerful influence on much of Deleuze's writing. For Uexküll, each living being lives in a world that is precisely the one to which its senses are adapted. See Jakob von Uexküll, *A Foray Through the Worlds of Animals and Humans*, trans. Joseph D O'Niel (Minneapolis: University of Minnesota Press, 2010), for a good introduction.

33. Irigaray could repeat the charge of matricide that she addresses to Nietzsche and Spinoza now to Deleuze: to replace one's natural birth, from a maternal body, with a birth through one's own self-production, whether it is through the advent of culture or the creation of a second nature, or, as here, through the endless adoption of events, is among the long-prevailing philosophical tactics for an evasion of the ineliminable debt to the mother's body and the event of one's birth, the event in which the subject is never a participant but only an effect. See Luce Irigaray, *An Ethics of Sexual Difference*, trans. Carolyn Burke and Gillian C. Gill (Ithaca: Cornell University Press, 1993), 91–92.

34. As Deleuze affirms, "Philosophical concepts are also modes of life and modes of activity for the one who invents them, or knows how to tease them out, give them consistency." Gilles Deleuze, "Zones of Immanence," in *Two Regimes of Madness*, 263.

35. Foucault asks what kind of life can resist the processes of governmentalization that regiment bodies. He suggests that it is partly possible through regimes of *askesis*, self-training and self-regulation—practices developed by the Stoics—that are simultaneously ethical and aesthetic exercises. See Michel Foucault, "On the Genealogy of Ethics: An Overview of Work in Progress," in Paul Rabinow, ed., *The Foucault Reader* (Harmondsworth: Penguin, 1984), 50.

36. Uexküll discusses in detail the lifeworld of the tick in both *A Foray* and in "A New Concept of Umwelt: A Link Between Science and the Humanities," trans. Gösta Brunow, *Semiotica* 134, nos. 1–4 (2001): 111–23.

37. Deleuze and Guattari discuss Uexküll's work on the simplified world of the tick ("Just three affects" Deleuze and Guattari claim can explain its world, *ATP* 256). Uexküll's work in theoretical biology has been used recently to conceptualize the worlds of many

living, and even nonliving, beings, from Martin Krampen's analysis of the autotrophic worlds of plants and the heterotrophic world of animals ("No Plant—No Breath" *Semiotica* 134, nos. 1–4 [2001]: 415–21), to the world of insects (Kalevi Kull, "Jakob von Uexküll: An Introduction," *Semiotica* 134, nos. 1–4 [2001]: 1–59, and "Uexküll and the Post-Modern Evolutionism," *Sign System Studies* 3, nos. 1–2 [2004]: 99–114), to the *Umwelt* of cells and protoplasm (Cheung 2004), the lifeworlds of humans (Floyd Merrell, "Distinctively Human Umwelt?" *Semiotica* 134, nos. 1–4 [2001]: 229–62; and Stephen Loo and Undine Sellbach, "A Picture Book of Invisible Worlds: Semblances of Insects and Humans," *Angelaki: Journal of the Theoretical Humanities* 18, no. 1 [2013]: 45–64) and the "lifeworlds" of robots and forms of artificial life (Tom Ziemke and Noel Sharkey, "A Stroll Through the Worlds of Robots and Animals: Applying Jakob von Uexküll's Theory of Meaning to Adaptive Robots and Artificial Life," *Semiotica* 134, nos. 1–4 [2001]: 701–46).

38.   Jakob von Uexküll quoted in Tobias Cheung, "From Protoplasm to Umwelt: Plans and the Technique of Nature in Jakob von Uexküll's Theory of Organismic Order," *Sign Systems Studies* 32, nos. 1–2 (2004): 140–41.

39.   Anthony Uhlmann, "Deleuze, Ethics, Ethology, and Art," in Nathan Jun and Daniel W. Smith, eds., *Deleuze and Ethics* (Edinburgh: University of Edinburgh Press, 2011), 155, explains the intimate relation between ethics and ethology in the Greek sources of Deleuze's work: "'Ethics' is etymologically linked to 'ethology' through the Greek word root, 'ethos.' The original meaning of 'ethos' is 'accustomed place,' or 'habitat' and by analogy it was quickly associated with 'custom, habit.' It evolved however to be understood as the 'character,' 'disposition,' or core values of individuals or groups. Ethology, then, links ethos and 'logos.'"

40.   Bogue, *Deleuze's Way*, 7.

41.   Not only the "disinterested" creation of knowledge, art, truths for their own sake but also capital, commerce, and the flows of economic power that address the intractable forces, and senses, of the world. But they do so differently, with little to no interest in the ontological orders that make them possible and which they cannot master. Knowledges of the order provided by the sciences and the humanities and sensations generated by art are both valued (insofar as they enable commerce) and reviled (insofar as they require capital investment) by capitalist flows.

42.   Deleuze, *The Fold*, 4.

43.   Ibid., 8. This term, while not infrequently used in philosophy, indicates, as Irigaray suggests in her reading of Merleau-Ponty in *An Ethics of Sexual Difference*, an unrecognized or unacknowledged elision of the maternal, the enfolding, invaginated condition for life.

44.   Marie François Bichat was an eighteenth-century anatomist who was among the first to understand that organ development occurs through the differentiation and specialization of tissue rather than through augmentation or addition. For Deleuze and Foucault (not to mention Ravaisson and Bergson), Bichat provides "what's probably the first general modern conception of death, presenting it as violent, plural, and coextensive with life. Instead of taking it . . . as a point, he takes it as a line that

we're constantly confronting, and cross in either direction only at the point where it ends. That's when it means to confront the line Outside." Gilles Deleuze, "A Portrait of Foucault," in *Negotiations: 1972–1990*, trans. Martin Joughin (New York: Columbia University Press, 1995), 111.

45. Ibid.

46. Deleuze acknowledges that he follows a tradition in philosophy that links it to neurology, one that includes the associationists, Schopenhauer and Bergson. See "On Philosophy," in *Negotiations*, 149.

47. Deleuze and Guattari (*WIP* 209) claim that the brain is inclined to *not* think, to avoid thinking, through the acquisition of opinion.

48. Gilles Deleuze, "The Brain Is the Screen," in Gregory Flaxman, ed., *The Brain Is the Screen*, trans. Marie Therese Guigis (Minneapolis: University of Minnesota Press, 2000), 366.

49. Bergson ascribes the notion of contraction, and the intimate relation between contraction and the habits necessary for the maintenance of life, to Ravaisson's *Of Habit*, trans. C. Carlisle and M. Sinclair (London: Acumen, 2008). See Henri Bergson, "The Life and Work of Ravaisson," in *The Creative Mind. An Introduction to Metaphysics*, trans. M. L. Addison (New York: Philosophical Library, 1946), 261–300.

50. *DR* 75.

51. Uexküll has claimed that the bodily organization of the sea urchin, a creature with no central nervous system and thus no singular point of self-regulation, functions through the autonomous operation of its organs, each acting as a little brain, an organ-brain: "If an external organ harbors a complete reflex arc, one can properly call this a 'reflex person.' Sea urchins have a great number of such reflex persons, which perform their reflex tasks without central direction, each on its own. In order to make the contrast of animals of this structure to higher animals more clear, I have coined the sentence, 'When a dog runs, the animal moves its legs. When a sea urchin runs, its legs move the animal'" (*A Foray*, 76).

52. Deleuze, "What Is a Creative Act?" 324.

5. SIMONDON AND THE PREINDIVIDUAL

1. Simondon defended his major dissertation, "L'individuation à la lumière des notions de forme et d'information" (Individuation in the light of the notions of form and information), hereafter ILFI, in 1958, published in part only in 1995. His minor thesis, *Du mode d'existence des objects techniques* ("On the Mode of Existence of Technical Objects") was also completed 1958 and published that same year.

2. His major dissertation was published in French as two volumes, *L'individu et sa genèse psychico-biologique* (The individual in its physico-biological genesis; Paris: Presses Universitaires de France, 1995 [1964]), hereafter *IGPB*, and *L'individuation psychique et collective* (Psychic and collective individuation; Paris: Aubier, 1989, 2007), hereafter *IPC*. Neither is yet published in English. Although only one of his articles is translated

in a short-book form (*Two Lessons on Animal and Man*, trans. Drew Burk [Minneapolis: Univocal, 2012]), there are many subterranean translations online, and a few texts on Simondon's work have now appeared in English, among them Pascal Chabot, *Gilbert Simondon and the Philosophy of the Transindividual*, trans. Thomas LaMarre (Cambridge: MIT Press, 2013); Muriel Combes, *Gilbert Simondon and the Philosophy of the Transindividual*, trans. Thomas LaMarre (Cambridge: MIT Press, 2012); and David Scott, *Gilbert Simondon's Psychic and Collective Individuation: A Critical Introduction and Guide* (Edinburgh: University of Edinburgh Press, 2014). See also Arne de Boever, Alex Murray, Jon Roffe, and Ashley Woodward, eds., *Gilbert Simondon: Being and Technology* (Edinburgh: University of Edinburgh Press, 2012); and five special journal issues: *Parrhesia* 7 (2009); *SubStance* 129 (2012); *Inflexions* 5 (2012); *Pli* (2012); and *Communication + 1* 2 (2013).

3. His graduate degree was on the writings of the pre-Socratics: Andrew Iliadis, "A New Individuation: Deleuze and Simondon," *Media Tropes* 4, no. 1 (2013): 100. See *Two Lessons on Animal and Man* for his overview of Greek conceptions of man's relation to nature and the animal.

4. Anaximander's (610–546 bce) concept *apeiron* is the infinite original principle of being that cannot be correlated with any particular thing but with every thing. It is the continuing source, a kind of feminine or maternal principle (!) that gives birth to whatever can be. It is both an indefinite and limitless origin temporally and an indefinite boundless space that is the origin and the final destination of all. Irigaray also invokes Anaximander in *In the Beginning, She Was* (London: Bloomsbury, 2013), 11.

5. Deleuze is two years younger than Simondon. His most direct analysis of Simondon's work, a rare review of one of his contemporaries, was written in 1964, "On Gilbert Simondon," in *Desert Islands and Other Texts, 1953–1974*, trans. Michael Taormina (Los Angeles: Semiotext(e), 2004), 86–89.

6. Elizabeth Grosz, *The Nick of Time: Politics, Evolution, and the Untimely* (Durham: Duke University Press, 2004).

7. Gilbert Simondon, "The Position of the Problem of Ontogenesis," trans. Gregory Flanders, *Parrhesia* 7, no. 4 (2009): 4–16, 6, hereafter PPO.

8. Combes, *Gilbert Simondon and the Philosophy of the Transindividual*, 3.

9. Becoming is only possible because a being cannot resolve itself as such without creation (PPO 6).

10. "One can . . . suppose that reality in itself, is primitively like the supersaturated solution, and even more completely so in the preindividual regime, where it is *more than unity and more than identity*" (PPO 6).

11. Simondon uses the work of quantum field theory to suggest that our corresponding concepts of "things" and "identities" need to become more complex, more involved in what they do than what they are (PPO 6–7).

12. "Concrete being, or complete being—that is, preindividual being—is being that is more than a unity. . . . Unity and identity only appear to one of the phases of being, posterior to the operations of individuation: these notions cannot help us to discover the principle of individuation: they do not apply to ontogenesis understood in its fullest

sense, that is to say, the becoming of being as a being that divides and dephases itself by individuating itself" (PPO 6).

13.   See *IGPB* 28.

14.   "If we pay much more attention to the processes involved in the preparation of the raw materials of both clay and mold, we must also become more attuned to the technical mediations that must be performed on each for the brick to operate as a brick. The technical preparation of the clay is in fact vastly simpler than the construction of the mold" (*IGPB* 28–29).

15.   The solution to which the seed is introduced is often called a "mother-liquid," in PPO 11; a "mother-solution," in Anne Sauvagnargues, "Crystals and Membranes," in de Boever et al., *Gilbert Simondon: Being and Technology*, 60; and as a "mother-water," in Chabot, *Gilbert Simondon and the Philosophy of the Transindividual*, 83, that is, while the form-matter relation has been shaken from its Aristotelian binarization, it retains Aristotle's association of (formless) matter with the maternal-feminine and the (forming) seed with the paternal and the masculine.

16.   Transductions are the operations by which a kind of unity or cohesion is attained through the dephasing or becoming of the different. Simondon borrows the concept from biology, where it explains how cells convey a stimulus, energy, or information between themselves, converting one kind of energy into another. See *IGPB* 30; also PPO 11.

17.   PPO 10.

18.   As Simondon explains: "This type of individuation . . . is accompanied by a perpetuated individuation, which is life itself, according to the fundamental mode of becoming: *the living conserves within itself a permanent individuation.* It is not the result of individuation, like in the case of the crystal or the molecule, but is a theater of individuation" (PPO 7).

19.   Sauvagnargues explains the significance of the membrane in the leap from inorganic to organic individuations: "The membrane thus defines the leap from the chemical to the living and promotes the emergence of this new property: the difference between exterior and interior, the result of its differentiating action. The fold simultaneously produces interiority and exteriority, inside and outside, the result of its differentiating action. . . . The selective membrane is thus productive of its own interiority" ("Crystals and Membranes," 67).

20.   Sauvagnargues, *Deleuze and Art*, 66. Sauvagnargues claims that Simondon restores Bergson's concept of the image and his understanding of the ways in which the present carries all of the past with it (ibid.).

21.   "We would have to define, over and above a topology of the living being, a chronology of the living being associated with this topology, just as elementary as it and as different from the physics form of time as topology is different from the structure of Euclidean space" (*IGPB* 226).

22.   In my understanding of Simondon, the entirety of materiality and ideality are immanent in or emerge from the preindividual. However, life and psychic organization are self-forming emergent properties that rely on ontologically prior individuations, such

that the complexity of life elaborates and develops itself from the relative simplicity of the materiality of the crystal's individuation. Life and the psychic are more than ideality, they are modes of organization and expression of ideality (and materiality).

23. "In reality, there is a very strong kinship between life and thought. . . . Living matter is far from being purely indeterminate or purely passive; nor is it blind aspiration. It is the vehicle of informed energy. Likewise, thought is composed of distinct structures such as representations, images, certain memories, and various perceptions." Gilbert Simondon, "Technical Individualization," trans. Alberto Toscano, in Joke Brouwer and Arjen Mulder, eds., *Interact or Die!* (Rotterdam: V2, 2007), 209–10.

24. Ibid., 210.

25. Simondon claims that the solitary subject is not doomed to freedom, as Sartre suggests, but to anxiety (*IPC* 256).

26. Combes, *Gilbert Simondon and the Philosophy of the Transindividual*, 34.

27. The passage is from "Zarathustra's Prologue" (*Z* #66). See Gilles Deleuze, "Bartleby; or, The Formula," in *Essays Critical and Clinical*, trans. Michael A. Greco and Daniel W. Smith (Minneapolis: University of Minnesota Press, 1997), 68–90. For a more detailed reading of Deleuze's analysis, see Arnaud Bouaniche, "Deleuze and Simondon: Community and Transindividuality," *Pli* 23A (2012): 23–31.

28. There is a certain discomfort in using Simondon's concept of transcendence here, in a book largely devoted to the movement of immanence. But I would suggest that Simondon's work is not transcendental in its focus and that transcendence may be understood in terms of the enfolding and complication of material-ideal relations rather than their movement to a beyond. If there is transcendence, it is only the increasing organization and complexity of the preindividual, not its replacement.

29. See Igor Krtolica's illuminating discussion of the transindividual, "The Question of Anxiety in Gilbert Simondon," trans. Jon Roffe, in de Boever et al., *Gilbert Simondon: Being and Technology*; see also Combes, *Gilbert Simondon and the Philosophy of the Transindividual*, 33–50.

30. Toscano argues that the transindividual holds the key not only to a new order of invention that returns to the charge of nature that individualization had left behind, but a new kind of sociality and collectivity, no longer normalized but open. See "The Disparate: Ontology and Politics in Simondon," *Pli* 23A (2012).

31. The magical mode characterizes the human's first anthropological attachment to an environment, described by Simondon as a mode of "magical unity" in which humans, a landscape, or environment and a divine order seem to imbue key points of a landscape—a mountain peak, a massive tree, a cliff—with a more than geological significance. He suggests that technologies and religions aim to restore some of the sense of this primordial belonging-together. See Gilbert Simondon, "On the Mode of Existence of Technical Objects," trans. Ninian Mellamphy, *Deleuze Studies* 5, no. 3 (2011): 408 hereafter METO.

32. METO 416. He elaborates: "At the beginning, technics are often content to develop a privileged place, as when constructing a tower at the summit of a hill, or placing a lighthouse on a promontory at the most visible point. But technics can also successfully

create the functionality of privileged sites. Of natural realities technics retains only the figural power, not the site and natural localisation on a determined ground given prior to any human intervention" (METO 417). Similarly, religion is a mediator between man and the world, rather than a mode of directing man beyond this world. But with this crucial difference: religion comes to represent the functions of totalization precisely as technics becomes a figure detachable from any place and usable everywhere. As reciprocal means by which, from two different angles, the relation between the individual and the world can be mediated, technics and religion cannot supplant one another but function in two different spaces or endpoints.

33. Gilbert Simondon, *Du mode d'existence des objects techniques* (Paris: Aubier, 1989), 179.

34. Simondon suggests elsewhere that the beauty of the technical object is very specifically about its relative place: "The technical object is beautiful when it encounters a ground that agrees with it, of which it can be the proper figure, that is, when it completes and expresses the world" (ibid., 185).

35. Simondon praises the "Le Corbusier Monastery" (Sainte Marie de la Tourette, near Lyon, constructed 1956–1960) as a beauty of design and conceptualization that prepares in advance for the changes it will need to undergo in the future. Gilbert Simondon, "Technical Mentality," trans. Arne de Boever, *Parrhesia* 7 (2009): 24–25.

36. Simondon gives us a simple example of the aesthetic resonances of technical objects: "A simple cadmium nut and bolt offers iridescences and variations that remind one a little of the colors of fluoride lenses: they're the colors of a pigeon's throat, which sparkles." Gilbert Simondon, "On Techno-Aesthetics," trans. Arne de Boever, *Parrhesia* 7 (2009): 3. The iridescences of cadmium are what forms of life, forms of technics, and forms of art may borrow from, elaborate, and reticulate, each in their own ways, capitalizing on its qualities.

37. Ibid.

38. "The aesthetic impression implies the feeling of the complete perfection of an act, a perfection that objectively gives it a radiance and an authority by which it becomes a key point of a lived reality, a knot of experienced reality. This act becomes a key point of the network of human life inserted into the world; from this key point to others a superior kinship is created that reconstitutes an analogue of the magical network of the universe" (Simondon, *Du mode d'existence des objects techniques*, 180).

39. See Combes, *Gilbert Simondon and the Philosophy of the Transindividual*, 65.

40. This is not to say that ethics is only about positive and enhancing encounters, for any ethics must also address what diminishes and impoverishes individuals and collectives.

41. Simondon explains: "Philosophy is its own condition [unlike science and ethics, which are conditioned by technics and religion, themselves the product of the division between figure and ground], for as soon as reflexive thinking begins, it has the power to perfect whichever of the geneses that has not been entirely achieved, by becoming aware of the sense of the genetic process itself" (METO 410).

42. Simondon, "Technical Mentality," 18.

43. Ibid.

6. RUYER AND AN EMBRYOGENESIS OF THE WORLD

1. See, for example, Laurent Meslet, *La philosophie biologique de Raymond Ruyer* (Paris: Harmattan, 1997) and *Le psychisme et la vie* (Paris: Harmattan, 2005); and Fabrice Colonna, *Ruyer* (Paris: Les Belles Lettres, 2007) for introductions to his work in philosophical biology.

2. Deleuze speaks of Ruyer in a number of his writings without developing his analysis. In *Difference and Repetition*, Deleuze places Ruyer alongside Bergson as one of the greatest theorists of actualization. Gilles Deleuze, *Difference and Repetition*, trans. Paul Patton (New York: Columbia University Press, 1994), 216; see also Gilles Deleuze and Félix Guattari, *Anti-Oedipus. Capitalism and Schizophrenia*, vol. 1, trans. Robert Hurley, Mark Seem, and Helen R. Lane (London: Athlone, 1983), 286; Gilles Deleuze and Félix Guattari, *A Thousand Plateaus. Capitalism and Schizophrenia*, vol. 2, trans. Brian Massumi (Minneapolis: University of Minnesota Press, 1987), 332–35; Gilles Deleuze, *The Fold: Leibniz and the Baroque*, trans. Tom Conley (Minneapolis: University of Minnesota Press, 1993), 102–4; and Gilles Deleuze and Félix Guattari, *What Is Philosophy?* trans. Hugh Tomlinson and Graham Burchill (New York: Columbia University Press, 1991), 20, 208–15, for Deleuze's reading of Ruyer.

3. Primarily in the work of Paul Bains, "Subjectless Subjectivities," in Brian Massumi, ed., *A Shock to Thought: Expression After Deleuze and Guattari* (London: Routledge, 2002), 101–16, and *The Primacy of Semiosis: An Ontology of Relations* (Toronto: University of Toronto Press, 2006). See also Ronald Bogue, "Raymond Ruyer," in Graham Jones and Jon Roffe, eds., *Deleuze's Philosophical Lineage* (Edinburgh: Edinburgh University Press, 2009), 300–20; Brian Massumi, *Parables for the Virtual: Movement, Affect, Sensation* (Durham: Duke University Press, 2010), and *What Animals Teach Us About Politics* (Durham: Duke University Press, 2014); and Elizabeth Grosz, "Identity and Individuation: Some Feminist Reflections," in Arne de Boever, Alex Murray, Jon Roffe, and Ashley Woodward, eds., *Gilbert Simondon: Being and Technology* (Edinburgh: University of Edinburgh Press, 2012), 37–56.

4. Ruyer claims that an idealism that requires the mediation of representations between consciousness and objects—as Kant develops, but also as the tradition of semiology asserts—misunderstands the nature of consciousness as impersonal or prepersonal, as the condition under which a human self-consciousness may be possible: "From post-Kantian idealists to Sartre, or even to a few scholars who want to put on an appearance of being philosophers, we flounder in the quicksand of subjective idealism. Realist materialists are correct to reject this academic concept, even though they are wrong to confuse subjective idealism and the realism of consciousness. For although subjective idealism is false, panpsychism is true." Raymond Ruyer, "There Is No Subconscious," *Diogenes* 36 (1988): 30.

5. Ibid.

6. Raymond Ruyer, "Person-God and Tao-God," trans. Kris Pender of "Dieu-Person et Dieu-Tao," *Revue de Métaphysique et de Morale* 52, no. 2 (1947): 6.

7. In "Person-God and Tao-God," Ruyer makes clear his departure from conventional religions that assume at their center the idea of a Person-God.

> The Person-God perhaps rules, undoubtedly rules, from the other side of the heavens; there, there will undoubtedly be a city of spirits; but, in this world, in Nature, the notion of a personal God is faced with incessant contradictions. We do not pretend to be capable of justly saying in what our life consists, but what we know is that it is not the life of a pure spirit which speaks to spirit, which receives answers from it in a purely spiritual exchanges. We live under the Law, and not under pure grace, we live under an Order, which is more than a material order, but which is not an order of personal relation. To believe in a Person-God, in this world, is to expose oneself to imagining an idol, and of finding this idol unjust.
>
> (1–11)

8. Raymond Ruyer, "Dialectic Aspects of Belief," trans. S. J. Greenleaves, *Diogenes* 15 (1967): 78.

9. See Ronald Bogue, *Deleuze on Music, Painting, and the Arts* (New York: Routledge, 2003) and "Raymond Ruyer" for further details regarding the relations between Ruyer and Uexküll.

10. Deleuze, *The Fold*, 116.

11. Ruyer began his philosophical career by elaborating a "mechanistic monism" in his writings of the early 1930s. Rolf A. Wiklund, "A Short Introduction to the Neo-Finalist Philosophy of Raymond Ruyer," *Philosophy and Phenomenological Research* 21 (1960): 187. But, with the publication of *La Conscience et le corps* (Paris: Alcan, 1937), Ruyer begins his work on neofinalism, on a directed materiality, a materiality of sense.

12. Ruyer commonly uses an argument ad hominem in challenging his critics. He claims that even presenting an argument in favor of determinism is the exhibition of freedom. If the determinist is fully determined, then there would be no purpose in mounting an argument for determinism. The determinist seeks a purpose with deterministic arguments that is his own, and is itself not determined by anything but a purpose. Raymond Ruyer, *Neofinalism*, trans. Alyosha Edlebi (Minneapolis: University of Minnesota Press, 2016), 5.

13. "The axiological cogito demonstrates that before there can be a search for a secure foundation for knowledge, before we can affirm that an 'I' exists, we must affirm that we search or seek, that we want, we set goals that we can follow, even as we seek to know what this I can secure" (ibid., 7).

14. Ruyer in Robert Champigny, "Translations from the Writings of Contemporary French Philosophers," *Journal of Philosophy* 54 (1957): 351.

15. This conception of autoaffection as self-proximity and self-enjoyment may link Ruyer's conception to Whitehead's understanding of life as self-enjoyment: Alfred North Whitehead, *Modes of Thought* (New York: MacMillan, 1938); see also Steven Shaviro, "Self-Enjoyment and Concern: On Whitehead and Levinas," in Roland Faber, B. Hennings, and C. Combs, eds., *Beyond Metaphysics? Explorations in Alfred North*

Whitehead's Late Thought (Amsterdam: Rodopi, 2010), 249–58. It is Whitehead's concept of God that Ruyer finds problematic.

16. Wiklund summarizes: "Primary beings are centers of finalist activity, and they obey the laws of the absolute domain with its unity surviewing a multiplicity" ("A Short Introduction," 192).

17. E. W. F. Tomlin, "The Philosophy of Life," *Dialectica* 13, no. 2 (1959): 128–29, explicitly links Ruyer's neofinalism to Spinoza's conatus.

18. Raymond Ruyer, "Dialectical Aspects of Belief," trans. S. J. Greenleaves, *Diogenes* 15 (December 1967): 74.

19. Ruyer, "There Is No Subconscious," 25.

20. Ruyer, *Neofinalism*, 95–100.

21. Bogue suggests, contrary to Husserlian phenomenology, that consciousness is 'not *of* something. Consciousness *is* something" ("Raymond Ruyer," 302).

22. Bains, in "Subjectless Subjectivities," provides the clearest explanation of the peculiar folds that link the interior of consciousness to the exterior of objects: "We have the strong impression that our sensorial/visual field is *in front* of us and that we *look at it* from a supplementary dimension. This is an error. Sensations are brain achievements and there is no brain behind the brain or eye behind the eye to look at its products. Vision or any other sensorial existence is existence rather than 'representation of'. There is no re-presentation of one world but only the multiple worlds our brains achieve. *This is not subjectivism—no philosophical or psychological subject is involved* The brain or organism as an autopoetic, self-referential, primary true form, is naturally producing a virtual world" (108).

23. Ruyer, "Dialectic Aspects of Belief," 78.

24. Ruyer, *Neofinalism*, 92.

25. See Raymond Ruyer, "The Status of the Future and the Invisible World," trans. R. Scott Walker, *Diogenes* 28 (1980): 37–53.

26. I believe that Ruyer's work could be used to rethink quantum field theory as Barad has done in some of her writings, perhaps to even more effect than Derrida. Much of quantum physics is surprisingly Ruyerian. See Karen Barad, "Quantum Entanglements and Hauntological Relations of Inheritance: Dis/continuities, SpaceTime Enfoldings, and Justice-to-Come," *Derrida Today* 3, no. 2 (2010): 240–68, and "On Touching—the Imhuman That I Therefore Am," *differences. A Journal of Feminist Cultural Studies* 23, no. 3 (2012): 206–23.

27. Tomlin claims that Ruyer's position is the inverse of Bergson's, at least regarding the relations of ideality and materiality. For Bergson, life intervenes in matter to enliven matter; for Ruyer, by contrast, matter is always already enlivened to the extent that it is self-forming and autoaffecting. E. W. F. Tomlin, *Living and Knowing* (London: Faber and Faber, 1959), 154.

28. Raymond Ruyer, *La Genèse des formes vivantes* (Paris: Flammarion, 1956), 58.

29. Raymond Ruyer, *Paradoxes de la conscience et limites de l'automatisme* (Paris: Albin Michel, 1966), 167.

30. Ruyer, "The Status of the Future and the Invisible World," 42.

31. As Ruyer explains, "Thanks to the invisible world, organisms learn how to act, to adapt; in a word, to live. Actual consciousness in its superficial aspects is the foam on a tidal wave created by the unceasing arrival of the waters of the invisible ocean on rivers already individualized and channeled which seem, falsely, to carry everything to the ocean, but which in fact have received everything in the past and which continue to receive everything still today" (ibid., 45).

32. Ruyer claims that the mnemic theme directs the mode of self-formation of primary forms:

> This theme, in embryonic formation, is manifested as the mnemic potential of the species. It is theoretically separable from the actual domain and actualized as the extended field in a localized domain. The actual domain is inseparable from the theme and without the theme would not at all be different from a non-living series of juxtaposed molecules. A cell, an embryo, fixed and colored for research purposes theoretically retains for the observer's eye the form of the cell of the living embryo. But separated from the theme, it is no longer a true form; it is no more than a snapshot of it. Every authentic form is in time as well as in space. It subsists in time by translating a potential, of itself untemporal, into space.
>
> ("There Is No Subconscious," 32)

33. "The resemblance of two actualizations of a single memory requires the idea of a mnemic theme; the organic resemblance of two individuals of the same species requires the idea of a specific potential" (Ruyer, *Neofinalism*, 131).

34. Ruyer, "There Is No Subconscious," 32.

35. See Félix Ravaisson, *Of Habit*, trans. C. Carlisle and M. Sinclair (London: Acumen, 2008); and Henri Bergson, "The Life and Work of Ravaisson," in *The Creative Mind: An Introduction to Metaphysics*, trans. M. L. Addison (New York: Philosophical Library, 1946), 261–300; See also Elizabeth Grosz, "Habit Today: Ravaisson, Bergson, Deleuze, and Us," *Body and Society* 19, nos. 2–3 (2013): 217–39.

36. "Habitual memory—which is thematic, delocalized, immaterial as the potential of an embryonic region, that does not depend on a physico-chemical trace in specifically determined nervous cells—can be easily transferred from one nerve center to another, retaining its form and its general meaning despite its transfers. On the other hand, image memory, despite an essential difference, most resembles a material image or a photograph, a material fact in mosaic form, localized" (Ruyer, "There Is No Subconscious," 35).

37. Ibid., 34.

38. Ibid., 37.

39. Bogue elaborates on the transpatial nature of the mnemic theme as a melody to be performed, a kind of irresistible memory ("Raymond Ruyer," 307).

40. Ruyer states his difference from tradition forms of theology and a traditional concept of a Divine creator: "The internal assemblage of the universe is such that finalist activity reigns everywhere within it: all beings are domains of activity; all 'agents' aim for an ideal or confirm to it in one way or another. As such, it matters little whether we

conceive God on the model of the human agent, the organic agent, or even the mineral agent" (*Neofinalism*, 239–40). The world itself has no single goal or aim; but each self-forming whole in the world aims itself to goals, ideals, that is, achievements. Like all true form, God is both agent and ideal, operating according to the logic of self-survey and self-production. Which is perhaps another way of saying that God is the name we give to the process by which each thing directs itself to ideals, as well as the name for the ideals to which they are directed.

41. For further details regarding the distinctions between Form I, Form II, and Form III, see Raymond Ruyer, *La Gènese des Formes Vivantes* (Paris: Flammarion, 1956); and Bogue, *Deleuze on Music, Painting, and the Arts*, 69 and "Raymond Ruyer," 312.

42. Uexküll was intrigued by the idea that each living being develops itself according to a musical theme, using the experiments of both Driesch and Spemann on the development of embryos in Jakob von Uexküll, "The New Concept of Umwelt," trans. Gösta Brunow, *Semiotica* 134, nos. 1–4 (2001): 121.

43. See Hans Driesch, *The Science of Philosophy of the Organism: The Gifford Lectures* (London: Adam and Charles Black, 1908) and *The History and Theory of Vitalism* (London: Macmillan, 1914).

44. Raymond Ruyer, "The Mystery of Reproduction and the Limits of Automatism," *Diogenes* 12 (1964): 54.

45. Preformism is a theory that, in its most extreme form, assumes the homunculus, a tiny representative of the being-to-come, already resides in the gametes, and gestation is a mere increase in size; today this is best represented by genetic reductionism, which suggests gestation merely brings to fruition a being already constituted from the fertilized egg.

46. The epigenetic view believes that the embryo uses complex and inventive ways to produce itself out of itself. Spemann was awarded a Nobel Prize in medicine in 1935 for his embryological research.

47. Spemann, Driesch, and the tradition of biological vitalism are discussed in some detail in the work of Mathias Guttman, "Uexkull and Contemporary Biology: Some Methodological Considerations," *Sign System Studies* 32, nos. 1/2 (2004): 169–86; Christian Kerslake, *Deleuze and the Unconscious* (London: Bloomsbury, 2007); and Jane Bennett, *Vibrant Matter: A Political Ecology of Things* (Durham: Duke University Press, 2010).

48. Ruyer, "There Is No Subconscious," 33.

49. Ruyer, "The Mystery of Reproduction," 54–55.

50. Ruyer, *Neofinalism*, 70.

51. Ruyer, "The Mystery of Reproduction," 66.

52. The place of the maternal body, that is, the body in which the egg, the embryo, or larva are produced, is designatable as or is nominally female. In fish this process occurs outside the body; spawn, eggs, and sperm are produced by both sexes and fertilize in water. But for most living beings above the level of the unicellular organism, the maternal body does not direct embryonic development but does provide it which sustenance, protection, and a dark milieu in which it is capable of forming itself. An embryo requires an embryonic or uterine home, as Irigaray reminds us.

53. Ruyer elaborates the parallels between the embryo and the unicellular organism: "A unicellular entity has neither hands nor eyes. It nevertheless forms pseudopods, a mouth, a stomach, and it excretes. An egg, an embryo in its earliest stages, acts like a unicellular entity. It deforms itself with regard to its overall form: an absolute overview without a point of external overview, which would be perpendicular to the surface or volume" ("There Is No Subconscious," 25)

54. Ruyer, "The Mystery of Reproduction," 68.

55. Ruyer explains: "The machine and the factory . . . extend the organ. Nowhere will it be suggested that there is an absolute metaphysical break with the primitive tool and the perfected factory [i.e., the perfectly automatic factory]. This amounts to admitting, therefore, that the perfected factory is still linked with the organism, in some indirect way though without break of continuity. The organism itself, even more than an assemblage of tools, is a perfected factory, where automatism is pushed to the extreme, even if a regulatory 'supervision' subsists which continues the instructional activity of embryogenesis." Raymond Ruyer, "Marx and Butler or Technologism and Finalism," trans. Kris Pender from "Marx et Butler ou Technologisme et Finalisme," *Revue de Métaphysique et de Morale* 55, no. 3 (1950): 302.

56. Ibid., 303–4.

57. Ruyer, "The Mystery of Reproduction," 63.

58. Ruyer, "There Is No Subconscious," 43. This is the basis for Ruyer's critique, much of it developed before the revolution in genetics that occurred with the mapping of the human genome, of genetic reductionism. There is no more reason to favor the genetic level than there is to privilege the molecular, cellular, or organic levels. Each exists in a relation of primary form, of immediate self-proximity, elaborating higher and more complex forms successively, and each could just as readily be identified as the "cause" or the "explanation" of life's emergence and development.

59. Ruyer, *La Genèse des formes vivantes*, 73.

60. Ruyer, "There is No Subconscious," 26.

61. Here Ruyer carefully distinguishes his position regarding mnemic themes from Platonic ideals, which require no material form and persist as they are in themselves without materialization. Platonic forms or ideals always remain distant and remote, incapable of localization, where the mnemic theme resides always in a region specific to form bodies and their capacities for acting and directs it even through its possible distortions through a plasticity that also directs concepts and thought.

62. Tomlin, "The Philosophy of Life," 150.

63. See Raymond Ruyer, "The Vital Domain of Animals and the Religious World of Man," *Diogenes* 5 (1957): 42.

64. While disputing traditional theological conceptions of God as a Person-God, a divine supernatural human with every imaginable power, a creator of the world from outside the world, Ruyer instead poses the idea of an immanent God, what he calls a "Tao-God," and the order in which we conceive of the value of our actions as "religious." "It is above all in the spiritual and moral order that action and reaction take a sense that can be called religious" ("Person-God and Tao-God," 2). I would prefer instead to

understand this order as immanent, a pattern of actions and affects that enhance, bring joy, affirm in a purely secular sense.

65.   "To respond, or to refuse to respond, to the call of an ideal that one perceives—these two contrary acts equally make us sense a divine order: the joy which accompanies even the pain of effort, the absence of joy which accompanies the absence of love, the disgust which follows incrimination, the taste of ashes in lies—these cannot be understood by psychological laws conceived in the manner of the physiological laws" (ibid., 3).

66.   Ruyer, "Person-God and Tao-God," 2–3.

67.   Like Spinoza, Ruyer criticizes the naïveté of those who pray for direct intervention by a personal God. See ibid., 8.

68.   As Ruyer says, "Whosoever says: 'I am God, I am the Way, the Truth and the Life,' guarantees nothing at all by this. But the beauty of music, be it Bach or Mozart, is self-revealing and has no need of a guarantee. In the end a Gospel cannot be considered 'divine' except, like the music of Mozart, for what it is." Ruyer, "Dialectical Aspects of Belief," 72.

69.   Ruyer, "Person-God and Tao-God," 78.

70.   Ruyer, in Champigny, "Translations from the Writings of Contemporary French Philosophers," 354.

71.   Ruyer, "The Status of the Future and the Invisible World," 42.

BIBLIOGRAPHY

Alaimo, Stacy, and Susan Hekman, eds. *Material Feminisms*. Bloomington: Indiana University Press, 2008.

Alliez, Eric. *The Signature of the World: What Is Deleuze and Guattari's Philosophy?* Trans. Eliot Ross Albert and Alberto Toscano. London: Continuum, 2004.

Althusser, Louis. *Reading Capital*. Trans. Ben Brewster. London: New Left, 1977.

Annas, Julia. "Ethics in Stoic Philosophy." *Phronesis* 52 (2007): 58–87.

Aurelius, Marcus. *The Meditations*. Trans. G. M. A. Grube. Indianapolis: Hackett, 1988.

Armstrong, Aurelia. "The Passions, Power, and Practical Philosophy: Spinoza and Nietzsche Contra the Stoics." *Journal of Nietzsche Studies* 44, no. 1 (2013): 6–24.

Atamer, Esra. "Dissipative Individuation." *Parrhesia* 12 (2011): 57–70.

Awad, Adel, Ahmed Farag Ali, and Barun Majumder. "Nonsingular Rainbow Universes." *Journal of Cosmology and Astroparticle Physics* 52 (October 2013), doi:10.1088/1475–7516/2013/10/052.

Badiou, Alain. *Deleuze: The Clamour of Being*. Trans. Louise Burchill, Minneapolis: University of Minnesota Press, 2000.

——. "Spinoza's Closed Ontology." In *Theoretical Writings*. Trans. Ray Brassier and Alberto Toscano, New York: Continuum, 2004.

Bains, Paul. *The Primacy of Semiosis: An Ontology of Relations*. Toronto: University of Toronto Press, 2006.

——. "Subjectless Subjectivities." In Brian Massumi, ed., *A Shock to Thought: Expression After Deleuze and Guattari*, 101–16. Routledge: London, 2002.

Balibar, Etienne. "Spinoza: From Individuality to Transindividuality." *Mededelingen vanwege het Spinozahuis* (1997): 11–59, http://www.ciepfc.fr/spip.php?article236.

Barad, Karen. "On Touching—the Inhuman That I Therefore Am." *differences: A Journal of Feminist Cultural Studies* 23, no. 2 (2012): 206–23.

——. "Quantum Entanglements and Hauntological Relations of Inheritance: Dis/continuities, SpaceTime Enfoldings, and Justice-to-Come." *Derrida Today* 3, no. 2 (2010): 240–68.

Barnes, Jonathan. "Nietzsche and Diogenes Laërtius." In Anthony Jensen and Helmut Heit, eds., *Nietzche as a Scholar of Antiquity*, 115–38. London: Bloomsbury, 2014.

Barthélémy, Jean-Hughes. "'Du Mort Qui Saisit Le Vif': Simondonian Ontology Today." *Parrhesia* 7 (2009): 28–35.

——. "Individuation and Knowledge: 'The Refutation of Idealism' in Simondon's Heritage in France." *SubStance* 41, no. 3 (2012): 60–75.

Beistegui, Miguel De. "Science and Ontology: From Merleau-Ponty's 'Reduction' to Simondon's 'Transduction.'" *Angelaki* 10, no. 2 (August 2005): 109–22.

——. "The Vertigo of Immanence: Deleuze's Spinozism." *Research in Phenomenology* 35 (2005): 77–100.

Bennett, Jane. *Vibrant Matter: A Political Ecology of Things.* Durham: Duke University Press, 2010.

Bergson, Henri. "An Introduction to Metaphysics." In *The Creative Mind: An Introduction to Metaphysics*, 133–69. Trans. M. L. Addison. New York: Philosophical Library, 1946.

——. "The Life and Work of Ravaisson." In *The Creative Mind: An Introduction to Metaphysics*, 261–300. Trans. M. L. Addison. New York: Philosophical Library, 1946.

——. *Matter and Memory.* Trans. N. M. Paul and W. S. Palmer. New York: Zone, 1988.

Bobzien, Susanne. "Logic." In Brad Inwood, ed., *The Cambridge Companion to the Stoics*, 85–123. Cambridge: Cambridge University Press, 2003.

Boeri, Marcelo D. "The Stoics on Bodies and Incorporeals." *Review of Metaphysics* 54 (2001): 723–52.

Boever, Arne de, Alex Murray, Jon Roffe, and Ashley Woodward, eds. *Gilbert Simondon: Being and Technology.* Edinburgh: University of Edinburgh Press, 2012.

Bogost, Ian. *Alien Phenomenology, or What It's Like to Be a Thing.* Minneapolis: University of Minnesota Press, 2012.

Bogue, Ronald. *Deleuze on Music, Painting, and the Arts.* New York: Routledge, 2003.

——. *Deleuze's Way: Essays in Transverse Ethics and Aesthetics.* Burlington, VT: Ashgate, 2007.

——. "Raymond Ruyer." In Graham Jones and Jon Roffe, eds., *Deleuze's Philosophical Lineage*, 300–20. Edinburgh: University of Edinburgh Press, 2009.

Bouaniche, Arnaud. "Deleuze and Simondon: Community and Transindividuality." *Pli* (special issue on Deleuze and Simondon) 23A (2012): 23–31.

Bowden, Sean. *The Priority of Events: Deleuze's Logic of Sense.* Edinburgh: Edinburgh University Press, 2011.

Braidotti, Rosi, *Metamorphoses: Towards a Materialist Theory of Becoming.* Cambridge: Polity, 2002.

——. *Patterns of Dissonance.* Cambridge: Polity, 1991.

——. *The Posthuman.* Cambridge: Polity, 2013.

Bréhier, Émile. *The History of Philosophy: The Hellenistic and Roman Age.* Trans. Wade Baskin. Chicago: University of Chicago Press, 1971.

Brunschwig, Jacques. "Stoic Metaphysics." In Brad Inwood, ed., *The Cambridge Companion to the Stoics*, 206–32. Cambridge: Cambridge University Press, 2003.

Bryant, Levi, Nick Srnicek, and Graham Harman, eds. *The Speculative Turn: Continental Materialism and Realism*. Melbourne: Re.press, 2011.

Chabot, Pascal. "The Philosophical August 4th: Simondon as a Reader of Bergson." *Angelaki: Journal of the Theoretical Humanities* 10, no. 2 (2005): 103–8.

——. *The Philosophy of Simondon: Between Technology and Individuation*. Trans. Aliza Krefetz with Graeme Kirkpatrick. London: Bloomsbury, 2013.

Champigny, Robert. "Translations from the Writings of Contemporary French Philosophers." *Journal of Philosophy* 54, no. 11 (1957): 313–54.

Cheung, Tobias. "From Protoplasm to Umwelt: Plans and the Technique of Nature in Jakob von Uexküll's Theory of Organismic Order." *Sign Systems Studies* 32, no. 1–2 (2004): 139–67.

Clough, Patricia, and Jean Halley, eds. *The Affective Turn: Theorizing the Social*. Durham: Duke University Press, 2007.

Colebrook, Claire. *Deleuze and the Meaning of Life*. London: Continuum, 2010.

Colonna, Fabrice. *Ruyer*. Paris: Les Belles Lettres, 2007.

Combes, Muriel. *Gilbert Simondon and the Philosophy of the Transindividual*. Trans. Thomas LaMarre, Cambridge: MIT Press, 2012.

Coole, Diana, and Samantha Frost, eds. *New Materialisms: Ontology, Agency, and Politics*. Durham: Duke University Press, 2010.

Copleston, Frederic. *A History of Philosophy*, vol. 9: *From the French Revolution to Sartre, Camus, and Levi-Strauss*. New York: Doubleday, 1994.

Curley, Edwin. *Beyond the Geometrical Method: A Reading of Spinoza's Ethics*. Princeton: Princeton University Press, 1988.

Debaise, Didier. "The Subjects of Nature: A Speculative Interpretation of the Subject" *Pli* (special issue on Deleuze and Simondon) 23A (2012): 18–37.

——. "What Is Relational Thinking?" *Inflexions* 5 (2012): 1–11.

DeBrabander, Fermin. *Spinoza and the Stoics: Power, Politics, and the Passions*. London: Continuum, 2007.

Deleuze, Gilles. "Bartleby; or, The Formula." In *Essays Critical and Clinical*, 68–90. Trans. Michael A. Greco and Daniel W. Smith. Minneapolis: University of Minnesota Press, 1997.

——. "The Brain Is the Screen." In Gregory Flaxman, ed., *The Brain Is the Screen*, 365–73. Trans. Marie Therese Guigis. Minneapolis: University of Minnesota Press, 2000.

——. *Difference and Repetition*. Trans. Paul Patton. New York: Columbia University Press, 1994.

——. *Empiricism and Subjectivity*. Trans. Constantine Boundas. New York: Columbia University Press, 1991.

——. *Expressionism in Philosophy: Spinoza*. Trans. Martin Joughin. New York: Zone, 1990.

——. *The Fold: Leibniz and the Baroque*. Trans. Tom Conley. Minneapolis: University of Minnesota Press, 1993.

——. "Lecture Transcripts on Spinoza's Concept of Affect" (1978). http:www.webdeleuze.com/php/sommaire.html.

——. *The Logic of Sense*. Trans. Mark Lester. New York: Columbia University Press, 1990.

——. *Negotiations, 1972–1990*. Trans. Martin Joughin. New York: Columbia University Press, 1995.

——. *Nietzsche and Philosophy*. Trans. Hugh Tomlinson. London: Athlone, 1983.

——. "On Gilbert Simondon." In *Desert Islands and Other Texts, 1953–1974*, 86–89. Trans. Michael Taormina. Los Angeles: Semiotext(e), 2004.

——. *Pure Immanence: Essays on a Life*. Trans. Anne Boyman. New York: Columbia University Press, 2001.

——. *Spinoza: Practical Philosophy*. Trans. Robert Hurley. San Francisco: City Lights, 1988.

——. "Supplement on the Work of David Hume." *Angelaki: Journal of the Theoretical Humanities* 16, no. 2 (2011): 181–88.

——. *Two Regimes of Madness: Texts and Interviews, 1975–1995*. Trans. Ames Hodges and Mike Taormina. New York: Semiotext(e), 2006.

Deleuze, Gilles, and Félix Guattari. *Anti-Oedipus. Capitalism and Schizophrenia*, vol. 1. Trans. Robert Hurley, Mark Seem, and Helen R. Lane. London: Athlone, 1983.

——. *A Thousand Plateaus. Capitalism and Schizophrenia*, vol. 2. Trans. Brian Massumi. Minneapolis: University of Minnesota Press, 1987.

——. *What Is Philosophy?* Trans. Hugh Tomlinson and Graham Burchill. New York: Columbia University Press, 1991.

Derrida, Jacques. *The Ear of the Other: Otobiography, Transference, Translatedation*. Trans. Peggy Kamuf. Lincoln: University of Nebraska Press, 1988.

——. *Positions*. Trans. Alan Bass. Chicago: University of Chicago Press, 1982.

——. *Specters of Marx: The State of the Debt, the Work of Mourning, and the New International*. Trans. Peggy Kamuf. New York: Routledge, 1993.

Descombes, Vincent. *Modern French Philosophy*. Trans. L. Scott-Fox and J. M. Harding. Cambridge: Cambridge University Press, 1980.

Domino, Brian. "Nietzsche's Use of *Amor Fati* in *Ecce Homo*." *Journal of Nietzsche Studies* 43, no. 2 (2012): 283–302.

Driesch, Hans. *The History and Theory of Vitalism*. London: MacMillan, 1914.

——. *The Science and Philosophy of the Organism*. London: Adam and Charles Black, 1908.

Dumouchel, Paul. "Gilbert Simondon's Plea for a Philosophy of Technology." In Andrew Feenberg and Alastair Hannay, eds., *Technology and the Politics of Knowledge*. Bloomington: Indiana University Press, 1995.

Epictetus. *The Discourses, The Handbook, Fragments*. Trans. Robin Hard. London: Everyman, 1995.

Epictetus. *The Handbook*. Trans. Nicholas P. White. Indianapolis: Hackett, 1983.

Faivre, Antoine. *Access to Western Esotericism*. Albany: SUNY Press, 1994.

Faucher, Kane X. *Metastasis and Metastability: A Deleuzian Approach to Information*. Rotterdam: Sense, 2013.

Flaxman, Gregory, ed. *The Brain Is the Screen: Deleuze and the Philosophy of Cinema*. Minnesota: University of Minneapolis Press, 2000.

Forth, Christopher. *Zarathustra in Paris: The Nietzsche Vogue in France, 1891–1910*. DeKalb: North Illinios University Press, 2001.

Foucault, Michel. *A History of Sexuality*, vol. 2: *The Use of Power*. Trans. Robert Hurley. New York: Vintage, 1990.

——. *A History of Sexuality*, vol. 3: *The Care of the Self*. Trans. Robert Hurley. New York: Vintage, 1988.

——. "On the Genealogy of Ethics: An Overview of Work in Progress." In Paul Rabinow, ed., *The Foucault Reader*, 340–71. Harmondsworth: Penguin, 1984.

——. *The Order of Things: An Archaeology of the Human Sciences*. Trans. Alan Sheridan. New York: Pantheon, 1971.

Frede, Dorothea. "Stoic Determinism." In Brad Inwood, ed., *The Cambridge Companion to the Stoics*, 179–205. Cambridge: Cambridge University Press, 2003.

Frisch, Karl von. *The Dancing Bees: An Account of the Life and Senses of the Honey Bee*. Trans. Dora Ilse. New York: Harcourt, Brace, and World, 1953.

Gatens, Moira, ed. *Feminist Interpretations of Benedict de Spinoza*. Pittsburgh: University of Pennsylvania Press, 2009.

Gillaert, Nel. "Determining One's Fate: A Delineation of Nietzsche's Concept of Free Will." *Journal of Nietzsche Studies* 31 (2006): 42–60.

Goodchild, Philip. "Deleuzean Ethics." *Theory, Culture, and Society* 14, no. 2 (1997): 39–50.

——. "Philosophy as a Way of Life: Deleuze on Thinking and Money." *SubStance* 39 no. 1 (2010): 24–37.

Gregg, Melissa, and Gregory Seigworth, eds. *The Affect Theory Reader*. Durham: Duke University Press, 2010.

Grosz, Elizabeth. *Becoming Undone: Darwinian Reflections on Life, Politics, and Art*. Durham: Duke University Press, 2011.

——. "Deleuze, Ruyer, and Becoming Brain: The Music of Life's Temporality." *Parrhesia* 15 (2012): 1–13.

——. "Habit Today: Ravaisson, Bergson, Deleuze, and Us." *Body and Society* 19, nos. 2–3 (2013): 217–39.

——. "Identity and Individuation: Some Feminist Reflections." In Arne de Boever, Alex Murray, Jon Roffe, and Ashley Woodward, eds., *Gilbert Simondon: Being and Technology*, 37–56. Edinburgh: Edinburgh University Press, 2012.

——. *The Nick of Time: Politics, Evolution, and the Untimely*. Durham: Duke University Press, 2004.

——. *Time Travels: Feminism, Nature, Power*. Durham: Duke University Press, 2005.

Guchet, Xavier. "Technology, Sociology, Humanism: Simondon, and the Problem of the Human Sciences." *SubStance* 41, no. 3 (2012): 76–92.

Guth, Alan. *The Inflationary Universe: The Quest for a New Theory of Cosmic Origins*. New York: Basic Books, 1998.

Guttman, Mathias. "Uexküll and Contemporary Biology: Some Methodological Considerations." *Sign System Studies* 32, nos. 1–2 (2004): 169–86.

Hadot, Pierre. *The Inner Citadel: The Meditations of Marcus Aurelius*. Trans. Michael Chase. Cambridge: Harvard University Press, 2001.

Hallward, Peter. *Out of This World: Deleuze and the Philosophy of Creation*. London: Verso, 2006.

Han-Pile, Béatrice. "Nietzsche and *Amor Fati*." *European Journal of Philosophy* 19, no. 2 (2009): 224–61.

Harris, Errol E. *The Substance of Spinoza*. Atlantic Highlands, NJ: Humanities International Press, 1995.

Harven, Vanessa de. "How Nothing Can Be Something: The Stoic Theory of the Void." In "The Coherence of Stoic Ontology." PhD diss., University of California, Berkeley, 2012.

Harvey, Olivia, Tamara Popowski, and Carol Sullivan. "Individuation and Feminism: A Commentary on Gilbert Simondon's 'The Genesis of the Individual.'" *Australian Feminist Studies* 55 (2008): 101–12.

Hayward, Mark, and Bernard Geoghegan. "Introduction: Catching Up with Simondon." *SubStance* 41, no. 3 (2012): 3–16.

Iliadis, Andrew. "Informational Ontology: The Meaning of Gilbert Simondon's Concept of Individuation." *Communication + 1*, 2, article 5 (2013).

——. "A New Individuation: Deleuze and Simondon." *Media Tropes* 4, no. 1 (2013): 83–100.

Inwood, Brad, ed. *The Cambridge Companion to the Stoics*. Cambridge: Cambridge University Press, 2003.

Inwood, Brad, and Lloyd P. Gerson, eds. *The Stoics Reader: Selected Writings and Testimonia*. Indianapolis: Hackett, 2008.

Irigaray, Luce. *An Ethics of Sexual Difference*. Trans. Carolyn Burke and Gillian C. Gill. Ithaca: Cornell University Press, 1993.

——. *In the Beginning, She Was*. London: Bloomsbury Academic, 2013.

——. *Marine Lover: Of Friedrich Nietzsche*. Trans. Gillian C. Gill. New York: Columbia University Press, 1991.

Jardine, Alice. *Gynesis: Configurations of Woman and Modernity*. Ithaca: Cornell University Press, 1986.

Jensen, Anthony K., and Helmut Heit, eds. *Nietzsche as a Scholar of Antiquity*. London: Bloomsbury, 2014.

Jones, Graham, and Jon Roffe, eds. *Deleuze's Philosophical Lineage*. Edinburgh: University of Edinburgh Press, 2009.

Jun, Nathan, and Daniel W Smith, eds. *Deleuze and Ethics*. Edinburgh: University of Edinburgh Press, 2011.

Kerslake, Christian. *Deleuze and the Unconscious*. London: Bloomsbury, 2007.

Krampen, Martin. "No Plant—No Breath." *Semiotica* 134, nos. 1–4 (2001): 415–21.

Krtolica, Igor. "The Question of Anxiety in Gilbert Simondon." In Arne de Boever, Alex Murray, Jon Roffe, and Ashley Woodward, eds., *Gilbert Simondon: Being and Technology*, 73–91. Trans. Jon Roffe. Edinburgh: University of Edinburgh Press, 2012.

Kuhn, Annette, and AnnMarieWolpe, eds. *Feminism and Materialism*. London: Routledge, 1988.

Kull, Kalevi. "Jakob von Uexküll: An Introduction." *Semiotica* 134, nos. 1–4 (2001): 1–59.

——. "Uexküll and the Post-Modern Evolutionism." *Sign System Studies* 3.2, nos. 1–2 (2004): 99–114.

Leibniz, Gottfried. "Comments on Spinoza's Philosophy." In *G. W. Leibniz: Philosophical Essays*, 272–80. Ed. and trans. Roger Ariew and Daniel Garber. Indianapolis: Hackett, 1989.

——. "Two Sects of Naturalists." In *G. W. Leibniz: Philosophical Essays*, 281–83. Ed. and trans. Roger Ariew and Daniel Garber. Indianapolis: Hackett, 1989.

Leroi-Gourhan, André. *Gesture and Speech*. Trans. Anna Bostock Berger. Cambridge: MIT Press, 1993.

Levinas, Emmanuel. *Totality and Infinity: An Essay on Exteriority.* Trans. Alphonso Lingis. Pittsburgh: Duquesne University Press, 1969.

Lichtenberger, Henri. "France and Germany Judged by Nietzsche." *Philosophical Forum* 40 (2009): 211–27.

Lloyd, Genevieve, and Moira Gatens. *Collective Imaginings: Spinoza Past and Present.* London: Routledge, 1999.

Long, A. A., and D. N. Sedley, eds. and trans. *The Hellenistic Philosophers,* vol. 1: *Translations of the Principal Sources, with Philosophical Commentary.* Cambridge: Cambridge University Press, 1987.

Loo, Stephen, and Undine Sellbach. "A Picture Book of Invisible Worlds: Semblances of Insects and Humans." *Angelaki: Journal of the Theoretical Humanities* 18, no. 1 (2013): 45–64.

Look, Brandon. "'Becoming Who One Is' in Spinoza and Nietzsche." *Iyyun: The Jerusalem Philosophical Quarterly* 50 (2001): 327–38.

Lorraine, Tamsin. *Deleuze and Guattari's Immanent Ethics: Theory, Subjectivity, and Duration.* Albany: SUNY Press, 2012.

Lossky, N. "The Metaphysics of the Stoics." *Journal of Philosophical Studies* 4, no. 16 (1929): 481–89.

Macherey, Pierre. "The Problem of Attributes." In W. Montag and T. Stolze, eds., *The New Spinoza,* 65–95. Minneapolis: University of Minnesota Press, 1997.

Mackenzie, Adrian. *Transductions: Bodies and Machines at Speed.* London: Continuum, 2002.

Magueijo, João, and Lee Smolin. "Gravity's Rainbow." *Classical and Quantum Gravity* 21 (2013):1725–36.

Massumi, Brian. *Parables for the Virtual: Movement, Affect, Sensation.* Durham: Duke University Press, 2010.

——. "'Technical Mentality' Revisited: Brian Massumi on Gilbert Simondon, with Arne de Boever, Alex Murray, and Jon Roffe." *Parrhesia* 7 (2009): 36–45.

——. *What Animals Teach Us About Politics.* Durham: Duke University Press, 2014.

Mates, Benson. *Stoic Logic.* Berkeley: University of California Press, 1953.

Matheron, Alexandre. "Ideas of Ideas and Certainty in the *Tractatus de Intellectus Emendatione* and in the *Ethics.*" In Yirmiyahu Yovel, ed., *Spinoza on Knowledge and the Human Mind,* vol. 2 of *Spinoza by the Year 2000,* 83–91. Trans. Jonathan Bennett. Leiden: Brill, 1994.

——. "Le moment stoïcien de l' *Éthique* de Spinoza." In Pierre-François Moreau, ed., *Le Stoïcisme aux XVIe et XVIIe siecles,* 302–16. Caen: Presses Universitaires de Caen, 1994.

Mellasioux, Quentin. *After Finitude: An Essay on the Necessity of Contingency.* Trans. Ray Brassier. London: Bloomsbury Academic, 2010.

Merrell, Floyd. "Distinctively Human Umwelt?" *Semiotica* 134, nos. 1–4 (2001): 229–62.

Meslet, Laurent. *La philosophie biologique de Raymond Ruyer.* Paris: Harmattan, 1997.

——. *Le psychisme et la vie.* Paris: Harmattan, 2005.

Miller, Jon. "Spinoza and the Stoics on Substance Monism." In Olli Koistinen, ed., *The Cambridge Companion to Spinoza's Ethics,* 99–117. Cambridge: Cambridge University Press, 2012.

Montag, Warren. *Bodies, Masses, Power: Spinoza and His Contemporaries.* London: Verso, 1999.

Montag, Warren, and Ted Stolze. eds. *The New Spinoza*. Minnesota: University of Minnesota Press, 1997.

Morrison, James C. "Why Spinoza Had No Aesthetics." *Journal of Aesthetics and Art Criticism* 47, no. 4 (1989): 359–65.

Nadler, Steven. *Spinoza: A Life*. Cambridge: Cambridge University Press, 2001.

Nematollahy, Ali. "Nietzsche in France, 1890–1914." Trans. Sheldon Huggins. *Philosophical Forum* 40 (2009): 169–80.

Nietzsche, Friedrich. *The Gay Science*. Trans. Walter Kaufmann. New York: Vintage, 1974.

——. *Human, All Too Human: A Book for Free Spirits*. Trans. R. J. Hollingdale. Cambridge: Cambridge University Press, 1988.

——. *On the Genealogy of Morals and Ecce Homo*. Trans. Walter Kauffman. New York: Vintage, 1969.

——. *The Pre-Platonic Philosophers*. Ed. and trans. Greg Whitlock. Chicago: University of Illinois Press, 2006.

——. *Selected Letters of Friedrich Nietzsche*. Ed. and trans. Oscar Levy. New York: Doubleday, 1921.

——. *Selected Letters of Friedrich Nietzsche*. Trans. C. Middleton. Indianapolis: Hackett, 1996.

——. *Thus Spoke Zarathustra: A Book for All and None*. Trans. Walter Kauffman. New York: Modern Library, 1995.

——. *Twilight of the Idols and The Anti-Christ*. Trans. R. J. Hollingdale. Harmondsworth: Penguin, 1972.

——. *The Will to Power*. Trans. Walter Kauffman and R. J. Hollingdale. New York: Vintage, 1968.

Piercey, Robert. "The Spinoza-Intoxicated Man: Deleuze on Expressionism." *Man and World* 29 (1996): 269–81.

Ravaisson, Félix. *Of Habit*. Trans. C. Carlisle and M. Sinclair. London: Acumen, 2008.

Roffe, Jon. *Badiou's Deleuze*. London: Acumen, 2012.

Rorty, Amélie Oksenberg. "The Two Faces of Spinoza." *Review of Metaphysics* 41 (1987): 299–316.

——. "The Two Faces of Stoicism: Rousseau and Freud." *Journal of the History of Philosophy* 34 (1996): 335–56.

Rozzoni, Claudio. "The Deepest Is the Skin: Deleuze and Simondon as Superficial Philosophers." *Pli* (special issue on Deleuze and Simondon) 23A (2012): 1–22.

Rutherford, Donald. "Freedom as a Philosophical Ideal: Nietzsche and His Antecedents." *Inquiry* 54, no. 5 (2011): 512–40.

Ruyer, Raymond. *La Conscience et le corps*. Paris: Alcan, 1937.

——. "Dialectic Aspects of Belief." Trans. S. J. Greenleaves. *Diogenes* 15 (December 1967): 64–79.

——. *Éléments de psycho-biologie*. Paris: PUF, 1946.

——. *La Genèse des formes vivantes*. Paris: Flammarion, 1956.

——. "Marx and Butler or Technologism and Finalism." Trans. Kris Pender from "Marx et Butler ou Technologisme et Finalisme." *Revue de Métaphysique et de Morale* 55, no. 3 (1950): 302–11.

——. "The Mystery of Reproduction and the Limits of Automatism." *Diogenes* 12 (1964): 53–69.

——. *Neofinalism.* Trans. Alyosha Edlebi. Minneapolis: University of Minnesota Press, 2016.

——. *Néo-finalisme.* Paris: PUF, 1952.

——. *Paradoxes de la conscience et limites de l'automatisme.* Paris: Albin Michel, 1966.

——. "Person-God and Tao-God." Trans. Kris Pender of "Dieu-Person et Dieu-Tao." *Revue de Métaphysique et de Morale* 52, no. 2 (1947): 1–11.

——. "The Status of the Future and the Invisible World." Trans. R. Scott Walker. *Diogenes* 28 (1980): 37–53.

——. "There Is No Subconscious: Embryogenesis and Memory." Trans. R. Scott Walker. *Diogenes* 36 (1988): 24–46.

——. "The Vital Domain of Animals and the Religious World of Man." *Diogenes* 5 (1957): 35–46.

Sauvagnargues, Anne. "Crystals and Memory." In Arne de Boever, Alex Murray, Jon Roffe, and Ashley Woodward, eds., *Gilbert Simondon: Being and Technology,* 57–72. Trans. Jon Roffe. Edinburgh: Edinburgh University Press, 2012.

——. *Deleuze and Art.* London: Continuum, 2013.

Schmigden, Henning. "Inside the Black Box: Simondon's Politics of Technology." *SubStance* 41, no. 3 (2012): 16–31.

——. "Thinking Technological and Biological Beings: Gilbert Simondon's Philosophy of Machines." Paper presented at the Max Planck Institute for the History of Science, Berlin, August 27, 2004, www.csi.ensmp.fr/WebCSI/4S/download_paper/download_paper.php?paper=schmidgen.

Schofield, Malcolm. "Stoic Ethics." In Brad Inwood, ed., *The Cambridge Companion to the Stoics,* 233–56. Cambridge: Cambridge University Press, 2003.

Schrift, Alan D. "Thinking About Ethics: Deleuze's Not-So-Secret Link with Spinoza and Nietzsche." *Philosophy Today* 53 (2009): 207–13.

Scott, David. *Gilbert Simondon's Psychic and Collective Individuation: A Critical Introduction and Guide.* Edinburgh: University of Edinburgh Press, 2014.

Scruton, Roger. *Spinoza.* Oxford: Oxford University Press, 1986.

Sellars, John. "*Aion* and *Chronos*: Deleuze and the Stoic Theory of Time." *Collapse III.* Ed. R. Mackay. Falmouth: Urbanomic, November 2007.

——. "An Ethics of the Event: Deleuze's Stoicism." *Angelaki: Journal of the Theoretical Humanities* 2, no. 3 (December 2006): 157–71.

——. "The Point of View of the Cosmos: Deleuze, Romanticism, Stoicism." *Pli* 8 (1999): 1–24.

——. *Stoicism,* Los Angeles: University of California Press, 2006.

Sharp, Hasana. *Spinoza and the Politics of Renaturalization.* Chicago: University of Chicago Press, 2011.

Shaviro, Steven. "Self-Enjoyment and Concern: On Whitehead and Levinas." In Roland Faber, B. Hennings, and C. Combs, eds., *Beyond Metaphysics? Explorations in Alfred North Whitehead's Late Thought,* 249–58. Amsterdam: Rodopi, 2010.

Simondon, Gilbert. *Du mode d'existence des objects techniques.* Paris: Aubier, 1989.

——. "The Genesis of the Individual." In Jonathon Crary and Sanford Kwinter, eds., *Incorporations,* 297–317. Trans. Mark Cohen and Sanford Kwinter. New York: Zone, 1993.

——. *L'individuation psychique et collective à la lumière des notions de forme et d'information, potentiel et métastabilité.* Paris: Aubier, 1989.

——. *L'individu et sa genèse physico-biologique.* Paris: Presses Universitaires de France, 1964.

——. "On Techno-Aesthetics." Trans. Arne de Boever. *Parrhesia* 14 (2012): 1–8.

——. "On the Mode of Existence of Technical Objects." Trans. Ninian Mellamphy. *Deleuze Studies* 5, no. 3 (2011): 407–24.

——. "The Position of the Problem of Ontogenesis." Trans. Gregory Flanders. *Parrhesia* 7 (2009): 4–16.

——. "Technical Individualization." Trans. Alberto Toscano. In Joke Brouwer and Arjen Mulder, eds., *Interact or Die!* 206–15. Rotterdam: V2 and Nai, 2007.

——. "Technical Mentality." Trans. Arne de Boever. *Parrhesia* 7 (2009): 17–27.

——. *Two Lessons on Animal and Man.* Trans. Drew Burk. Minneapolis: Univocal Press, 2011.

Smith, Daniel W. "Deleuze and the Question of Desire: Toward an Immanent Theory of Ethics." *Parrhesia* 2 (2007): 66–78.

Solomon, Robert. "Nietzsche on Fatalism and 'Free Will.'" *Journal of Nietzsche Studies* 23 (2002): 63–87.

Sommer, Andreas Urs. "Nietzsche's Readings on Spinoza: A Contextualist Study, Particularly on the Reception of Kuno Fischer." *Journal of Nietzsche Studies* 43, no. 2 (2012): 156–82.

Spencer, M. E. "Spinoza and Nietzsche—a Comparison." *Monist* 41 no. 1 (1931): 67–90.

Spinoza, Benedict de. *Ethics.* Trans. Edwin Curley. London: Penguin, 1996.

——. *Theological-Political Treatise.* Trans. Michael Silverhorn and Jonathon Israel, Cambridge: Cambridge University Press, 2007.

——. *Works of Spinoza. On the Improvement of Human Intellect; The Ethics; Selected Letters.* Trans. R. H. M. Elwes. New York: Dover, 1951.

Spivak, Gayatri Chakravorty. "Can the Subaltern Speak?" In Cary Nelson and Lawrence Grossberg, eds., *Marxism and the Interpretation of Culture,* 271–313. Chicago: University of Illinois Press, 1988.

Stiegler, Bernard. *Technics and Time 3: Cinematic Time and the Question of Malaise.* Trans. Stephen Barker. Stanford: Stanford University Press, 2011.

——. "The Theater of Individuation: Phase-Shift and Resolution in Simondon and Heidegger." *Parrhesia* 7 (2009): 46–57.

Tinbergen, Nikolaas. "On Aims and Methods of Ethology." *Zeitschrift für Tierpsychologie* 20 (1963): 410–33.

Tomlin, E. W. F. *Living and Knowing.* London: Faber and Faber, 1955.

——. "The Philosophy of Life." *Dialectica* 13, no. 2 (1959): 144–59.

Toscano, Alberto. "The Disparate: Ontology and Politics in Simondon." *Pli* (special issue on Deleuze and Simondon) 23A (2012).

——. "Gilbert Simondon." In Graham Jones and Jon Roffe, eds., *Deleuze's Philosophical Lineage.* Edinburgh: University of Edinburgh Press, 2009.

——. "Technical Culture and the Limits of Interaction: A Note on Simondon." In Joke Brouwer and Arjen Mulder, eds., *Interact or Die!* 198–205. Rotterdam: V2 and Nai, 2007.

——. *The Theatre of Individuation: Philosophy and Individuation Between Kant and Deleuze.* London: Palgrave Macmillan, 2006.

Uexküll, Jakob von. *A Foray Into the Worlds of Animals and Humans: With a Theory of Meaning*. Trans. Joseph D O'Niel. Minneapolis: University of Minnesota Press, 2010.

——. "A New Concept of Umwelt: A Link Between Science and the Humanities." Trans. Gösta Brunow. *Semiotica* 134, nos. 1–4 (2001): 111–23.

Uhlmann, Anthony. "Deleuze, Ethics, Ethology, and Art." In Nathan Jun and Daniel W. Smith, eds., *Deleuze and Ethics*. Edinburgh: University of Edinburgh Press, 2011.

Ure, Michael. "Nietzsche's Free Spirit Trilogy and Stoic Therapy." *Journal of Nietzsche Studies* 38 (2009): 60–84.

Viljanen, Valterreri. "Spinoza's Ontology." In Olli Koistinen, ed., *The Cambridge Companion to Spinoza's Ethics*, 56–78. Cambridge: Cambridge University Press, 2012.

Vries, Marc de. "Gilbert Simondon and the Dual Nature of Technical Artifacts." *Techné* 12, no. 1 (Winter 2008): 23–32.

Whitehead, Alfred North. *Modes of Thought*. New York: MacMillan, 1938.

Wiklund, Rolf A. "A Short Introduction to the Neo-Finalist Philosophy of Raymond Ruyer." *Philosophy and Phenomenological Research* 21 (1960): 187–98.

Wilson, Elizabeth A. *Affect and Artificial Intelligence*. Seattle: University of Washington Press, 2010.

Yovel, Yirmiyahu, ed. *Nietzsche as Affirmative Thinker*. The Hague: Martinus Nijhoff, 1992.

——. *Spinoza and Other Heretics: The Adventures of Immanence*. Princeton: Princeton University Press, 1989.

Zbebik, Jabuk. "Gilbert Simondon, Gilles Deleuze, and Sobriety." *Semiotic Review of Books* 17, no. 2 (2007): 1–5.

Ziemke, Tom, and Noel Sharkey. "A Stroll Through the Worlds of Robots and Animals: Applying Jakob von Uexküll's Theory of Meaning to Adaptive Robots and Artificial Life." *Semiotica* 134, nos. 1–4 (2001): 701–46.

Žižek, Slavoj. *Organs Without Bodies: On Deleuze and Consequences*. London: Routledge, 2003.

INDEX

Quantum field theory, 3, 222, 284*n*11, 290*n*26

Rabinow, Paul, 281*n*35
Rationalism, 88, 103
Rationalist forms, 16
Rational ordering principle, 24
Ravaisson, Félix, 228, 283*n*49
"Raymond Ruyer" (Bogue), 290*n*21, 291*n*39
Real, preindividual ordering, 174
Reality, 186, 284*n*10
Reason, 48, 68–69; of finite things, 74; human beings influenced by, 19, 45–53, 57; as order's part, 58; passion tinging, 108–9; Stoics on, 22, 265*n*12, 265*n*20
Reductionism, 5, 11, 17, 250–51, 292*n*45, 293*n*58. *See also* Spinoza, Benedict de
Reductive determinism, 36–37
Reference (*Bedeutung*), 41–44, 137, 148, 279*n*16
Referent, as body, 40–41
Reflexive thinking, 207–8, 287*n*41
Reflex person, 283*n*51
Regulation, political struggle linked to, 134
Regulative fictions, 104–5
Religion, 12, 286*n*32; Abrahamic, 243; art influencing, 203; mediation through, 201–4, 207–8; philosophers and, 98–100, 102–14, 207–8, 245–46, 293*n*64. *See also* Christianity
Remote causes, 73
Res cogitans. *See* mind
Resentment (*ressentiment*), 51, 277*n*36
Res extensa. *See* body
Responsibility, 27–28, 267*n*40
Ressentiment. *See* Resentment
Rest, of finite things, 74. *See also* Mediated infinite modes
Revelation, *EH* on, 128
"Richard Wagner in Bayreuth" (Nietzsche), 130–31
Roman Empire, 19–20
Roman Stoicism, 19–20
Roman Stoics, 6, 19–20, 44
Rome, 19, 98
Room (*chora*), 33
Rope, 195–98
Rutherford, Donald, 270*n*9
Ruyer, Raymond, 134, 162, 169, 257–58; on aesthetics, 243–48; on Agent, 244–45,

291*n*40; on artists, 245–46; on atoms, 221–27, 229–30; autoaffection conception of, 289*n*15; axiological cogito as foundational for, 214; on brains, 225–31, 239–42; on cells, 225–31; on consciousness, 210–31, 288*n*4; Darwinism objected to by, 225; on desire, 228–29; on determinism, 289*n*12; on embryo, 231–39, 293*n*53; embryogenesis and, 209–48, 288*nn*1–71; on ethics, 243–48; ethology understood by, 211; on Euclidean space, 185; on future, 247–48; genetic reductionism criticized by, 293*n*58; God for, 229–30, 243, 247–48, 289*n*7, 289*n*15, 291*n*40, 293*n*64, 294*nn*67–68; on habit, 227–29, 291*n*36; on Ideal, 244–47, 294*n*65; ideas for, 210; on individual, 210–11; invisible world talked of by, 225–30, 242, 244–48, 291*n*31; life conception of, 211–42; matter for, 290*n*27; on melody, 212, 216–17, 226, 227; on memory, 227–29, 291*n*33, 291*n*36; mnemic themes, 221–24, 226–39, 234–37, 238–40, 244–45, 247–48, 291*nn*32–33, 293*n*61; on molecules, 223–24; on nature, 221, 226, 227; Neoplatonism of, 243; on organism, 293*n*55; on organs, 225–31; overview, 10–11, 209–14; on perception, 218–21; philosophers and, 210–11, 212–14; philosophy of, 10–11, 209–48, 288*nn*1–71; primary forms conceived by, 212–48, 250–51; quantum field theory rethinking of, 290*n*26; religion turned to by, 245–46, 293*n*64; on seeing, 218–21; on self-creation, 229–39; on self-survey, 230–39; as subjective idealist, 222, 288*n*4; tablecloth example of, 218–21; Tao-God interest of, 211, 246–48, 293*n*64; on values, 227, 243–48; on vision, 218–21; will to power understood by, 212. *See also* Neofinalism; Primary forms

Sadness, 82, 83
Sage, 44, 91
Sauvagnargues, Anne, 184, 285*n*19, 285*n*20
Sayables (*lekta*), 30–32, 37–44, 267*n*41
Schofield, Malcolm, 268*n*54
Schopenhauer, Arthur, 283*n*46
Sciences, 282*n*41; affirmation of, 104–5; art and, 95–96, 104–9, 125; brain as subject of, 163; faith in, 105–7; forces